John Hen

GREAT SCIENTISTS WAGE THE GREAT WAR

THE FIRST WAR OF SCIENCE
1914–1918

WILLIAM VAN DER KLOOT

FONTHILL

For Bannus and Harry

Fonthill Media Language Policy

Fonthill Media publishes in the international English language market. One language edition is published worldwide. As there are minor differences in spelling and presentation, especially with regard to American English and British English, a policy is necessary to define which form of English to use. The Fonthill Policy is to use the form of English native to the author. This case is not straightforward: William Van der Kloot was born in the USA but has spent a fifth of his life in Britain. He was educated and has published books and papers in both countries, so his English presentation is inexorably hybrid.

Fonthill Media Limited
Fonthill Media LLC
www.fonthillmedia.com
office@fonthillmedia.com

First published in the United Kingdom and the United States of America 2014

British Library Cataloguing in Publication Data:
A catalogue record for this book is available from the British Library

Copyright © William Van der Kloot 2014

ISBN 978-1-78155-402-9

Typeset in 10pt on 13pt Sabon Lt Std
Printed and bound in England

Contents

About the Author

A book about history and science should be written by someone with feet planted firmly in both camps. William Van der Kloot was born in the US and served in the US Navy at the tail end of the Second World War. He studied Biology at Harvard, with shorter periods at the University of Chicago and the University of Cambridge. He researched and taught at Harvard, Cornell, NYU School of Medicine, and Stony Brook University, where he became Distinguished Professor of Physiology and Biophysics. He has published some 160 papers, including several on the history of neuroscience. His interest in the Great War began in childhood from the tales of his father and uncles; as he worked in science he studied the War on the side. Later in life he left the laboratory bench for the archives and libraries, where step by step he uncovered how much scientists had altered the course of the war. A surprise because so little has been written about it. In the past decade the Royal Society has published five of his articles on science in the the First World War and he has published two books on other aspects of the War. It is hard to imagine a better preparation for writing the present book, which tells general readers what six deeply involved, preeminent scientists did. The final chapter shows how two of them prepared British science for its crucial role in the Second World War while the German protagonist, who in the interwar years discovered nuclear fission—the basis of the atom bomb—remained on the side-lines longing for the defeat of the Nazis and after the war leading in the reestablishment of international science.

Preface

For many years I worked as a scientist; for relaxation I read about the Great War. It seemed quite unlike WW2. Scientists—other than Fritz Haber with poison gas and nitrogen fixation—seemed to be nonexistent. Consequently when I stumbled across the fact that five future Nobel laureates worked in the German poison gas program I published an article pointing this out. I was naïve. Pursuing the subject I learned that every nation mobilized distinguished scientists during WW1. They solved crucial problems. It is simply that their efforts have not been described satisfactorily in the histories.

This book fills part of this gap, telling how the academic-military complex evolved. I use the case history method to follow six eminent scientists through the war, based on autobiographies, letters, reports, and the like. Along with their intellectual gifts they had vivid personalities. The emphasis is on the scientists; their science is described for the general reader. The major events in the war on land are recapped in chapter 2; those at sea in chapter 5; those in the air in chapter 7.

The final chapter shows how some of our British scientists prepared for the effective mobilization of their scientific talent that occurred in WW2, while some of the best German scientists sat on their hands.

Acknowledgements

I am indebted to T. M. C. Van der Kloot and to the staffs of the following: the London Library; Professor Frank James and Jane Harrison at the Archives of the Royal Institution; Caroline Herbert at the Archives of Churchill College, Cambridge; the Archives of Christ's College, Cambridge; the Archives of the Royal Society, the Wellcome Library; the Bodleian Library, Oxford; the Imperial College Library; the Science Museum Library; the Archives of the Science Museum at Swindon; the Library and Archives of University College, London; the Archives of the Imperial War Museum, London; the Public Record Office; the Cambridge University Library; the National Army Museum, London; the New York Public Library; the Stony Brook University and Health Sciences Libraries. I am grateful to Susannah Bramley for information about her grandfather A. V. Hill, to Meg Weston Smith for information about her father E. A. Milne, and for John Henderson for information about Starling and Bayliss. Many years ago Otto Loewi often told me about his meetings with Starling and Dale.

Abbreviations

AA: Anti-aircraft
ADP: Adenosine diphosphate
AEF: American Expeditionary Force
ANZAC: Australian and New Zealand Army Corps, British Army
ASD: Anti-Submarine Division, British Admiralty
ASDIC: Anti-Submarine Division-ics' (sonar)
ATP: Adenosine triphosphate
BIR: Board of Invention and Research, UK
C.B.E.: Commander of the British Empire
C.C.S.: Casualty Clearing Station
DER: Director of Experiment and Research, British Admiralty
DSIR: Department of Scientific and Industrial Research
FRS: Fellow of the Royal Society
F.S.C.: Field Service Company, Royal Engineers, British Army
GB: Great Britain
GHQ: Headquarters of the British Army in France
K.B.E.: Knight Grand Cross of the Order of the British Empire
KWG: Kaiser Wilhelm Gesellschaft, Germany
KWI: Kaiser Wilhelm Institute, Germany
M.C.: Military Cross, UK
MM: Ministry of Munitions, UK
MPG: Max Plank Gesellschaft
MPI: Max Plank Institute
NAS: National Academy of Sciences, US
NCO: Non-commissioned officer
NPL: National Physical Laboratory, UK
NRC: National Research Council, US
O.B.E.: Most Excellent Order of the British Empire
OHL: German Imperial Headquarters, *Oberste Heersleitung*
OP: Observation Post
OTC: Officer Training Course, UK

RA: Royal Artillery
RAMC: Royal Army Medical Corps
RE: Royal Engineers
RFA: Royal Field Artillery
RGA: Royal Garrison Artillery
RHA: Royal Horse Artillery
RMA: Royal Marine Artillery
RSFWC: Royal Society Food [War] Committee
UCL: University College, London

1

From Victory to Iron Duke

The coming of war in August 1914 was celebrated jubilantly in London, Berlin, and other European cities. The revellers were clueless about what they faced. A century of hitherto unparalleled economic and scientific advances had profoundly transformed warfare. Lord Moulton, who served as Britain's high explosives tsar, put it well: 'In scale and in intensity alike, this war represents the results of the totality of scientific progress ...'. [1]

One example illustrates the point. Compare HMS *Victory*, the flagship of Admiral Horatio Nelson during the Napoleonic wars, with HMS *Iron Duke*, the flagship of Admiral Sir John Jellicoe a century later. *Victory*, launched in 1765, was manned by 800 men. The maximum work output of a fit man is 0.35 hp. Therefore, her captain deployed 284 hp, about the power of a pickup truck today. He ingeniously used his men's energy to harness the wind, which in the best of conditions propelled the vessel at 10 knots. *Victory*, huge for her time, displaced 3,500 tons. Her captain also expended chemical energy, she fired 1,148 lb of metal in her broadside; her largest guns had a range of 2,600 yards, but 800 yards was the upper range for a broadside.

Iron Duke was launched in 1912 and had a slightly larger crew, 925 men. She was propelled by four steam turbines delivering 29,000 hp—more than 100 pickup trucks. The turbines spun four propellers that drove her at a flank speed of 21.25 knots. The crew's muscles were augmented by motors that raised her anchor and small boats, hoisted shells and explosives from the magazines, pumped salt and fresh water and the like. Interior spaces were lit by electricity. They spoke from compartment to compartment by telephone. *Iron Duke* displaced 25,000 tons, more than seven times *Victory*. Her main armament was ten 13.5-inch guns; one shell weighed 1,400 lb—each shell was heavier than Nelson's total broadside and was packed with high explosive. Maximum range was 23,800 yards, an increase of more than nine-fold; at the Battle of Jutland she fired at targets 18,000 yards away.

Nelson treasured *Victory*'s stout oak sides; he would have been astounded by the 11-inch band of steel armour that girdled *Iron Duke* and baffled by her gyrocompasses, optical rangefinders, four submerged torpedo tubes, and the wireless apparatus for communicating over hundreds of miles. Nelson's battle orders travelled only as far as a string of sharp eyes peering into spyglasses could make out signal flags. Our list of innovations in the flagship could go on and on. They had been devised by thousands of trained brains, thinking scientifically. The crews were also dramatically transformed. Most of *Iron Duke's* men were well schooled technicians, experts in trades not conceived of a century before.

Growing populations and wealth

The changes in the British flagships reflect profound changes in European life during the nineteenth Century. Population skyrocketed: in Britain, it increased 2.5-fold, despite the departure of more than 7.7 million émigrés from 1840 to 1900.[2] There were more people because there was more food and better public health—both products of science. Of course, only a small fraction of these advances were made by people who thought of themselves as scientists, many were done by enthusiastic farmers, metal workers, or engineers who had been trained as apprentices. Inspired by the spirit of the age, they communicated their results in an expanding number of books and journals. Yet all of them were standing on the broad shoulders of Arab investigators, Galileo, Newton, Volta, Ampere and the others who had shown so convincingly how questions can be answered by carefully controlled experiments.

Wealth increased even faster than population, the gross domestic product per person in the Netherlands, for which we have the best data, increased 2.7-fold in the century.[3] Rich societies could afford *Iron Dukes* as well as improved universities and institutions for scientific research. Science gradually became a profession. Much of the new wealth was created by using energy from oxidizing coal to generate steam to drive factory machinery, locomotives, printing presses and the like. Thanks to fast printing presses, fast distribution by rail, and the elimination of a heavy tax that the Government had imposed to discourage readers, the number of newspapers printed in London increased from 18,000-a- day in 1821 to more than seven million a century later.[4]

Explosives

Advances in the chemistry of explosives and of steel changed naval warfare profoundly. Gunpowder, a mixture of carbon, sulphur, and saltpetre, had been used for centuries to shoot projectiles from tubes, to shatter rock and to excavate earth. Saltpetre is either sodium nitrate from the mines in Chile or potassium nitrate from Asia, where it is obtained from urine. When a gram of gunpowder is burned it releases less energy than a gram of coal, but releases it swiftly because the oxygen comes from the nearby nitrate in the powder, not from the air. The hot gases produced—carbon dioxide and sulphur dioxide—drive the projectile up the barrel. In mid-century Ascanio Sobrero, a professor in Turin, discovered that when glycerine is slowly dripped into a mix of concentrated sulphuric and nitric acids an oil is formed that explodes far more powerfully and rapidly than the same weight of gunpowder, because the oxygen is built into the exploding molecule. The oil is nitroglycerine. Its oxygen atoms are strongly attracted by nearby carbons and hydrogens. A pressure wave that pushes molecules closer together can trigger the reaction, so nitroglycerine is all too easily set off by a jolt. There were frequent, horrifying accidental explosions. But perhaps surprisingly nitroglycerine is not that easy to detonate when you want to.

Both problems were solved by Alfred Nobel.[5] He invented a gunpowder detonator that reliably set off nitroglycerine, so it was widely used despite the hazards of transporting it. Then Nobel showed that when nitroglycerine is absorbed on the silica from fossil diatom shells (diatomaceous earth), which has an enormous surface area, it is no longer detonated by a bump. Dynamite largely replaced gun powder in mining and construction.

Another chancy high explosive, discovered early in the century, was guncotton, prepared by treating cotton waste with nitric acid. Powerful but unstable. Nobel tamed it in 1876 by devising blasting gelatine: a colloidal suspension of nitroglycerine in guncotton. His next brainwave was to make the colloidal suspension with 45 per cent nitroglycerine, 45 per cent guncotton and 10 per cent camphor. It is so stable that it can be heated and rolled into sheets or forced through sieves to form threads. (Celluloid is a close relative.) He called it Ballistite. Detonated by heat moving through the charge; it explodes without producing smoke and fouls barrels far less than gunpowder. He tried to sell it to the major powers as a propellant for driving shells out of gun barrels. The British established a committee on explosives that included the chemists James Dewar FRS and Frederick Abel FRS, the chief chemist at the Royal Military Academy in Woolwich. Nobel told them exactly how to make Ballistite. They changed the mix to 58 per cent nitroglycerine, 37 per cent guncotton and 5 per cent Vaseline. First the nitroglycerine and guncotton are gingerly mixed by hand, then the mix is dissolved in acetone and stirred for hours mechanically. Named cordite, it was adopted by the British Government as their propellant. The Nobel Company sued for patent infringement and lost. (Lord Moulton, later the British explosives tsar during the War, was their lead counsel.)

After cordite is dried it is made into finely ground powder. The granules burn from outside in so burning speed depends on particle size. Large granules take 40 msec to burn. Slow burning makes guns with long barrels feasible: propellant gases are generated throughout the burn, all of the time that the shell is in the barrel. A further advantage is that less pressure is generated at the moment of ignition to stress the gun's chamber.[6]

The properties of explosive molecules depend on how they are packaged. A solid block is a high explosive: a shock wave detonates the charge almost instantaneously, just like nitroglycerine. The high explosive the British packed into shells was picric acid, but just weeks before the war they decided to switch to TNT (trinitrotoluene).

Gunpowder was only used as a detonator in fuses and to explode the canister containing shrapnel bullets, which requires little force and gives a puff of smoke that helps gunners see where the shrapnel has been let loose. Other smoke-producing chemicals were often added to the charges in high explosive shells, for visibility and to induce fear and choking.

Steels

The first major advance in cannon design during the century had been by making wrought iron guns more powerful, increasing the strength of the chamber by wrapping a series of iron cylinders around it. Some were breech loading. Soon these guns were made obsolete by newly developed steels; alloys of iron formulated with different desirable features. For example, steel alloys containing manganese are used for safes, railroad rails, and armoured plating. Huge, breech-loading long guns made with tough alloys were prefect for the new propellants.

Fisher

The man who led the major step in the transformation of the flagships was First Sea Lord John Arbuthnot Fisher, appointed in 1904, known throughout the fleet as 'Jackie'.[7] He first came to public notice when as the commander of HMS *Excellent,* the Naval Gunnery School in Portsmouth Harbour, he campaigned vigorously for the development of steel long guns. In colourful language he warned that Britain would soon lose command of the seas because penny-pinching prevented the navy from matching the technical innovations of their rivals. His campaign was well timed. British manufacturing was in depression; so industrialists enthusiastically rallied to his cause. Parliament increased the naval appropriation 150 per cent. The next infighting was over where to spend the money. Traditionally most guns were made at the Woolwich Arsenal, the huge Government arms complex in East London. The rub was that the start-up costs for the new technologies were enormous, so even with an increased budget it would take the Arsenal years to get into production. Private companies with contracts in hand could raise huge sums on the capital markets and start fast. Fisher was appointed head of naval ordnance in 1886, with authority to contract private companies.[8] The British military-industrial complex was coming together nicely.

From 1860 to 1910 the British *per capita* investment in defence increased more than two-fold, with of course a spike during the South African War.[9] Until the Boer War allocations for the army and the navy were roughly equal, but by 1910 the navy spent one-third more than the army.[10] The well-paid corporate boards of the armaments companies included MPs and Lords.

Armstrong paid dividends of between 10 and 20 per cent yearly, but the highest return was from the Harvey Steel Company, which from 1894–98 yielded 30 per cent.[11] These firms had many well-paid employees; the economy of Newcastle relied on the 40,000 employees on Armstrong's payroll. The companies also had well-supported research and development units and educated engineering students, whose tuition added to income.

Figures for how much was invested in armament's research are hard to come by. In 1878 Krupp had 803 white collar employees, of whom 276 were technical. Vickers in the first decade of the twentieth century had a research staff of 300 to 400, supported by 6–12 per cent of the budget.[12] In 1913 Dupont de Nemours in the USA had 250 employees in research and development. Research was also done in Government facilities. In Britain in 1907 the centre was at the Royal Arsenal where there were divisions of explosives, ballistics, and metallurgy, whose costs were equally divided between the War Office and Admiralty. The Arsenal and its three divisions were commanded by serving military officers.[13]

First Sea Lord Fisher appointed a committee to study recent innovations in metallurgy, explosives, gun design, optics, propulsion systems and the like. Looking at the whole picture, they envisioned a revolutionary new battleship: a fast, armoured gun platform that could demolish any of its forerunners.

The Admiralty's principal scientific advisor was William Thomson, first Baron Kelvin. He was Second Wrangler in the mathematical tripos at Cambridge in 1845. Wrangler calls for a digression because these examinations were crucial milestones for some of our British protagonists. Initially the university required a single examination, called the tripos, for a degree.[14] Most was in Latin and every degree candidate was required to demonstrate some competence in mathematics. A mathematical tripos was introduced as a specialized subject in the nineteenth century. Most instruction was by private coaches who worked through problems while their tutees scribbled notes. The examination began with relatively easy questions; calculus was not required during the first three days, but only a fast worker could get through all of the problems set for each session. After a hiatus for grading, those whose scores were high enough to compete for honours were examined further. Now the questions were formidable, some almost impossible. None of the five examiners could answer all of the questions. The last paper was on Friday afternoon. A week later the list of those who passed was read at the Senate Hall in order of merit. By tradition those who won first class honours were known as Wranglers, the first was Senior Wrangler, the last was unofficially known as the Wooden Spoon, who again unofficially received a special salute and a badge of office when the degrees were awarded.

As a Second Wrangler at age-22 the future Lord Kelvin was appointed professor of natural philosophy at the University of Glasgow. He made notable contributions to thermodynamics—the absolute temperature scale is named in his honour—while becoming even better known for calculating the parameters required for the successful trans-Atlantic telegraph cable. Kelvin loved both science and the sea and was happy to consult with the Admiralty. The complex was becoming academic-military-industrial.

Throughout the century science in the universities was expanded and strengthened. They started from an almost implausibly low level. Richard Watson, who was elected professor of chemistry at Cambridge in 1764, admitted that he: '… knew nothing at all of chemistry, had never read a syllable on the subject; nor seen a single experiment in it.' He studied and learned enough to lecture. Watson was so successful as a chemist that seven years later he was elected to the Regius Chair of Divinity which paid better. His successor in chemistry never learned enough to lecture.[15] Early in the nineteenth century the German universities began to build distinguished science faculties, after a lag of decades the British universities followed suit.

The Dreadnought

The result of the committee's planning was a great leap forward in naval construction. To propel the ship, they gambled on new turbine engines developed at the Parson Marine Turbine works in Newcastle, which hitherto had been only installed in small vessels. A turbine uses the velocity of steam to spin a series of rotors, instead of using the pressure of steam to drive a piston. Steam velocities are high: it escapes from an opening in a boiler to the outside air at 2,500 feet per sec, far too fast to spin a rotor effectively.[16] An earl's younger son Charles F. Parsons was eleventh Wrangler, who then apprenticed as an engineer for four years at Armstrong's. He saw that steam could be kept at useful velocities if its pressure could be dropped stepwise. To do so, he flowed steam through a series of rotors within a turbine casing. At each step the pressure difference is between the steam entering the gap between the rotor blade and the casing and the steam in the chamber on the far side of the rotor. (His first steam turbine, a beautiful example of precision machining, is displayed in the Science Museum in London.) It took another leap of imagination to move from this relatively small engine to the huge turbines needed to propel a warship.

The great long guns and the turbines driving the first of Fisher's creations, HMS *Dreadnought*, made every other battleship in the world obsolete—they would be sitting ducks for *Dreadnought*. She was at sea in less than a year after her keel was laid. She had a major impact on the international arms race. The Germans saw that they were only one ship behind in a race for naval parity and laid keels for their own dreadnoughts. The British kept their lead by spending twice as much *per capita* on defence than either the French or Germans.[17] (This statistic is uncomfortable for those who maintain that Germany entered the Great War prepared to conquer the world, or at least Europe.) Fisher, a fan of speed, also constructed relatively lightly-armoured, fast battle cruisers, which mounted the huge guns of a battleship.

The new British battleships and battle cruisers were designed to burn both fuel oil and coal. Oil is a more concentrated power source than coal. Another advantage is that when was ploughing forward at flank speed it is almost impossible to feed enough coal into the boilers to maintain steam pressure, but oil can be rapidly pumped directly to the burners. *Dreadnought* carried 2,900 tons of coal and 1,120 tons of oil.[18] Oil had to be purchased from the US. Obtaining new oil supplies from the Middle East became a major objective of British foreign policy. The Germans, who in wartime would not have a secure route to oil supplies, stuck to coal.

As Jackie worked with the engineers and naval architects he entertained his co-workers with prattle about the imaginative and bloodthirsty enterprises that their ships would undertake when the day for action came: seizing German coastal islands or sweeping the Baltic clean of the German Navy and then landing Russian hordes on the coast near Berlin. His language was as colourful as his ideas; he was the sort of fellow who signed letters to friends, 'Yours til death'.

The navies also built submarines, which relied on rechargeable batteries, discovered by Gustav Planté in 1859, which powered the electric motors that propelled the vessel when submerged. On the surface, she was driven by internal combustion or steam engines that also recharged the batteries. Fisher thought that eventually submarines would dominate wartime seas, but most naval men thought this notion laughably farfetched.

Changing armies

Land warfare was also revolutionized by scientific advances. Smokeless propellants meant that battles were no longer fought in an almost impenetrable cloud; in South Africa the British infantry, standing shoulder to shoulder in their time-honoured line of battle, were given a harsh tutorial when shot down by almost invisible Boer farmers in foxholes rapidly operating steel, breech-loading rifles firing clips of cartridges propelled by cordite. Machine guns fired still faster. Steel field guns were breech loading and quick firing. They used the energy in their recoil to throw open the breech so that the used casing dropped out and a new shell could be thrust in immediately. Sophisticated carriages rocked the gun back into firing position.

The German Army was ready to employ heavy artillery in the field, primarily howitzers that lobbed shells down on their target. The manual about how they were to be used was written in 1889–93 by Major Paul von Hindenburg, a general staff officer serving in the War Ministry. (It was translated into English by William Robertson and his wife; he rose from the ranks to become chief of the Imperial General Staff during much of the War.) Hindenburg was also responsible for the manual on field fortifications; the howitzers were to be used to smash the enemy's field works.[19] Major decisions that prepared the Germans well for the coming war.

The Germans and Austro-Hungarians built mobile siege guns that hurled enormous shells capable of smashing the concrete of enemy border fortresses. Some of these monsters were towed into action by tractors. The caterpillar continuous track had been invented in 1904 and was used on farm machinery and a few, advanced military vehicles. Aeroplanes, dirigibles and kite balloons were obtained for observing the fall of shot and for scouting. The European powers spent freely on arms.

Improved communications sent commander's orders travelling at the speed of light for thousands of miles. By 1917 Field Marshal Hindenburg was supreme commander of 13 million soldiers from four nations fighting on three continents. The reverse side is that telephones kept generals close to their central switchboard in snug command posts miles behind the battle lines, which they rarely visited. It is said that in the last weeks of the Battle of Passchendaele in 1917 Field Marshal Haig's chief of staff, Lt Gen. Sir Launcelot Kiggell, for the first time motored far enough forward to see the slimy morass behind the battle line. He tearfully choked out, 'Good God, did we really send men to fight in that?'[20] This may be a fable but surely many commanders were shielded from the realities of no-man's-land. (In the Second World War improved wireless enabled aggressive generals in command tanks to advance with their spearheads.)

In 1918 on an average day a British field army was kept in step by 10,000 telegrams, 20,000 telephone calls, and 5,000 messages forwarded by their dispatch riders and runners.[21] But as soon as attacking infantry left their trenches they lost contact with higher commanders and their artillery support, except for rudimentary appeals conveyed with flares and rockets and signals to aeroplanes. It was murder to order a staff officer to ride forward with orders or to report on the situation. Command and control also broke down within the assault units. Traditional drum messages and bugle calls were swamped by the din of exploding chemicals. Even whistle blasts with their limited vocabulary were often incoherent in the racket. Officers commanding by gesture were immediately targeted by defenders. By the end of the war experienced storm troops relied on small sections of men, often led by a well-schooled non-com, attacking with a light machine gun, a portable mortar, or a bag of grenades.

If the attackers successfully occupied an enemy trench they were unable to direct their fire support—crucial in an artillery war. A telephone cable might be run across no-man's-land, but it was often cut by the intense enemy fire. Until the very end of the war, wireless sets and their batteries were too heavy, cumbersome and delicate to be brought along.

The point is that most of the tools for the catastrophe were already on hand, evolved over a century thanks to open-handed allocations of public funds for research and development, even though most of the statesmen, admirals, and generals who signed or forwarded the cheques could scarcely conceive of their capacity for carnage.

Bringing scientists to war

When the war came, interested Governments could look for past examples of how to mobilize scientists to confront new problems.[22] Following the revolution of 1789 France was invaded by an alliance pledged to restore monarchy. The desperate Convention appealed for help to the Paris Academy of Sciences. Among the notable scientists called on were Charles Augustin de Coulomb, a pioneer in electricity, and Pierre-Simon Laplace, a mathematical astronomer. When the young Napoleon returned from his triumphs in Italy he spent some of his time at their research centre testing devices under development and discussing scientific problems. Then he mobilized a group of distinguished savants for his expedition to Egypt, where he signed orders as: 'Le Membre de' l'Institut,' Général en Chef'.

President Abraham Lincoln incorporated the US Academy of Sciences in 1863 for scientific assistance during the Civil War. The academicians worked on signalling, especially at night, on the prevention of corrosion, the more efficient use of steam as a power source, and other projects. Lincoln attended some night signalling experiments conducted from the tower of the Smithsonian Institution.

Despite long years of meticulous, expensive preparation, once the Great War was underway there were bolts from the blue: unexpected problems needing solutions. In Germany the Imperial General Staff was responsible for mobilizing needed scientific talent. The French Government started a new organization for this purpose at the outbreak of the war. The British lackadaisically stumbled and groped for ways to tap their scientific riches: muddling through. The Americans, who entered the war after 32 months, wisely mobilized scientists in advance. The following chapters will show how these systems worked by relating the case histories of six eminent scientists. Six may seem few, but because science is a social enterprise many others appear in each chapter, including those from allied countries. Finally we will see how some of the Britons who had done science for the first war ensured that it was organized effectively in the second war, during which many German civilian scientists sat on their hands.

Gas Warfare
Otto Hahn

Otto Hahn, his young wife Edith, and her father were strolling in Berlin on Sunday 28 June 1914 when the special editions hit the streets. The Austro-Hungarian Archduke Franz Ferdinand and his wife had been shot dead in Sarajevo, Bosnia-Herzegovina. They were horrified by the murders and father predicted war.[1] Hahn thought his pessimism excessive.

The murderers were youthful Bosnian terrorists armed and abetted by Serbian military intelligence. Their goal was to have the Bosnian Serbs governed by Serbia—a dream that still smoulders today. The Austro-Hungarian Government decided that they should go to war to stamp out Serbian state-sponsored terrorism. The German Kaiser was enraged by the slaughter of close friends—he had stayed with them in Bohemia just two weeks before—so he agreed that the Austrians should do whatever they thought necessary. Secretly the Austro-Hungarians wrote a stiff ultimatum to provoke the Serbs. The Serbs accepted it all except for clauses permitting Austrian police to enter Serbia to identify Government officials who had given the green light to military intelligence. Without another word, the Austro-Hungarians declared war on 28 July. The Germans secretly urged them to limited objectives.

The Russians had mobilized part of their army to give Serbia moral support. From then on all was fore-ordained by treaties and secret engagements between the major European powers. The Germans demanded that the Russians stop mobilizing. The Russians did not stop. Germany issued an ultimatum to the Russians and when it was rejected declared war on Russia on 1 August. To fulfil their treaty obligations, the French had also ordered mobilization, so the Germans declared war on them too—they must fight a two-front war.

First the Germans mobilized men who had finished full-time training less than five years previously; they re-joined their regiments each summer for manoeuvres. Hahn's class of older trained men, ages 27 to 39, would muster later when the railways could take them. They were organized into *Landwehr* regiments and divisions, second-line troops. At age 40, reservists were assigned for five years to the eldest group, the *Landstrum*.

The Kaiser Wilhelm Institutes

Hahn, aged 35, and nominated that year for the Nobel Prize, was torn away from Edith, his bride of little more than a year, their comfortable flat in Berlin, and his beloved laboratory at the Kaiser Wilhelm Institute (KWI) for Chemistry, a splendid new building in the suburb of Dahlem. The Institutes had been brought to life by vastly wealthy Leopold Koppel who offered to fund a KWI in Berlin for Physical Chemistry and Electrochemistry if Fritz Haber (Nobel Laureate 1918) would direct it—Haber was enticed from Karlsruhe by an annual salary of 15,000 marks (£720; roughly £144,000 today). The value of the £ has increased roughly 200-fold from then to 2014. Haber also received a house and other benefits. The Kaiser donated seven-and-a-half acres in Dahlem from his lands as King of Prussia. Haber planned his new laboratories as well as those in a neighbouring building for a KWI for Chemistry, to be directed by Richard Willstätter (Nobel Laureate 1915).

Hahn was an associate in the Chemistry Institute, overseeing a radioactivity unit with a salary of 4,000 marks (£190). He and his co-worker Lise Meitner had state-of-the-art laboratories on the ground floor, including a room for measuring radioactivity. The second woman to obtain a doctorate in physics from the University of Vienna, she came to Berlin in 1907 to attend Max Planck's (Nobel laureate 1918) lectures.[2] She also hoped to do research in Berlin, but feared that she was too shy to do well under any of the stars in the physics department. In Vienna she had worked briefly on radiation from radium. So Hahn was a possible mentor, even though he was a chemist. They were similar ages and she could bring herself to ask him scientific questions.

He had come to radioactivity by a similarly circuitous route. After taking a chemistry degree he applied for a commercial position in a German chemical company; the prospective employer insisted that first he must polish his English. In the autumn of 1904 Hahn went to University College London (UCL) as an unpaid volunteer in the laboratory of Sir William Ramsay (Nobel laureate 1904 for discovering the noble gases). Hahn expected that he would do organic chemistry but disconcertingly Ramsay handed him a porcelain dish holding a white powder containing a trace of radium, which Pierre and Marie Curie (Nobel laureates 1903) had discovered the year before. Hahn was to purify the radium and then make salts with large organic anions for precise determinations of radium's molecular weight.

Antoine Becquerel (Nobel laureate 1903) discovered radioactivity in 1896. He found that photographic film carefully shielded from light was fogged by uranium placed on the black paper wrapping. This showed that uranium releases energy that penetrates the paper and reacts with the film. Energy release by radioactive substances is palpable: they are warm, phosphorescent, certain other crystals glow when placed nearby, and they ionize the nearby air. Ionization is the easiest to quantify. They used an electroscope, a small metal box containing two rectangular strips of thin metal foil fastened together at one end and insulated from the box.[3] The strips and the box are charged to opposite polarities with a battery. The strips with the same charge repel one another so that the free ends spring apart. They stay apart for days because the air between them and the container wall is an insulator. Radiation entering the container ionizes the air within. Ionized air is a conductor, so electrons flow from the strips to the wall. As the charge difference between the strips diminishes they swing closer together. The distance between the strips is measured at set time intervals by looking at them through a glass window in the chamber wall, using a microscope with an ocular micrometre.

Following progress with his electroscope, Hahn purified 10 mg of radium by fractional crystallization. He also isolated another hitherto unknown radioactive substance which was named radiothorium. Its half-life is about two years, while radium's is roughly 1,600 years. At that time each new radioactive substance was assumed to be a new element, and was named accordingly. A few years later Frederick Soddy (Nobel Laureate 1921) found it impossible to separate radiothorium from thorium. Hence they must have the same number of electrons and therefore the same chemistry, but different molecular weights. He had discovered isotopes.

Ramsey told Hahn not to be a fool, a man who had discovered an element should aim for a professorship. He wrote to Ernest Rutherford (Nobel laureate 1906), the leading investigator of radioactivity. Rutherford was a New Zealander who was now at McGill University in Montreal as a research professor of physics. He invited Hahn to Canada.

The Curies believed that radioactivity is an intrinsic, timeless property of certain elements. They release energy ceaselessly, somehow the energy lost is replenished from their environment. Rutherford and Soddy, then a young colleague in the McGill chemistry department, sucked a radioactive gas out from an ore containing radioactive thorium (it is an extremely short-lived isotope of the noble gas radon). The gases' radioactivity declined by half every few minutes. They had discovered that radioactive isotopes have half-lives.[4] They showed that radium decays with a half-life of 1,590 years, and that one of its decay products is a radioactive radon isotope with a half-life of 3.82 days. The atoms of radioactive elements are unstable; they release energy when they disintegrate.

Rutherford discovered that radioactive elements release energy in three forms. Heavy, powerful alpha rays, which are helium atoms stripped of their electrons so they have two positive charges; beta rays, which are electrons, and gamma rays, which are electromagnetic radiations like x-rays.

Rutherford was an irrepressible, vivid personality; you could hear him speaking several rooms away. Behind his back he was known as the 'croc' after the crocodile in Peter Pan that heralds its approach by the swallowed clock ticking in its belly. In Montreal Hahn discovered two new radioactive isotopes. Rutherford roared with laughter in 1906 when he was notified that he would receive the Nobel Prize for chemistry, a subject he gaily proclaimed he knew nothing whatsoever about.

After Hahn returned to Berlin, he identified new radioactive isotopes, eventually he and his colleagues discovered eleven of them. He became a professor in 1910. By the time that they moved into the new KWI for Chemistry, Meitner had been appointed as one of Planck's assistants, the lowest academic rank, and was no longer living on her parent's largesse. In 1913, she became an associate in the Institute. The following year, to outbid a tempting offer from Prague, her salary was doubled to 3,000 marks (£144). The Hahn-Meitner Laboratory had an annual research budget of 2,000 Marks (£96); half for equipment and half for assistants.

Meitner was formal, 'lady-like', and decorous. Until Hahn married they met only in their workroom and at the weekly physics colloquium and ate together only at official functions. 'And yet we were really very close friends'. While they worked she hummed songs by German composers, but when things were going really well they sang together, usually songs by Brahms. Scientifically they were a well matched duo because radioactivity is on the interface between physics and chemistry. As Hahn put it: 'I never really managed to understand thermodynamics, far from ever being able to make anything of thermodynamic equations'. Furthermore, she had to learn how to separate elements by dissolving preparations in acid and then precipitating the constituents as insoluble salts.

Mobilization

Meitner was even more of a Godsend when he was called back into the army. She could keep their radioactivity measurements going. She also promised to keep him up-to-date on new papers and lab gossip, and she would try to comfort his wife. Hahn knew that Edith, with brittle nerves, would be distraught while he was in the army. He assured her that the *Landwehr* would not get near the fighting and that it was a just war. They had plenty of money because he had received a royalty of 66,000 marks (£3,168) on the sales of mesothorium purified by his method. There was a strong medical market for radioactive substances, and mesothorium was more effective and cheaper than radium. Ten per cent had gone to Meitner, who had helped with the crystallizations, but he was left with a lovely nest egg. (In 1915, he received 40,000 marks (£1,920), but payments stopped after the blockade cut off ore imports.)

The Austrian author Stefan Zwieg caught the mood: 'It was the war of an unsuspicious generation, and the greatest peril was the inexhaustible faith of the nations in the single sided justice of their cause'.[5] From the Institutes, James Franck (Nobel laureate 1925), Gustav Hertz (Nobel laureate 1925), and Hans Geiger were also called up as reserve officers.[6] Railway stations overflowed with wildly cheering crowds pressing bouquets and bottles on their heroes.

The Germans were outnumbered. They could field 97 divisions; the Austro-Hungarians added a further 60 divisions. They were opposed on two fronts by 90 French, 150 Russian and 12 Serbian divisions.[7] Allied propaganda charged that the Germans started the war to conquer Europe, or perhaps the world. If so, they were incredibly miserly and incredibly optimistic.

The Imperial General Staff, still basking in their glory earned in the defeats of Austro-Hungary and France almost two generations before, devised the Schlieffen plan to cope with the two-front war. Confident that Russians mobilization would be slow, they would crush the French first, with their spearhead a powerful right wing that would bypass the fortified, mountainous frontier by an end-run through neutral Belgium—even though this would add the British Empire to their foes. It is a measure of German statesmen that they assented to such recklessness. Inevitably their left wing facing the French would be weak; if pushed it should give ground slowly. Schlieffen's successor, the elderly Helmut von Moltke, the nephew of the brilliant general who had led the Prussians against Austria and then the Germans against France, found the plan too audacious. He weakened his *schwerpunkt* by transferring forces from right to left and permitting the left wing to counterattack rather than withdrawing. When the Russians invaded East Prussia the commander of the Germany army there briefly considered withdrawing behind a defensible river line. Moltke replaced him by Hindenburg with Erich Ludendorff as chief of staff. He also sent two unasked-for corps from the right wing, who arrived after the Russian invaders were crushed. His final folly was when the right wing glimpsed the top of the Eiffel Tower on the horizon. Imperial Supreme Headquarters, OHL (*Oberste Heersleitung*), was in Luxembourg, where they were connected by telephone to both Eastern and Western fronts, but the spearheads were only in contact by coded wireless messages. Concerned that they were overextended, Moltke sent a staff lieutenant colonel who had never seen a battlefield to decide what to do. He ordered the right wing to withdraw to a defensive line along the River Aisne. The crucial Battle of the Marne was between the retreating German rear-guard and cautiously advancing Allied troops, who believed they were compelling their enemy to give way. If the Germans had stood firm they probably would have won the war.[8]

Moltke was superseded by the Prussian War Minister, Erich von Falkenhayn—at first secretly. The Allied pursuit was bloodily halted along the river Aisne, where the retreating Germans holed up on the hilly north bank behind strands of barbed wire in a hastily prepared trench line.

The first casualty from the KWI was James Chadwick (Nobel laureate 1935), who had studied with Ernest Rutherford who had moved to Manchester. Now he was working with Hans Geiger, who had returned to Germany from Manchester two years before. Soon after Geiger left for the front, Chadwick was imprisoned at a racetrack on the west of Berlin—eight men in a stall built for two horses. Five thousand Britons were rounded up and interned in similar shoddy conditions. To pass the tedious hours they started a scientific discussion group. One participant, a young Royal Engineer officer Charles D. Ellis, who was in Germany studying the language, became enchanted with atomic physics. After the war Ellis studied with and then collaborated with Rutherford. He was elected to the Royal Society at the age of 34.[9] Planck, Meitner and others tried to improve the scientific prisoner's living conditions, provided publications, some experimental apparatus, and visited. Later the captives were permitted occasional return visits.

Offiziers-Stellvertretern (candidate officer) Hahn reported to his regiment in Wittenberg. He commanded an infantry platoon, about 85 men. Around half of the eligible German lads were called up for two years of mandatory military training; farm boys preferred because they were strong and obedient. Some educated young men, like the Hahn boys, volunteered for a year of training, paying part of the cost. At the end of his year Hahn passed the examination for a commission, but opted not to continue officer training when he left for England.

In his battalion the other officer candidates were invited to eat in the officers' mess—Hahn was not, because he had no right to wear a university duelling cap. His father was a successful glazier in Frankfurt who sent his four boys to university. The social side of university life was dominated by the fencing societies—*Burschenschaft*—whose members, distinguished by distinctive, rakish caps, drank beer and duelled against other societies. Father Hahn would not permit his sons to join a *Burschenschaft*. Otto was allowed to join the National Scientific and Medical Association whose members did not duel and were not entitled to wear caps. Hence Hahn did not eat with the officers. He did not let on that he had duelled with a lout who had called him a coward; the sabre scar was on his arm.

Hahn was prepared for snobbery but did not expect to be out of shape. Of course facial wrinkles showed that time had passed since his first stint in the army. His moustache was trimmed short and shaved to the length of his mouth, no longer his youthful boar's tusk. His hairline had receded almost to the top of his skull, leaving him with an impressively high, slightly sloping forehead that emphasized his bushy eyebrows and deep-set eyes. His chin was neither weak nor prominent; he had an amiable, slightly lopsided grin, with the left side of his mouth curved up just a bit more than the right. His body had aged less than his scalp. He jogged, ran long distances, and attended a weekly gymnastics class, but a few years before he had wrenched a knee severely while skiing. Each day as they marched west this knee swelled painfully. His soldier servant Rehfeldt massaged it every night, but it grew worse. Finally the medical officer ordered him back to Aachen for treatment. When he returned to his unit, he was permitted to 'organize himself' a bicycle to keep up. He loved to join in the singing as they marched. In Dahlem he sang in a glee club called the 'Hoarse Pheasant', and shortly before the war Max Planck persuaded him to take singing lessons.

Soon after they crossed the frontier, Hahn shoved aside the rifle one of his men was aiming at a Belgian civilian running off in the distance. The outraged soldier insisted that he had been thwarted from killing a sniper who had discarded his uniform. As evidence, he pointed to a Belgian army tunic lying in a wet ditch, which any fool could see must have marinated there for days. Most of the invaders were sure that they would be ambushed by partisans, just as their grandfathers had been in France.

One night there was an alarm—500 Belgians were about to attack. None came. There were similar alarms on following nights and a rattled sergeant shot one of his own men. After that they had a few quiet nights. With the next alarm, Hahn loudly inquired whether the same formidable 500 were at them yet again. Laughter relaxed trigger fingers.

When they marched into Louvain the devastated city centre was still smouldering. On the sixth night of German occupation the central part of the city had burnt, including the historic library of the ancient university and its priceless collection. Germans claimed that the arson and chaos was triggered by a premeditated sniper attack on their troops. Belgians said that two German columns had encountered one another unexpectedly, exchanged shots and then set fire to buildings they thought sheltered snipers. Hahn considered the Belgian version more likely. The Allies portrayed the Germans as sadistic, barbaric Huns.

Newspapers on both sides revelled in accounts of the depraved evils of their foes. German intellectuals rushed to their country's defence; in September they issued a *Proclamation to the Civilized World* defending the invasion of Belgium, the conduct of their troops, and pompously arguing that the Allies were petrified by German intellectual and economic superiority. Among the 93 signers were Fritz Haber, Emil Fischer (Nobel Laureate 1902), Walther Nernst (Nobel laureate 1920), Wilhelm Ostwald (Nobel laureate 1909) and Richard Willstätter. (A few biologists argued against the war publically. They retained their academic positions during the war, but were fired after the Versailles Treaty.)

The Allies charged that the German Army gave their troops free rein to loot, rape and murder. American newspaper correspondents were the largest group of neutral observers in Belgium. They issued a joint statement that the German troops were controlled by their officers and were behaving properly; civilians were slaughtered in accord with military regulations against civilian sniping, not by men running amok.[10] Roughly 5,000 Belgian civilians were killed during the invasion, most accused of sniping. Word of the reprisals spread rapidly and there was little civilian sniping when the German Army entered France.

Hahn and Rehfeldt were transferred to another battalion, where Hahn ate amiably with the officers. When they were allocated captured Belgian and French machine guns—a mystery to all—they turned to their scientist. He figured out how to load, how to release the safety, and then fired a few shots, before coaching his platoon.

They marched across the border to the fortified city of Lille, which the French had evacuated so it would not be levelled by artillery fire. Lise Meitner had mailed him two letters, but neither came through. She had enrolled as a part-time student of anatomy and x-ray techniques at the Lichterfelde Hospital near Dahlem.[11] Hahn's division was assigned to the newly formed Sixth Army. Its commander, the handsome Rupprecht Crown Prince of Bavaria, was cheered when he was driven slowly through the streets of Lille in his gleaming, open automobile.

After the French and British assaults on the line along the Aisne were bloodily repulsed, Falkenhayn felt free to return to the offensive in France, striking toward the channel ports, throwing everything he had into the pot, including newly formed, scarcely trained, volunteer divisions. Tens of thousands of untrained young men who had enlisted, many of them students, were chucked into the cauldron.

After a few days Hahn's regiment left Lille marching southwest toward the roar of gunfire. Along the front they lay on their bellies on soggy ground, straining to see the men they were to kill. About 300 metres ahead a line of men in field grey was   lying on the ground; presumably they would lead the attack. The bugles blew, the officers shouted 'onward', the men shouted 'hurrah', and they rushed forward. The grey line in front of them did not budge—slaughtered earlier. Hahn and his platoon bypassed cadavers, body parts, and pools of blood: what remained of a volunteer regiment.

Their attacks failed. Unable to break through the French in Artois, they were marched up into Belgium to attack a salient shielding the rail centre of Ypres. They were opposite the village of Kruiseke, which was at the base of a mini-salient extending into the German lines; it was garrisoned by the British 20th Brigade. The first German attack was repulsed. At 09:00 on 26 October, heavy howitzers began dropping high explosive shells onto the two companies of the Scots Guards defending the apex of the salient. About 50 German infantrymen infiltrated between the Scots and the battalion on their left. Many of the infiltrators were captured, killed, or struck down by their own shells; the survivors hid in the woods.[12] An hour later the Germans attacked with Hahn's machine guns spitting out covering fire. According to the British *Official History* the infiltrators hidden in the woods shouted 'retire', so some of the British abandoned their trenches. True or not, about noon the Germans broke into the salient and swept into the village, capturing nine officers and 300 other ranks. The commander of the First Army, Sir Douglas Haig, rode up the road toward the front at about 15:00 and was 'astounded at the terror-stricken men coming back'.[13] General Ruggles-Brise rallied the survivors, who formed a new line along the base of the former salient. The 20th Brigade had lost more than 1,000 men; their foes probably had comparable losses.

Hahn's division was shifted to another part of the Ypres front, as Falkenhayn brought in unbloodied troops to continue his murderous attacks. The Allies fought for every metre while the attackers, especially those scarcely trained, paid a heavy price in what Germans still refer to as the 'slaughter of the innocents'. Hahn was mentioned in dispatches. At the impressive ceremony when the first decorations were distributed to his regiment he was awarded the Iron Cross 2nd Class. When the weather became impossible, Falkenhayn ordered his army in the west onto the defensive, they dug in. As Falkenhayn later wrote this '... first gave time to exploit science and engineering to their full extent in the interests of the war.'[14]

Toward the end of December, Hahn received his first letter from Lise Meitner. We have copies of her letters, but not his. She wrote about progress in the laboratory and about their comrades. Hahn's first student, who had just received his degree, and a professor had been killed. She was about to visit her family in Vienna, her younger brother was serving in Austrian Poland and had been promoted to first lieutenant. The Austrians began the war by striking Serbia to teach them their lesson. Instead the experienced Serbian army more than held their own and soon many of the Austrians had to be shifted to Poland to face a forceful Russian attack.

On Christmas Eve Hahn's unit was in the trenches near the town of Messines. No-man's-land was about 50 m wide. The artillery fell silent, so men on both sides occasionally poked their heads over the parapets. Finally a particularly bold fellow stood in full view. Almost immediately the trenches on both sides emptied, and the foes walked forward to shake hands and to clap one another on the back.

They exchanged gifts. The English gave cigarettes, prized for their high quality. The Germans reciprocated with candied fruit and beer. Hahn was in his element: with his excellent English and a musical repertoire in both languages, he led the singing with élan. The fun went on until late that night and continued next morning. Flabbergasted generals were terrified that the war might end spontaneously, so staff officers were rushed to the front to reinstate hostilities. At noon on Christmas day Hahn's regiment was ordered to open fire. Hahn told his company commander that he saw no enemy, so he did not know where to shoot. The war began again on Boxing Day.

Two days later Hahn's regiment was withdrawn from the front, no longer an effective fighting force. They celebrated New Year's Eve in a Belgian army barracks in Brussels. Hahn contributed to the merriment by singing a ditty derogatory to troops on the line of communications, who were known as 'down the line dodgers'.

> Who turns his back on German gels, And picks up flighty mad'moiselles, Who never sleeps alon-i-o, The dodger down the line, we know[15]

Early in 1915 he was commissioned as a lieutenant. Meitner wrote distressing news: in December Fritz Haber and two of his KWI staff were synthesizing a potential tear gas. Haber had just left the room when the reaction exploded, one man lost a hand, and Otto Sackur was killed. Sackur and Hahn had been close friends since they met at UCL.

Haber and poison gas

In the middle of January, Hahn was ordered to report to Fritz Haber. The last Hahn had known Haber was a *Landstrum* vice-sergeant, now he was an army captain. In some photographs, Haber looks like the stereotype of a Prussian officer, with shaven head and duelling scar on his chin. In person he was an unmilitary type: 47-years-old, plump, with sagging flesh, a cigar perpetually propped in his jaw, his pockets bulging with notebooks and other paraphernalia, an embodiment of civilian clutter.

Without Haber's chemistry the Germans could not have lasted more than a few months. Nitrates are essential components of fertilizers and explosives. The Germans imported them from saltpetre mines in the Alacama Desert of Chile, which would be emptied by 1930. Perhaps the nitrogen from air could be transformed into usable compounds. Prominent chemists had tried and failed. In 1905, Haber's thermodynamic calculations proved that the reaction is feasible and he succeeded in synthesizing ammonia by heating together nitrogen and hydrogen at extremely high pressure using uranium or osmium as a catalyst. His industrial sponsors, the Badishche Anilin und Sodafabrik screened 2,500 substances for the most effective catalyst, iron is best. A brilliant chemical engineer, Carl Bosch (Nobel laureate 1931), adapted the process for industry. OHL based their plans on monthly ammonia production.

At the outbreak of war Haber and Willstätter asked the director of the KWG how they might help the war effort. He had no suggestions, though Haber was named Head of the Chemistry Division of the Prussian Ministry of War.

Haber's next bright idea was evoked by Walther Nernst, professor of chemistry in Berlin, 50-years-old, an ardent patriot and a lover of motor cars.[16] As a volunteer he had driven almost to Paris with the German right wing. When the troops vanished into trenches shielded by thick barricades of barbed wire, he foresaw stalemate. He thought about how chemistry might end the deadlock and discussed the possibilities with Major Max Bauer, a 45-year-old general staff officer at OHL.[17]

German general staff officers, identified by a carmine collar flash, were intelligent, studious, and rigorously selected. The usual climb to the general staff started at the War Academy, where admission was won though a stiff competitive examination graded by senior officers who were not allowed to know the candidate's names or regiments. Professors from the University of Berlin, just across the street, taught some of the courses. After three years' intensive study, the top one-third was appointed to the general staff. In 1915, there were 352 general staff officers: 113 in Berlin and the rest in the field. (The British had 80 general staff officers for their much smaller army.) Bauer's route to the Staff was exceptional. From a poor family, he became a foot [heavy field] artillery officer. After ten years' service, he was appointed adjutant to the commission that tested guns, which included naval officers and civilian engineers. As an observer of the Russo-Japanese War he watched Japanese heavy guns smash Russian fortifications. In 1905, he was appointed to the General Staff. Disguised as a wood merchant, he reconnoitred the Russian forts in Poland and the Belgian forts.

Then he and Erich Ludendorff planned an assault on Liège, to crack open the gate into Belgium. Enormous guns would be needed to demolish the ring of forts surrounding the city. But first infiltrating infantry must prevent the Belgians from dynamiting the vital railway bridges over the river Meuse. (By chance Ludendorff was on the scene in August 1914. When the infantry commander was killed he led the successful attack.) In 1906 the Krupp works was commissioned to design a huge mortar. Bauer worked closely with the Krupp research department, headed by Professor Rausenberger, as they designed the 42 cm mortar that became famous in 1914 as Big Bertha. He also worked with chemical companies on explosives, and was responsible for evaluating the economic problems that would be posed by a long war. It is hard to conceive of an officer better primed to listen to Nernst's idea—they agreed to try shells filled with tear gas.

Haber was invited to their trial, held on the artillery range near Cologne. He was unimpressed. Tears only streamed down his cheeks when he stood on the edge of the shell hole. Tens of thousands of shells would be needed to make a sufficient length of front uninhabitable; at that time such numbers were beyond belief. Better to use the wind to blow a cloud of poison gas at the enemy. A heavier than air gas would creep down into trenches and dugouts. Phosgene would be ideal, it was very poisonous, but only a small amount was produced for dyeing. There was plenty of chlorine, they were producing 70 tons per day, a few deep breaths of air containing chlorine at 1,000 parts in a million are fatal, and it is two-and-a-half times as dense as air.

Bauer arranged for Haber to brief Falkenhayn on how to win the war with a surprise chlorine attack. Surprise was indispensable, because countermeasures would be straightforward. Falkenhayn authorized Haber to go ahead and on the spot promoted him to captain. The German chemical cartel was glad to pitch in. Their academic-military-industrial complex was gelling nicely.

Hahn reported to Haber at noon in a Brussels hotel. Haber lolled in bed in pyjamas as he explained his project before asking Hahn to join his team. Hahn protested that it was a terrible thing to poison men. Haber replied: 'Someone will smash your head in. We are only responsible for the chemistry and technical implementation.'[18] Was it more atrocious than cutting men in half with a machine gun? This was a chance to end the war straightaway. What about international law? No problem. The First Hague Convention banned the use of shells releasing asphyxiating gas, but did not mention gas from cylinders. The French had already used non-lethal gases at the front. Hahn signed on. Bauer transferred him to Field Weather Station No. 2, a temporary unit to bring together the scientists recruited for gas warfare. Haber announced that there would be a meteorology congress in Brussels, as cover for the influx of so many well-known scientists, including Hahn's friends James Franck, Gustav Hertz, Erwin Madelung, and Wilhelm Westphal.

The first attack

Renamed the 'Disinfection Unit', they were almost surely the most scientifically distinguished military unit in history. In Berlin they attended a short course on the properties of chlorine, the use of protective breathing devices, and meteorology. A regular *pionier*, Colonel Peterson, took command in March, so the unit now became *Pionierkommando* Peterson.[19] Soon they had 500 men facing the British along the road from Menin to Ypres.

Meitner had not heard from Hahn for four anxious weeks. She begged him to reassure her with a postcard. He wrote a letter in which, judging from her reply, he seriously breached security. She assured him that he is a compassionate man—this may be a merciful weapon to end the dreadful war. As always she wrote formally; it was a decade later when they began to 'du' one another.

The *Pionierkommando* expanded to 1,600 men; on 27 April 1915 it became *Pionier Regiment* 35. A few weeks later *Pionier Regiment* 36 was added to the order of battle. They conducted a small-scale test at the Belgian army grounds at Beverloo. Haber and Bauer rode into the edge of the chlorine cloud, their horses bucked and foamed with sweat. Both men spent several days in bed recuperating. A leader of the chemical cartel, Carl Duisberg, was also slightly poisoned.

At the railhead in Flanders they filled cylinders from tank cars of chlorine. The cylinders were 1.2–1.5 m tall, weighed 85 kg and were as 'unwieldy as a corpse'. They were manhandled into the trenches at night. Twice cylinders were ruptured by British shell fire, the released gas killed three men and injured 50. After the second incident Regiment 35 was equipped with standard miner's oxygen breathing apparatus, 3,000 were available and more were on order. The cylinders were plumbed so that liquid chlorine siphoned out; if the gas expanded within the cylinders they became freezing cold and were likely to obstruct.

When almost ready, sharp-eyed subordinates warned Peterson that in their present position regardless of wind direction a gas cloud would sweep over their own as well as the enemy trenches. They shifted front to the northwest of Ypres, facing the French, where a wind in the correct direction would only poison enemy. By 11 April 1915, 1,600 large and 4,130 small cylinders were in place grouped as batteries of ten plumbed together so that they released through a single outlet. The cylinders were spread along seven kilometres of front. The attacking infantry would advance far enough behind the cloud so they would not require protection. After the accidental deaths, the infantry were provided with cotton pads soaked with sodium thiosulphate solution, which would filter out the chlorine; this was how workers in the chemical industry were protected. The pads did not arrive until 15 April, and many lacked tapes to tie them on, so they had to be held over the nose with a hand—awkward for an attacking infantryman.

Belgian intelligence learned that pads had been issued. The French were informed about the cylinders by prisoners and by a deserter, probably an Alsatian. British medical officers were warned that a chemical attack was possible, but not told how to respond. Allied commanders had good reason to shrug off warnings. There was no intelligence that reinforcements or guns were arriving. Falkenhayn had refused to reinforce the attackers or even to provide additional artillery ammunition, which was in short supply. Most likely he thought breakthrough was scientific hyperbole— he does not even refer to the attack in his memoirs. His plan for the west was to kill more than they lost. In the east he would try for a break-through to buck-up the flagging Austro-Hungarians, by using every available shell.

The gas attack was scheduled for 07:00 on Tuesday 22 April, but it was dead calm.[20] Finally a late afternoon breeze blew gently from the northeast. At 17:00 the stopcocks were opened. Within ten minutes, 150 tons of chlorine flushed from the cylinders. The cloud formed in front of the German line, and then crept slowly toward the enemy, at about 0.5 m per sec. It started white and then became yellow-green. The earth was warm, so the heated gas rose until its crest was 10 to 30 m above ground level. The Algerian defenders leapt out of their trench and ran toward the rear, leaving six kilometres of trench line undefended. After the lingering patches of gas blew away, the German infantry advanced cautiously. On their flanks opposition was spirited, but there was almost no one in front, within an hour they occupied their objectives, the villages of Langemark and Pilkem. Once there they followed orders and halted, having taken 2,000 prisoners and 51 guns. Ypres was a little over three kilometres further on.

The Allies rushed up troops to plug the gap. The Germans were repulsed when they attempted to move forward the next morning. More gas was released on the flank of the initial attack, against trenches held by Canadians, who the day before had watched the sun turn a sickly green and identified the gas as chlorine because it stank like their drinking water.[21] They fought regardless of the poison, so on day two the Germans gained little. The Germans reported that they treated 200 gas casualties in their hospitals, twelve of whom died. The Allies asserted that the gas killed 5,000 and wounded 15,000. After this, gas could never be the decisive weapon—surprise was gone. Falkenhayn had chucked away his chance for an early victory.

The world raged at a new barbarity. As the military historian Liddell Hart wrote: '... it was novel. The world condones abuses but detests innovations.'[22] The British Cabinet agreed to retaliate in kind. The Germans attacked with gas clouds six more times during the Second Battle of Ypres, but gained little ground and were not impressed with their new weapon. By 20 May almost every man in the Allied forces carried a gauze mask capable of filtering chlorine out of inspired air.

Hahn did not witness the first attack, because Colonel Peterson had perceived that he understood poison gas clouds and had a soldier's eye for ground and fields of fire. He and James Franck were sent to Champagne, where the French were attacking ferociously; they are likely to have been the sharp eyes that saw the flaw in their first position in the salient. They inspected the entire frontline in Champagne without finding a site where a gas cloud release would help the defence.

Meitner wrote from Vienna to congratulate Hahn on the success at Ypres. Her brother and brother-in-law were both home on leave and optimistic that they would beat the Russians in the Carpathians. Geiger was with the field artillery at the front in Lorraine. She signed herself *Institutskameraden*.

In Dahlem the scientists at the KWI searched for volatile poisons by plodding page by page through the *Beilstein Handbook of Organic Chemistry*, which lists the properties of every carbon compound described in the literature since 1771.

Gas in Poland

Regiment 35 was sent east to support a joint, German-commanded attack on the Russian flank between the towns of Gorlice and Tarnow. By the time the gas arrived the Russian defensive line, more ditches than trenches, had been smashed by high explosive and the Russians were retreating headlong, scorching the earth behind them. A few days later Hahn photographed the Kaiser standing in front of his automobile in full dress uniform. Haber also came east; leaving Berlin shortly after his wife killed herself with a shot to her chest. She detested gas warfare, but it seems unlikely that it provoked her suicide.

Regiment 35 moved north to take part in an attack on Warsaw. They bivouacked in a burnt town, even more miserable than the usual filthy, verminous Polish village. Gustav Hertz tried to cheer his comrades with his favourite beverage, 95 per cent laboratory alcohol, but Hahn could not develop a taste for it. Rehfeldt and Hertz's batman disputed about whose lieutenant fed the most lice.

Meitner returned to the lab, where something had gone wrong with their measurements of the half-life of mesothorium, so she was starting again. She was busy refereeing scientific manuscripts submitted to the journals, because few reviewers were available. Geiger had been promoted to first lieutenant.

On 12 June 1915, after several bumbled attempts when the wind failed, they released a mixed cloud of chlorine and phosgene: chlorine acts promptly, while phosgene often takes a day to kill or incapacitate, but is ten times more toxic. The Russians vanished—either stricken or bolting—but some gas blew back, which so frightened the German infantry that they huddled in their trenches even after the cloud dispersed. Hahn and a few others, without using their breathing apparatus, walked through the former Russian line waving their arms to show they were alive and unopposed. The infantry were goaded into moving, but meanwhile Hahn had an upfront view of his victims: men dying with purple faces and black tongues protruding grotesquely as they hacked up bits of lung. He tried to save some with oxygen from his breathing apparatus, but to no avail. The German Official History states that 350 Russians died of gas poisoning. Hahn felt 'profoundly guilty and disturbed'.

Relatively little is known about how these poisons act.[23] Chlorine attacks the air tubes leading into the lungs. A few breaths are enough to produce intolerable distress. Phosgene has little effect on the larger tubes, but in time destroys the alveoli: tiny, terminal sacks in the lung where oxygen is taken up and carbon dioxide is released. The damaged lungs fill with fluid. Blood volume drops markedly before death.

Gas masks

Hahn was recalled to Berlin to set up a 'gas-protection' organization for training troops. Their gas mask was going into mass production. It was a tight fitting leather mask, treated with coal tar and tallow and fitted with eyepieces. A strip of rubber sealed the mask to the face. The wearer breathed in and exhaled through a circular filter, which screwed onto the front of the mask, so it was easily replaced. The screw fitting had the dimensions used for German light bulbs and their sockets, so they were spewed out by available machinery.

Haber had started the search for an effective filter, beginning with charcoal, the chemist's favourite absorbent. Charcoal is produced by heating wood in the absence of oxygen and then is activated by heating in steam. A millilitre of charcoal may have a surface area of more than 1,000 square metres. Many chemicals stick to its surface, which is why it is used in filters to absorb cooking odours and liquors are aged in casks with charred linings. It absorbed chlorine well, but does less well with phosgene. They tried to improve performance by absorbing other chemicals onto the charcoal, but this made them less effective for chlorine. Haber asked Willstätter for help. They were friendly next-door neighbours, even though their dogs persisted in snarling at one another through the boundary fence. Willstätter would not work on poisons but would defend against them. His group began with diatomaceous earth impregnated with potassium carbonate and dusted with activated charcoal. It absorbs chlorine, but a little phosgene leaks through. He tested his filters by breathing in a room containing a low concentration of phosgene.

The Russians introduced chloropicrin. It produces nausea, so if some gets through the filter the mask is pulled off. German filters did not trap it. Willstätter's group came up with a three-layer filter: first treated diatomaceous earth, second charcoal, and third pumice granules impregnated with potassium carbonate and hexamine, which binds any remaining phosgene or chloropicrin. Willstätter could not explain why he tried hexamine, which has a box-like structure that serves as a trap—it just came to him. They used high quality charcoal prepared from vegetables; later in the war it was impregnated with zinc oxide. Initially the layers were separated by thin gauze, which later was replaced by paper impregnated with chlorinated naphthalene.[24] Thirty million three-layer filters were manufactured by early 1916 and Willstätter was awarded the Iron Cross 2nd Class.

Better still, in 1915 he was awarded the Nobel Prize for his work on plant pigments. He showed that the green photosynthetic pigment chlorophyll contains magnesium held in a structure similar to that holding iron in haemoglobin. The yellow pigments are carotenoids, made from 40 carbon atoms, while the blue and reds are anthocyanins, complicated ringed structures containing sugars. He had beautified the KWI site by planting the empty space between the institutes with dense banks of colourful flowers. When he left to take the chemistry chair in Munich, he harvested the blooming tulips and gentians and sent them to hospitals.

The chemists also inspected filters from captured enemy gas masks; any alteration signalled that a new poison might be in the works.

Hahn was sent to Berlin, but did not see Meitner because she had left for Vienna to volunteer as an x-ray nurse-technician in the Austro-Hungarian army. Hahn became a human guinea pig. There are marked species differences in sensitivity to poisons. Both sides began by testing on dogs, a poor choice. The French found that low concentrations of hydrogen cyanide poison dogs; they amassed a massive stockpile of shells filled with it, planning a surprise attack. In Britain the physiologist Joseph Barcroft and a dog entered a closed chamber containing a 1 in 2,000 concentration: the dog convulsed and died in 33 seconds, Barcroft was unaffected after ten minutes. Later the British did their preliminary tests on goats and their decisive tests on primates.

Filters and gases were tested in wooden, gas-tight huts built behind the KWI. The tester put on a gas mask and stayed in the chamber until convinced that gas was getting through. His time inside was measured with a stopwatch. Gases were tested by entering without a mask and breathing in a low concentration of the chemical until the tester was positive that he was being poisoned. They must react to gas, not fear. One of Hahn's fellow testers stayed in too long and died. Hahn noticed that after exposure to low levels of phosgene a cigarette tasted frightful. His observation was publicized and used at the front as a useful warning gauge, because phosgene is odourless. Another of Hahn's dangerous tasks was to walk through test gas clouds while taking samples for determining the concentration of the poison. Franck was also a guinea pig.

Hahn's work in Berlin kept him away from the next German gas attack in Poland. Again the gas blew back on their own lines, poisoning Hertz, who spent months in hospital and ultimately was discharged. He returned to the physics department in Berlin where he was soon joined by Franck, discharged due to severe dysentery. Together they studied the flow of electrons passing through a tube filled with low concentrations of gases or of vaporized metals. Their results are predicted by the Bohr model of the atom, in which electrons move from one orbit to the next by gaining or releasing a quantum of energy. Quanta had been envisioned by Planck and Einstein, now they were made real.

Warsaw fell on 4 August 1915. The Germans and Austro-Hungarians drove the shattered Russian army out from most of Poland. In September, Hahn returned to Regiment 35, which was preparing a new attack near Riga (now the capital of Latvia). Before the attack was launched he was on a train west where on 19 October they carried out a large but not very effective attack near Reims, followed by several more cylinder attacks on the French.

The British retaliate

The Allies planned a joint offensive for September. The British were to attack near the village of Loos. Their infantry would have to advance across open ground spread out like a stage before German observers perched on the superstructures of coalmine elevators. They planned to screen their infantry with smoke candles and chlorine released from 5,000, 200 lb cylinders. Haig, who commanded the attacking Army, considered the gas crucial. At 05:00 on D-day an aide lit a cigarette. Haig watched the smoke lazily drift toward the enemy line and ordered the attack. The author Robert Graves, who was with the Royal Welch Fusiliers in the assault trenches, wrote that gas was released little by little because many of the men detailed to open the valves had been issued spanners that did not fit the nuts on the valves.[25] Finally they were opened with the few variable spanners on hand. This is not cynical, literary whimsy. Charles H. Foulkes, the Royal Engineer who commanded the 1,404 men responsible for the release, reported that some of their fixed spanners were of soft metal that split and some of the nuts on the valves were round rather than square and were not fit by the issued spanners.[26] The wind was so light that the chlorine cloud hovered just in front of the British trenches. The advancing infantry emerging from the stationary cloud of gas and smoke were slaughtered by machine guns. The Germans remembered it as the *Leichenfeld von Loos* (corpse field of Loos).

Hahn was back in Berlin in December 1915, preparing to leave for Turkey. Bulgaria had entered the war that autumn. In a few months the Germans, Austro-Hungarians and Bulgarians overran Serbia, Montenegro and Albania.[27] Bulgarian belligerency also opened the rail line to Turkey. The British and French had landed on the Gallipoli

Peninsula in the spring, after their old battleships failed to force the straits, but the invaders were pinned close to the beaches by the Ottoman army, forewarned by the naval attack and assisted by a few German officers and specialists. Now the Germans shipped them heavy guns and planned a gas cloud attack as well—Hahn was to decide where to release it. The Allies did not wait to be pushed off; they slipped off the beaches in two stages, without casualties—thanks to General Sir Charles Monro, who was sent there to pull out the chestnuts and did so brilliantly. [28] Churchill deprecated him as the general who 'came, saw, and capitulated'. Subsequently Monro was appointed commander of the Indian Army; during a great European war this seems like poor use for outstanding military talent. Hahn's trip east was scrubbed and he wintered in Flanders.

Meitner's medical work

Meitner was now a radiological technician at Reserve Hospital No.1 in Lemberg (now Lviv, Ukraine). She had lieutenant's perks and was paid £180 a year. The hospital was only 40 km behind the front, so they received critical cases. Most of the ward attendants were prisoners who poked fun at their Tsar and claimed that they were keen to fight infidel Turks—not fellow Christians. Her brother was safe and now was fighting the hated Italians, who had entered the war in spring 1915. (The leading young Austrian theoretical physicist, Fritz Hasenöhrl, was killed on the Italian front.) By the end of November she had taken more than 200 x-rays, assisted in the operating theatre, sometimes as anaesthetist, and had repaired the hospital's electrical system. They received their first patient with frozen feet. At their Christmas party, they entertained 1,000 patients; Hahn celebrated at home with Edith. Meitner weighed only 50 kg and wished she might gain a bit. Worse of all, she felt so out of touch that she 'no longer knew what physics is'.

In France Marie Curie equipped 20 donated vehicles with x-ray equipment to be used when needed at field hospitals and also helped to set up radiological units in 200 clearing stations. Years later when her bones were disinterred to be reburied in the Pantheon their radioactivity was measured. Too low to attribute her early death to radium poisoning, as had been suspected, instead she probably died early from over-exposure to x-rays.

Appropriately, Ludwig Haber, Fritz's son by his second marriage who became an economist in England specializing in the chemical industry, wrote a comprehensive book about gas warfare.[29] He evaluates the 13 or 14 German gas attacks in 1915 as almost useless; delivery by cloud was too chancy.

Verdun and the Somme

In the first months of 1916 Hahn tested mixtures of gases, first in Dahlem and then at the Bayer Chemical Works in Leverkusen, where the Hahns stayed in a comfortable guesthouse. The Germans learned about the French hydrogen cyanide shells and added silver oxide to their filters to absorb it. Then Hahn was sent to Verdun.

Falkenhayn had attacked the fortified city in February, not intending to break through the French line but to chew them up with his superior artillery. The main railway line into the city had been cut in 1914, so the French would struggle to bring in supplies, though desperate to hold the city. Neither side was aware that the Verdun forts were made of stouter concrete than those in Belgium and northern France, which the huge mortars had converted into death traps. Consequently, most of their guns had been removed for use elsewhere. One of the largest, Fort Douaumont, withstood the huge mortar shells but was captured by a patrol that slipped in through an unguarded embrasure. Despite this minor success before long German losses matched French because the commander of the attacking army, Imperial Crown Prince Wilhelm, pictured himself riding in triumph through Verdun and pushed infantry forward before his guns had done their work. Falkenhayn did not rein him in. Meanwhile the French artillery was growing stronger, reinforced with excellent new heavy guns. A continuous motorcade kept supplies and reinforcements moving up the only highway into the city. Some British and French generals are accused of being injudicious killers; Falkenhayn is of the same ilk.

The French flung their illegal gas shells into the battle. The Germans were ready; they had stockpiled shells filled with diphosgene. Phosgene must be liquefied by cooling before it can be poured into a shell, but diphosgene is liquid at room temperature so shells could be filled in the field. Hahn was sent to Verdun to brief the commander of the next attack, whose command post was in Fort Douaumont. He did not reach the fort because shelling was so heavy that he was refused a guide, he must wait until morning. That night hand-grenades stored in a casement in the fort exploded. The blast ruptured tanks that contained oil for flame-throwers. The blazing oil flowed down the passageways until it reached a store of French 15 cm shells. When they exploded 39 officers and 650 men were killed.

Hahn was methodical and precise, but while filling an experimental shell with phosgene a tiny droplet splashed into his eye, which required sustained medical treatment. In May, he attended a conference held in the lecture theatre of Haber's KWI for Physical and Electrochemistry, which now was devoted to chemical warfare and was supported by the army. Forty attended; the 25 scientists included the future Nobel laureates Haber, Willstätter, Franck, Heinrich Wieland (1927), and Hahn, who represented the army's gas unit. Also there were the managers of the five largest German chemical works and four representatives from the Ministry of War. As Haber later wrote: 'In Germany generals, scientists and technologists lived under the same roof. They greeted one another on the staircase ... '.[30] Their academic–military–industrial complex was thriving.

As the toll mounted at Verdun there was a gradual reversal of fortune, by late autumn the French had retaken most of their lost ground. The Austro-Hungarians believed that their field fortifications in Russia were impregnable, so in the spring of 1916 they transferred troops to attack the Italians in the Tyrol, hoping to take

Verona. To help their beleaguered Allies, the Russians attacked in the Ukraine with an army commanded by Gen. Aleksei Brusilov. They broke through a long section of the Austro-Hungarian line, routed the defenders and captured 200,000 men in three days. A new defensive line was finally held by German reinforcements and men rushed back from Italy.

In July the British and French attacked in the valley of the River Somme, starting with a seven-day barrage, which rained almost 600 kg of steel on every square metre of enemy line. Nonetheless, in some positions where the British finally formed line in front of their trenches and walked forward they were checked by uncut barbed wire. The Germans rushed up from their deep dugouts to man their machine guns. The attackers had 50 per cent casualties on the first day, including 19,240 killed. The bloodbath dragged on day after day—the capture of the remaining rubble of a village was hailed as a major victory.

Romania declared war on Austro-Hungary on 27 August 1916, adding 700,000 trained men to the Allied side. The Allies pledged them eastern Hungary and parts of Bulgaria. The Kaiser turned ashen at the news; Falkenhayn had assured him that Romania would remain neutral. For months General Staff officers, including Bauer, had grumbled disparagingly about Falkenhayn's bad judgments: the attack at Verdun, ignoring intelligence that they would be attacked on the Somme and insisting on rigid defensive tactics sacrificing men for meaningless ground. Falkenhayn was dismissed—his friend the Kaiser wept. He was replaced by the successful team from the Eastern Front, Hindenburg and Ludendorff. They began by organizing a two-pronged assault on Romania: up from the south by Bulgarian, Austro-Hungarian, Ottoman and German troops commanded by the German Field Marshal August von Mackensen, and from the west through the Carpathians, with troops commanded by Falkenhayn. (Hindenburg had a deft political touch.) Bucharest fell on 6 December.

Hindenburg's appraisal by many English language historians is baffling. Laurence Stallings describes him as 'an old military booby'.[31] Most dismiss him more moderately although the evidence is that he was one of the most effective military leaders in the war. Part of the reason is that for a general he was astoundingly self-effacing. When appointed supreme commander he agreed to his chief of staff Ludendorff's demand to be co-commander. He permitted Ludendorff to sign all orders and the daily press release; he was the public face of OHL. When they did disagree Hindenburg had the final word, mostly in private. In the long term this was to his advantage. Ludendorff was blamed for the defeat and Hindenburg was twice elected president.

Militarization of the Institutes

Meitner received few letters from Hahn. She passed along scientific gossip and asked for his reaction to the victory in Romania: 'One must be glad about it, if one still has the capacity to be glad.' In October 1916, she resigned from the Austrian service and returned to Dahlem. She was as thin as a rake, but could not gain because the food at the Station Restaurant and the *Rathskeller* was so revolting. It was the beginning of what was remembered bitterly as the 'turnip winter' when their staple food, potatoes, almost disappeared from the German diet. At the Planck's she enjoyed hearing Einstein play his violin in Schubert and Beethoven trios, but found his opinions on politics and the war eccentric and naive. She considered 'an educated man who in these times does not look at a newspaper surely a curiosity'.

Combatants took over more and more of the institute's space. Meitner wrote: 'The Haber people have treated us like conquered ground.... I wish that I could creep into a hole and see nothing and hear nothing ... '. Haber had nine departments working in Berlin; at the end of the war they were staffed by 150 academics and more than 1,300 NCOs, soldiers, and women. He offered Meitner an attractive job—she turned it down. Haber wanted his group to become a KWI for The Sciences of Military Technology, funded by the Army, who demanded that several officers be appointed to the KWG governing board. The board refused. They compromised on a plan for a new building that would be part of the KWI for Physical Chemistry and Electrochemistry, for which the Army promised 6 million marks (£48,000).

Hahn spent the rest of 1916 shuttling between the western and eastern fronts. He was awarded the *Albrechsorden* of the Kingdom of Saxony and the Hessian Medal for Bravery. In December Peterson was promoted to general and transferred to OHL to direct gas warfare. Hahn and six other officers went with him. According to Hahn: 'Malicious gossips declared that I was there because I could sing the Bavarian soldier's song *Schwalangerscher* so extremely well'.

The British were now firing gas-filled grenades from trench mortars, and even more tellingly, hurling small barrels of poison from a device invented by William H. Livens, a Royal Engineer, to throw canisters of flaming oil. His projector was an unadorned eight-inch diameter steel tube, two feet nine inches or four feet long. The tubes were buried in the earth at a 45 degree angle and a cordite charge ignited by an electrical spark shot out the canister—scores of projectors could be fired simultaneously. Range was determined by the quantity of cordite used. The bursting canisters covered a large area with a high concentration of poison; it was a long run to safety and gas mask filters might be saturated before they got out. Moreover wind direction and velocity were less critical when launching an attack. The projectors first saw action in July 1916 on the Somme, and within weeks Livens boasted that if used on a large scale the cost of killing Germans would be reduced to 16s a head—a real bargain, only about £165 today.[32] The British primarily used gas to harass the enemy.

A decisive mistake

The German Navy maintained that if U-boats were allowed to sink without warning all shipping approaching the British Isles and in much of the Mediterranean the starving British would be compelled to sue for peace in less than a year. They bolstered their case with tables of slanted statistics—challenged by expert civilians. They also assumed that neutral shipping would be too terrified to enter the prohibited zones and scoffed at the idea that the Allies might be able to protect their merchantmen.

Nernst had designed trench mortars and developed propellants and explosives for them; during the war the Germans manufactured 80,000 mortars and 30 million rounds.[33] As a personal friend of the Kaiser he was permitted to address the council considering unrestricted submarine warfare. Almost surely it would bring the US into the war. He knew the US and warned that they would be formidable foes. The military scoffed. US economic strength was already all-out for the Allies. The US had a tiny army with a tiny officer corps; it would be years before they could be a serious opponent on the ground. The admirals promised to drown every American soldier who ventured to cross the Atlantic. When Nernst tried to offer counter-arguments Ludendorff refused to listen to this presumptuous civilian and shouted him down. Nernst's two sons had been killed in their war—now he threw up his hands, withdrew from military work, and returned to his laboratory. The Germans announced that unrestricted submarine warfare would begin on 1 February 1917.

Meitner's own laboratory

On 1 January 1917 Meitner was appointed head of a new physics section in the Chemical Institute, with the same salary as Hahn, but her additional personnel and laboratory space must wait for peace. Prices for goods made irreplaceable by the blockade soared, Meitner paid 22 marks (£1) for three metres of desperately needed rubber tubing. Hahn spent most of January in Dahlem, again testing gas masks and potential poisons and slipping off to work in their laboratory. Their goal was to isolate protoactinium, the parent-substance of the actinium series formed when the earth was born. Imagine their songs when the radioactivity of their precipitates increased. Hahn departed in February, leaving her to carry on with the chemistry.

The Russians rose up in March, forcing the Tsar to abdicate. The provisional Government pledged to continue the war. Hindenburg decided not to attack them, fearful that an advance into Russia would rally the people to fight for their country, as in 1812. So the Eastern Front was hushed until the provisional Government unleashed a summer offensive, which killed many Russians, gained little, and eroded people's confidence in their new leaders.

The French disaster

General Robert Nivelle, an artilleryman who had regained some of the lost ground at Verdun, replaced Joffre as commander of the French Army. He pleased British politicians because he spoke excellent English and French politicians because he was a Protestant and a firm republican, a rarity in their officer corps. Nivelle claimed that he could break the German line with skilfully programmed artillery fire, pledging that his troops would advance 33 km in three days. Part of the German line in France was a huge salient, with its apex at the point where the line curved from running northward toward Flanders to running eastward into Champagne. Nivelle planned a two-pronged attack to pocket its defenders by pinching them off. Before he moved the Germans withdrew from the salient to strong new fortifications across its base—which the Allies called the Hindenburg line. Undeterred, Nivelle threw the cream of the French Army against the hills on the north bank of the Aisne, on a front known as the *Chemin des Dames*, after a road built along the summit by Louis XV for his daughters. The attack, launched in an unseasonable snowstorm, failed. Not more miserably than past attempts but this time the fired-up troops anticipated victory. There were too few medical clearing stations, so untreated, tormented wounded lay in the open on stretchers along the roadsides while the next wave of attackers trudged past. Soon units refused to continue the hopeless onslaught; mutiny spread like a chain reaction. All told, 115 regiments refused orders. A British general put it nicely: 'The French Army is in a state of indiscipline not due to losses but disappointment.'[34] Nivelle was replaced by General Henri Pétain who stopped attacking, enforced discipline and assuaged legitimate grievances. Astoundingly, the Germans learned little about the disorders and stood passively by while Pétain mended his almost broken army.

The Americans entered the war in April, drafting one million men while keeping needed industrial workers and farmers on their jobs.

Meitner was working all-out in the laboratory and her letters were crammed with data. In May, she wrote the sad news that one of Planck's daughters had died in childbirth. (Later her twin sister married the widower and she met the same fate.) Malnutrition was increasing maternal and infant mortality. One of Planck's sons, Karl, had died the year before in France.

Fumigation

At the KWI they also developed gases to poison rats, mice, beetles and their ilk; beasts that ate too much of the grain stores. The gas must not leave a toxic residue. Hydrogen cyanide was best; it enters cells and binds to iron atoms in an enzyme that is the final step in oxidative metabolism. All organisms that depend on oxygen are killed by cyanide. At first they released it from cylinders, which are bulky and hard to transport. It was more efficient to generate it on site by reacting sodium cyanide with acid. Yet better is to adsorb the hydrogen cyanide on diatomaceous earth and release it by heating. This blend was named Zyklon B.[35] It was used extensively on sealed-in humans in the Second World War; it was the gas of mass destruction.

Mustard gas

To draw attention away from the reeling French army, the British prepared for a massive offensive in Flanders, intending to liberate Belgium and to occupy the U-boat pens along the coast. They were still massing their guns when the Germans fired 50,000 shells into the British positions on the warm, windless night of 12–13 July. The shells exploded with a soft plop and released gas that smelled like mustard. The casualties had novel symptoms. Most striking was agonizing burning of the eyes, followed in some cases by blindness. Hours later many of those exposed developed bronchitis and huge skin blisters, most often in the armpits and groin. It is a testimony to British grit that they did not panic. The blisters healed in a week or two and the conjunctiva of the eye repaired itself, so the blinded could see. Unexploded shells were rushed to the gas warfare laboratory at British GHQ in Flanders where the properties of the oily filling were compared with the entries in Beilstein (their copy was on loan from Balliol College, Oxford). After three days of intensive investigation, they identified the gas as dichlorodiethyl sulphide, commonly known from its smell as mustard gas. Its chemical precursor was used in German industry for the synthesis of indigo dye.[36]

The Germans only realized how nasty their new weapon was when they interrogated prisoners. They knew that inhaled mustard gas is very toxic, but had not anticipated the burning eyes and skin that drove men beyond distraction. The mustard lingered for days as liquid on the ground so contaminated areas or equipment were unapproachable. The Germans did not use mustard during the rest of 1917; they expanded production and planned how to use it most effectively. It took the Allies almost a year to figure out how to make the horrible stuff.

The Flanders offensive began on 21 July 1917, when 2,300 British guns opened fire—the bombardment went on for ten days, tearing asunder the ancient drainage system in the low-lying fields, the rains came, and the rest of the great battle was fought in the slime. Men and horses drowned on the battlefield. The low ridge on which the village of Passchendaele perched was taken after 143 days—the maximum British advance was 8.3 km.

In August regiments 35 and 36 were reformed into four autonomous battalions, all under Peterson's command. Each Army on the Western Front had a staff officer for gas; each division had a gas officer, as did every second battalion. Every second company had a gas NCO.

Caporetto

Meitner had failed to isolate protactinium, so during the summer she shifted to a new starting material, 43 g of pitchblende with radium and uranium already removed, but she was unable to separate the remaining radioactivity. Hahn did not answer letters so: 'With all due respect for your reasons for not writing, don't you think that others beside yourself are also pressed for time? You are thrifty with everything, even with friendly words.' He replied three weeks later, apologized perfunctorily, but only discussed radioactivity. She replied: 'I am still of the opinion that a friendly line from time to time is not a great sacrifice for friendship ... '. To make amends, he sent a bottle of schnapps for 'her spiritual needs'. Paper was so scarce that she wrote briefly in tiny characters.

Hahn had been in Italy on a top secret mission. For two years, the Italians had been struggling to break through the Austro-Hungarian line along the valley of the river Isonzo, which runs north from the Adriatic into the high Alps, near to the present-day Italian-Slovenian border. After 11 major battles, their furthest advance was 24 km. Even the Slavs in the Austro-Hungarian army, who had little taste for battling their Russian 'cousins', fought the Italians furiously; but now the hungry, battered, outnumbered defenders were close to cracking. To keep them fighting Hindenburg decided to lend enough German troops to give the Italians a bloody nose, aware that he could not muster the strength to knock them out of the war. Hahn led three German officers, disguised in Austrian uniforms, to the Isonzo valley to look for a sector where gas might be decisive. They knew that Italian gas masks were effective for four hours at best and that their anti-gas training was slipshod.

They toured the length of the front, from the green plain alongside of the Adriatic—too exposed to enfilading artillery—up the river valley across the Carso, a rugged limestone plateau that had seen bitter fighting, and then into the mountains, snow-capped as they travelled north, where entrenchments were blasted into precipitous slopes. The Italians had a small bridgehead across the Isonzo River near the town of Tolmin (now in Slovenia), in a mountain valley where gas would linger nicely. This bridgehead was to be pinched off when the Italian line on the other side of the river, in front of the town of Caporetto, was assaulted. A perfect target for gas bombs thrown by their new *Gaswurfminen*. These mortars, modelled on the Livens projector, were tubes 18 cm in diameter and 45 cm long, they could throw a canister containing 600 ml of gas for a distance of 1,800 m.

A new Army was formed from seven German divisions, including the Alpine Corps, and three Austro-Hungarian divisions. It was commanded by the German Otto von Below, who had a first-rate record in offensive operations. His chief of staff was a Bavarian expert on mountain warfare. Their skilful plan was first to empty the Italian trenches before passing through. The *Gaswurfminen* were dug into the rear side of a slope along the valley. Canisters were brought in at night. German troops and materials were brought to the front by 2,400 trains pulling 100,000 cars. Artillery positions were dug at night and cannon sneaked in during the six nights immediately before the attack: 1,800 guns, 420 howitzers, and 1,000,000 shells. The first day a gun was in position, it was permitted a few registration shots and then remained silent, so there was no suspicious increase in casual shelling. The infantry occupied their assault positions on the last two nights before the scheduled attack. Their supplies were brought up by mules with hoofs muffled by sacking.[37]

After a two-day delay due to foul weather, a mixed chlorine and phosgene bombardment was launched at 02:00 on 24 October. Eight hundred and ninety four *Gaswurfminen*, ignited electrically, fired simultaneously with an ear-shattering whoosh—the sky turned as red as flame. The gas settled beneath the thick mountain mist. Terrified defenders fled to the rear, abandoning trenches and guns. After the gas cloud settled in, mortars dropped explosive on the Italian trench line to encourage anyone still there to join the retreat. Then there was a two hour lull in the firing, during which a huge mine sent part of the Italian line sky-high. As day dawned, Italian reserves were double-timing up to plug the gap when 2,200 artillery tubes opened drumfire on them. At 08:00 the infantry followed a creeping barrage into the almost undefended Italian positions, while alpinists advanced along the crests of the adjoining ridges to protect their flanks. The main body of attackers marched almost unopposed along the excellent valley roads toward Italy, some advanced 16 km on the first day. After the breakthrough the German troops returned to the Western Front. In the next 17 days the Austro-Hungarians advanced 130 km, stopping when their men and animals were exhausted, their supply lines too extended, and by French and British divisions rushed in to avert catastrophe. The Italians had five times as many casualties as their opponents.

Hahn returned to Germany before the attack. Many Allied historians writing about what became known as the Battle of Caporetto say little or nothing about the gas attack, but German historians considered it a 'sweeping success'.[38] Hahn was awarded the Iron Cross 1st Class.

Passchendaele

He returned to the Western Front, again looking for sectors favourable for gas. The German frontline in Flanders consisted of scattered strong points manned by small sections armed with light machine guns, often huddled in shell holes covered with tarpaulins or corrugated iron. Behind them were concrete blockhouses sheltering heavy machine gun crews. Still further back were shallow dugouts with thick concrete roofs to house reserve infantry who counterattacked if the enemy penetrated the frontline. The Germans aspired to 'the invisible battlefield', on which it was almost impossible to detect where defenders were lying in wait.

The indistinct front made it harder to evaluate the prospects for a gas attack. In one sector the commanding general concluded that gas would be useful. Hahn disagreed respectfully but firmly. Later he was reprimanded by his immediate superior for contradicting a general. This encounter still rankled when Hahn wrote about it in his memoirs: 'I was not saved from a ticking-off even by being the proud possessor of a pass with the following wording: "Lieutenant Hahn is a staff member of the Gas Warfare Section, Imperial Headquarters, and is not required to undergo delousing"'.

General Peterson's adjutant taught him a useful lesson on how to handle brass. One day out of the blue the general asked what time the night train left for Münster. The adjutant answered like a shot: '19:45 hours Sir'. Astonished, Hahn privately asked his comrade how he knew such out-of-the-way data. Simple: he invented the departure time. Should the General actually decide to go, he would telephone for the time and report that the schedule had altered.

Meitner wrote that she was heartened by the revolution in Russia. She had visited the Planck's to greet their son who had been wounded and imprisoned in a French camp for three years before being exchanged.

Hahn came home on leave and they were together again in the laboratory, evaporating off the sulphuric acid in which she had concentrated the radioactivity. Before they could analyse the residue his leave was over and she left for Christmas in Vienna with her family.

Plans for 1918

The Germans and their allies had thrashed the Serbians, the Romanians and the Russians. Now they outnumbered their adversaries on the Western Front. They had tested innovative offensive tactics in Italy and in their last attacks in Russia; during the winter they taught them to their best divisions. Despite this superficially rosy picture, in February Haber convened his co-workers to warn them that the war was lost. Most Germans were more concerned with feeding their children than with victory. They had no more rubber, so brand-new gas masks would not seal to soldier's faces—and everyone knew this. They must face reality.

In 1914 most Germans were convinced that they were defending their country from an encircling enemy nutcracker. Success gave their Kaiser and his circle more ambitious goals: they coveted French coal mines, the Belgian seacoast and Poland. In July 1917 the anxious Reichstag voted 212 to 126 for a peace without annexations. Their resolution concluded: 'The Reichstag strives for a peace of understanding and the permanent reconciliation of people. Forced territorial acquisitions and political, economic and financial oppressions are irreconcilable with such a peace.'[39] They should have followed up by refusing to vote the needed credits, but they waffled and provided the funds, they would 'not let the troops down'. The new imperial chancellor flouted the peace resolution.

A whistle-blower gave Allied citizens a dose of grimy reality. The Russian Bolshevik Government published the Allied secret treaties, like the one dividing up the Ottoman Empire, perfect illustrations of the ambitions, cynicism and hollow rhetoric of their leaders. Woodrow Wilson seemed the exception. When the US entered the war he refused to become an ally, instead identifying the US as an 'associate' to make it crystal clear that it was not in the secret deals. He presented fourteen points, which he later added to, as criteria for a peace that would make this the last great war. Many on both sides found his points reasonable—even inspirational. Their leaders had deep reservations. Could the Imperial German Government renounce Alsace and Lorraine? Could the blockading British advocate freedom of the seas? Though not his aim, his points were terrific propaganda.

Gas as a super weapon

Another German gas battalion was formed in February 1918 and two more were added in June. They were equipped with rifled mortars for projecting gas canisters with increased range and accuracy. By then as Hahn later wrote: '... our minds were so numbed that we no longer had any scruples about the whole thing'. Their new poisons would penetrate the enemy's filters. They were compounds of arsenic: diphenylchloroarsine and ethyldichloroarsine. They are so toxic that testers are unable to tolerate 0.0012 mg per litre for more than a minute. Far lower concentrations made men listless and lethargic, draining them of the will to fight—almost perfect weapons. They were solids. For tests they were heated until they vaporized into microscopic particles with diameters of $10^{-4} - 10^{-5}$ cm, which penetrated every filter then in use. Arsenicals are corrosive, so scarce resources were diverted to manufacture corrosion-proof shell casings, which were filled with arsenicals suspended in phosgene; the Germans stockpiled 14 million of them for use in 1918. Four per cent of the gas they produced during the war was arsenicals. Hahn does not tell us whether he worked on arsenical chemistry, subsequent events suggest he did. He insisted that he never worked on mustard gases.

They assumed that the arsenicals would be vaporized when the shells exploded. They were not. Explosions spewed out arsenicals, but usually without reaching the temperature required to form the deadly minute particles. Enemy gas masks would easily filter them out. They had not bothered to measure particles formed by test explosions. And the enemy was ready. The Germans issued their troops a particle filter that clipped over the filter on the gas mask. Capturing these showed the Allies what to expect. The British developed a filter that strained out particles and the fortnightly meetings of their gas warfare committee focused on particulate clouds.[40]

Meitner wrote good news in January. She was working late measuring the radioactivity of their precipitates and was succeeding. One letter started with a warning: 'Hold your breath before beginning to read, this will be a very long one'.

OHL intended to destroy the British army, which they thought weaker than the French, by a series of smashing blows.[41] Each attack would start with a few hours of ferocious bombardment on an unprecedented scale to stagger the enemy and break their will to resist—shock and awe. Shells would fall out of the blue because German guns no longer had to register on their targets by observing where trial shots fell. Instead, each gun was calibrated in advance on a practice range and a night or two before D-day was emplaced in a precisely surveyed position. They fired at map coordinates. This made gas shells especially useful because they impacted without scoring a direct hit. The ground around enemy artillery positions was smothered in gas, driving the gunners and their animals off, or forcing them to toil while gasping to breathe through respirators with eyepieces misted over. Mustard gas drove defenders away from entrenchments and walled off lanes for advancing storm troops. The German artillery expert Colonel Georg Bruchmüller and his staff issued elaborate schedules for firing different varieties of gas shells at different times during the attack, carefully calculated to keep the concentrations of poisons at effective levels.[42]

The first German attack on 21 March 1918 hit the British front near St Quentin; the preliminary bombardment lasted five hours, during which 3,200,000 rounds were fired by 6,608 guns, one-third were gas shells. As Haber watched, the infantry advanced in small units, armed with light machine guns and portable mortars. Modified field artillery pieces were manhandled forward to deal with strong points. Airplanes roared overhead, machine-gunning Allied positions.

The Germans broke through a long length of fortified front and almost eliminated the British Fifth Army as an effective fighting force, storming forward without tanks or other innovative heavy weapons but with exemplary organization, effective training, and shrewd tactics. Trench lines could be pierced if you knew how. The stunned, desperate Allies named General Ferdinand Foch to coordinate the Allied armies, rushed reinforcements to plug the gap, and drafted more Americans.

Knowledgeable German officers were less impressed. The attack was planned to create a pocket by slicing through at two points, snaring tens of thousands of the finest British troops. The trap did not spring because the northern *schwerpunkt* was resisted so stoutly that it took several days to break through. The end result was that the Germans failed to gain any strategic objective, only a vast salient that substantially lengthened their defensive line. Its defenders had to be supplied by hauling everything across the recent battlefield, then the old Somme battlefield and finally the dismal landscape devastated during the withdrawal to the Hindenburg line. Frontline troops were short of food and ammunition and had too few guns. German general staff officers were trained to understand when they had achieved as much as possible with the resources at their disposal. Some thought that they had reached that point, but OHL remained committed to total victory.

They attacked again, this time in Flanders along the river Lys. Once again, they breached British and Portuguese lines, in a few days regaining all of the ground lost the previous autumn. They seized the strategic Kemmel Ridge after covering it in a cloud of gas laid down by *Gaswurfminen*, but failed to take the railway centre that was their strategic goal or to overwhelm the resilient, determined British Army.

They struck next in Champagne, along the *Chemin des Dames*, as a feint to draw Allied reserves south. Afterwards they planned to shift fronts once again to finish off the British in Flanders. In Champagne the Allies were taken completely by surprise on the misty morning of 27 May. The French commander in the sector violated Pétain's instructions by massing defenders in the frontline. They were immersed in a vast cloud of gas, laid down by *Gaswurfminen*, just as 3,719 guns opened up at them. The defenders were half-suffocating in their masks as the high explosive rained down and their dugouts filled with poison. Once again, the Germans demonstrated that gas could be used to break through trench lines. The defenders melted away as the German infantry thrust forward. OHL ordered their troops to push on—it was too spectacular a success to abandon. They crossed the Aisne and then the Marne, so they were less than 70 km from Paris.

The Allies' backs to the wall.

The advance stalled because Allied resistance stiffened and the Germans were unable to bring sufficient supplies forward on the single railway line that ran to the salient front, so they attacked to obtain additional railway lines by widening the salient. The magic was gone. They were decisively defeated by brilliant French defensive tactics—the bombardment struck empty trenches and the real line of resistance was beyond the range of the German field artillery—and by fresh American troops. Then it was the Allies turn. They attacked repeatedly at points all along the front. OHL turned to the defensive, planning a new, shorter line in France and Belgium; in the worst case, they would stand on the Rhine. They retired slowly to give time to evacuate their wounded and supply dumps. Allied blows kept pushing them backwards. The German army had sustained enormous casualties, they were famished, and 20 per cent of the troops transported from Eastern to Western Front deserted along the way. Tens of thousands of soldiers were striking by loitering in the rear.

Protoactinium

Five days before the first German offensive, Hahn and Meitner submitted their paper on 'The Mother Substance of Actinium'. It is protactinium with a half-life of 34,300 years. Hahn then returned to duty, but soon walking became an effort and climbing stairs impossible. He was probably poisoned with phosgene and was sent to Bad Nauheim to recuperate, and Edith joined him. He took the waters, bathed, and exercised for all of July. In the countryside he obtained additional food for friends. Meitner thanked him for six eggs and cheerfully reported that she had gained 1.3 kg. Two of the eggs had gone to the Francks, because he still looked so poorly. In July, it was so cold that they sat in wool jackets sipping hot acorn 'coffee'.

She visited Vienna and when back in Dahlem presented their work at a colloquium in the Physics Institute, with the bigwigs lining the front row. She followed Hahn's coaching and addressed the audience rather than the blackboard. Planck relaxed her with an early, friendly jest and Einstein pleased her with a comment about the psychology of her shyness. A week later, Haber escorted her to a dinner of the Dahlem civic body, after which she travelled to Sarajevo to stay with her brother Walter during his 14-day leave.

Revolution

Hahn was ordered to report in mufti to Wilhelmshaven in October. He led a small group of soldiers who were taken by ship to an isolated peninsula near Danzig (now Gdansk, Poland). On board he exercised his contingent in gas mask use, making the dismal discovery that wearing a mask while tossing on the sea is a sure recipe for seasickness. On the peninsula, they tested a top-secret experimental weapon, a large pot from which arsenicals were released as a huge cloud, a *Gas Büche* that released arsenicals as 10µm particles.[43] After the successful tests he telephoned to Wilhelmshaven to arrange for their return transport. It was difficult to get the call through. When it was finally answered, he spoke with an apparatchik of the Workers and Soldiers Soviet.

While his back was turned the Empire crumbled from top and bottom. Hindenburg and Ludendorff finally conceded that they could not win, and demanded that the Government negotiate an armistice immediately. Ludendorff was under the care of a psychiatrist, who had him walk in a peaceful garden while singing folk songs. Both generals resigned; Hindenburg's was not accepted. Bauer left OHL. The Government asked Wilson for an armistice based on his fourteen points. The Bulgarians and Ottomans signed armistices and Austro-Hungary disintegrated. Wilson refused to negotiate so long as the Kaiser remained in power. The German navy mutinied and there were general strikes in the industrial centres. Ludendorff's successor volunteered to accompany the Kaiser to the front so they might die as heroes, but the Kaiser opted for exile in the Netherlands. Germany was proclaimed to be a republic with a Social Democratic Government. It was a virtually bloodless, almost a velvet, revolution, but the new Government was violently assaulted by revolutionary communist spartacists and counter-revolutionary rightists. Hindenburg told the new Government that the army would support them, but would not fire on fellow Germans. Instead, he supplied volunteers and weapons to *Freicorps*, which had been used in the fight against Napoleon and which were the model for the illicit private armies that battled sporadically in the German streets until the Nazis emerged victorious.

The troops replaced their officers by elected committees. After the armistice Hindenburg cooperated with the committees to get the field army back over the Rhine before the cut-off date when they would become POWs.

Hahn made his own way home. He travelled in mufti, because officers were liable to be manhandled. In central Berlin there was rifle and machine gun fire, but the trams kept running, after dark turning off their lights when there was shooting. A few days later his batman and friend Rehfeldt knocked on the door of his flat. He was wearing the red cockade of the revolution and carrying Hahn's kit: 'I don't know how much of this stuff is yours Sir, but I thought I might just bring it.' He reported that when the gas *pioniers* rebelled they treated General Peterson respectfully, but their lieutenant colonel skedaddled to escape retribution: he was a martinet who had finagled with their rations. Ludendorff fled to Sweden. Hahn and Meitner went to their lab.

Food and Wound Shock
Ernest Starling

When war came both admirers and enemies wondered how Starling would react—he was an outspoken Germanophile.[1] His wife Florence was of German stock, had studied in Germany, and accompanied him on the piano when he sang Lieder. Six of his 60 scientific papers were written in German and he campaigned passionately for restructuring British medical schools on the German model, with clinical departments led by fulltime physician-scientists, rather than by part-time practitioners. This crusade made many enemies. Knowing that he was impetuous and emotional, close friends were not flabbergasted by his responses. 'He was so appalled by the barbarity of the invasion of neutral Belgium that he vowed never to speak German again.' Even more dramatically he proposed to enlist in Kitchener's new army as a rifleman, even though he was 48-years-old with four children. It was not a totally outlandish idea, he was fit enough. He jogged around Regent's Park before dinner, took serious walking vacations, and every year climbed Alps with ropes and guides.[2] He might pass for a man ten years younger. Finally, as a friend wrote, he was 'Persuaded, if not convinced, that this was not the most suitable manner in which to satisfy his strong tribal instinct'.[3] He would do the Huns more harm as a medical officer. Here are the qualifications he presented to the Royal Army Medical Corp (RAMC) when he applied for enlistment.

His qualifications

He was educated at Guy's Hospital Medical School, accumulating so many honours a friend claimed: 'If he had liquidated the many gold medals awarded to him he would have been able to enjoy comparative affluence'.[4] A dynamic young teacher sparked his interest in physiology. After finishing his training he became a demonstrator in physiology at Guy's, raising outside funds to support research and enable him to work full-time. The other members of the department were practitioners. His close friends were Charles Martin and Frederick Gowland Hopkins (Nobel laureate, 1929), who had worked as a chemist before tardily studying medicine.[5] Starling's first paper was co-authored by Hopkins.[6]

Then he collaborated with William Maddock Bayliss at UCL, elder by six years and with an impressive beard—he is said to have never shaved in his life.[7] Before long they were also brothers-in-law. They fit like hand and glove. Bayliss was deliberative, Starling was impulsive. Bayliss thought slowly, Starling thought swiftly. Bayliss was wealthy, Starling earned his bread. Bayliss was clever with his hands, he patiently built apparatus and was a dexterous surgeon; Starling was impatient to get on with it, it took him years to become skilful with the scalpel. Bayliss was calm and loved to laugh, Starling was high-strung and ambitious.[8] Bayliss smoothed over differences, Starling pressed toward his objective. Both found science a splendid game: Bayliss played for fun, Starling played to win.

In 1899 Starling became the Jodrell Professor of Physiology at UCL. A 33-year-old human dynamo, in odd hours—lounging with feet on his desk—he dictated a textbook, which established him as the arbiter of physiology in the English language. A tireless fundraiser, he upgraded the physiology apparatus to the best modern standard, and then built an Institute of Physiology, followed by buildings for anatomy and pharmacology, which UCL had inaugurated by appointing the first chair in GB. (Biochemistry was yet to come as an independent discipline.)

In his efforts to transform medical education he worked closely with Richard Burdon Haldane, an MP and prominent London lawyer. Haldane became secretary of state for war in the Liberal Government of 1906, with a mandate to bring the army up to date.[9] He reorganized the small professional army into a British Expeditionary Force (BEF), able to embark within days. He backed them up with a volunteer reserve known as the Territorial Force and established Officer Training Corps (OTC) in the universities.

In his spare time Haldane chaired a Royal Commission on the University of London. The University established curricula, examined students and awarded degrees for a set of colleges, including twelve London medical schools. The Commission had considerable input from Abraham Flexner, an American who was studying medical education for the Carnegie Foundation for the Advancement of Teaching.[10] He testified that the British schools were subpar to the German and the new American and Canadian schools whose clinical departments did trailblazing scientific work, while the British were trade schools'.[11] It was not hopeless because led by physiology the British had now caught up with the Germans in pre-clinical sciences. Starling testified and wrote reports in a similar vein.[12] In the letters columns of medical journals and newspaper their antagonists blasted them for pro-German bias.

The Commission recommended that the medical schools should give up teaching physics, chemistry, and biology, which should be prerequisites for admission. Hitherto applicants had been rated largely on their proficiency with languages. The medical course was shortened to four-and-a-half years. The basic sciences should be taught by fulltime teachers paid salaries on the university scale. In Germany the entire class sat in a lecture theatre watching their clinical professors examine patients who were rarely touched by a student. One of the strengths of the London hospitals was that the medical students were involved in and needed for patient care, giving them extensive hands-on experience. The Commission wanted each school to establish three clinical units led by professors of medicine, surgery, and obstetrics–gynaecology. Units were anathema to the part-time clinical instructors in London. Their stipends were modest but academic titles brought lucrative consulting. The war put most of the Commission's recommendations on hold.

Above all, Starling was a superb scientist. In 1901 he and Bayliss in one brilliant day's work found that the pancreas secreted fluid after an extract from the lining of the small intestine was injected into the bloodstream. They had discovered that the body employs chemical messengers—which they named hormones—to coordinate its activities. When the acidic bolus of digesting food passes from the stomach into the small intestine, the acidity elicits the release of the hormone which triggers the pancreas to secrete bicarbonate solution, which neutralizes the acid, and additional digestive enzymes. Two other examples of Starling's major discoveries will be given later since they explain wound shock.

This finishes the synopsis of what Starling offered the RAMC: a foremost medical scientist, administrator, and scientific statesman with the knack of explaining what science is about to non-scientists. How would the RMAC take advantage of such gifts?

The call to the colours

While waiting to be called up, Starling briefly refreshed his clinical skills at Guy's Hospital. Commissioned as a Captain, he was stationed at the Herbert Hospital in Woolwich as a pathologist; presumably because the RAMC was not confident he could safely treat living patients. Such squandering of genius speaks for itself.

The Royal Society formed a War Committee to help to solve emerging problems. Its ten distinguished members first met on 12 November 1914.[13] The Committee sent a letter announcing their readiness to assist to the War Department, which responded 55 days later. The Army was too busy to think about science.

The green chlorine cloud in Flanders changed their minds. The following day John Scott Haldane, the director of the research establishment of the Doncaster Coal Owners Association and fellow of New College, Oxford was called to the War office. A respiratory physiologist, for years he had advised the Government about gases in mines, in the London Underground, and in deep sea diving.[14] Two days later he was in France. He advised troops attacked by gas to breathe through moistened earth held in a bottle with its bottom knocked out or through socks soaked in urine: the acid in the urine reacts with chlorine. On 1 May 1915 a variety of simple configurations for masks were tested in the Oxford Physiology Department; the best protection was given by pads of cotton waste held in place by black netting and dipped into sodium thiosulphate solution.

The Cabinet, the Royal Society, the War Office, and the RAMC each set up a committee to confront the new horror, some of their members overlapped. Starling was promoted to major and appointed director of a chemical warfare research unit, housed at the Royal Army Medical College on the Millbank adjacent to Tate Britain. He continued living at home with Florence, their son, and three daughters. UCL, like many patriotic employers, brought his military salary up to his professorial stipend of £260 and with the royalties from his bestselling textbook, there was no economic squeeze.

Starling also was consulted by Royal Society war committees. In April 1915 he wrote a short report for the Engineering Committee on 'The acceleration the human frame can stand without injury'.[15] The War Committee built up steam slowly. In June—10 months after the beginning of the war—they wrote all Fellows to ask whether their expertise would be available. The following month they set up a sectional committee on Physiology: Starling as chair, Bayliss, A. R. Cushney, W. M. Fletcher, J. S. Haldane, L. Hill, and F. G. Hopkins. The War Committee published a short note in *Nature* to inform the world of science, in veiled language, about their activities.

In May 1915 a German U-boat sank the liner *Lusitania*, killing 1,100 including children. Starling became yet more bellicose. A manuscript written by the Danish physiologist August Krogh (Nobel laureate 1920) went down with the ship. He wrote to Krogh: 'No victory will be of any use that does not mean absolute abolition of the Prussian power—and that implies going on to the bitter end—at the expense of half our men.'[16]

In October, Starling was assigned to teach gas defence to Kitchener's new army units. Groups of 50 medical and brigade gas officers came to London to hear his lectures on protection and treatment. The pad had been replaced by a helmet, a flannel bag that covered the head and pinned tightly around the neck. To absorb chlorine the helmet was soaked before use in a solution of sodium thiosulphate and glycerine (to keep it moist). The wearer breathed in though his nose and expired through a rubber mouthpiece leading to a one-way valve. He peered out through celluloid circles that soon misted over.

To teach the 100,000 men training in Kitchener's camps, four young RAMC physicians experienced in physiology were assigned to Starling: Francis Bainbridge, Edward Cathcart, Bertram Collingwood, and Charles Lovatt Evans. They travelled from camp to camp lecturing to groups of about 150 officers and NCOs, often shouting through a megaphone. Then troupes of students donned helmets and entered a closed room containing a chlorine concentration of 1 in 1,000, where they marched and then trotted. Next they moved into a room containing tear gas, where after a minute or two they were ordered to remove the helmet—gushing tears drove home the message of how well the hood worked. Starling specified that students should not be forewarned that all of their brass buttons and insignia would turn green by chlorine reacting with copper—it was a souvenir that drove home the menace.

There were many problems inordinately difficult to resolve.[17] They had too few practice helmets and many had defective valves, which undermined student confidence. His instructors complained indignantly to Starling and he harassed his superiors in turn; he wrote to General Atkins: 'Is there no-one responsible for gas training who can stir up matters as regard to supplies? Why cannot the army council put someone definitely in charge of this whole gas business? At present no-one seems responsible for anything.'

He also advised the RAMC about trace nutrients. The 1912 edition of his textbook does not mention any need for trace substances in a satisfactory diet, not even the longstanding naval use of limes to prevent scurvy. Some work on trace nutrients was being done in Britain; there was little interest in Germany or Austria.[18] In December 1915 a British force advancing up the Tigris towards Baghdad was surrounded by the Ottomans. They could not break out, so they dug in and awaited relief. The British soldiers ate horseflesh, white bread and a little oatmeal, which lacked thiamine (vitamin B1) so some developed beriberi.[19] The Indian troops subsisted on barley and a little ghee (clarified butter). They obtained thiamine from their barley but because they would not eat meat and had no fresh vegetables they lacked ascorbic acid (vitamin C) and risked scurvy. When the 9,000 men capitulated in April 1916, 1,100 of them had severe scurvy and 150 had beriberi. Not enough was known to airdrop them foods rich in vitamins—instead they dropped opium to stem hunger pangs.

Starling's old friend Charles Martin had returned from Australia to London in 1903 as the first director of the Lister Institute of Preventive Medicine. When war came, he became a major in the Australian Medical Forces, stationed on the island of Mudros, where the sick and wounded from Gallipoli were evacuated for treatment. The hospitals were overflowing with men suffering from dysentery and paratyphoid A and B. Sharp-eyed Martin also picked out patients with beriberi. He wrote to Starling that officers were more likely to suffer 'because they do not eat sour bread or beastly fresh meat. ... they substitute sardines and nice biscuits and have tinned peas and tomatoes, and various luxuries, all super-heated'. (Heat destroys vitamins.) He fed yeast to his beriberi patients.[20] In February 1916 Starling wrote a report on beriberi for the RAMC: 'It is a deficiency disorder found in races whose staple food is rice. The rice husk contains undetermined substances that are called vitamins'.[21] One-half ounce of yeast per week is an effective preventative for those subsisting on polished, husk-free rice.

Bayliss and shock

Bayliss was holding the fort at UCL, teaching, administering, sitting on university and external committees, while still making time for some science. In 1915 he published his monumental *Textbook of General Physiology*, a compendium of the titbits he had culled from years of study of the physiological processes common to all living organisms. It inspired a generation of investigators.

Probably he heard about an interesting medical discovery made at the front. Generations of military medics faced wound shock with no idea how to treat it.

Victims became ashen and listless, sweating profusely, with a rapid pulse, and dilated pupils. Surgeons knew that they would surely die on the table so they were triaged and consigned to moribund wards. Captain Ernest Cowell RAMC was a young pacesetter who used a sphygmomanometer to measure blood pressure; most medics just felt the pulse to estimate rate and strength.[22] (In the Second World War Cowell was a major general directing allied medical services in North Africa.[23]) He teamed up with Captain John Fraser, from CCS (Casualty Clearing Station) No. 33, to systematically measure blood pressures. Soldiers in rest areas had normal systolic pressures: between 110 and 120 mm Hg. After a few days at the front facing death or wounding soldiers were short of sleep, poorly fed, thirsty because water was strictly rationed, and often cold and wet—even in winter they were not permitted to bring up their great coats. Their pressures rose to about 140 mm Hg, reasonable considering hardships and stress. Blood pressures of the wounded varied. Some were elevated by their emergency reactions, which release hormones from the adrenal medulla and a neurotransmitter from the sympathetic nerve fibres innervating the organs. The chemicals increase the force of contraction of the heart and constrict the arteries, raising blood pressure.

Their eye-opener was that shocked men have pressures of 90 mm Hg or even less. Some wounded men show no signs of shock when first seen and have normal blood pressures, but the symptoms appear over the next few hours and their pressure falls. Once in shock pressures usually fall further. If they decline to 50–60 mm Hg men die because blood to sustain the heart is not pushed through the coronary circulation. During the Somme battles in 1916 medics tried to save wound shocked men by infusing salt solutions, blood pressures rose and they rallied, but then pressure fell again and they died, for reasons that will be discussed shortly.

Bayliss removed about half of an anesthetized cat's blood while monitoring its blood pressure. Pressure fell markedly. This was just as predicted by 'Starling's law of the heart'.[24] Working with an Australian student named Sidney Patterson (who became a son-in-law) and Hans Piper, a German who was killed in the war, Starling showed that when more blood flowed into the heart during relaxation (diastole) its chambers were enlarged by stretching out their muscle fibres. The next contraction (systole) is more powerful, forcing more blood out of the heart. Conversely, when less blood enters the heart, less blood is ejected at the next contraction. Hence, the heart is a self-regulating pump, which is why it is so difficult to manufacture mechanical replacements. Starling's law also explains how the output of the right side of the heart, pushing blood into the lungs, matches the output of the left side of the heart, pushing blood into the systemic circulation.

In Bayliss's cats, the decrease in blood volume decreased the filling of the heart, so output decreased, and therefore blood pressure fell. He could check this interpretation by replacing blood lost with saline solution. At first blood pressure increased, because more fluid entered the ventricle making contraction stronger. However, as the minutes passed blood pressure gradually fell back down to the disastrously low level.

This transitory effect of infusing saline is exactly what the 'Starling Mechanism' predicts. Gases and small molecules are exchanged between the blood and the tissues in the capillaries, whose walls are a single layer of cells that separate the blood plasma from the interstitial fluid. Small molecules can move through tiny pores between the cells in the capillary wall; large molecules, like the plasma proteins, cannot. Starling showed that water and small molecules are pushed out from the plasma when it enters the capillary, driven by the hydrostatic pressure that drives blood through the circulation. Because the large proteins are retained in the plasma, they generate an osmotic pressure, known as the 'colloid osmotic pressure'. Colloid osmotic pressure pulls water from the interstitial fluid into blood. When blood enters the capillary the hydrostatic pressure pushing water out exceeds the osmotic pressure drawing water in, so water is lost. This increases the colloid osmotic pressure. The hydrostatic pressure declines as the blood flows through the capillary. By the end of the capillary the hydrostatic pressure is lower than the colloid osmotic pressure, so water moves back into the blood. Normally overall there is little net water movement between blood and interstitial fluid. Excess interstitial fluid is drained away though lymphatic vessels, which collect it and return it along with any escaped plasma proteins to the veins. This is vital; preventing the return of lymph to the blood kills an animal within a day. Diluting the blood with saline solution reduces its colloid osmotic pressure so fluid leaks out of capillaries into the tissues until the concentration of plasma proteins returns to normal level.

It was clear what Bayliss should do next. In 1911 Frank P. Knowlton, a professor from Syracuse University in New York who was on sabbatical leave in Cambridge, published work on the kidney based on the Starling mechanism.[25] The kidney is largely made up of tiny tubules. Each tubule has a tuft of capillaries at one end, at the other end urine flows out on its way to the bladder. Knowlton measured the rate of urine formation in anesthetized cats. When he diluted the blood by infusing salt solution it decreased its colloid osmotic pressure. Fluid is still pushed out of the tufts of capillaries by hydrostatic pressure but less is pulled back by colloid osmotic pressure and therefore urine flow increases. When the excess water and salt is filtered out of the blood the plasma osmotic pressure returns to normal and so does the rate of urine formation. The reduced colloid osmotic pressure is why saline solution infused into shocked wounded restores blood pressure only transitorily.

Knowlton also injected salt solution containing large molecules to generate an osmotic pressure like the plasma proteins. This infusion does not increase urine formation—just as Starling predicted. The large molecule Knowlton added to generate osmotic pressure was either gelatine or gum acacia (also known as gum arabic). Gelatine is a protein derivative of collagen; it is manufactured from bones and hides. The gum is exuded from acacia trees; it accumulates as gobbets on the bark. Commercial supplies come mostly from Sudan. It is made up of long, high molecular weight chains of sugars and of acids derived from sugars. It has many uses, including in the adhesive used on postage stamps, the binder in watercolour paints, and in chewing gum. After Cambridge, Knowlton went to UCL to work with Starling, publishing two more papers from his productive sabbatical.

Following this lead, Bayliss replaced the volume of blood he had removed with saline containing six per cent gelatine or gum acacia. Blood pressure recovers. The rise is sustained because the colloid osmotic pressure is at its normal level. In the spring of 1916 Bayliss presented this work at a meeting of the Physiological Society, speaking for the allotted ten minutes followed by five minutes for discussion. Printed abstracts were circulated before the meeting and if the members present voted approval they were published later in the *Journal of Physiology*.[26] By today's standard Bayliss's abstract is unpublishable. He did not even tell what animal he worked on; the missing information must be pieced together from his later publications. Bayliss, always a model of caution, emphasized that the large molecules gave his infusion solutions the viscosity of blood—a red herring that he should have tested and eliminated. Knowlton showed that soluble starch increases the viscosity of the blood but not the colloid osmotic pressure. Urine flow increases only transitorily after infusing starch in saline solutions, hence viscosity is unimportant. Bayliss's abstract does not hint that his work might save wounded men. Perhaps he was cautious because some wounded who went into shock had lost little blood.

Salonika

The gas instruction schedule eased when many of Kitchener's new divisions were moved to France for the great offensive on the Somme. An army gas laboratory was set up at St Omer, with a staff of 30 and facilities to analyse new chemicals used against them.[27] Each British army had a staff officer for gas, so did each corps, division and battalion. Corps gas schools became training centres, where selected NCOs attended two-week courses and regimental officers were given briefer instruction. In June 1916 gas helmets began to be replaced by box respirators, which had a close fitting, rubberized mask with eyepieces. On the inner face of the mask there is a nose clip and a rubber mouthpiece attached to an extensible rubber hose that leads to a metal box pierced with air holes and containing absorbents: charcoal, potassium permanganate and soda lime. A problem is that the rubber hose increases the 'dead space', the volume of air that is expired from the lungs but then re-inspired—so does a snorkel. You re-breathe some of the carbon dioxide you had expired. The box could be replaced after use or if an improved mixture of absorbent chemicals was developed. Artillerymen were issued a larger box and goggles instead of eyepieces. The new respirators were so prized at the front that few were spared for training in GB, so most instruction was done at the new schools in France. When the Americans entered the war they adopted the box respirator. The French and Germans masks were more comfortable without a nose clip or mouthpiece and without the dead space.

Starling was promoted to lieutenant colonel; in autumn 1916 he was sent to Salonika (now Thessaloniki) in neutral Greece, as Chemical Advisor. According to both Martin and Evans he had '... nothing in particular to do'. Apparently he went alone; experience had shown that gas defence instructors did not really need much scientific knowledge, so instructors could be trained on the spot.

The Allies had landed in Salonika to prop up their Serbian allies. In August 1914 the Austro-Hungarians invaded Serbia to punish them for murdering the Archduke. The tough, experienced Serbian army repulsed them and the Austro-Hungarians had to hurriedly redeploy to present-day Poland to stop the Russians from invading Hungary. In the fall of 1915, after the Russians were driven back, the Austro-Hungarians turned on the Serbians again, this time with German reinforcements and commanders. The Allies were forewarned so on the day the enemy attacked French and British troops landed at Salonika.[28] A few days later by prearrangement the Bulgarians entered the war and attacked the Serbian right flank. The single line of railway running north from Salonika was so decrepit and Greek railwaymen so grudging that few French troops reached Serbia. Those that did were promptly driven out. The British stayed behind; their orders were not to cross the Greek frontier.

The enemy occupied Serbia, Montenegro and Albania (which had been under Italian control), but stopped at the Greek frontier. The Allies fortified Salonika and evacuated the shattered remains of the Serbian army to the Greek island of Corfu—despite furious protests from the neutral Greek Government. The 120,000 Serbians were fed, rested and then brought to Salonika. The Allied commander was the French General Sarrail, who owed his appointment to strong republican credentials. Past experience had taught the French Government to fear military coups—remember the two Napoleons. The Allied entrenchments were 110 km long, manned by five British and three French divisions, the Serbians, two Russian brigades, and an Italian division—half a million men. The Germans jeered, Salonika was their 'largest internment camp'.[29] Georges Clemenceau, then a newspaper editor and later French premier, detested overseas distractions from the battle for France and dubbed the defenders 'the gardeners of Salonika'.[30]

Conditions in the Balkan Mountains were too harsh for action during winter, during which there was an upheaval in the Serbian army.[31] A cabal of dissident officers was arrested for plotting against the Prince Regent. One of them was Col. Dimitrievic, who had provided the weapons and backup for the youthful assassins of the Austrian Archduke and his wife. The accused officers were tried and convicted on the evidence of two convicted murderers who years later admitted their perjury. Dimitrievic was executed and 180 other officers were removed from their commands. There was also unrest among French and Russian troops, sparked by the revolution in Russia and the abdication of the Tsar. Nonetheless, the Allies resumed their attacks. Both sides fired gas shells.

The violation of neutral Belgium had solidified the British public behind the war—now they saw that it depended on who violated whom. The occupation of Salonika was winked at by the charismatic and captivating Greek Prime Minister, Eleftherios Venizelos, who dreamt of incorporating all of the lands in the Ottoman Empire with Greek speakers into a larger, greater Greece. To do so Greece must join the Allies.

The Greek king, Constantine I, had been educated at Heidelberg and the Prussian Military Academy and was married to a sister of Kaiser Wilhelm II. He thought that the Central Powers were likely to win and was unwilling to gamble the future of his kingdom for more land. When Bulgaria entered the war the Greek parliament, led by Venizelos, voted to declare war on them. The king refused to sign the declaration and forced Venizelos from office; many of his party took refuge in Salonika. Allied fleets blockaded Greece. After months of internal strife and prodded by a French incursion, the king abdicated in favour of his son, Venizelos returned to power. The Greeks joined the Allies in July 1917.

Starling surely also heard much chat in officers' messes about what parts of the Middle East would be rewards for the victors—also a popular subject in the British war cabinet. When foreign minister Sir Edward Grey suggested that the Empire was already large enough, he was politely ignored.[32]

Starling wrote to his mother that he was content in the city, billeted in an attractive house on a peninsula on the shore of the magnificent harbour, but we know little about his work there. He followed current events in the ever-optimistic *Balkan News*, printed daily for the army in Salonika. When Starling arrived, the gardeners were moving out of their trenches to attack, trying unsuccessfully to ease enemy pressure on Romania, which joined the Allies in August 1917. Bucharest fell in December.

Starling's belligerency waned. His black and white view of the war turned grey. He applied for discharge on the ground that he was over 50. He was ordered home in June 1917 but with a stop in Italy to inspect their gas warfare program. He spoke some Italian.[33] The night before he left Salonika, he dined with the British commander, Gen. Milne. 'He seemed very satisfied with my work—agreed that it was finished'.[34]

In Italy he found that their best-equipped soldiers tied a perforated metal can holding absorbent over the nose; they were poorly trained in their use.[35] Their best filter protected for less than four hours. Most of their soldiers still made do with a snout made of 32 layers of muslin impregnated with absorbent.[36] The Italian scientific advisors thought British standards unreasonably high.[37] A few months after his visit, the enemy broke through at Caporetto, moving forward behind a cloud of gas—after which the Italians took gas seriously.

When he arrived in London, Starling reported to Lt-Gen. Furse, master general of the ordnance. The next day he wrote to the general about how sorry he was that they did not have time to discuss 'our own gas organization, or rather absence of organization'. He also reminded the general that in the spring of 1916 he had reported experiments on mustard gas, no action was taken on his memo, a lapse due to '… pseudo-administrative but really irresponsible committees.'[38]

His son John had enlisted and was a cavalry officer, apposite because he loved horses. He remained in the army for some years after the war and then settled in rural Ireland.

When Starling retired from the army, he was appointed as a Companion of The Most Distinguished Order of Saint Michael and Saint George (CMG). This order of chivalry honours diplomats and others for extraordinary or important non-military service in a foreign country. Wags maintain that the initials represent 'Call Me God'. It was awarded to senior figures in the RAMC, for whom a military medal was inappropriate.

The MRC

Back in London he was appointed to two new war jobs—both more suited to his talents than anything he had done for the RMAC. Ironic that he had to become a civilian to truly help the war effort. We will consider his jobs in turn. On 17 August 1917 he chaired the first meeting of the Medical Research Committee's (MRC) Special Committee on Shock and Allied Conditions, among its members were Bayliss, and Charles S. Sherrington (Nobel laureate 1932). Its secretary was Henry H. Dale (Nobel laureate 1936), a 41-year-old investigator now employed by the MRC.[39] As a junior member of the UCL Physiology Department he disliked teaching microscopic anatomy, then a responsibility of British physiology departments, so he moved to the Burroughs Wellcome Pharmaceutical Company and then to the MRC, which was established in 1913 under the chairmanship of Lord Moulton to allocate research funds from the monies collected by the National Insurance Act enacted two years previously. (Later the name changed: Committee was replaced by Council.)

Bayliss reported on a recent, exciting journey to France undertaken on their behalf. Shortly after arrival he was separated from his minder and arrested as a spy.[40] When freed they went to CCS No. 23 to learn about wound shock from Captain Ernest Cowell. Cowell knew Bayliss from his student days at UCL, where he received the MD in 1909; Bayliss may have remembered such a bright student.

Shocked patients also have a lower body temperature, partly due to profuse sweating. Stretchers were carried back to a CCS by relays of bearers. Along the way wounded men were seen by three or four medical officers. Cowell and Fraser prescribed hot tea and 16 mg of morphia by mouth, higher doses might be lethal. As soon as possible they were fed hot soup. Blankets were provided for the stretchers and Cowell designed a blanket covered with waterproof sheeting to cope with the mud and filth. The bearers were taught how to wrap patients, like stewards on ocean liners wrap passengers on deck chairs. Stoves kept the reception tent at the CCS warm on all but the hottest summer days and stretchers could be placed above heaters for additional warmth. Bayliss was asked to bring a report written by Cowell and Fraser to the Committee.

Bayliss then moved on to CCS No. 33, where he met Colonel Cuthbert Wallace (on leave from his position as dean and principal surgeon at St Thomas's Hospital London), Fraser (later professor of surgery at Edinburgh), and Captain Walter B Cannon USAMC. He was Higginson professor of physiology at the Harvard Medical School and was the authority on the body's reaction to emergencies, precisely the physiological changes Cowell had seen in the trenches. Cannon named it the 'fight or flight' reaction.[41] Soon after the American declaration of war, foreign secretary Arthur Balfour brought to Washington a British wish list. Military physicians were a top priority. Several American field hospitals were dispatched to France and ultimately 1,200 American physicians served with the RAMC.[42] Cannon, aged 46, was with a Harvard unit.

He had reviewed the perplexing literature on shock. There was some evidence that even patients who had not haemorrhaged had a lowered blood volume. Cannon thought that missing blood might accumulate in the great veins in the abdominal cavity.[43] Abdominal veins contract when exposed to an extract of the pituitary gland, so he brought along some ampoules of extract when he visited CCS No. 23 to see wound shock first-hand. When casualties from the battle of Lens poured into the station Cannon was permitted to infuse pituitary extract into the abdomen of a moribund shocked German with a gaping chest wound. The man died two hours later. The autopsy showed Cannon that blood had not pooled in the abdominal veins, as British surgeons had long known. They also knew that the blood of many shocked men had an abnormally high concentration of red blood cells, which suggested that plasma had leaked out of the circulation. (In 1918 blood volume was measured by injecting a high molecular weight dye that cannot penetrate the capillary wall and later withdrawing blood and measuring the dye's concentration. Blood volume is decreased in shock, whether or not the subject had lost large quantities of blood.)

Productive scientists bounce back from failure. One of the few pieces of lab apparatus available to Cannon was an arrangement of tubes and flasks for measuring how much bicarbonate there is in blood plasma. He found that shocked patients have low levels of bicarbonate, which means that their blood is acidic. (The pH meter was invented later.) He waited impatiently for several weeks to exploit his discovery until the intensity of the fighting rose. When shocked soldiers again flooded the wards, he fed two of them spoonfuls of sodium bicarbonate to neutralize acid, they both survived. He infused three shocked patients with a litre of warm sodium bicarbonate solution. Immediately they became more chipper and all of them survived. Euphoric with success, he wrote to his wife that cooking soda cured shock. Bayliss and two others assessed Cannon's data, they thought the work sound. At the time standards for research were almost unbelievably low—today five uncontrolled cases would not get you a listen. The Committee decided to invite Cannon to come to work in London. At their next meeting they defined wound shock as: 'A condition of circulatory failure due to deficient entry of blood into the heart'. The definition smacks of Starling's clear thinking.

At their third meeting they were joined by two of Dale's co-workers, Francis Bainbridge, released from the army by poor health and now professor of physiology at St Bartholomew's Hospital, London, and A. N. Richards, a 41-year-old professor of pharmacology at the University of Pennsylvania, present as a guest because he was working with Dale. They were experimenting with histamine, which Dale had discovered almost a decade before. Injecting histamine triggers a drastic fall in blood pressure. Anaphylactic shock occurs when sensitized individuals are exposed to a foreign protein to which they have become immunologically sensitive—for instance to proteins in bee venom. In sensitive persons the foreign protein releases histamine stored in specialized cells, blood pressure plummets so they collapse and may die from circulatory failure. Blood pressure falls even though cardiac output is normal because histamine relaxes the arteries and reduces resistance to blood flow. Injecting adrenaline constricts the arteries and restores blood pressure; it can save the patient's life. Histamine also makes capillary walls permeable to plasma proteins, so water leaves the blood and tissues swell.

Adrenaline does not help wound shocked, so it is not caused by histamine. Nonetheless Dale felt sure that wound shock must be caused by a histamine-like molecule. Once the offending molecule was identified they could develop a drug to block its action. The histamine speculation was described in an article published by the MRC in the spring of 1917 in the *British Medical Journal* and also in a shorter paper in the *Lancet*, which solicited ideas from physicians treating wound shock.[44] Both of these papers end with an afterthought mentioning that Bayliss had done work 'which may be valuable'. In the *Lancet* they noted that in both shocked animals and men a much higher proportion of the blood was made up of red blood cells, demonstrating that plasma had been lost. The recovery with gum acacia infusion in animals was mentioned, but it was suggested that seven per cent gum acacia is probably too high a concentration. Dale seems to have had no clear idea of the role of colloid osmotic pressure in maintaining plasma volume. The Committee: '... decided to ask Dr. Bayliss to resume his study of various transfusion fluids ...'. The Dale group was asked to see whether acid injections produced shock in experimental animals.

At this stage anyone with the advantage of hindsight wonders why they did not immediately urge that gum solutions should be transfused into unconscious, doomed, shocked patients. What was there to lose?

At the fourth meeting Bayliss presented his data, passing around the table his long sheets of rather bewildering tracings of cat blood pressures, showing that blood pressure was restored in haemorrhaged anaesthetized animals infused with six per cent gum acacia in saline or in bicarbonate solution—the bicarbonate was to neutralize the acid that so concerned Cannon, but it did not seem to make a difference. The Dale group reported that infusing acid did not decrease blood pressure in anaesthetized cats.

Cannon joined the Committee at its sixth meeting on 2 November. They decided to do animal experiments on cold and shock, which demonstrated that cold does not cause shock, but does decrease the amount of blood that must be withdrawn to put an animal into shock. More data about histamine was reported by the Dale group. Bayliss satisfied Cannon by reporting that five per cent gum in bicarbonate worked well. Sterile solutions were being prepared for clinical tests.

Finally at the meeting on 29 November they had a report from France that 33 cases infused with gum-saline had done well. Some recoveries seemed almost miraculous— like Lazarus rising from the dead. This was 614 days after Bayliss had reported his experiments; during the war the British averaged 1,282 men wounded per day, 106 of them died. The exhilarating result was undercut by Cannon's irritation that the solution did not contain bicarbonate. The Committee made amends by recommending six per cent gum in two per cent sodium bicarbonate, it seemed like a minor concession. Five hundred ml should be given, followed by a second 500 ml if blood pressure remained dangerously low. At the next meeting Bayliss passed around bottles containing sterile gum-bicarbonate. They had a biophysical therapy for wound shock.

Before the war Canadian and American physicians had experimented with blood transfusions, using the method developed by Karl Landsteiner (Nobel laureate 1930) to make sure that donor and recipient had compatible red blood cell types. Incompatible red blood cells clump together. At first they transfused directly from donor's artery to recipient's vein. Astonishingly, the first transfusions reported for wound shock were done without typing the blood; nonetheless transfusions were given a ringing endorsement: 'We have seen patients who were blanched and shocked and with a pulse hardly perceptible brought back to life in the most astonishing way ...'.[45] Five of the 16 moribund patients they transfused survived. They also cited two successes by Fraser, who typed his donors and recipients. Now there were two ways to treat wound shock. Gum solution was easier to obtain and to infuse but blood seemed a more 'natural' therapy. The next step should have been to determine if one was better than the other. This was not done.

The Food Committee

Starling and Bayliss were also members of the Royal Society's Food (War) Committee (RSFWC), along with Walter Fletcher (the director of the MRC), Noel Paton, who had studied the nutrition of Glasgow's poor, and Starling's old pal, Gowland Hopkins.[46] Hopkins had left Guy's in 1897 for Cambridge; they wanted to develop 'chemical physiology' and Starling convinced them that Hopkins was their best choice for doing so.[47] The Food Committee was chaired by Sir Alfred Kempe, a successful barrister whose hobby was mathematics; he was also the treasurer of the Royal Society.

The RSFWC was the brainchild of William Bate Hardy, the biological secretary of the Royal Society, who was also the Committee's secretary. Hardy started as a zoologist interested in blood cells, then studied colloids, then lubricants, and finally food production and storage. One admirer described him:

> ... with his black beard and commanding air, looking rather like an Elizabethan pirate, was one of the great men of his time. I never met a man so exactly fitted by knowledge and intellect and force of character to be a leader in industrial research.[48]

The RSFWC based their recommendations on a strong scientific base begun during the French revolution by Antoine Lavoisier and Pierre-Simon Laplace. They placed guinea pigs or burning candles in a chamber surrounded by snow and measured the rate at which melted water dripped out. They showed that both candle and guinea pig produced heat by reactions with oxygen. Later investigators showed that all living organisms produce heat. By the early twentieth century physiologists could measure precisely the heat produced by humans of different ages and sexes while resting or undertaking varying levels of physical activity. The subjects were placed in a chamber whose walls had copper plates on the inside and outside. The plates were kept at precisely the same temperature, so heat would not move across the wall—in effect the chamber was a huge thermos flask. Heat produced by the subject warms water flowing through the chamber in a pipe. The rise in water temperature measures most of the subject's heat output. The remainder is determined by absorbing water from sweat and expired air and converting the total into calories. The energy content of foodstuffs is determined by measuring the rise in temperature when they are burnt in a vacuum flask, and then subtracting the heat from any by-products that would be excreted un-metabolized, like the urea from proteins excreted in the urine and the un-digestible cellulose excreted in the faeces. A vast body of precise experimental evidence agrees that over the long term energy in is equal to energy out—unless the organism is changing size.

It is easier to measure metabolic rate from the quantity of oxygen used. The ratio of oxygen uptake to carbon dioxide production indicates the relative amounts of carbohydrates, fats, and proteins being burned. All of this magnificent science is nicely presented in the 1912 edition of Starling's textbook.[49]

How much food a country needs is calculated from the census by subdividing the population into different groups, based on age, sex, body weight and daily work. Each group is assigned a coefficient expressing their fraction of the daily requirement of the 'average 70 kilogram man'. The number in each group is obtained from the census, and then total energy need is calculated.

Only forty per cent of the food eaten in Britain in 1914 was home-grown—the rest came by sea. The Government did little about food until Lloyd George became prime minister in December 1915. In 1916, the RSFWC calculated that the country had sufficient food for soldiers and sailors to receive 3,859 Cal with 140 g of protein, still leaving the civilian 'man' with 4,009 Cal with 113 g of protein—there was plenty of food so long as they could keep bringing it in. The Government spurred production at home by fixing prices to be paid for future crops and keeping agricultural labourers on the land by mandating a minimum wage of 25s per week.

Lord Devonport was appointed food controller, responsible for distribution and use. On paper he was ideal. The tenth son of a plumber, Devonport had created International Foods, a chain of 200 grocery stores.[50] In the flesh he was a calamity. He knew no science, but thought he did. In February 1917, he issued a voluntary rationing plan. The Royal Household pledged to comply, but surprisingly photographs of them over the following year show no weight loss—baffling because the ration specified a starvation intake of 1,300 Cal per day. He compounded his foolishness by publishing a *Food Economy Handbook* stuffed with howlers. He asserted that the entire country could subsist on the food wasted in peacetime, insisted on prolonged chewing to extract all of the energy, and advised that meat and bread should not be eaten at the same sitting because this would 'double the stomach's work'. Next he advocated a voluntary meatless day, which patriots adopted. Meat consumption fell and cereal consumption rose. This was dim-witted because at the time they had more meat on hand than cereals. He banned baking of crumpets and other tasty delicacies, and cut beer production by 50 per cent. Imagine the grumbling. In May, his Ministry was authorized to control food supplies. Hardy described their activities as 'of incalculable use to the German Government'.[51]

Hardy wrote tactfully to Devonport, discreetly pointing out scientific blunders, and advocating a cull of farm animals because they consumed needed cereals to produce more meat than was needed. It was essential to keep the lid on food prices: 'The Committee, as physiologists, desire to lay stress on the fact that in buying food the labouring population is buying energy—the power to do work'.[52]

The RSFWC emphasized that fruit was not a luxury, because it contained needed 'essential subtle principles'. As much as possible should be imported. The committee sponsored nutritional experiments, for instance seeing whether onions are anti-scorbutic. Edward Mellanby had been raising dogs on oats, mimicking the diet of the poor in Scotland.[53] By chance, he kept his dogs indoors, without sunlight, and they developed rickets. He cured them by supplementing their oatmeal with cod liver oil; for half a century there had been sporadic reports that it prevented rickets. The Lister Institute was a centre for nutrition research.[54] Most of the male scientists were in the forces; Martin replaced them with brilliant women. The secretary of the Food Factors Committee, Harriett Chick, was from the Lister, and occasionally she met with the RSFWC.

In February 1917, when the unrestricted U-boat campaign began, Great Britain had on hand stocks of beef and mutton for two weeks, bacon for four days, butter and margarine for three days.[55]

Devonport, overwhelmed and ineffectual, resigned on doctor's orders (he lived for another 17 years). Lloyd George knew that rationing and price controls were inevitable and tried to recruit a Labourite to administer such socialism. None of them took the bait, so Lord Rhondda became food controller. He was the 15th of 17 children of a Welsh coalmine owner, who had studied mathematics at Cambridge before entering Welsh politics. His rise in the Commons was blocked after a bitter quarrel with Lloyd George, so he focused on his successful coal business. He knew what science was about, sought advice, and delegated authority. Beer production was restored, but with lower alcohol content. In June, he was given control of food prices.

Starling, still in uniform, attended his first meeting of the RSFWC in November 1917. The chair, Kemble, was off seriously ill. The second week Starling was there as a civilian, the third week he was appointed chairman. He was not an immediate success. After a few meetings Hardy cautioned that '... he must take better control of the discussions and move them along.' (Judging from their minutes the same criticism applied to his chairing of the wound shock committee.) He also became principal scientific advisor to the Ministry of Food. Other members of the Committee had worked on nutrition, but Starling had the nod because he could communicate effectively with non-scientists. The RSFWC decided what foodstuffs should be rationed and how much should be allowed. Starling brought their recommendations to the Ministry. Long queues stretched outside food stores selling coveted items. Rhondda solved this by requiring shoppers to register at a shop and to buy all of their foodstuffs there—queues vanished. Bayliss wrote a book explaining nutrition to the public, with the message: 'Mind the calories and the proteins will take care of themselves'.[56]

After the Americans entered the war, Herbert Hoover, who had fed the Belgians, was appointed food commissioner for the Allies and the US, their new 'Associated Power'. He refused to accept orders from individual Allied countries; they must evaluate their needs together and make a single request.[57] The evaluation would be done by an Inter-Allied Scientific Food Commission, with two representatives each from Great Britain, France, Italy and the US. As Hardy wrote to 10 Downing Street:

> The representatives must be chosen carefully, the Committee, if given adequate backing, will be invaluable in dealing with America. The food question there is in the hands of men, some of whom have that degree of knowledge that is more deadly dangerous than complete ignorance.[58]

He feared that they would allocate fewer calories than the British required, because Americans were accustomed to work and to sleep at higher temperatures and therefore required less energy for body heat.

Hardy was responsible for setting up the commission. The British representatives were Starling and T. B. Wood, professor of agriculture at Cambridge. Hardy wrote to the French Academy and the Italian Academy Lincei helpfully suggesting names—they were duly appointed. Professor Bottazzi from Rome was the Italian physiologist; he had no qualifications in nutrition, but had worked with Starling at UCL. Hardy believed that the Italians troops at Caporetto folded because they were semi-starved. Their diet was concocted by a single, unqualified 'expert'. Hardy did not try to manipulate the American choices; the National Research Council designated Professors Lusk and Chittenden.

More acid and shock

The Wound Shock Committee's first meeting in the New Year was on 19 January 1918. They learned that no gum-bicarbonate solution had reached France. Dale had commissioned his old associates at the Burroughs Wellcome Company to prepare it, but when they sterilized the solution the gum precipitated. They were trying to sort it out. Cannon insisted that bicarbonate was indispensable. He and Bayliss had put anesthetized cats into shock by infusing somewhat more hydrochloric acid than the Dale group had used.

Lieutenant Oswald H. Robertson USAMC, who had worked at the Rockefeller Institute, was asked for a memo on transfusion methods. Techniques were improving rapidly. Donor's blood was collected in a bottle containing sodium citrate.[59] Citrate chelates the calcium required for blood clotting, so the collected blood remains fluid. From a bottle they could transfuse a known volume. Robertson found that refrigerated citrated blood remained usable for days. Donors were easy to get, they were rewarded with a week's home leave. Before a big trench raid Cowell would be in the front line with a few litres on ice.

Captains Cowell and Frazer came over from France for the next meeting. Gum solution was still unavailable because of the acid problem. Dale and Richards reported that infusing Cannon's dose of hydrochloric acid did not shock their cats. They used light ether anaesthesia; Bayliss and Cannon's cats were deeply anesthetized. The committee decided that acid should be infused into an un-anesthetized cat, and agreed that the four would do so the next day in Dale's laboratory at the Lister Institute.

Dale injected a local anaesthetic, cocaine, into the skin of the cat's elbow. He knew how to reassure laboratory animals, and the cat did not struggle as they infused the acid. The small wound was bandaged and the cat set free to wander about the room. At first it panted rapidly because acid stimulates the respiratory centre, but before long its breathing was normal. There were no symptoms of shock. After an hour or so the four scientists adjourned for lunch. When they returned the cat was lively and playful. Dale saw that 'they were ready to throw up the sponge'.[60] Acid does not cause shock. Once in shock failing circulation leads to acid blood.

The Committee next met on 13 March. Cannon was missing—face-saved by being ordered back to France. Starling told them that his other duties took so much time that he could not continue in the chair. Bayliss was elected to replace him. With acid no longer a worry, they voted to use gum-saline solution and to establish their own production facility in France. This was two years after Bayliss's paper.

In March 1918 Starling published a report on the work of the Surgical Shock Committee, stating that gum acacia solution was being bottled in sterile vials and would soon reach France.[61] The best gum was sold as 'Turkey elect'. The solution was stored in bottles commonly used for sterilized milk.

Starling was sent back to Italy. After the defeat at Caporetto the Italians purchased 1.6 million British box respirators, half provided from stock and the rest available in the spring. General Herbert Plumer, commander of the British army in Italy, insisted that the Italians improve their anti-gas measures.[62] Hence Starling was sent there, accompanied by Captain Charles Lovatt Evans, now aged 34, who had been studying how much the added resistance of breathing through the box respirator limited heavy work. Evans left us a merry account of their expedition.[63] When they met at the London station, Evans was not surprised to find his former commander in mufti, but was impressed with Starling's handsome, fur-lined overcoat, which exuded such an aura of wealth that *en route* their luggage was repeated rifled in the vain hope of uncovering similar riches. They visited Rome, Padua and Italian HQ. British divisions brought their gas schools with them to Italy and enrolled Italian students who then instructed their own.

While they were in Rome, Starling disappeared every afternoon without explanation. Evans had his first clue when they left Italy; Starling was carrying a wooden box which he declined to discuss. Much later Evans learned that it contained a small bust, unhappily a poor likeness, which eventually graced Evan's office when he became Jodrell Professor at UCL. The sittings had been arranged by a physiologist who was a friend of the sculptor. The travellers left Padua for home during an air raid. On the train, Starling was horror-struck to discover that he had left his passport behind—he was smuggled across the French border. The passport re-joined them in Paris. When they arrived in Boulogne to catch the leave boat to Dover, they found that his passport did not include permission to leave the war zone, so they lingered for hours until London vouched for his right to step onto the ferry.

For the rest of the year Starling missed the Wound Shock Committee meetings. At their 14th meeting on 6 June 1918 Colonel T. R. Elliott RAMC, from the Third Army, reported that gum solution was quite effective if given to shocked men when they arrived at the CCS, but if infusion was delayed for eight to twelve hours blood seemed better. This was his impression—not the outcome of a proper clinical trial. A German manual sent to their field hospitals in May 1918 stated that injections of saline or adrenaline or blood transfusions were ineffectual for treating wound shock. (They probably transfused too little blood.) The most promising approach was the infusion of gum acacia solution, developed by Professor Otto Kestner of the University of Hamburg, but it should be used cautiously.[64] Surely Kestner had read Bayliss's paper.

Some gum-saline was produced at the Boulogne Base Hygienic Laboratory and no problems were reported with it, but much of it had to be made in the field.[65] In August 1918 the chief medical officer in Italy prohibited gum-saline because of untoward reactions and there were some similar incidents in France with locally-prepared solutions. Cannon examined some of the batches giving nasty results, and found that they were acidic, probably from the tap water they were made from. Bayliss thought the problem was more likely to be inadequate sterilization. The Committee recommended that they try again in Italy, taking care to use 'Turkey elect' gum acacia.

Surgeons who infused one per cent or two per cent gum acacia reported failure. They were wary of putting glue into their patients and did not understand the biophysical rationale. They were in good company. At the Rockefeller Foundation in New York, Joseph Erlanger and Herbert Gasser (joint Nobel laureates 1944) produced shock by constricting the veins returning blood to the dog heart and then failed to counteract it with small volumes of 25 per cent gum acacia, the committee suggested they should try the concentration used in the field and infuse much more, after all the aim was to restore blood volume. Their colleague Peyton Rous (Nobel laureate 1966), found that seven per cent gum acacia-saline worked.[66]

Cannon and Bayliss induced shock by crushing muscles in anesthetized animals, even when there was little haemorrhage. Crushing works when the nerves from the muscle are cut, but not if the circulation is tied off. When the circulation is restored the animal goes into shock. They thought that the trigger was a chemical formed in the damaged muscle, an idea that pleased Dale, but they did not consider the possibility that the muscle capillaries might have been made leaky by crushing, so proteins were lost from the plasma when the circulation was restored.

Immediately after the armistice, on 15 November, the RAMC convened a conference of surgeons and pathologists at Boulogne to consider the treatment of shock and haemorrhage.[67] Bayliss, Dale and Cannon were there. The clinician's reports were slipshod. There was no data on the number of cases treated, blood pressures before and after infusion, number of survivors or the like. Most of their evidence was anecdotal. A few instances were reported of bad effects from gum-saline, none with the 4,000 bottles prepared at the base. In the First Army they learned that it was important not to run in the solution too rapidly, it should take 15 minutes, and the solution should be at body temperature. At least 750 ml should be infused, 500 ml was too little. The other British reports were also positive, though often men stabilized with gum-saline required a later blood transfusion to get them out of the woods. This must be taken with a grain of salt because a second gum-saline infusion was rarely used, so the case for the superiority of blood was weak.

The American experience in July and August was good: 200 cases treated, with only minor side effects.[68] But in September and October results were so poor that they considered stopping infusions. Oswald Roberson investigated and concluded that the failures were with men too far gone to be helped; the weather was cold and because of the rapid advance some wounded travelled for 40 hours before they reached a CCS. In the British First Army, Cowell was trying to infuse wounded as close as possible to the front, anticipating the procedures adopted in the Second World War.

The final Committee meeting was on 24 March 1919. Starling was with them once again. They discussed the Boulogne meeting with six surgeons, and agreed that while most thought blood superior, gum-saline should be given further trials in civil practice. They did not ponder about how long it had taken for Bayliss's discovery to be given the chance to save lives.

Another example illustrates how slipshod the RAMC was in introducing new therapies. The Royal Engineers established a gas warfare research centre at Porton near Salisbury. In early 1917 Joseph Barcroft set up a physiological lab there, which gradually grew to five professionals. Barcroft was a Quaker civilian, his colleagues were RAMC. They kept in close touch with the MRC, its Department of Applied Physiology was directed by the physiologist Leonard Hill. They improved the design of an oxygen breathing mask designed by J. S. Haldane for treating accidently gassed munitions workers. If seriously gassed soldiers were dying because their lungs were too damaged to take up enough oxygen, then breathing pure oxygen instead of air might keep them alive while damaged tissues repaired themselves. Clinical tests were promising and by the end of the war 4,000 masks and oxygen tanks were in France. They arrived without clear instructions for use or spelling out the physiological rationale. Many physicians assumed that oxygen reverses the damage, so they only treated the patient for an hour or so. Of course when the mask was removed the patients were no better, so the therapy was clearly a failure. No data was collected on the number of cases given proper, prolonged assistance with oxygen or how they fared.[69]

Edgar D. Adrian (Nobel laureate 1932) was another physiologist who became involved in the war. At Cambridge he had done excellent work in sensory neurophysiology. Adding an MD would help his academic career so he matriculated at St Bartholomew's Hospital in 1914. When he graduated in 1915 he joined the neurologist L. R. Yealland in treating war-induced hysterical disorders: mutism, paralysis, sensory deficits. Before starting treatment they confidently assured their patients that they would be cured. Then they showed the patient that he could perform the missing function, inducing movement with electrical stimulation of a motor nerve, evoking sound by probing the back of the throat, or the like. Before the patient had time to think over what had occurred, they were ordered to repeat it. They treated 250 cases with 95 per cent success.[70]

Precious food

Sugar rationing began in January 1918; everyone had 0.5 lb per week. The following month, meat, butter and margarine were rationed in London and the Home Counties, and later throughout the country. Following the RSFWC's advice bread was never rationed, though wheat was milled to extract more from each seed and other cereals were added to the flour. Bread was less tasty, but there was enough for all, and it contained more vitamins than white bread.

Rationing—with affordable prices—improved many diets. During the preceding century, many poor urban dwellers had too few calories and, unbeknownst to all, were vitamin deficient.[71] When roller mill flour was introduced to make tempting white bread, more were malnourished because the vitamins are in the discarded husk. And the poor scrimped by replacing expensive butter with the newly-developed margarine which contained few vitamins. Thirty per cent of the population was malnourished. Public school boys were on average five inches taller than boys from state schools.[72] Forty to fifty per cent of the men who volunteered for service in the Boer War did not meet the Army standard, so minimum height had to be lowered from 5 feet 3 inches to 5 feet. Malnourished mothers were unable to nurse, so they fed their babies canned skimmed milk, lacking vitamins. The war rations gave almost everyone enough calories and a better chance to acquire vitamins. What is more, most people judged the system fair and there was almost no black market for food. The French did not do as well: food intake fell from the pre-war 3,800 Cal per day to 2,900 Cal per day.

The Inter-Allied Scientific Food Commission met first in Paris on 25 March 1918. Hardy's apprehensions about the Americans were unwarranted, because they arrived with the best measurements yet at different environmental temperatures and convinced the group to raise the recommended ration slightly. The Commission established a permanent secretariat in Paris. The next meeting was in Rome at the end of April. There was a Belgian observer—they had no representatives because all of their competent scientists were behind enemy lines. The Commission recommended that cereals be regarded primarily as human, not animal, food and agreed that meat is not essential but 75 g of fat per day is. Troops at the front should have 3,900 Cal per day, with more for men at high altitude and for those under the age of 20. They recommended an average wheat extraction of 85 per cent, even though that made bread barely palatable. Prices paid for meat should make it unprofitable for farmers to feed cereals to livestock. Propaganda to save food should be vetted by scientists, to avoid the cant spread by the likes of Lord Devonport.

Their third meeting was in London, and their final meeting, a month after the armistice, was in Rome and Naples, where they estimated the food required for victualing the liberated countries, which included much of the former Austro-Hungarian Empire. They did not consider the needs of Austria or Germany.[73] Some Europeans would surely starve unless all available food was centrally controlled and carefully distributed. Herbert Hoover came to London to see to it. His first meeting with the Allied ministers:

> ... was at once an enlightenment in national intrigue, selfishness, nationalism, heartlessness, rivalry and suspicion, which seemed to ooze from every pore—but with polished politeness.[74]

Food was a powerful political weapon so there was endless haggling. On 19 December, Colonel Edward M. House, President Wilson's friend and frequent surrogate, wrote to Foreign Minister Balfour that because of the delay President Wilson:

> ... wishes me to inform you that he is instructing the United States Food Administration to take measures at once to furnish food supplies and to establish an organization to this end in certain places outside of Germany.

Without further bargaining Hoover moved to Paris and went into action.

President Wilson arrived at the peace conference as the world's most admired leader, cheered rapturously by adoring crowds as the personification of a better future. Hoover was named director of relief and rehabilitation. They had 400 million people to feed in what would soon be 28 nations. In 1919 Europe would need 31 million tons of food—32 million tons was available, 18 million from the US. In a year his organization brought to Europe 27 million tons of food and 420,000 tons of clothing and medical supplies. It was distributed by former workers in Hoover's Belgian relief organization and experienced administrators discharged from the US armed forces.

Primed by four years of hate propaganda, now was the time for revenge. Lloyd George called a 'khaki election' in 1918 to ride into office on the back of victory; his coalition promised to squeeze the Germans like a lemon until her pips squeaked— they won overwhelmingly. The Allied leaders knew little and cared little about food for their enemies. The British representative at the signing of the armistice, Admiral Sir Rossyln Wemyss, was surprised by the reiterated German pleas for an immediate end to the food blockade. All they got was Article 26 which stated:

> The existing blockade conditions set up by the Allied and Associated powers are to remain unchanged. ... The Allies and the United States contemplate the provisioning of Germany during the Armistice as shall be found necessary.[75]

In fact the noose was drawn tighter when the Royal Navy stopped Germans from fishing in the North Sea and the Baltic. Food for European neutrals remained blockaded until the US threatened that their navy would escort American food shipments through.

The RSFWC had tracked the food situation in Germany as best they might. They had data published in 1914 by German scientists to alert their government about their vulnerability and they monitored German medical journals and newspaper reports. The Committee anticipated that the enemy would suffer from deficiencies in protein and fat, which would fall below the level required for 'maintaining the health and efficiency of the German nation'.[76] They did not foresee that during the last two years of the war: 'there was an absolute insufficiency in the caloric supply, and that the greater part of the civilian population during this time were in a state of chronic starvation'.

Hoover sent two food experts, Vernon Kellogg and Alonzo Taylor, into Germany.[77] They found that since the armistice urban dwellers had even less food because the transportation network was on its knees, with railway loadings only 40 per cent of normal. The Social Democratic Government, which took power in the revolution of November 1918, could not control the farmers or get the rationing system working fairly and were derided for their failure to get the blockade lifted. To add to their troubles the Government was battling a Bolshevik (Spartacist) uprising with equally dangerous right-wing free corps.

Many Britons were happy to continue to withhold food 'until the Germans learn a few things'. A German entreaty to buy food was headlined in the *Daily Mail* as 'Hun food snivel'. The French were unwilling for the £266 million of remaining German gold to be squandered for food when it was needed to repair their ravaged country. Wilson did not press the Allies. Finally Lloyd George realized that something must be done. After weeks of bitter infighting, the 'Big Four'—Wilson, Lloyd George, Clemenceau, and Vittorio Orlando—agreed to permit representatives to meet with the Germans in Brussels on 13 March. The Germans were permitted to import 270,000 tons of grain and 70,000 tons of fats monthly, which would increase available grain by 40 per cent and fat by 180 per cent. In return the Allies took over the entire German merchant marine, even though all food delivered was paid for in gold. Hoover disembarked food in German ports before an ounce was handed over. The fallout from the post-armistice food blockade was poisonous. The eminent German military historian Max Delbrüch concluded that it had created burning hatred—fuel for the right-wing.[78]

The starving foe

Vienna was hit hardest by the post-war blockade.[79] When the Austro-Hungarian Empire fell apart the new-born nations would not sell scarce food to their detested former masters. The Viennese pulled through thanks to a trainload of food from the Swiss and another from British parents whose POW sons had been treated compassionately by Austrian captors.

Rickets was a severe, ongoing problem throughout northern Europe. In 1914, about half of the children in the industrial towns of England were affected. In March 1919, Harriett Chick and two of her fellow workers at the Lister Institute, Elsie Dalyell and Margaret Hume, were sent to Vienna.[80] Hospitals overflowed with children with severe rickets: bent limbs, swollen bellies and square heads. Babies were born with rickets because the mothers lacked vitamin D and so did their milk. Austrian specialists believed that rickets was a bacterial disease endemic to northern Europe, because it was not found in the south where diets were similar. The visitors added cod liver oil to baby formula and fed spoonful's to older children on the wards. It tastes awful but is a rich source of vitamin D and it cured quickly. Then a German physician discovered that rickets could be cured by sunlight or artificial UV light, which promotes the synthesis of vitamin D in the skin, explaining why rickets is rare in the sunny south.

We know that Starling secretly visited Germany in early June 1919, because the trip created a fluster.[81] The British Army of Occupation reported that:

> Germans want more particulars and ask by whom he is accredited, what organization he is working for, and why it is desirable to keep his visit out of the Press.

He was sent by the Supreme Economic Council and was accompanied by Mr McDougall (Chief Live Stock Commissioner for Scotland) and Mr Guilleband of the Foreign Office. Surely while there he broke his vow never to speak German again—we do not know when he returned to singing *Lieder*. The Germans claimed that they could not afford to purchase their next allotment of grain and pork. Pork was costly, because in 1917 Hoover had promised farmers a set, generous price for the duration. Now the world was overloaded with expensive pork with a short shelf life. Starling kept his visit secret; there is no hint of it in his later publications.

Later that year Starling published *The Olive-Sharpey Lectures on the Feeding of Nations: a Study in Applied Physiology, etc.*[82] It included a section on 'Vitamines' (they had been named by Hopkins who supposed that they would all be amines; the 'e' was soon dropped). At least two water-soluble substances are needed to prevent scurvy and beriberi, and a fat-soluble factor is required for normal growth. The same information appeared in the next edition of his *Principles of Human Physiology*, published in 1920.

On Tuesday 1 February 1920, Starling lectured the Royal Statistical Society on nutrition in Germany during the food blockade.[83] The RSFWC had not predicted German starvation because before the war they had imported only 13.7 per cent of their food, mostly oils and animal fats. 'No one could foresee the fall in harvests during the war due to foul weather and the shortage of fertilizers.' Nonetheless, the available food:

> might have been sufficient to maintain the whole people in fair health, though in a lean
> condition, if its distribution could have been controlled and effected on equitable lines.

The Government failed to make farmers decrease their cattle herds; though they were skinny they still ate grain. Almost 20 per cent of the bread cereals were illegally diverted to feed livestock. Rationing was blatantly unfair. Operators of profitable war industries fed their workers and their families with food purchased at black market prices—up to ten times those mandated by the Government. By 1918, 25 to 33 per cent of total food energy passed through illicit channels and unprivileged urban dweller's body weight was down by 20 to 25 per cent—they were teetering on the edge. Military stomachs also growled. American handbills scattered over their trenches to encourage desertion itemized the rations provided to POW's.

The shortage of protein produced a symptom predicted by the Starling mechanism. A low intake of amino acids depresses the synthesis of blood proteins, so the colloid osmotic pressure of the plasma decreases and fluid accumulates in the tissues, grotesquely swelling legs and children's bellies.

There were only half of the predicted number of children in the age groups from 1 to 3 and from 10 to 15. Starling summarized how the food blockade affected unprivileged civilians:

> Food filled their thoughts by day and their dreams by night, and the only desire was
> to end the War by any possible means that might lead to a slackening of the blockade
> and the free entry of food into the country. No means could have been more effective
> in breaking the spirit of a nation which had been regarded as a danger to European
> civilization.[84]

Public folly

Starling did not wait for the war to end to give his bitter assessment of his government's failure to use science:

> It is the absence of science and scientific method, not ignorance of chemistry, which has been responsible for our failures of leadership in the conduct of the war, whether at home or on the Western Front ... It is indeed regarded almost as heresy to demand of a government minister a special knowledge of the work he is appointed to direct, and the idea of promotion by merit in the army or other public service arouses feelings of horror in the majority of these services. [85]

He argued that the sons of the elite should not squander endless hours being ineffectually drilled in ancient languages:

> An expenditure of money equal to that devoted at the present time to the provision of gas masks to the Army would cover all the needs of education for many years to come.

4

Explosives
Chaim Weizmann

Two of the 2,108 pages of David Lloyd George's *War Memoir* are given to scientists—all devoted to a single hero. He extols Professor Weizmann who did a 'great service to the state' by discovering how to make the acetone needed to make cordite by fermentation.[1] His Weizmann touting became more vivid over the years: how he had been offered every facility—a battleship if needed—to make the crucial molecule and how he was rewarded with the Balfour Declaration that opened Palestine for Jewish settlement.[2] Weizmann's autobiography is equally slippery with the facts: spinning is an indispensable political skill.[3]

Ideas wanted for war

Shortly after the outbreak of the war Weizmann and other British scientists received a printed letter from the War Office inviting ideas. Weizmann, a 39-year-old reader in biochemistry at the University of Manchester, wrote a detailed, multi-page reply. The explosive cordite is a colloidal suspension produced by prolonged mixing of nitroglycerine and guncotton. For safety, mixing is started cautiously by hand, when mixed enough to be safe acetone is added and then mixing is continued mechanically. More than half a pound of acetone is needed for each pound of guncotton. Some of the acetone is recovered during drying, but nonetheless large quantities are consumed. In Britain acetone was produced by 'destructive distillation', in which wood chips from broadleaf trees are heated in a retort; the volatile components liquefied in a still are acetone, methanol, and acetic acid.[4] The British had a distillery in the Forest of Dean, but it could make only 400 tons p.a. Expansion was impracticable.

Weizmann produced acetone in his laboratory by fermenting maize with a bacterium he called BY; later it was classified as *Clostridium aceto-butylicum Weizmann*. Fermentation is a sequence of enzyme-catalysed reactions that break carbohydrates into smaller pieces without using oxygen. During the sequence energy is transferred to transform ADP (adenosine diphosphate) to ATP (adenosine triphosphate). The energy in the third phosphate bond is used to do the cell's work. The end product of the fermentation pathway is pyruvic acid. The next reactions vary. Animals transform pyruvic acid into lactic acid. Yeasts transform it into ethyl alcohol. Bacteria produce a variety of products. Weizmann asked for funds to scale his fermentation up for industrial production. He posted his letter with high hopes. Like most other responders he heard nothing more.

H. B. Speakman, a chemistry honours student, had taken Weizmann's lectures and laboratory; now he was helping to win the war by slogging through hours of rifle drill.[5] He volunteered to assist Weizmann instead. Weizmann taught him how to cope with bacteria—Speakman was an apt pupil. BY converted 7.5 per cent of their maize mashes into acetone.

C. P. Scott

Meanwhile, Weizmann made an influential friend who transformed—not too strong a word—his scientific, political, and financial careers. On 16 September 1914 he attended an evening party given by a philanthropic Jewish couple in Manchester. His physician wife Vera worked on maternal health; some of her projects were supported by the wealthy hosts. He was introduced to a gentleman, 68-years-old but spry, who commuted by bicycle to the offices of the *Manchester Guardian*, which he had edited for 42 years. C. P. Scott was an ardent Liberal, had been an MP, and knew every politician worth knowing. Scott asked whether he was Polish, if so he had some questions for him. Weizmann replied: 'I am not a Pole and I know nothing about Poland. I am a Jew, and if you want to talk about that, Mr Scott, I am at your disposal.'[6]

Scott invited him to his home a few days later. He learned that Weizmann was born in Russia, educated in Germany and Switzerland, and was an ardent Zionist who had moved to England to promote his cause. Several hundred thousand Jews had migrated to Britain fleeing Tsarist restrictions. They entered freely until the gate was shut by the Alien's Bill passed in 1904 in the last days of Arthur Balfour's Unionist Government. (Unionist refers to keeping Ireland as part of the United Kingdom. Their Liberal opponents were for Irish home rule.)

Weizmann taught Scott about Zionism. The international Zionist organization had been founded by the Austrian journalist Theodore Herzl, with the goal of returning Jews to the Holy Land. In 1901 Herzl travelled to Constantinople to offer the Ottomans 20 million Turkish pounds—which he would have to raise—to open their border to Jewish immigration. It would have paid off their national debt, but they refused.

The following year Herzl came to London to see colonial secretary Joseph Chamberlain, hoping to obtain permission for Jews to settle on Cyprus and in Egypt in the El Arish valley along the border with Palestine. The answer was 'no', but they might consider the British East Africa Protectorate, which was now served by a new single-track railway.[7] Jewish wealth could develop the land rapidly. The indigenous Blacks could be shunted elsewhere. In Chamberlain's outpouring of geography Herzl caught the word Uganda, the terminus of the railway, and thereafter referred to the proffered territory as Uganda.

At the next Zionist Congress Herzl proposed that a commission go to Uganda to access its potential as a way station for Palestine. Weizmann fervently opposed any thought of Africa. The delegates argued bitterly for days. When they voted, 295 were for the commission, 175 were opposed. If Herzl went ahead the movement would split. The Zionists were still disunited when Herzl died of heart failure at the age of 44. Some blamed Weizmann and his followers for breaking his heart.

Scott asked why Uganda would not do, was it not more promising than the deserts of Palestine? We do not know precisely how Weizmann answered, but invariably he spoke with calm dignity, as an expositor not a salesman. His affect was heightened by looking like a fit subject for El Greco, with a dark complexion, lean face and upright body, long straight nose, trimmed moustache and chin whiskers. His thrust was spiritual, not geopolitical. A devoted Jew prayed three times every day to return to Zion. Uganda was not Zion. True Jewish life was deeply satisfying, a people bound together by language, blood and belief, practicing together their daily rituals and celebrating together their Holy Days. But this life could not be lived properly by Jews surrounded and demeaned by gentiles. God promised that they would return to Zion. Of course God did not mean all of the Jews spread over the earth. A strong Jewish community in Palestine would change Jews everywhere, eliminating *Schlamperei,* the chaos, self-contempt and lack of dignity that cast a deep shadow over Jewish life.[8]

Weizmann had visited Palestine and foresaw excellent prospects for perfumes, tinned fruit and essential oils. Science could build a flourishing economy and hence university education was a priority. British support was crucial. Scott pointed out that there was a Jew in the Government: Herbert Samuel. Weizmann scoffed; positive that Samuel was another rich, assimilated Jew who looked down his nose at Zionism. Scott asked for references about Palestine and Weizmann loaned books and gave him a map showing the few Zionist settlements. He was sure that under British protection a million Jews would settle in Palestine, providing a bulwark that would shield the Suez Canal from attack from the east. Won over, Scott became an ardent Zionist and a staunch friend.

Meeting Lloyd George

On 3 December 1914 Weizmann was staying in London on Zionist business. Scott arrived by the night train; by pre-arrangement they met at Euston Station. Scott told him that at 09:00 they were invited to breakfast at 11 Downing Street with Chancellor of the Exchequer David Lloyd George, a close friend and political ally. (Lloyd George was also a friend of other proprietors of major newspapers. He was the first British politician to appreciate the power of the press and cultivated it assiduously.)[9] Herbert Samuel was also at the breakfast. Lloyd George, informal and with a light humorous touch, was easy to talk with. Occasionally he displayed his flair for mimicry. (His take on Weizmann's accent and upright deportment must have been a treat.) He threw questions about Palestine at Weizmann, who was astonished when Samuel added helpful, supportive comments, and even more surprised when Samuel mentioned that he was writing a memo to Prime Minister H. H. Asquith urging for a Jewish State in Palestine.[10] Samuel thought that a Jewish University was needed there, Weizmann strongly agreed. He had already obtained support for one from Jewish financiers including Baron Edmond de Rothschild in Paris. Rothschild insisted that Paul Ehrlich (Nobel laureate 1908), the great pioneer of chemotherapy, must head the committee to plan the University. Ehrlich lived in a scientific cocoon and showed little interest in Jewish problems but somehow Weizmann had talked him into taking the chair. The war stopped planning.

Lloyd George suggested that Weizmann call on Arthur James Balfour, the Unionist leader. Samuel Alexander, professor of philosophy at Manchester, arranged a meeting in December 1914; Alexander and Balfour both wrote and lectured on philosophy. Weizmann was surprised when Balfour recalled that they had met in 1905, after Prime Minister Balfour had lost a vote in the Commons and dissolved parliament. He was running again for the seat in Manchester East. Weizmann's friend Charles Dreyfus chaired the Manchester Unionist Party. He arranged for a short meeting. Later events made this meeting legendary, but at the time neither regarded it as noteworthy, so their accounts were written years later and can only be hazy recollections. Balfour had not answered subsequent letters from Weizmann. Now he spoke of Zionism sympathetically and invited Weizmann to call again.

The Zionist cause was strengthened early in 1915 when the Ottomans sent two columns from Palestine across more than 200 km of desolate, almost waterless desert to the bank of the Suez Canal. The 18,000 attackers, who lugged all of their water, food, and ammunition, did not seriously threaten the 90,000 well-supplied troops defending Egypt. Nonetheless the British trembled at the vulnerability of their lifeline—the spine of their Empire—and kept all of these troops in Egypt when 20,000 of them might have tipped the scales during the invasion of the Gallipoli Peninsula.

Explosives for war

In the autumn of 1914 the new secretary of state for war Field Marshal Horatio Herbert Kitchener formed a War Office committee to oversee and expand the production of explosives. They had only projected to make enough for the Navy and the small Army. As its chair he appointed Lord Justice of Appeal John Fletcher Moulton, who was 70-years-old. It sounds daft—it was not.[11] Moulton, the third son of a Wesleyan minister, was Senior Wrangler in 1868 with the highest score hitherto obtained. While studying law he experimented on electricity; his experiments gained him an FRS. As a patent lawyer he represented or cross-questioned many scientists.

He became an expert in explosives as lead counsel for the Nobel Company when it sued the Government for infringing on their patent by making cordite; the case was lost in the Lords in 1895. The Government argument was on narrow ground: they used insoluble guncotton in acetone while the patent specified 'the well-known soluble gun-cotton'. As a Liberal MP and as an attorney Moulton worked closely with R. B. Haldane and knew Kitchener socially. He took as gospel Kitchener's disquieting forecast that the war would last for years and set out to make every ounce of explosive for which they could obtain precursors. From the start his organization included expert explosive chemists and he hired the chief engineer of the de Beers mining company in South Africa, K. B. Quinan, at the extraordinary salary for that time of £4,000 yearly. Vast quantities of explosives were used in Africa, especially in the gold mines. Moulton built three huge national factories: for TNT at Oldbury, for guncotton at Queen's Ferry, and for cordite on an isolated site at Gretna near Carlisle, where they hired and trained the staff and managed production. He was a man who 'thought in tons when others thought in pounds' and exemplified how they should have mobilized scientists. During the war they made more explosives than shells to hold it.

For decades picric acid was the British high explosive. Just months before the war they chose to switch to less expensive TNT. Moulton continued picric acid production and commissioned the chair of Colour Chemistry and Dying at the University of Leeds, Arthur George Green, to develop a cheaper way to make it. He was provided with research funds and a salary for an assistant. Green's new synthetic pathway brought the price down from £500 per ton to £67, which saved the British £3m per year—a huge sum at the time. Production of picric acid and TNT was limited by precursor availability. Moulton anticipated they would need more. He pressed his explosive chemists to test mixtures of TNT with ammonium nitrate, which could not be used by itself because it is hydroscopic. They found that 80 per cent ammonium nitrate, 20 per cent TNT was excellent. The Navy refused to accept the combination; he battled the Army for months before they gave way. Named amatol, it became the British standard. Moulton gave a lesson in how scientists should be mobilized for war, which was disregarded by his peers.

Into the Admiralty

Weizmann complained bitterly to his colleagues at Manchester about the War Office's silence. Harold Dixon, director of laboratories, was an expert on the chemistry of explosions. He had proved that they are exceedingly rapid chemical reactions, not—as others had argued—some unique form of transformation. He advised Weizmann to write to Dr William Rintoul at the Nobel Dynamite works. Unannounced, Rintoul strode into Weizmann's laboratory on 9 Feb 1915 and asked to examine his notebooks. He returned a fortnight later with a team of Nobel's experts, who spent several days going over the data and watching demonstrations by Weizmann and

Speakman. Impressed, Rintoul advised Weizmann to apply immediately for a patent and proposed favourable terms for a contract with the dynamite works.

Rintoul wrote about Weizmann to the Admiralty's advisor on cordite supply, Sir Frederick Nathan. A former artillery officer, he had managed one of Nobel's plants. Nathan invited Weizmann to call at the Admiralty on 21 April 1915. Acetone was on the world market from distilleries in the US and Canada, but a cartel kept the price sky-high and a cheaper source would be timely. In April 1915 the British Kynoch Company contracted to make 500 tons a year from lime acetate, but their production peaked at 400 tons. A company led by Halford Strange, a British industrial chemist, and Auguste Fernbach, the director of the fermentation department at the Pasteur Institute, produced acetone by fermentation for the French Government, which did not make cordite; they only needed it as a solvent for the cellulose acetate they used to coat the canvas on aeroplane fuselages. They used an organism BF (*Bacillus Fernbach*). Its disadvantage is that it does not break down the starch in the starting vegetable so the process had to be started with an organism that broke the starch into usable pieces. Weizmann's BY does the entire job. In England they had an acetone plant at Rainham, fermenting—at the insistence of the War Office—potatoes, not the maize they preferred.[12] They opened a second plant at King's Lynn in September 1914. Only four per cent of the potato was converted into solvents and 25 per cent was not fermented at all.

Weizmann had worked with Strange and Fernbach in the past, but now relations were strained. At the outbreak of war Fernbach and his assistant Moses Schoen, were made responsible for the bacteriology of the Paris water supply—the French were worried about germ warfare.[13]

To see whether BY fermentation could be scaled up Nathan agreed to provide £500 for expenses and for an assistant's salary for Harold Davies, a collaborator since 1910, who was now employed by Strange (So much for Lloyd George offering him—if needed—a battleship.) Then Nathan walked Weizmann down the hall of the Admiralty to meet First Lord Winston Churchill, who enthusiastically told him his goal should be to produce 30,000 tons of acetone. Weizmann took leave from Manchester University.

In August the Nobel plant at Ardeer in Scotland suffered its third accidental explosion in 1915. This time three workers were killed, 19 were injured and there was extensive damage to the facilities. Windows were smashed in all of the nearby villages. Rintoul wrote that it would be many months before they could resume production and meantime they could not sign an agreement with Weizmann, he should continue to work directly with the Admiralty.

At first Weizmann split his time between Manchester and London, where he set up a laboratory in three rooms rented from the Lister Institute for £500 per year. His wife and son stayed in Manchester while she served out her contract as a physician. He hired Ida Smedley, who was a lecturer at Manchester, and Miss Fisher. (Manchester chemistry enrolled female students, a few years before Weizmann had three of them.) Speakman joined them when they moved to spacious facilities owned by the Lister Institute in Wandsworth, South London, where there was a five gallon fermentation vessel. They were able to grow sufficient bacteria in pure cultures to successfully inoculate five gallons of maize mash. As was his custom, in the laboratory Weizmann dressed immaculately in suit and tie and chain-smoked cigarettes.

Now they were ready to try industrial scale production. He informed Nathan that they could produce acetone for £180 per ton, the sale of the butyl alcohol would bring it down to £100. At that time the Italians were buying acetone from the US for £500 per ton. He also reminded Nathan that in less than a year he must inform Manchester University whether he would return from leave. (As will be seen, returning to Manchester was anathema to him.)

They moved to the Nicholson Gin Factory at Bromley-by-Bow in east London, where there was a large new fermentation vessel. They were to ferment the maize mash and the professional distillers were to capture the products. Their first attempts failed because of contamination with unwanted organisms. The impatient and rather contemptuous brewers were liberal with ignorant advice; for example that the profs should begin by crossing their fussy bacteria with reliable yeast cells. Weizmann was convinced that the distillers were not properly sterilizing the vessel. Finally they were successful with 100 gallons of mash and then with 300 gallons. Both runs transformed 7.5 per cent of the maize into organic solvents. Scott and Nathan were both given frequent progress reports. Weizmann also published two unrelated scientific papers in 1915.

The Ministry of Munitions

The British launched a Ministry of Munitions (MM) in May 1915, headed by Lloyd George. He had a huge job. Starting with a staff that could easily fit into a sitting room, they eventually filled 100 hotels, clubs and houses in central London. Lloyd George recruited men of 'push and shove' to move beyond the long-established suppliers to the War Office by obtaining arms from hundreds of competent manufacturers. He selected all of the top staff except for Moulton who moved from the War Office as the Explosives Division, which retained much of its independence.

On 30 June 1915 Scott wrote to Weizmann:

> I saw Lloyd George this evening. He asked me to ask you to call on Mr Wolff [LG's private secretary at the MM] at the Munitions Office on Monday.[14]

Scott had been lobbying about acetone. A lunch was scheduled. At their second meeting Weizmann was pleased that Lloyd George—blessed with a politician's capacious memory—remembered Zionism and its advocate. The minister was captivated by the prospect of oceans of acetone, and henceforth boasted that Weizmann was his own scientific discovery. After lunch Lloyd George introduced

Weizmann to his under-secretary Dr Christopher Addison: an anatomist, Liberal politician and the sort of administrator who seemed always to know where every needed scrap of paper is filed. He instructed Lord Moulton to see to it that Weizmann had ties with the MM as well as the Admiralty. Weizmann warned Lloyd George that there were too few scientists in Britain, he offered to recruit more in France and Switzerland.

Weizmann extended his leave from the University in Sept 1915 and was named temporary honorary technical advisor to the Admiralty on acetone supplies with £2,000 yearly for supplies and expenses. Scott had briefed him on what to ask for. He served as Weizmann's scientific agent, just as actors, musicians, sports stars and writers have agents. He had discovered that neither Chaim nor Vera had any sense about money. They decided on an agreeable standard of living and then struggled to pay the bills, often relying on loans from friends to tide them over.

Weizmann was also appointed for one year as Chemical Advisor to the Ministry of Munitions on Acetone Supplies with a salary of £1,500 p.a. and £500 for removal expenses to London (which cost just under £45). This more than doubled his salary. Scott negotiated the high payments on the ground that Vera must give up her position to move to London.[15] Henceforth experimental expenses were divided between the MM and Admiralty. His eight assistant's salaries ranged from £125 to £350 yearly.

Addison and Moulton vetoed Weizmann's proposed recruiting trip abroad. Britain had plenty of brainpower and they guessed that his business abroad was more personal than official. Weizmann complained to Scott about their intransigence. When Scott next lunched with Lloyd George he mentioned that Weizmann was barred from travelling abroad, even though he had been invited by the French Government (which does not seem to be true). Twelve days later Scott, Weizmann, and Herbert Samuel lunched with Lloyd George. According to Scott they discussed Moulton's 'incompetence, vanity, and obstructiveness'.[16] After lunch Lloyd George met with Scott, Nathan and Weizmann. Nathan had been transferred from the Admiralty to direct cordite production and was Weizmann's immediate superior. Before that meeting Nathan told Scott that his friend was 'a little difficult to work with'. Lloyd George authorized Weizmann's travel, but his passport remained locked in Moulton's safe. Again Scott complained to Lloyd George, urging him to remove acetone from Lord Mouton's bailiwick. Instead Lloyd George stamped his foot and the passport was released. Two weeks later at breakfast Lloyd George boasted to Weizmann and Scott that he had ticked off Moulton, Nathan, and Quinan for their highhanded treatment of Weizmann and told them that he would gladly accept their resignations, which were not forthcoming. Probably just another of his self-serving yarns, it is hard to credit that he would risk his most successful unit. In his diary Scott fumed that they treated Weizmann poorly because he was a Jew and a foreigner.

Weizmann spent part of December in France, not recruiting anyone. Strange wrote to Weizmann and suggested that they meet to resolve their differences. Weizmann replied that he did not think a meeting worthwhile, but would entertain written proposals.

The fermentation procedure

For full-scale production in early 1916 Weizmann's group moved to a newly constructed wooden shack on the grounds of the Navy Cordite Plant at Holton Heath. (Another facility was constructed at Nazik in India.) They isolated BY by inoculating soil samples into a sterile mash of two per cent maize meal and allowing it to ferment for four to five days at 37 degrees C.[17] Cultures that smelled of butyl alcohol were then heated to 100 degrees C for one to two minutes. BY is a spore-former. High temperature kills most bacteria but spores survive, so the next culture is more likely to be uncontaminated BY. Pure cultures are sub-cultured 50 to 100 times to obtain enough bacteria to seed a large fermentation. At Holton Heath they had a flat-bottomed, 1,000 gallon iron fermentation chamber, a former acid mixing vat. They filled it with maize mash, which was sterilized with steam at elevated pressure: this also broke up the granules of starch in the maize. After nineteen hours it was cooled and inoculated.

All too frequently the mash was contaminated with bacteria that produced butyric acid, which stinks. Spoiled brews were siphoned onto the surrounding heath, to the intense disgust of their neighbours. Desperate, on the sly the scientists hung a heavy spanner on the safety valve that released steam when the pressure reached the danger level for the iron vessel. The higher sterilizing temperature did the trick. (Later when they had better fermentation vessels they sterilized at temperature of 130–140 degrees C at two to three atmospheres pressure.[18]) BY fermentation occurs in two stages. First, the multiplying bacteria transform carbohydrates into organic acids. Second, they ferment the acids and the remaining carbohydrates into the solvents.[19] The gases that bubble out are hydrogen and carbon dioxide. When gas production stops the brew is heated with steam and about 10 per cent of the liquid is boiled off, which takes 15 hours, this fraction contains the acetone and butyl alcohol. When they had their first success Weizmann telegraphed Scott who travelled down to London to give Lloyd George the great news. The volatile fraction they obtained from the fermented mash was re-distilled to separate acetone from butyl alcohol. The scientists were struck by how professional distillers worked by smell, taste and touch, not bothering to measure pressure, temperature, or specific gravity. The butyl alcohol was stored in drums, in hope that someday a use would be found for it.

Weizmann grumbled to Scott that he was still merely 'a temporary and anonymous worker' in the MM.[20] Scott negotiated with Nathan and Addison; Weizmann was given the title of superintendent of the Lister Institute Government laboratories.

Lloyd George summoned the heads of all of the British distilleries to a meeting in February 1916, giving them only three days advance notice. He told them that their stills were needed for war production.[21] He assured them that they would not lose money and, after some prodding, agreed that their staff would be badged as war workers to protect them from conscription. There were two types of stills. Kettle stills have chambers in which the mash is heated and the alcohol and other volatile spirits, which add flavour, waft into a simple cooling tube. They are used for making whisky and gin. (In Britain they produced about 43,000 tons of gin per year.) Patent stills utilize a complicated cooling apparatus, which makes it easier to collect each volatile component one by one. Six of the Patent distilleries were taken over for acetone production.[22] Nathan directed Weizmann to stay clear of the distilleries; his job was at the Lister.

Strange and Graham produced so little acetone from potatoes at King's Lynn that the MM took over the plant in March 1916 to make acetone from maize.[23] Weizmann was asked to oversee the conversion. Before agreeing he consulted his patent advisor, Atkinson Adam, who suggested that first he should tell the MM all about his previous dealings with Strange. When Weizmann arrived in Great Britain in 1904 he was given a place to work in the Manchester Chemical Laboratories by William Henry Perkin, one of the world's leading organic chemists. As Weizmann demonstrated his abilities in the laboratory and in the classroom he rose in the department. In 1910 Strange approached Perkin with a project to make synthetic rubber.[24] The emerging automobile industry needed vast quantities of rubber for tires. The supply of latex from wild rubber trees was limited, so the price of rubber was skyrocketing—a ton cost £1,200. Heated rubber releases isoprene, so rubber must be an isoprene polymer. Perkin should develop methods to synthesize and to polymerize isoprene.[25] The University permitted outside work during a defined fraction of a faculty member's time. Strange offered Perkin a share in future profits, a supplement to his salary, funds for supplies, and a salary for a confidential assistant. Perkin offered the assistantship to Weizmann, who signed a confidentiality agreement, in return for an extra £250 per year and one-third of Perkin's profits.[26] Isoamyl alcohol was an apt precursor, but was in short supply, so their first step should be to discover an inexpensive way to obtain it.

During the summer break the Weizmanns usually spent some time in Paris with Vera's sister. To prepare himself for the day when Manchester would need a new professor to inaugurate a biochemistry department, Weizmann had enrolled in a short course in bacteriology at the Pasteur Institute, and the next year spent some weeks perfecting these skills. Now Weizmann consulted with Auguste Fernbach, the distinguished director of the Pasteur's fermentation laboratory, about the possibility of obtaining isoamyl alcohol by fermentation. Fernbach was sure it could be done. Strange contracted with Fernbach, who appointed Schoen as his assistant. Everything was going so well that Weizmann demanded a larger part of Perkin's pie, threatening to peddle his knowhow elsewhere. Perkin fired him as assistant in the project. (It never produced riches because plantations of cultivated rubber trees began to flood the market with latex.)

Weizmann wrote an account on these proceedings to Lloyd George, who passed it on to Dr Addison for their files. Addison and Moulton concluded that there was no serious problem and requested Weizmann to provide cultures of BY for King's Lynn. Acetone production there rose from 0.5 ton per week from potatoes to 4 tons from maize. In July 1916 the MM estimated that they could produce 18,000 tons per year.

Strange's solicitors wrote to Lord Moulton alleging that Weizmann's acetone process belonged to their clients. In a second letter they warned that Weizmann was trying to sell the process to the French Government. (Weizmann had hoped to sign contracts with the French and Italians, but negotiations stalled.) Moulton, experienced in this game, ignored their letters.[27] Then the solicitors demanded a hearing, so on 16 May 1916 Moulton and Nathan met with Strange, Fernbach, and their solicitors. Moulton's conclusion was that the dispute was between the contending parties and should be settled by arbitration.[28] Strange threatened to sue Weizmann, who stood firm—it was his bacterium.

To avoid shipping maize across the Atlantic the MM purchased a distillery in Toronto, incorporating it as the British Acetone Company. Weizmann sent Speakman and Mr Legg over to get production going; he was confident of his youngster's skills. The University of Toronto recruited the rest of the scientific staff. They were in production by April 1916. (In time Speakman became professor of bacteriology at the University of Toronto.)

The MM did their job brilliantly. At the end of the Battle of the Somme the BEF had more guns and ammunition than at the start, and explosives supply never limited the British war effort.

Early in 1917 Vera resigned from her job and moved to London. Their second son Michael was born that November. They had no intention of returning to Manchester.

Scott busied himself with negotiations for his friend's royalties for the acetone. He started at the top with another old friend, Chancellor of the Exchequer Reginald McKenna. At their second negotiating session they agreed on £50,000, which was endorsed by First Lord of the Admiralty Balfour, but the Admiralty dragged their feet and did not pay.[29] There was a massive Cabinet shake-up at the end of 1916: Lloyd George became prime minister, Balfour foreign secretary, and McKenna was out. They were replaced respectively by Edwin Montagu, Edward Carson, and Andrew Bonar Law (who had succeeded Balfour as Unionist leader). Scott was on good terms with them all. They agreed that the acetone issue should be resolved by an *ad hoc* committee chaired by McKenna. In July 1917 the committee set the rate. Weizmann wrote that he was paid a 'token award' of 10s per ton produced, which brought him about £10,000. If this is correct then 20,000 tons of acetone was produced by his process.[30] He informed Scott that the Admiralty settled on £4 per ton, which if his production figure is correct would have netted him £80,000.[31] It is not crucial to nail down how much the British taxpayers paid Weizmann, the bottom line is that in time fermentation made him very wealthy.

He resigned from Manchester. His last years there had been clouded by the dispute with Perkin. The cloud seemed to lift when Perkin moved to Oxford with the promise of a new building and the resources to build a strong department. Weizmann regarded himself as the logical successor. The search committee listed him on the names of prospects that they asked outside referees to comment on; none of whom rated him as an outstanding candidate. Instead he was offered a senior lectureship in Biochemistry. He was deeply offended, announcing that he would be off as soon as possible. He would have jumped at an offer to join the Zionist bureaucracy in Berlin, but Vera was irrevocably opposed. He must not give up science. 'Our road to Palestine will not be through Berlin.'[32] She held her ground and he did not speak to her for three weeks. Now the whole sorry mess was behind them.

Fermentation in Germany

Some of Weizmann's ardent admirers echo Lloyd George's whimsy that his acetone kept Britain in the fight. Untrue, but it did save the nation money.

Fermentation did keep Germany in the war. Glycerol is an indispensable precursor for explosives. Fats are esters in which three long-chain fatty acids are strung from the short glycerol framework. When fat is heated with alkali to make salts of the fatty acids for soap, glycerol is a by-product. The Germans had imported most of their fats, and with the blockade what they had must be eaten. There was little fat to spare for soap, so they had little glycerol. They were saved by the biochemist Karl Neuberger, director of the KWI for experimental therapy, who found that with sodium sulphite in the solution glycerol is produced when yeast ferments sugar. His discovery was secretly patented in 1914 and was developed for industrial production. The Germans set up 53 factories that produced 1,000 tons per month.[33] Lord Moulton produced glycerol by taking over all of the soap boilers in Great Britain. They also produced 9,000 tons per year from vast quantities of whale oil.[34] The US used yeast to ferment strap molasses in an alkaline solution: 20 to 25 per cent of the sugar was converted to glycerol.

Palestine's future

The British had goaded the detested Ottomans into war in 1914, confident that they would be a pushover. The Russians were happy to join in: they coveted Constantinople and the Dardanelles. To apportion the spoils, in March 1915 Asquith set up a post-Ottoman planning committee chaired by Sir Maurice de Bunsen. War Secretary Kitchener's representative on the committee was Sir Mark Sykes, an expert on the Middle East. Sykes proposed to partition the southern Ottoman lands into spheres of influence with the British getting Palestine and Mesopotamia. The committee was chary about Palestine. There were so many religious and national groups with daggers drawn that they foresaw a hornet's nest. Sykes was sent to the Middle East to explore the prospects, when he returned six months later he advised the committee that an impending Arab uprising might drive the Turks out of Syria, Palestine and Mesopotamia, so it was high time to divvy up the region with the French. The French negotiator was their long-time consul in Beirut, François Georges-Picot. Sykes and Picot reached agreement in January 1916. The part of

Palestine south of a line drawn from the port of Acre to the Sea of Galilee (about 17 km south of the present border between Lebanon and Israel) should be administered by an international condominium. Palestine north of Acre would be incorporated into Syria, which would go to the French. The British would construct a railway from Haifa to Baghdad—they were to have what is now known as Iraq with its vital oil wells. The agreement was top-secret and the Zionists knew nothing about it.

In March 1916 Samuel told Weizmann that the Cabinet was sympathetic to a Jewish presence in a British Palestine, but in May the Sykes-Picot agreement was secretly ratified by Great Britain, France and Russia, Palestine would not be British.

As acetone production became a routine industrial process Weizmann had more time to work for the Zionist Political Committee.[35] In 1916 he edited a short book with a number of contributors: *Zionism and the Jewish Future*. Edmond de Rothschild underwrote its publication, it sold well and Weizmann made sure copies reached the power brokers—many of their doors were open to Lloyd George's scientist.

When Weizmann moved to London in 1916 the Zionist Committee rented an office at 175 Piccadilly, across the street from the Royal Academy building, for £150 per year. A volunteer, Israel Sieff, set up the office assisted by a cadre of bright young men from Manchester who had been drawn to Zionism by Weizmann's magnetism. Sieff had enlisted in 1914 but was released because his father needed him in the branch of the large family business that brokered cotton waste for making guncotton.

In the autumn of 1916 Maurice Hankey, a 39-year-old Marine officer serving as secretary of the Committee on Imperial Defence, floated the idea of establishing a small War Cabinet to run the war, taking over from the 30 or more members of the Cabinet. Many of the political leaders who endorsed the idea also stipulated that the prime minister must not be a member. Asquith indignantly rejected his demotion. He was toppled. Lloyd George became prime minister in December 1916, assuming the powers of a 'constitutional dictator'.[36] He was determined to fight to the finish, it must end in a knockout. He shored up his political base by appointing four of the great press barons to high positions in the coalition Government.

Lloyd George chaired the new War Cabinet, seconded by Andrew Bonar Law, who as the new Chancellor of the Exchequer was a neighbour living in No. 11 Downing Street—he had lost two sons in the war. Initially the other members were Lord Curzon, former viceroy of India; Lord Alfred Milner, an imperialist and Liberal politician who was a journalist before settling the peace terms with the Boers and organizing the South African Government; and Arthur Henderson, a Labour politician (and Nobel laureate for peace in 1934). Henderson had also lost a son. When Scott asked about Palestine Lloyd George replied, 'Oh! We must grab that.'[37] Hankey was secretary, at top-secret meetings he kept the notes in his own hand and in his own safe. Sykes was one of two assistant secretaries. Lloyd George's feel for organization also changed the way that the Cabinet did its business: for the first time minutes were kept of their discussions and decisions were recorded. But as was the convention neither the Cabinet nor the War Cabinet voted: they operated by consensus.

Balfour was foreign secretary; he agreed with Lloyd George that the British should have Palestine. Now they had to win over a consensus. Zionism might help to persuade foot draggers. He arranged for Simon Marks, another young Mancunian, to be seconded from the Royal Artillery to join the Zionist office in Piccadilly.[38] His father had begun with a market stall in Leeds with the famous slogan 'Don't ask the price, it's a penny'. After he formed Marks and Spencer they expanded to 60 stores, in their early years the top price for any item sold was 5s. Young Marks took charge of the Piccadilly office, while Sieff served as Weizmann's personal assistant. The two got along famously—they were both pals and brother-in-laws. The Committee published the weekly newspaper *Palestine*. The first issue appeared in January 1917. Sykes advised them to restrain their rhetoric if they intended to win the public relations battle.

The new Government faced a grave, top-secret crisis—they were on the verge of bankruptcy. On 22 February 1917 a treasury official, John Maynard Keynes, calculated that their available financial resources would not 'last more than four weeks from today.'[39] In the US the British had to pay all of Italy's bills, two-thirds of France's, half of Belgium's, and most of Russia's. About half of the invoices in the US were covered by American loans, but the balance was paid from the dwindling British gold hoard and the sale of British-owned securities. The British were still afloat because they had obtained further credits from American banks who would go under if Great Britain became bankrupt, and by cutting back on orders. Lloyd George remained serene: lenders would lend as long as the British seemed to be winning. His sanguine conviction was not put to the test. The US entered the war—now they were backed by the US Treasury.

In February 1917 Weizmann was elected president of the English Zionist Federation. Sykes, emphasizing that he was acting as a private person, asked for a memorandum stating their objectives, and after it was presented was lobbied by Lord Rothschild, his nephew James, and Weizmann. Later—in the same unofficial capacity—Sykes met with larger groups of prominent Zionists. Nahum Sokolow, the representative to Great Britain from the International Zionist Committee, visited Picot in Paris and was received sympathetically by Pope Benedict XV in Rome.

The War Cabinet dealt with pressing problems and set long term goals. Outside experts advised on thorny issues. In Palestine British troops had advanced from Suez to Gaza, where the Ottoman line held firm—they still were far tougher than the Allies had anticipated. The advance drew Ottoman reserves away from Baghdad; its capture by the British in March 1917 was trumpeted as a major Allied triumph. The energetic General Edmund Allenby, commanding in Palestine, was methodically preparing to break through the Gaza line. He moved HQ from Cairo to Gaza and was building roads and a water pipeline to provide for swelling troop numbers. Palestine kept popping up on the War Cabinet agenda, thanks in part to Hankey's interest. Perhaps they had given away too much with Sykes-Picot's internationalized Palestine. A British garrison there would shield the flank of the vital Suez Canal. Jews were enlisting in the British Army and the Zionists promised to help defend a British Palestine that allowed Jews in. They could reopen negotiations with the French by endorsing the Zionist dream, which cloaked British ambitions with a patina of compassionate selflessness. And of course Zionism was a noble cause.

It would not be easy to modify Sykes-Picot, though the French were flagging militarily and financially. Every creed with a claim in Palestine would have to be assured that their rights would be preserved. The reeling Russians could not oppose a rewrite that did not touch on their Turkish ambitions. When the Tsar was toppled in February 1917 all restrictions on Jews in Russia were swept away and the newly legal Zionist organization came above ground to recruit many new members. The War Cabinet set up a committee on the future of Palestine, which in April recommended that the British should have both Palestine and Mesopotamia.

Scott stumbled across the top-secret landmine of the Sykes-Picot agreement in April 1917 when visiting Paris. The Zionists were flabbergasted—they had no inkling of a secret treaty. Herbert Samuel pressed the War Cabinet to act. His cousin Edwin Montagu, now minister of munitions, was strongly opposed, arguing that establishing a home for Jews in Palestine said that Jews had no home in England. The generals in the Middle East were apprehensive about the Arab allies shielding their right flank, who had been promised post-war kingdoms.

Pressuring the War Cabinet

Thanks to Scott's finger on the pulse of government, Weizmann knew the ins and outs of debates about Palestine and saw to it that Zionists lobbied energetically, stressing the influence of Jews on world opinion and the power of Jewish capital. The Piccadilly office mobilized the mass of their supporters while Weizmann and his big guns personally pressed the case. As he proudly wrote later: 'Starting with nothing, I Chaim Weizmann, a Yid from Motelle and an almost-professor in a provincial university, have organized the flower of Jewry in favour of the prospect ...' .[40] Sykes met unofficially with the Zionist Committee to brief them on the counter-arguments they faced. The War Cabinet was warned repeatedly that the Germans might soon announce their own commitment to a Jewish future in Palestine. This was not fantasy, despite the horrors to come in the Nazi epoch. In Germany there was sympathy for the Zionist dream and appreciation of the worldwide might of Jewish opinion and financial clout.

Pressure ratcheted up when Sykes received a telegram from Egypt reporting a pogrom in Palestine; 10,000 Jews were without food and water and would soon be massacred like the Armenians. He urged the War Cabinet to send Weizmann to Palestine immediately. Instead they appealed to the King of Spain, their neutral contact with the Germans. The Germans replied that military operations required civilians to be evacuated from Gaza and Jaffa for their own safety. The Jews had organized their relocation; regrettably two had died on the march. The Chief Rabbi of Jerusalem refuted the reported outrages.[41]

In June 1917 Weizmann learned from his principal American informant Supreme Court Justice Louis Brandeis that a US commission was heading toward Egypt. The Americans had not declared war on the Ottoman Empire and meant to bribe them to make peace with the Allies. The initiative was led by Henry Morgenthau, their former ambassador to the Porte. If the Ottoman Empire survived the war both Allied and Zionist dreams would be dashed. Balfour flabbergasted Weizmann by asking him to serve as the British representative to persuade the American delegation that it was a rotten idea. Weizmann took leave from the Admiralty. At Waterloo Station he was handed a British military passport. In a few tumultuous years he been transformed from an exotic outsider into a trusted British agent—a remarkable demonstration of diplomatic skill. He travelled with a bodyguard and was trailed across Spain by German agents. They met at Gibraltar. The Americans carried their heavy weapon in wooden crates: $400,000 in gold for bribes. Their party included Professor Felix Frankfurter, later an eminent justice of the Supreme Court. They conferred for two days in a sweltering casement in the Rock until it became crystal clear that Morgenthau did not have a plan, only vague hopes. The commission returned home. The Foreign Office was relieved; Weizmann's stock soared.

The debate raged on. Anti-Zionist British Jews published a letter in *The Times,* arguing that Judaism is a religion—not a nation. Their thesis was contested by the Chief Rabbi of the British Empire and other prominent letter writers, who argued that God had given Palestine to the Jews. Lord Rothschild mailed his rebuttal to Balfour who forwarded it to the War Cabinet. Henderson had been replaced by George Barnes, another Labour politician who had also lost a son in the war. Edward Carson, the new Unionist leader, and Jan Christian Smuts, a former Boer general, were added. The peace treaty of Vereeniging that ended the Second Boer War specified that black enfranchisement would only be considered after the whites had self-rule: it set them on the road to apartheid. The treaty worked so well for whites that 15 years later Smuts sat at the British War Cabinet table. He saw no reason why Arabs should not be the blacks of Palestine.[42] Weizmann had already cultivated Smuts' friendship.

Milner was asked to produce a declaration on the future of Palestine. He was assisted by two young diplomats, William Dunlop and Harold Nicolson. In a dark basement in the Foreign Office they worked throughout the summer writing draft after draft, sure that they were enunciating a noble ideal that would in small part justify the senseless carnage of the war. Mark Sykes and Naoum Sokolow often dropped by to assist. Balfour also red-pencilled drafts, impressing Nicolson 'by a fervour of conviction alien to his temperament'.[43] The War Cabinet still teetered in the balance. They invited Montagu to present his anti-Zionist arguments. The Zionist Political Committee submitted to Balfour a draft resolution that recognized 'Palestine as the National Home of the Jewish people'.[44] Lord Rothschild lobbied for it. Weizmann persuaded Lloyd George to place the declaration on the War Cabinet agenda for 4 October. Montagu was present, still fighting, but was outfaced by Balfour who rebutted his arguments proposition by proposition with a trained philosopher's skill. The latest version of the declaration called for: '... the establishment in Palestine of a National Home for the Jewish people ... it is clearly understood that nothing will be done which may prejudice the civil and religious rights of the existing non-Jewish communities in Palestine or the rights and political status enjoyed by Jews in any other country'. The wording satisfied the War Cabinet but prudently they decided to consult further with Jewish leaders and to make certain that President Woodrow Wilson agreed.

The wording was a bitter pill to the Zionists because it did not acknowledge the historic right of the Jews to the land given them by God. After passionate debate the majority decided that it was the best they could hope for. Weizmann and 175 Piccadilly shifted into top gear. Three hundred synagogues and other organizations were mobilized to pass resolutions supporting the declaration. Scores of supporting letters were solicited from notables. Public meetings and demonstrations were organized, but President Wilson decided that a declaration was premature. Brandeis and other prominent American Jews were marshalled. They convinced the president to issue an unequivocal endorsement, although he emphasized that the US was not party to the declaration.

When Palestine was next on the War Cabinet agenda Lord Curzon, whose extensive travels between 1887 and 1895 had made him an authority on the East, presented a lengthy, scholarly memorandum elucidating what was at stake.[45] The Biblical 'land of milk and honey' meant goat's milk and the juice of the small native grape. Inhospitable as the land was, its inhabitants would fight to keep it. He dryly stated a case for realism, but did nothing more to sway his colleagues. Sykes submitted a memo about the imminent likelihood of German endorsement of Zionism. They must not shilly-shally. The War Cabinet next met on 31 October 1917. Balfour argued that the declaration would be persuasive propaganda and would establish the British claim to Palestine. Weizmann waited anxiously outside the meeting room; Sykes emerged and said, 'Dr Weizmann, it's a boy.'

On 2 November 1917 Balfour sent the approved declaration as a letter to Lord Rothschild, it was published a week later. British propaganda distributed hundreds of thousands of copies in Germany, Austro-Hungary, and Russia. The German Government affirmed that they also favoured Jewish settlement in Palestine.[46] The declaration came in the nick of time. A few weeks later the new Bolshevik Russian Government published the secret treaties, including Sykes-Picot, which now had been recast from a cynical land grab into an idealistic vision. The British broke through the Ottoman defences at Gaza and drove north toward Jerusalem.

So much for Lloyd George's fairy tale that the Balfour Declaration was Weizmann's reward for acetone. Weizmann's tart rejoinder was: '... history does not deal with Aladdin's lamps.'[47]

Acetone production in the US

When the US entered the war the MM purchased the Commercial Distillery in Terre Haute Indiana, which became British Acetone, and the US bought the Majestic Distillery in same city. Fermentation equipment was designed in Toronto and the Canadians provided trained scientific staff to get the new facilities operating. Once they were producing, the MM stopped fermenting maize in Britain, where grain was needed for food; shipping acetone across the Atlantic took far less cargo space. Weizmann proposed to continue production in Britain using horse chestnuts and acorns. During the summer of 1917 3,000 tons of chestnuts were collected, mainly by patriotic boy scouts, but acetone yield was poor,[48] and they could not control foaming in the fermentation vessel.[49] The MM needed less acetone because they developed a new version of cordite known as RDB that used ethanol and ether as the solvents during mixing.[50] The British estimated that in 1918 they would require 15,950 tons of acetone for making cordite in Britain, Canada, and India and for the dope that sealed the canvas on aeroplanes.[51] This was only three quarters of the previous year's output. In 1918 British Acetone's factories in Toronto and Terre Haute produced 2,563 tons.

Zionism triumphant

Early in 1918 the War Cabinet decided to send a Zionist Commission to Palestine. Sykes was to set it up and Weizmann was appointed chair. There were five other Britons, an Italian, and a French opponent of Zionism. Israel Sieff came along as Weizmann's aide. The Russian Bolsheviks were not invited, which did not bother them because liberated Russian Jews no longer needed Palestine. Before leaving in March Weizmann had an audience with King George, suitably hallmarking his rise up the British pyramid. He relinquished his Admiralty salary and nominated Harold Davies and Dr Ida Smedley MacLean as co-directors for the acetone project, which was closed in June 1918.

Weizmann's first meeting in Palestine with Allenby was chilly; during wartime the general regarded Zionism as an unwelcome side issue. The next morning Weizmann was standing in front of his tent when Allenby's car came by. It stopped and the general announced that he was driving to Jerusalem. Would Weizmann like to join him? Weizmann politely declined, explaining that it might be embarrassing for the general to enter the capital in his company. Allenby was silent for a moment and then said: 'You are quite right—and I think we are going to be great friends.'[52] Characteristically Weizmann '... was calm, paternal, imperturbable, certain of himself' in such circumstances.[53] The brief exchange exhibits the sensitivity of his diplomatic antennae.

The cornerstone for the Hebrew University was laid on Mount Scopus on 23 July 1918. Allenby and his staff were among the dignitaries on the podium. After the speeches they sang the Zionist anthem *Hatikvah* and *God Save the King*. The ceremony epitomized Weizmann's vision for Palestine's future: '... a framework to be filled in by our own efforts.'[54] He went into the desert to meet the Emir Feisal, a leader of the Arab revolt and the son of the Sharif of Mecca. The Emir was assured that Jewish immigration would not derail the promised Arab kingdoms.

When Weizmann returned to England he booked an appointment to report to Lloyd George. He was asked for lunch on 11 November 1918. When the day dawned he was sure that he would be scrubbed but it was confirmed. Naturally it was not an everyday, relaxed lunch, and there was no time for Zionist business; Lloyd George left early for a thanksgiving service in Westminster Abbey.

Lloyd George called an election that autumn. He and his coalition campaigned on the proposition that the defeated Germans had enough money to completely reimburse the Allies for the cost of the war. He surely realized that this was not true, but kept repeating the lie after Scott vehemently protested. Their friendship ended.

Chaim and Vera agreed that for the foreseeable future he must give up science. He went to Paris to shepherd the cause through the peace negotiations. Significant portions of the Balfour Declaration were included in the Mandate for Palestine written by the new League of Nations, despite Arab opposition.

One of the casualties in the great flu pandemic was Sir Mark Sykes, 39 years old.

5

Locating Submerged U-boats
William Henry Bragg

On the first day of the war the French Government created a commission for scientific warfare directed by Paul Painlevé, a celebrated and productive mathematician, who had entered politics because he was infuriated by the injustice done to Dreyfus.[1] When elected to the Chamber of Deputies in 1910 he specialized in the military, especially aviation. Under his leadership the new commission evolved into the *Bureau de l'Instruction Publique des Beaux Arts et des Inventions intéressant la Défense Nationale*, with a substantial budget and generous quarters in central Paris. He established six sections, each with two or three distinguished advisors. They evaluated suggestions from the public and coordinated research. The naval section did submarine research at naval bases in Toulon, Cherbourg, and Brest. Thanks to universal military training many scientists were on active service, as they were in Germany.

The British were satisfied with their small existing War Office and Admiralty laboratories. Soon accounts of German technological feats filled the newspapers: they smashed Belgian and French concrete fortresses with heavy mortars firing high explosive, poisoned Allied troops with gases, and sank shipping with U-boats. The troubled public bombarded the War Office and the Admiralty with thousands of letters suggesting countermeasures—unanswered, they were consigned to file boxes.

The celebrated author H. G. Wells launched a newspaper campaign in June 1915 demanding that the Government take advantage of the nation's scientific talent, protesting bitterly that: 'On our side we have not produced any novelty at all except in the field of recruiting posters'. An editorial in the leading scientific journal *Nature* made the same point less colourfully. A political earthquake finally got the Government involved with scientists: the Liberal Prime Minister H. H. Asquith and the Unionist opposition formed a coalition government. In the reshuffle Winston Churchill lost the Admiralty. He was detested by Unionists as an apostate from their party and as the architect of the botched campaign to force the Dardanelles.

His successor as first lord, 66-year-old Arthur Balfour FRS, was familiar with scientists.[2] His brothers-in-law were the physicist Lord Rayleigh FRS (Nobel laureate 1904) and the anatomist Henry Sedgwick FRS. Balfour appointed a fellow FRS, Admiral Sir Henry Jackson, as first sea lord. Jackson was a pioneer in wireless radio transmission. Balfour knew that the Navy had failed to meet expectations, they must change.

The Royal Navy's problems

Things had not gone well on Churchill's watch, even before the disaster in the Dardanelles. The public had assumed that a war would open with a gigantic naval battle to smash the upstart German High Seas Fleet, after all the odds were heavily in the Allies favour. The Germans awaited attack, while most of the British capital ships bobbed at anchor in northern bases. The Grand Fleet was commanded by Sir John Jellicoe in Scapa Bay in the Orkneys and the Battle cruiser Squadron under Vice-Admiral David Beatty in the Firth of Forth. Churchill champed for action but the professionals on the Admiralty Board refused to order major attacks. Churchill explained their caution: 'Jellicoe was the only man on either side who could lose the war in an afternoon'.

Churchill was keen for secrecy, which undercut public trust. On 27 October 1914 the British dreadnought *Audacious* struck a mine and sank slowly off the coast of Ireland. The news was suppressed to keep the Germans in the dark, but a Philadelphia newspaper published a photograph taken from a passing liner of the floundering battleship. On 1 November a flotilla of British cruisers stumbled into the German Pacific Squadron off the coast of Chile. The British lost two cruisers, an admiral and 1,500 men. The Government kept this calamity to themselves while they assembled a strong fleet that destroyed the German Squadron near the Falkland Islands. The public welcomed victory but were incensed that once again bad news had been kept from them. The Government pledged that henceforth the Admiralty would tell the truth however unpalatable. Later we shall see unanticipated upshots from mandated candour.

When the war began both sides regarded submarines as too slow to be offensive weapons, they planned to use them for scouting and minelaying. Twenty German U-boats were operational. Most of them lurked as pickets outside the naval harbours, a few scouted in the North Sea. *U-15* encountered the cruiser screen shielding the Grand Fleet as it was making a brief sortie; she was rammed and cut in half by *Birmingham*. Nonetheless, the Grand Fleet turned tail to find shelter. The British stationed three old cruisers, known to their crews as the 'live-bait patrol', cruising off the Dogger Bank near the German coast: 'live-bait' because they would be easy prey for fast, modern warships. Early in September a U-boat sank all three and 1,400 seamen drowned in an afternoon, more men than Nelson lost in all of his battles.

Another capability of submarines was demonstrated in late October when the British merchantman *Glitra* was stopped by *U-17*. The Germans boarded her and opened her sea cocks. Her crew manned their lifeboats which the U-boat towed close to shore. This was all according to 'cruiser rules', the international convention for seizing merchant ships. After this unlooked-for success, the German high command debated whether to let U-boats loose on merchant vessels. Events decided for them. In November the British, to enhance their blockade, declared the North Sea a war zone. In retaliation U-boats captains were authorized to sink enemy merchant ships following cruiser rules.

Churchill counterattacked pugnaciously, thereby making it impossible for the enemy to follow the rules. One hundred merchantmen were armed. By law they could be attacked without warning. Some were converted into 'Q ships', vessels with hidden guns to ambush an unwary submarine. U-boat captains began to torpedo without warning any vessel that might be a danger. Merchantmen were encouraged to fly neutral flags and ordered to try to ram U-boats—which made them combatants.

On 12 December 1914 German heavy cruisers bombarded Scarborough, Whitby and Hartlepool on the east coast of England, killing 40 civilians. The British fleet could not protect British homes.

In 1915 the Germans offered to stop attacking merchantmen if the food blockade was lifted. The Allies refused—they were committed to beating the U-boats. Thereafter the Germans sank without warning Allied merchantmen and neutrals suspected of carrying military supplies to the Allies. The German Navy predicted that within six weeks the British would be forced to abandon the blockade. On 7 May *U-20* torpedoed the liner *Lusitania*, drowning 1,198 people, including women and children.[3] World opinion excoriated German brutality, wavering Americans became pro-Ally, and the hubbub convinced the Kaiser to rein in his U-boats. Despite this, in September 1915 151,800 tons of shipping was sunk by U-boats, 67 per cent British. Seventy-seven merchant sailors perished.

The Board of Invention and Research

Balfour urged his colleagues in the new Cabinet to set up a scientific advisory committee. There was no support, so in July 1915 he appointed a Board of Invention and Research (BIR) to respond to the public's suggestions and to advise the Admiralty.[4] There was a three man central committee: J. J. Thomson (Second Wrangler, 1880), Sir Charles Parsons (Eleventh Wrangler, 1887), who was regarded as Britain's greatest engineer since Watt, and Dr (later Sir) George Beilby, a noted industrial chemist.[5] They were supported by an eminent consulting panel of twelve scientists (all FRS), three engineers and a metallurgist. Among the consultants was William Henry Bragg, 53-years-old, who had recently been appointed Quain Professor of physics at UCL and was moving from Leeds, and Sir Ernest Rutherford, 44, now professor at Manchester.[6] They were old friends.

Then Balfour bungled. He appointed Lord John Arbuthnot Fisher, 74-years-old, to chair the BIR. He was paid £1,000 yearly; committee members were reimbursed for their expenses. Fisher's credentials were paper perfect. Before retiring in 1910 he had applied science and technology to the Navy and set up the educational system to train the specialists needed to man sophisticated vessels. In late 1914, he was reappointed First Sea Lord because Churchill was certain that he would support bold and imaginative offensive schemes, like an amphibious landing on the German Baltic coast near Berlin. The Admiralty Board had vetoed them all.

Back in office, Fisher refused to risk the Grand Fleet, but agreed to Churchill's idea of forcing the way through the Dardanelles with obsolete battleships. Most senior naval officers strongly opposed the adventure; were angry at Fisher for supporting the madman; and were insulted by his nasty, demeaning dismissals of contrary opinions. Any officer who thwarted him would: 'find his wife a widow and his home a dunghill'.[7] On a single, black day six obsolete British and French battleships attacking the straits were sunk or put out of action. Fisher resigned. He did not begrudge the aged ships, but their expert crews were needed to man new battleships under construction. British and French troops landed on the Gallipoli Peninsula to take the forts in the rear were pinned down on the beaches by defenders who had been amply forewarned by the bombardments. Fisher's resignation contributed to Churchill's fall, so his resurrection at the BIR was a deft kick in Churchill's political pants. Balfour should have been more prudent. Regarding Fisher, Asquith thought that: '… the old man is rather unbalanced.'[8]

The BIR was housed in Cockspur Street, just around the corner from the Admiralty. Fisher was authorized to spend up to £10,000 for investigations.[9] The BIR's panel members soon had Fisher's measure. He was eager to find ways to win the war, but, as J. J. Thomson wrote, he had: 'an inordinate love of getting even with those who in any way opposed him'.[10] He dominated meetings, often ranting on about how stupidly the war was being fought. His audience included naval officers and clerical staff, who regaled their shipmates in the Admiralty with his choicest barbs. The Admiralty responded by often pigeonholing BIR recommendations and stonewalling requests for information. Fisher fought back with relish, soon the BIR was celebrated in the Admiralty as the 'Board of Intrigue and Revenge'.

The advisor's started to plough through the public's suggestions—eventually they reviewed an impressive 37,500 of them. Thomson recalled:

> I have just written one letter to a man with a perpetual motion machine, and another to a charwoman who was much upset by a bad smell and thinks it might be bottled up and used against the Germans.[11]

The panel was split into six sections. Bragg and Rutherford were appointed to Section II, whose responsibilities were 'Submarines, mines, searchlights, wireless telegraphy, and general electrical, electromagnetic, optical and acoustic subjects'. It was chaired by the Duke of Buccleuch, whose qualification was that he had served in the Navy as a young man, and its secretary was Sir Richard Paget, an expert on sound. They met on alternate Tuesday mornings at 10:30, their first meeting was on 13 August 1915.[12] Three officers represented the Admiralty.

Bragg, Rutherford, and Thomson

It is time to sort out the Bragg family because the elder son, William Lawrence, soon comes into the story and if nomenclature is not settled there will be a muddle. In the family father was called 'Will' and the first son was 'Willie'.[13] Their affectionate daughter, the youngest by some years, was baptised Gwendolyn; like her family I will call her Gwendy, which seems in keeping with her engaging and clear-eyed outlook on life. She wrote about father, as I shall, as WHB. To avoid confusion, the elder son signed most of his scientific papers as Lawrence Bragg, and later became Sir Lawrence; I shall adopt his sister's WL. The younger son, Robert John, was known as Bob. The mother was the artistic Gwendoline, née Todd. In 1915 both WL and Bob were artillery officers, they had received military training before the war while students at Cambridge.

Although Rutherford was younger he played a major part in Bragg's career, who was a late starter in the laboratory. They met in 1895 when Rutherford visited Adelaide, Australia, where WHB was professor of physics. Rutherford was travelling from his home in New Zealand to Cambridge, to enter a programme that would allow him to earn a Cambridge degree in two years; he was to study under J. J. Thomson. WHB knew Cambridge and J.J. well, so he could brief his visitor.[14] Surely he also told how J.J. had got him to Australia.

WHB had been Third Wrangler in the Mathematical Tripos Part I in 1884.

> I had never expected anything so high, not even when I was in my most optimistic mood. I was fairly lifted into a new world. I had a new confidence: I was extraordinarily happy. I can still feel the joy of it!

The top three had been coached three times a week by Mr Routh, their portraits and short biographies were published in an illustrated paper, *The Graphic*. The next year he did well in the advanced examination. Shortly thereafter, he was chatting with J.J. Both were at Trinity College. J.J. was the Cavendish Professor of Physics and the discoverer of the electron but was only six years older and they often played tennis together. They were walking toward Thomson's lecture. Thomson asked whether the Senior Wrangler in WHB's year was applying for the professorship in mathematics and physics at Adelaide, which had just fallen vacant. Bragg answered 'no', and then, summoning up all of his courage:

> ... asked J.J. whether I might have any chance and he said he thought I might. It had never occurred to me that anyone so young might be eligible. After the lecture was over I went and telegraphed an application—it was the last day of entry.

There were 23 candidates. J. J. Thomson was on the committee which consulted Sir Charles Todd FRS, Postmaster General and Government Astronomer of South Australia, who was in London at the time. They were considering whether a First with a liking for the bottle would be preferable to a temperate Third. Todd favoured moderation, so Bragg had the job. A few years later Todd became his father-in-law.

WHB was aged 41 when he did his first original experiment in 1904, 18 years after he arrived in Adelaide. He had delivered a presidential lecture to the physics section of the Australian Association for the Advancement of Science, in which he reviewed the recent exciting work on radioactivity and on the properties of the electron. Electrons are tiny compared to atoms, which at that time were envisioned to be like a plum pudding: a mass of unstructured dough with electrons dotted about like raisins. When a beam of electrons is sent hurtling through a gas those that collide with a larger particle lose most of their energy and almost stop, so the intensity of the beam diminishes as it goes along. The same proportion of moving electrons is stopped in each section of the path, so the intensity of the electron beam falls off exponentially with distance.

Large alpha particles behave differently. Marie Curie had found that in air the number of alpha particles in a beam remains constant until the beam reaches a critical distance at which they all seem to disappear. WHB reasoned that such large, heavy, particles must collide frequently with air molecules, losing some energy each time but pushing onward. All of the particles in the beam should collide about the same number of times. Consequently, the energy of the alpha particles falls almost uniformly until the beam no longer has enough energy to be detected by an electroscope. He predicted that the distance travelled should depend on the size of the atoms they encountered.

To test his idea a generous sponsor donated funds for a sample of an ore containing radium as an alpha source. He and a student, Richard Kleeman, set out to measure the 'stopping power' of gases and solids for alpha particles. At first they were frustrated because their careful measurements showed that their ore was emitting alpha particles at four different energies. They had to have a single energy. Fortunately they were visited by Frederick Soddy, who taught them how to extract the radioactive contaminants with water.[15] Using alpha particles with a single energy they measured the stopping power of seven gases and six thin metal films. WHB's measurements were careful, precise and reproducible. Stopping power increases with atomic weight, as would be expected because larger atoms are more likely to be struck.

WHB sent their data to Rutherford in Montreal who thought the work first-rate. Rutherford and Soddy helped to get their work published promptly. WHB was elected to the Royal Society.

Meanwhile Rutherford had moved to Manchester, where physics undergraduates in their third year did a research project. Ernest Marsden was supervised by Hans Geiger, a German who was an assistant in the department.[16] Rutherford suggested that they should shoot alpha particles at thin metal foils, as WHB had done, but see whether any are scattered backwards. A few are. The higher the metal's atomic weight, the more particles scatter back. Rutherford saw the implications in a flash. If atoms were—as Thomson had proposed—amorphous balls of matter like plumb puddings, alpha particles would rip through, not bounce back. Positively charged alpha particles would only bounce back if most of the atomic mass is packed into a tight, dense ball containing all of the positive charges. Rutherford's dense ball soon became known as the nucleus. Only a small fraction of particles bounce back because the nucleus is tiny. Even in high atomic weight uranium the nucleus occupies only 1/23,000 of the volume. The remaining space is sparingly occupied by the negatively charged electrons spinning in their orbits. Rutherford's new model of the atom was elaborated further by Niels Bohr, who developed a plausible hypothesis to explain why the negatively charged electrons are not pulled into the positively charged nucleus.

News: devastating and wonderful

When in London WHB stayed at the Hotel York while he attended BIR Section meetings. He searched for a house in the city, and set up his laboratory at UCL, assisted by his instrument maker C. J. H. Jenkinson, who was moving with him. Mother and daughter Bragg were away at their rural retreat, a cottage they rented for £10 yearly in Wharfedale. Father brought them the dreadful news. Gwendy, eight-years-old at the time, described it:

> But one morning as I was standing by the shallow stone sink in the kitchen, looking out into the garden, my father unexpectedly passed the window, came in, said to me quickly in a low voice 'Bob's gone' and then went upstairs to my mother. I heard her cry out.[17]

Gwendoline was never quite the same after her younger boy's death. As Gwendy later wrote:

> She was always happy painting, nothing in life gave her so much direct pleasure … But the First World War and the loss of her younger son dealt her a grievous blow from which she never really recovered. Her gaiety vanished ….

Bob had died of wounds on 2 September 1915 at Suvla Bay on Gallipoli.

The British had landed there on 6 August to break the deadlock by outflanking the Ottoman entrenchments, but once again were pinned on the beach. Bob wrote home: 'We had an awful mix-up when we landed; the arrangements here are perfectly scandalous … someone ought to get the sack.'[18] The landing was commanded by Lieutenant General Sir Frederick Stopford, who had no experience in amphibious operations and had never been in battle.[19] He had been serving as constable of the Tower of London until given the command because he was the ranking general on the Army List.

Bob was sitting in a dugout censoring letters when a shell struck. It did not explode but severed his leg. He died on a hospital ship. By that time WL was in France, seconded to the Royal Engineers (RE). WHB sadly accepted the condolences of his fellows in the BIR, and was more determined than ever to beat the Huns.

Condolences changed to enthusiastic congratulations on 12 November 1915 when WHB and WL were jointly awarded the Nobel Prize for Physics for their work on x-rays. The presentation ceremony was postponed until 1 June the following year. The Bragg's pleasure was poisoned by their fury that the Swedes had awarded the chemistry prize to a German, Richard Willstätter, for his investigations of natural pigments.

The road to the Nobel

They had a foretaste six months before when they were jointly awarded the Barnard Medal of Columbia University, a distinguished prize presented once every five years. Rutherford wrote his congratulations, assuring them that it was a handsome medal and asking whether he had ever shown them his?

Physicists were astounded when Roentgen discovered a ray that could pass through flesh; its nature was a mystery to be solved. WHB and his instrument maker in Australia built an x-ray generator. It consisted of an elongated, evacuated glass tube containing a negatively charged cathode, which released electrons that were drawn to a positively charged metal plate, the anti-cathode or target, at the other end of the tube. When electrons smash into the target they release x-rays. WHB used his tube for an oversubscribed popular public lecture in Adelaide on the latest marvel. Some clergymen, upset because the rays could see through clothing, denounced: 'the revolting indecency of the invention.'

WL had a tricycle accident that shattered his left elbow. The physician was not sure which bones were fractured and thought it best to fix the elbow so that it would heal immobile. Father's x-ray image enabled the physician to set the nasty, complicated break so that the elbow still flexed, though it remained stiff and his left arm was slightly shorter.

WHB began to study x-rays, measuring intensity with an electroscope. Obviously they were beams of energy, but what carried the energy? The beams are not deflected by magnetic or electrical fields, so he proposed that they are streams of tiny, neutral particles. Charles G. Barkla (Nobel laureate, 1917), who worked in Edinburgh, argued that the beams are waves because he could polarize them like light.[20] Bragg was unable to polarize his x-rays because they used different metals as the targets in their tubes: Barkla generated relatively low energy 'soft' x-rays, while WHB studied high energy 'hard' x-rays. They argued inconclusively in the weekly journal *Nature* until the editors refused to publish more. While this was going on WL was a physics student in the University of Adelaide, spending his time between classes in father's office reading new journals and discussing new ideas.

Neither WHB or Barkla had read Albert Einstein's paper of 1905, on the properties of ultraviolet light, showing that somehow waves and particles are two sides of the same coin. WHB later excused his omission because the paper was written by an obscure patent clerk and he did not read German. Most of those who did read the paper at the time ignore the idea; wave-particle duality does not appeal to common sense.

Then WHB accepted the Cavendish Chair in Physics at Leeds. It was not an altogether happy move. Gwendoline and the children missed informal, sunny Australian life and hated the sooty North. Adelaide students relished his lectures, Leeds students stamped their feet in displeasure. In time he adjusted his delivery to suit their taste. He became pro-vice-chancellor of the university; perhaps he was considering becoming a full-time administrator. The x-ray work seemed at a dead end, he fretted unhappily that he was not fulfilling Leeds' expectations.

In 1912 his particle interpretation of x-rays was demolished. Max von Laue (Nobel laureate, 1914) showed that an x-ray beam aimed at a crystal produces a reproducible pattern of spots on a photographic plate. The Germans interpreted the spots as the diffraction of x-ray waves by a three-dimensional grating formed by the atoms in the salt. To fit the data they assumed that the x-ray beam contains certain specific wavelengths—no one knew how to measure the wavelengths of real x-rays.

WL was at Cambridge, where he had won first-class honours in the mathematical tripos (the numerical ranking of Wranglers had been abandoned and the coaches had retired). He switched into physics and was a research student in the Cavendish Laboratory. He also thought about Laue's spots. The chemists supposed that the atoms forming simple crystals are arranged in sheets, running parallel to the crystal's face. If this is so, imagine what will happen when a thin beam of x-rays hit the face of the crystal at an angle. Most of the beam will go straight through the spaces between the atoms, but at every sheet some of the x-ray waves will hit an atom and be deflected. With most impinging angles the waves reflected from the different parallel layers in the sheet will be out of phase, and therefore will cancel one another out—no energy will be reflected.

(Anyone uncomfortable with the idea of the destructive addition of out-of-phase waves should recall that noise-cancelling earphones record the outside noise, shift it to be totally out of phase and then play it through the earphone to the listener. The noise penetrating into the head set is cancelled by the out-of-phase signal.)

WL realized that a mono-chromatic beam hitting the surface at precisely the correct angle will travel precisely a wavelength between reflecting sheets, so reflections will be in phase and will produce a beam of energy. In other words, a monochromatic x-ray beam should produce a detectable refection only at a set series of angles. There is a series because waves can be reflected in-phase from every layer, every other layer, every third layer and so forth. He wrote an equation describing the relationship between the beam's wavelength, the distance between the parallel plates of atoms in a simple crystal, and the angles at which a pencil beam of x-rays would reflect an in-phase beam. He tested the idea by varying the angle at which an x-ray beam struck a crystal of mica plate and obtained 'a lovely series of reflections'.[21]

The equation could be tested by varying the angle at which an x-ray beam struck a crystal and measuring how much energy was reflected. WHB and Jenkinson constructed an x-ray spectrometer, in which a crystal is rotated stepwise though precise angles while being struck with a thin pencil of x-rays. The intensity of the reflection was measured with an electroscope. WL commuted to Leeds to help with the measurements. Every observation fitted the equation perfectly. They remembered it as '... a glorious time when we worked far into every night with new worlds unfolding before us in the silent laboratory'.

They estimated the distance between the layers by measuring the volume and weight of simple crystals, calculating the number of atoms it contained by Avogadro's number and assuming that the atoms are equally spaced. This enabled them to calculate the wavelengths of reflected x-rays. Once they knew the wavelength they could determine the spacing of the atoms in crystals, starting with substances like sodium chloride, assembled from simple cubic cells, and then moving onto more complicated structures. They also showed that different metallic targets generate x-rays with different wavelengths.[22] X-rays contain two sharp peaks at frequencies that are characteristic of the material of the target, along with a dimmer background smeared over a range of frequencies.

As soon as they pushed the door ajar others rushed in. WHB had taught Henry G. H. Moseley, one of Rutherford's students, how to coax x-ray tubes into action.[23] Moseley and a Manchester colleague, Charles Galton Darwin (bracketed Fourth Wrangler, 1909, the eldest son of the astronomer Sir George and a grandson of Charles and Emma),[24] measured the wavelengths of the radiation from targets made of thirty different elements. The heavier the atomic weight the shorter the two principal wavelengths. They found that the wavelengths shift by the same amount between each adjacent element in the periodic table. This suggested that adjacent elements differ by one proton in the nucleus and supported the Rutherford-Bohr picture of the atom: a punctuate, positively charged nucleus surrounded by electrons. Moseley's series had gaps disclosing elements yet to be discovered. Henry Moseley was an RE lieutenant; he was killed by a sniper's bullet on Gallipoli while telephoning an order. Rutherford tried to arrange a safe scientific berth to save his talent for the nation, but mailed the letter on the day Moseley shipped out.

Science and U-boats

So WHB and Rutherford sat at the BIR conference table as old pals; they often vacationed together in Rutherford's motor car. At first glance they even looked rather alike: rectangular faces with chins sagging into the neck, elevated foreheads rising to balding pates, bushy eyebrows and greying moustaches. But the postures of the moustaches were like chalk and cheese. Rutherford's thrust assertively outward, while WHB's was held in modestly because his upper lip pressed firmly against his front teeth. WHB's angle may have developed along with his flute-playing embouchure, but surely it also reflected personality. Rutherford spoke loudly and forcefully—the 'Croc'. WHB spoke softly and precisely, preferring to communicate in writing. Rutherford's attitude was: 'It is such a great thing life, I wouldn't have missed it for anything.'[25] At times WHB was not too sure.

When Section II began to consider how to deal with U-boats, Rutherford surely had first say. In his usual way he clearly defined the problem and noted possible solutions, jotting them down with one of the pencil stubs stockpiled in his right waistcoat pocket. Submerged U-boats were deadly because they were unseen. Even an underwater observer could not see one at any distance in the murky seas around the British Isles, detecting them with dangling cables or disturbances in electrical fields emitted from hunting vessels would have too short a range. They might be located by echoes from a sound source; just a few years before an iceberg had been detected by its echo, but to locate an object as small as a submarine requires a sharply focused sound beam. This calls for a high frequency beam, because the angle of dispersion for sound radiated from a speaker is inversely proportional to frequency.[26] Echo location might be possible some day; ships were torpedoed every day. It would be more realistic to listen for submarines stealing through the depths. They must learn more about the physics of underwater sound and devise sensitive, directional hydrophones. This time the Admiralty returned a prompt, self-satisfied response: shortly after the outbreak of the war they had established an experimental and developmental station, newly developed hydrophones were already in action.

Rutherford had a water tank built in the cellar of the Manchester physics laboratory. Little was known about underwater sound. The best measurements of velocity had been made in Lake Geneva in 1827. A submerged bell was struck by a hammer at the instant that a gunpowder charge was ignited to give a flash. An observer on the far side of the lake activated a quarter-second stopwatch when he saw the flash and stopped it when he heard the underwater sound. They reported the velocity at 8.1 degrees C as 1,435 m per sec.[27] Not bad at all, today's value is 1,436.4 m per sec. Sound travels 4.3 times faster in water than in air, and therefore the wavelength for a given frequency is 4.3 times that in air. The pressure of a wave of the same amplitude in water is 60 times that in air. It should be possible to hear fairly distant U-boats. Rutherford was optimistic:

> If we prove at all successful, I think it will mean the practical elimination of the submarine as a serious factor in modern warfare.[28]

The Admiralty experimental station was on the Firth of Forth, on a rocky promontory called Hawkcraig. It was commanded by a retired officer returned to service: Commander Cyril P. Ryan, who was 41-years-old. Ryan had been noted in the navy for having 'a great turn for mechanical instruments'.[29] His work with wireless telegraphy had been lauded by Their Lordships, but he was less adept at commanding a flotilla of destroyers, so he had been retired in 1911, going to work for the Marconi Company.

Working with a staff of half a dozen able seamen, his first hydrophone went into action in January 1915.[30] His operation expanded rapidly as he installed shore listening stations near harbour entrances. In time, each shore station listened to 8 to 16 hydrophones, most mounted on tripods on the sea bottom. At H.M. Experimental

Station *Hawkcraig* he trained listeners and maintenance crews. By summer 1915 Ryan commanded 20 officers and 80 petty officers. The officers were mostly 'wavy navy', so-called because reserve officer's gold wrist stripes of rank were wavy rather than straight. The ship's company included Ryan's brother, from the African Civil Service, who was nicknamed 'The Great White Chief'; Brett, a famous violinist; Rose, a London theatre manager; Ashby Froude, a son of the famous historian; and Hamilton Harty and his wife Agnes Nichols, both well-known musicians.[31]

Rutherford, Paget, and the Duke of Buccleuch visited Hawkcraig on 15 September. They reported that Ryan was doing good work, but had too little money. He should be permitted to spend more than £1 on an experiment without authorization from London.

Ryan's hydrophones were modifications of instruments developed by the American Submarine Signalling Company. The company rang underwater bells at lighthouses and lightships that could be heard through hydrophones on vessels nine miles away. The case was a thick, hollow brass disc with a diameter of about 35 cm. On one face there was brass diaphragm 4.4 cm in diameter and 1 mm thick. It could be that thick because underwater sound waves are so powerful. Inside the case a short metal bar coupled the diaphragm to a 'carbon button' microphone, consisting of carbon granules packed between two metal plates. When one plate moves it changes the distance between the granules, altering the electrical resistance of the carbon layer. In time the carbon granules clump together, so hydrophones had an electromagnetic knocker triggered by the listener to shake the granules apart. Underwater sound waves are long, so these hydrophones respond to sounds coming from all directions. Hydrophone diaphragms respond all too well to the background noises in the sea, but are less sensitive to the low frequency purr of a U-boat's propellers, so later they coupled diaphragm to microphone with a metal lever, which transmits low frequencies best.

Ryan also mounted hydrophones in minefields; when the listener heard a U-boat he exploded the mine, but the rub was that the intruder comes into earshot while far away and it is hard to judge when to fire. (This problem was solved when vacuum tube amplifiers became available by replacing the high sensitivity carbon button with an ordinary, magnetic telephone receiver, which reduced the range to less than 200 yards.) They were beginning to install hydrophones on submarines and on former fishing boats to hunt for the enemy at sea.

In November 1915 Section II sent two civilian scientists to Hawkcraig: Albert B. Wood, who had been in Rutherford's group and was now a lecturer at Liverpool, and Harold Gerrard, an electrical engineer at Manchester. They were accompanied by F. W. Pyle, an instrument maker from Liverpool. Wood's memoirs are the source for much of what we know about how the BIR did research.[32] The scientists were paid £1 per day, which 25-year-old Wood regarded as handsome. Their workroom was a wooden shed with a concrete tank at one end. They had almost no equipment.[33] Nearby lodging was so expensive that Section II had to pay part of the mechanic's housing costs. Their lathes were on loan from the universities of Leeds and Sheffield.

The Battle cruiser Squadron was based in the Firth off the town of Rosyth, just a few miles west of Hawkcraig, on the other side of the Forth Bridge. The shore facilities included two enormous dry-docks. The huge, sleek vessels and their host of smaller auxiliaries made a magnificent sight when spread across the anchorage and a magnificent parade when they headed out to sea. The scientists listened to the cruiser's screws with one of Ryan's hydrophones; they could follow them for 20 miles.

The man commanding this naval might, Vice-Admiral David Beatty, often visited and strongly supported Ryan's work. Beatty was instantly recognizable, postcards with his photograph flooded the nation, decorating store windows and pinned inside back doors. He was a small, dapper, handsome man, looking younger than his 44-years, impeccably dressed in uniforms of his own design, and with his cap always tipped to a rakish angle. He was the youngest British admiral since Nelson, and he had already distinguished himself in actions off the German coast.

He escorted his moneyed wife Ethyl, the only daughter of the Chicago retailing genius Marshall Field. She resided at the nearby, impressive Aberdour House whose stables, tennis courts and garages she enlarged for her husband's pleasures. To be ready for action, he bunked on his flagship, HMS *Lion*. Beatty was her second husband. She had been divorced for desertion, losing her young son, but Beatty was not named as correspondent, which saved his career. Her nephew aptly and discreetly described her as 'free ranging in her affections'.[34] One memorable day Beatty turned back on his way to *Lion* to retrieve his cigarette case and found Ethyl in bed with an officer. Ryan was her discovery, as she wrote to her husband in early 1915: 'But it always seemed to me the few times you met Commander Ryan you were displeased.'[35] Beatty firmly vetoed her inviting Ryan to live in Aberdour House, there had to be some discretion. Nonetheless the Beatty's visited Hawkcraig frequently to see Ryan's latest wares.

Ryan saw little use for the reports the scientists provided on how sound waves are reflected at a water–air interface or a complete mathematical description of the vibrations of diaphragms in water.

Paget was an expert on human speech who used his knowledge of vocal anatomy to teach the deaf how to speak.[36] He spiced his lectures with a plasticine model of the human vocal apparatus, which he blew through while manipulating it to produce a potpourri of sounds. He made his name at Hawkcraig when a submarine was nearby by being immersed upside-down in the sea, with Rutherford holding his ankles. To determine the primary frequency generated by the submarine's screws he tapped his head when he surfaced, which gave his G# 'skull note', from which he sang stepwise to the note he heard beneath the water. Unfortunately, this information was of little use because the frequencies generated by hydrophones depend on the properties of the diaphragm as well as of the source, but as Wood delicately put it: 'at least he did not catch pneumonia'. The scientists made little impression on the seamen at Hawkcraig, because Ryan kept them in a separate compartment.

The scientists set two major goals: to develop seagoing hydrophones that could hear intruders above the racket produced by their own ship's engines and the water they were shoving through, and to develop hydrophones that could determine the target's bearing.

On 2 February 1916 *The Times* printed a two column letter denouncing the Government's failure to mobilize science for war, while the Germans were using science brilliantly. Two radical remedies were proposed. The Board of Trade should be converted into a Ministry of Science, Commerce, and Industry. And in future the civil service should give:

> a preponderating—or at least equal—share of marks in the competitive examinations to natural science subjects ....

It was signed by 36 eminent scientists, including Oxford professor of medicine Sir William Osler, Ernest Starling, Sir William Ramsay, W. H. Perkin and Lord Rayleigh. WHB did not sign. He was for a minister of science, but thought the stringent scientific qualifications for civil servants unachievable and off-putting. Science must gain its rightful place by showing what it could do.

Naval co-operation was slow and grudging. In February 1916, Wood and Gerrard finally received certificates acknowledging that their work was indispensable for the war effort and armbands showing their status. In March, after five months on the job, they had their first chance to listen to a submarine with a hydrophone. A submarine running on its electric motors sounded like the sawing of wood; a torpedo sounded like a clucking hen; porpoises like chattering children.[37]

In 1915 seventeen U-boats were lost. The Germans had stepped up production and had 69 in service at the beginning of 1916. They built 346 during the war, fewer than they could gainfully use, they mistakenly diverted scarce resources to less useful ventures.

Support for science

British science took a great stride forward in 1915 when a Committee of the Privy Council for Scientific and Industrial Research was established, chaired by William Symington McCormick, a noted Scottish Chaucer scholar. Not as odd a choice as he might seem. A talented committee man and vigorous education advocate, in 1901 he had been appointed by Andrew Carnegie—a beneficent Scot who made a vast fortune in the US—to direct a trust of £2 million to benefit the four Scottish universities and their students. McCormick's imaginative leadership of the trust led the Liberal Government to appoint him to a committee set up in 1905 to provide grants to British universities, which he eventually chaired. He played a major role in Haldane's Royal Commission on the University of London. A committee he chaired about how to enhance university research led to the formation of the new Council. Scientists, first appalled by a Chaucerian at the helm, soon appreciated his affable fairness, good sense and willingness to help. He complained to the money men: 'You send me to preach the Gospel to hungry men, with a Bible in one hand but no bread in the other.'[38]

His plea was heeded. The Committee was replaced by a Department of Scientific and Industrial Research (DSIR) in 1917. Its responsibilities included fuel, low temperatures, building, forest products, chemistry, radio, the Geological Survey and the National Physical Laboratory (NPL). The DSIR submitted their budget estimates directly to parliament.

Jutland

On 30 May 1916 Hawkcraig was treated to a stirring spectacle as Beatty's ships headed out to sea: six battle cruisers, four fast battleships, 14 light cruisers, 27 destroyers, and a seaplane carrier, all billowing dense black smoke from their funnels. Within hours, the rumour spread that Jellicoe's Grand Fleet also had sailed from Scapa Flow.[39] Some destroyers returned to the Firth on 1 June because they were low on fuel. Next the battered dreadnought *Warspite* limped up the waterway. Tugs nudged it into dry-dock No. 1. The rest of the heavy ships steamed in the following morning—some in appalling condition. The hushed observers on the shore saw twisted metal and paintwork scorched black. Beatty's flagship *Lion* had been hit by thirteen heavy shells and two light, starting six fires. The thick layer of armour plate on the top of her midship gun turret was twisted grotesquely upward, like the top of an opened food tin. *Lion* went into dry-dock No. 2. Their battle cruisers were unexpectedly vulnerable to German shells, as Beatty put it: 'there seems to be something wrong with our bloody ships today'—pause—'and something wrong with our system'.[40] Fires ignited in gun turrets by German shells flashed down through the ammunition conveying tunnels to detonate the magazines. It was not bad design, it was bad usage. They fastened the flash barriers open to get cordite to the guns faster.

The shore leave boats scuttled about the anchorage bringing the wounded ashore. The dead, as specified by regulations, had been buried at sea. Were they sacrifices for victory or testaments of defeat?[41] Balfour issued a communiqué briefly describing the battle between the two great fleets off the coast of Jutland in Denmark, giving losses factually—which infuriated Jellicoe, who thought this intelligence a gratuitous gift to the foe. Balfour announced that the British lost three battle cruisers, three armoured cruisers and eight destroyers to one German pre-Dreadnought battleship, four light cruisers and five torpedo boats. He was unaware that the Germans had also lost a battle cruiser. The perturbed public feared that the Admiralty, true to past form, was holding back bad news. Winston Churchill was brought in to review all of the reports and issue a second communiqué. Meanwhile the Germans announced their loss of a heavy cruiser and Churchill stressed that the enemy had fled to the shelter of their coastal batteries and that the blockade held firm.

Fisher despaired: 'They've failed me. They've failed me. I have spent 30 years of my life preparing for this day and they've failed me, they've failed me.'[42] Who to blame:

Jellicoe or Beatty? The first part of the battle was fought between battle cruiser squadrons. A signalling failure placed Beatty's fast battleships too far behind to fire effectively, taking 40 fifteen-inch guns out of the free-for-all in which the British lost more vessels. But Beatty strutted jauntily like a hero, while Jellicoe looked like a harassed accountant in naval uniform, so in the public eye he became the goat.

Directional hydrophones

The Duke of Buccleuch formally protested the Admiralty's foot-dragging on hydrophone development. Balfour met with representatives of Section II. He agreed to increase their budget, bring three more physicists to Hawkcraig and appoint WHB as resident director of research. The Admiralty negotiated with UCL to give him a six month leave (later extended to the duration) and to reimburse UCL for his salary. In July they rented their London house. He brought along his secretary, Miss Winifred Callis, and Jenkinson—who worked by WHB's side for life. C. H. Mertz, an engineer on Section II who worked in industrial research, offered WHB astute advice: 'don't pinch pennies as you did in academia'. Eventually Section II spent £6,508 13s 3d, of which 56 per cent went to acoustic research.[43]

The Bragg family set up house in a village overlooking the Firth, the views were superb. WHB expanded the scientific staff and even managed to add instrument makers—in short supply because so many were in the forces. Paget was a welcome, entertaining visitor: for instance, his audience would select a newspaper advertisement which he would use as the theme for an improvised oratorio. He was nine-year-old Gwendy's special favourite.

When Wood married in June there was a low-key celebration but generally the scientists were depressed and frustrated. To preserve secrecy Ryan refused to show Section II his monthly reports and rarely shared reports from hydrophone operators. The scientists had no feedback from the users about how their products performed.

WHB was kept on a tight leash. One day he was testing a new hydrophone on an experimental ship that was manoeuvring as specified by Ryan. WHB asked the vessel's captain for additional movements. Ryan watched incredulously from the shore and confined the captain to quarters for two weeks. WHB apologized and took full responsibility but the captain remained incarcerated. Edith Beatty stood firm in Ryan's corner. She wrote to her husband:

> I have just heard that the B.I.R. are now exerting themselves to interfere with the fitting of hydrophones in submarines, making suggestions and advocating changes without any reference to Captain Ryan.[44]

Their styles were poles apart. Ryan tested a new model by putting on earphones and listening to passing vessels. The scientists generated standardized sounds with a 'rattler', a thick steel plate hit by a hammer 20 times each second, or a 'rumbler', a drum containing miscellaneous bits of metal rotated by an electrical motor. They measured a microphone's sensitivity by rectifying its electrical output and measuring the DC current with a galvanometer. By inserting filters in the circuit they measured the currents generated by different sound frequencies. At long last on 28 October, 1916 they were permitted to borrow a submarine for one day. WHB wrote to Wood:

> So we must be quite ready: have all of the apparatus seen to, and spares in case they are wanted! We have enough films? Get a couple of more rolls if you can. You have everything else? We must see to stop-watches.

The next major advance was the development of a bidirectional hydrophone by J. T. McGregor Morris, Professor of Electrical Engineering at East London College and student assistant A. F. Sykes.[45] They tested their designs in the nearby swimming bath. In May 1916 they came to Hawkcraig for two days to test one of their models. Sykes reported in detail to WHB, mannerly letters in precise, slanting script. Morris's and WHB's letters were typed; except for the equations WHB penned in when he gently upgraded Sykes's physics.

Sykes was wounded by white feathers handed to him by patriotic young ladies. The BIR requested an 'Admiralty Badge' to show that he was engaged in the war effort; the Admiralty refused. Finally the Royal Society provided a lapel badge. Sykes worked without pay and the BIR was slow in reimbursing Morris who was paying expenses from his own pocket: by 28 July he had laid out £182 6s 6d, including £3 3s 8d for winter heating of the swimming bath. Despite repeated invoices to the BIR he had received only £20 as a personal advance from WHB. In August Morris wrote that:

> Sykes is getting rather difficult in his attitude to the Admiralty and I want to thrash things out with him.

This time the Admiralty helped: a Lieutenant James stopped by to assure Sykes that his service to his King was valued. Morris's account was finally settled on 3 October; Sykes received £200. (In 1917 they were awarded £12,000.)

The Sykes and Morris bidirectional hydrophone has a diaphragm in contact with the water on each side of the case containing the microphone. Sound waves hitting the diaphragm on one side elicit a small signal because the pressure is slightly higher on the side facing the source. When both diaphragms are in line with the sound source the pressures on the two sides are equal and there is no response. In practice the operator rotated the hydrophone until the sound disappeared. At that point the target was in line with the diaphragm, off either to the right or left—hence bidirectional. An analogy is a drum made by stretching a membrane over a hoop.[46] Striking the membrane radiates sound waves, but a listener in line with the plane of the membrane receives vibrations in opposite phase and hears almost nothing.

WHB and his group tried to modify the bidirectional hydrophone by blocking sound from hitting one side of the membrane with a baffle. After months of trials, they discovered that effective baffles must contain a layer of air. The clue came from Rutherford who had found that greasing metal diaphragms to preserve their shine decreased sensitivity due to trapped air bubbles. The distance between the baffle and the closest diaphragm had to be painstakingly adjusted to a critical value: about five centimetres.[47] Now they had a directional hydrophone whose output was maximum when the un-baffled side was pointing directly at the target. They worked well from shore or from a stationary vessel, but were useless due to extraneous noise when the ship's engine was running or when it was moving through the water.

Listening was a difficult art because in the sea propeller sounds were obscured by high frequency, background racket. Sometimes listeners were plagued by whales whistling messages to one another.[48] Trainee listeners were selected for high auditory acuity; they were screened by 'distinguished physiologists', and then they were thoroughly trained, starting with gramophone recordings of underwater sounds.[49] A major improvement was made when vacuum tube amplifiers became available at the end of 1917. They replaced carbon microphones with less sensitive magnetic microphones like those used in telephones, which are less sensitive to high frequencies that were further reduced by a filter in the amplifying circuit.

The French

The poor fit between British seadogs and scientists was exemplified by relations with the French. At the end of 1915, the *Bureau* proposed to exchange information with the British Admiralty—the offer was rejected. They thought they were comfortably ahead and worried about patent rights and security—after all the French might be the next foe and undoubtedly would be competitors after the war. In May 1916 Lieutenant Duc Maurice de Broglie, was allowed to visit Hawkcraig. He was a physicist who had started as a naval officer; he knew WHB and Rutherford. (De Broglie's younger brother won the Nobel physics prize in 1929.)

De Broglie told Section II that the French were trying to echo-locate submarines. Rutherford had considered this possibility but thought it impractical because a high frequency sound source would be needed to produce a narrow enough beam to be effectual.[50] Paget and William DuBois Duddell, an engineer in Section II who was an expert in wireless and the generation of high frequency waves, went to France to learn more.

The French had started work on echo location in early 1915, when the idea from an exiled Russian physicist in a Swiss tuberculosis sanatorium, Constantin Chilowsky, for a high-frequency system was passed along to Painlevé.[51] He was so impressed that he asked the eminent physicist Paul Langevin, 42-years-old, who had studied with the Curies and J. J. Thomson before becoming a professor at the Collège de France, to see what he could do. De Broglie was one of his students. Langevin considered echo detection impractical, but bowed to the minister's urging.[52] They were old friends, four years earlier Painlevé had been Lagevin's second at a duel held in the Bicycle Stadium, where Langevin fought a journalist who had been writing lurid accounts of his relations with the widowed Marie Curie. They squared off with pistols at 25 paces. Both duellists fired at the ground; honour was satisfied.[53]

Langevin and Chilowsky started work at the Collège de France. To generate a high frequency signal they used two metal plates separated by a 20 micron vacuum, the plates oscillated when an alternating voltage obtained from a spark gap like that used in wireless transmitters was applied. This was abysmally inefficient, so they replaced the vacuum with a thin insulating sheet of mica, which produced a signal that could be detected on the opposite bank of the Seine by a carbon microphone—both emitter and receiver were too delicate for service at sea. Then Chilowsky left the project because he could not endure Langevin's careful, step-by-step tactics. In 1916 Langevin moved to the experimental station at the Toulon Naval Base, where two vessels were placed at his disposal. He worked with two other academic physicists and a technical staff.

The French had a head-start in the fabrication of three electrode vacuum tubes, which had been developed in the US by Lee De Forest and his competitors. In 1914 the German Telefunken company sent a representative, Paul Pichon, to purchase samples of the latest US models. On his way home Herr Pichon arrived in London on 3 August and promptly hijacked his precious cargo to Calais where he became Monsieur Pichon. He had deserted from the French Army fourteen years previously and fled to Germany, but war reawakened his patriotism. (After the war he returned to Germany and continued his business career there.)[54] The French soon developed an improved model at the *L'Ecole Centrale* of the French Signal Corps.[55] By the end of the war they were producing 1,400 tubes per day. The fine wires for the screens in the tubes were drawn by skilled workers who in peacetime made metal gauzes for elegant clothing. They also developed amplifiers using as many as nine tubes, which were no noisier than British amplifiers with three tubes developed at the NPL. (During the war the Americans manufactured more than one million vacuum tubes.) Langevin amplified the echo and then converted it to audible frequencies by mixing it with a low frequency signal in a vacuum tube. The result was two new frequencies, one the sum of and the other the difference between the two inputs. This 'heterodyne method' had been devised in the US.

At a meeting in July Section II agreed to get involved in echo-location. Chilowsky had moved to Britain and offered his services, which were not accepted. Bragg reported that he had been permitted to examine the hydrophone on a captured U-boat, which was inferior to current British designs.

In September a distinguished French deputation, including Painlevé and Jean Baptiste Perrin, was permitted to visit Hawkcraig. Perrin (Nobel Laureate 1926) was a leading physicist now serving as an officer of engineers and was designing hydrophones. This meeting entered Bragg family legend.[56] The morning of the visit WHB received telegraphed orders from the Admiralty: 'On no account show them anything'. He appealed to Admiral Beatty's flag lieutenant:

Who organized such a lunch on board the flagship that their party were in no condition to notice what they were *not* shown after lunch when they went round Hawkcraig Point.

A good story, but it would be astounding if some science was not swapped behind naval backs. The incident highlights the Admiral's ignorance about science and how it is done. It took many distressing months to teach them better.

Section II asked Balfour for help; in October 1916 he signed a sharing agreement with the French and de Broglie was appointed liaison officer, but the Admiralty was adamant that information to be shared required specific approval. Richard Threlfall FRS was added to Section II. He had been professor of physics in Sydney and had befriended Bragg when he came to Australia. Now he was working for the company that produced most of Britain's phosphorus.

Harwich

Ryan was promoted to acting captain. When WHB returned from a short trip he found that the cable connecting a small island to the mainland had been removed without explanation by captain's order. It was used in experiments on a photophone, a device for transmitting voice messages underwater. One can imagine how futile it was for quiet, controlled WHB to protest to the forceful, confident, dashing captain.

WHB and Paget complained to Balfour, who offered WHB command of Hawkcraig. A more aggressive man might have seized victory, but WHB knew that Ryan was doing useful work and was well liked by his ship's company. Moreover Hawkcraig was too remote from submarines or their pursuers. They desperately needed feedback. Balfour agreed to establish an independent BIR anti-submarine research centre directed by WHB. It was set up at Parkeston Quay at Harwich, which was the base for U-boat hunters in the North Sea. They started with a staff of 30 civilians and eight wavy navy men to assist in sea trials. Initially they had five instrument makers, by the end of the war there were 50. The Harwich naval commander was supportive, but still restrained by his superiors. The scientists ate in the officer's mess on HMS *Maidstone*, a clipper ship that now served as the depot for a flotilla of E class submarines. Temporary wooden huts were erected as laboratories and a small flotilla of test vessels assembled. In September 1917 they were allotted the submarine *C-2* for their experiments.

The staff included R. W. Boyle, a former student of Rutherford's and now professor of physics at the University of Alberta. Boyle and a younger man, B. S. Smith, were assigned to work on echo location, keeping in close touch with Langevin. (After the war Smith became the Royal Navy's foremost authority on submarine echo location.)

In December Lloyd George became prime minister, Balfour became foreign secretary and Sir Edward Carson took over as First Lord. Jellicoe transferred his flag to London as First Sea Lord and Beatty took command of the Grand Fleet.

Unrestricted U-boat warfare

The Germans raised the stakes. On 9 January 1917 they declared the seas around the British Isles and in most of the Mediterranean to be war zones, any vessel entering them after 1 February would be sunk without warning—the British would starve. The German Navy promised to sink at least 600,000 tons of shipping each month.[57] They had 111 U-boats; 18 in the Mediterranean, 53 based in Germany and 33 in Flanders. Eighty more would be in service by the end of the year. Their new models carried enough fuel to patrol far out into the Atlantic.

With more ships going down the desperate scientists pulled out all of the stops. WHB investigated the mechanism of fish hearing, but learned nothing worthwhile. Wood was reluctantly participating in experiments, run by the director of the Plymouth Marine Laboratory, in which sea lions from Hengler's Circus were trained in swimming baths in Glasgow to move toward faint sounds—rewarded with bits of fish. But when returned to the sea they contentedly fished on their own, so eventually they were allowed to 'return to their legitimate business', as Rear Admiral Allenby aptly put it.[58] They were so magnificently streamlined that Wood could not hear them even when they swam just past a hydrophone. Sea lions were top secret, but nonetheless found their way into mocking German newspaper cartoons before the end of the year. Seagulls were trained to follow a fake periscope, but they proved to be too easily distracted. Sir Oliver Lodge, professor in Birmingham, suggested that they try a dowsing rod, not to detect water but to detect metal in water. Section II agreed to underwrite expenses.

On 15 May 1917, with national survival hanging in the balance, the War Cabinet received a printed 'Memorandum on submarine hunting' by Professor Bragg.[59] It was a pioneering effort to analyse military operations scientifically. Some recipients surely were dismayed by his few simple equations, but his idea was straightforward. He calculated the area that a hunter could sweep for a submerged U-boat in an hour from the distance the hunter travels and the distance on either side at which it can detect a submerged submarine. From the area of the war zone and the number of U-boats on patrol he calculated the probability that a U-boat would be in the swept area assuming they are randomly distributed. For example if the hunter's speed is ten miles per hour and its detection range is one mile on either side and if 40 U-boats are in the war zone around the British Isles, on average the hunter would stumble across a prey once every 500 hours. With 500 hunters at sea the U-boats should be in serious trouble. Hydrophones had a detection range of a mile or more.

The rub was that to hear a U-boat the hunter had to heave to and turn off her engines. A U-boat could hear them coming and easily outrun a stop-start hunter. The fleet needed new, fast hunters or, better yet, hunters propelled by paddle wheels or by water jets, from which one could listen while underway. Even if they were available hunters could be foiled by U-boats who heard them, switched off their engines and lay quiet. Hopefully the strain of silent sitting would be too much for German nerves. The problem seemed almost insurmountable.

He described one encouraging breakthrough: a destructor of U-boats. A pair of hunters equipped with the new directional hydrophones would find the exact position of a submerged U-boat. Then they would drag a powerful permanent magnet at the end of an electrical cable over the target until it was pulled onto the iron hull. As it swings toward the iron an electrical current is generated in an attached coil of wire. On this signal the hunter detonates a charge attached to the magnet, it could be small because it explodes directly on the hull. The destructor was being developed in the Admiralty laboratory by J. C. McLennan, professor of physics in Toronto, and also in Harwich. It was given high priority and lavish support, but this ingenious weapon never went into action, presumably it failed sea trials.

Depth charges remained their only reliable weapon. The D-type depth charge with 300 lb of explosive had first been used in June 1916, but production was slow, a year later most U-boat hunters carried only one or two. In December 1916, 30 depth charge throwers were ordered; they tossed the 'ashcans' well away from the hunter. A U-boat might be damaged if one exploded within 100 feet; a series of such close explosions might shellshock the crew.[60] Section II's experiments showed that it must explode within 44 feet of a U-boat to inflict a mortal wound.

In the agonizing months during which British backs were pressed against the wall, Section II meetings must have been depressed and tense. Bragg firmly protested that the scientists would not work effectively without feedback about how their instruments were performing at sea. The Admiralty only let them see reports of engagements in which they believed a U-boat was destroyed or damaged. They needed to evaluate all action reports. By this time the senior naval representative on Section II was Commodore William Reginald Hall, the head of Naval Intelligence; known as 'Blinker' because of a facial tic.[61] He thought WHB's request outrageous:

> The B.I.R. can carry on research on lines suggested by the Admiralty. The extension of circulation of these reports is to be deprecated. It will only lead to irresponsible criticism.

All that the scientists need know is that U-boats were at sea and must be found.

France seemed their only hope, but Langevin was struggling with the erratic performance of his microphones. He decided to try piezoelectricity—scarcely surprising for a student of the Curies, the brothers had discovered it. Some crystals—quartz and sodium potassium tartrate tetrahydrate (Rochelle salt) are the best—change shape when conducting an electrical current and generate an electrical potential when deformed. (They are used in clocks and to generate sparks from portable, squeeze-triggered gas stove lighters.)

Early on Rutherford had tried using quartz crystals connected to an earphone to listen underwater, but the signal was too faint.[62] Langevin persuaded an optician friend to cut thin slices from a glorious quartz crystal kept as an ornament in his shop. When connected to a powerful amplifier it made an excellent underwater microphone. Then they tried the same quartz sheet as the source of high frequency sound. A vacuum tube oscillator applied a powerful 150,000 Hz electrical potential across the slice. It resonated with a power of 10 watts per square cm: the output from the entire slice was close to a kilowatt. Fish placed in the beam were killed. With appropriate circuitry the sheet could be briefly oscillated to produce a sound pulse and then switched to receive an echo.

Section II sent William Henry Eccles (professor of Applied Physics and Electrical Engineering at the City and Guilds College, Finsbury) to France to learn more about their methods for producing and using vacuum tube amplifiers. The British were only making 100 tubes per day.

After a visit to Toulon, Boyle and Smith obtained quartz crystals from the Geological Science Museum, which were cut by a tombstone maker, and bought vacuum tubes from the French. Large slices of quartz were impractical for operational instruments because they were scarce and the voltage needed to oscillate them was prohibitively high. Langevin's group solved this snag cleverly by fabricating a mosaic of small bits of thin quartz that were glued between two square steel plates. The quartz bits could have irregular outlines. They were driven with a potential between 3,000 and 5,000 V at 40,000 Hz. The mosaic was also the receiver; the incoming signal was fed into an eight vacuum tube amplifier. Both pulse and echo were converted to audible signals producing the familiar ping-ping.[63] The first successful trial was in February 1918.

Boyle and Smith moved to Dartmouth for ready access to deep water. To construct instruments for use at sea they obtained quartz from a stockpile of chandelier pendants stored in the attic of a warehouse in Bordeaux.[64]

Convoys

Section II only heard about the profound changes in anti-submarine tactics by rumour and an occasional hint in a newspaper. When the Germans announced their campaign the secretary to the War Cabinet Sir Maurice Hankey, a Royal Marine, proposed that they convoy merchantmen, as they had in past wars.[65] The Germans successfully convoyed freighters carrying iron ore from Sweden across the Baltic. Military traffic between Dover and France was guarded effectively by destroyers and airships. On 13 February 1917 First Lord Carson and Admirals Jellicoe and A. L. Duff, the director the Anti-Submarine Division, breakfasted at 10 Downing Street. Lloyd George showed them Hankey's paper on a 'system of scientifically organized convoys'.

The Admirals thought it a wretched idea. They needed their destroyers to protect the fleet. A convoy must sail at the speed of the slowest ship. Merchant captains would be unable to keep position or to zigzag in synchrony. Subsequently Jellicoe met with ten merchant skippers who confessed that they lacked the skill to keep position in a convoy.[66] Even should these problems be solved, there were far too many vessels to convoy. This was easily documented, because the reluctantly truthful

Admiralty issued weekly an accurate report of losses to U-boats. To coat the bad news they also reported how many ships left and entered British ports: an average of 2,500 vessels every week. Only a small fraction of them were torpedoed—but how could you convoy 2,500 ships? They agreed to experiment by convoying freighters sailing to Norway—which was tried in April and judged a failure[67]—and to convoy colliers across the channel, which could be done with small, slow vessels useless to the battle fleet.

The French imported coal from England and Wales because most of their coal fields were in enemy hands. In November 1916, 600 colliers made the trip independently. In February 1917 Commander Reginald Henderson was appointed to convoy colliers with 30 armed trawlers. It was an immediate success. Henderson distrusted the Admiralty's figure for vessels that needed to be convoyed. He consulted the card index of the Ministry of Shipping which showed that only 160–180 of the vessels leaving port each week were ocean-going, the rest were fishermen, ferries and the like. He passed his figures on to his commander, Admiral Duff. Henderson may have been one of the '... junior officers who went to, and were received by, Mr. Lloyd George, and who formulated to him ideas for dealing with the submarine menace', who Jellicoe complained of bitterly. (In the long run whistle-blowing did not prevent Henderson from becoming an admiral.) Jellicoe, like many in high office, knew that he was accessible and open-minded without conceiving how his rigid, impassive stance and fixed eyes staring through spectacles dried the mouths of juniors tempted to argue a point.

On 30 April with losses still mounting a desperate Lloyd George went to the Admiralty to chair a session of the Board. Girded for confrontation, he was gratified to learn that Admiral Duff:

> ... finds the number of ships for which convoy will have to be supplied more manageable than he thought.

It was a dramatic reversal from what Lloyd George brilliantly characterized as a 'fateful error in accountancy'. In fact the Admiral:

> had completely altered his view in regard to the adoption of a system of convoy, and I gather that the First Sea Lord shared his views, at any rate, to the extent of an experiment.

An 'experiment, which he warned might involve a great disaster.' They were already assembling a group at Gibraltar—it arrived safely on 20 May.

Convoys were only one item in the prime minister's busy day in the Board Room of the Admiralty, sitting before the great fireplace topped with a compass arrow that followed a vane on the roof. He had the bad news that: 'The directional hydrophone has not yet proved a success except at shore stations.' He announced a reorganization of the naval staff to ease the burden on the First Sea Lord. A civil lord would be appointed to the Admiralty Board; a position pencilled in by Churchill when he set up the naval staff but which never had been filled. The prime minister was reinforcing them with a man of business.

The Admiralty budged, but slowly. Paymaster-commander Manistry was named 'organizing manager of convoys' on 6 June (according to Lloyd George) or on 25 June (according to Jellicoe, who gives his rank as Paymaster-captain). He was not allocated office space or staff; he was to 'scrounge' for them. Jellicoe had 279 destroyers in home waters. He could spare 20 to 30 for convoy duty. As Lloyd George put it: '... there is no wrath like the cold fury of the professional spirit proved wrong by outsiders ...'. This is unfair because an insider, Henderson, had helped to break the logjam.

They asked the US for destroyers and the first American flotilla arrived on 4 May. American naval liaison was by Rear-Admiral William Sims.[68] He had commanded the Naval War College before being sent to London secretly—in mufti—to lay the groundwork before the US declared war. He was for convoying. Sims had a sharp eye for people, he described Lloyd George 'as a great, big, exuberant boy ...'.

Three days after visiting the Admiralty Lloyd George proposed to the War Cabinet that Major General Sir Eric Geddes be appointed as the civilian lord.[69] Geddes was a 42-year-old, boyish-looking wizard.[70] Sims described him:

> His mighty frame, his hard and supple muscles, his power of vigorous and rapid movement, his keen eye and his quick wit—these qualities, in the opinion of those best qualified to judge, would have made this stupendous Briton one of the greatest heavyweight prize-fighters in the annals of pugilism.

More prosaically, Geddes had been the traffic manager of the North Eastern Railway when Lloyd George recruited him to the MM in early 1916. In seven months Geddes increased the output of high explosive shells five-fold. His shells piled up on the French docks because their railways could not cope with the flood. Geddes was sent over to investigate. General Sir Douglas Haig reacted: '... I am glad to have practical hints from anyone capable of advising.'[71] Haig found him a 'most pleasant and capable man.' Geddes was appointed director of military railways and brought over locomotives, railway men, and port operators. The fellow Scots often worshipped together in the Church of Scotland. Geddes was commissioned as a major general and then was named inspector general of transportation in all theatres of war.

Their congeniality undermines the widely accepted caricature of Haig as a not overly bright cavalryman, as in Richard Attenborough's film *Oh what a Lovely War*. General Sir Ian Hamilton, who knew him well, more credibly writes that Haig:

> was not born into the world with a silver spoon in his mouth; but possibly with a silver pencil in his hand ready to start his calculations.[72]

He rated Haig as the ablest staff officer of his generation. This a double-edged tribute; elsewhere Hamilton argued that staff officers do not have the temperament for high command since they lack the capacity for spur-of-the-moment, decisive action. (Hamilton, who invariably categorized himself as a staff officer, commanded the ill-starred operations on Gallipoli.) Haig surely deserves credit for building an effective staff for the enormously expanded BEF, though some weak reeds obtained top positions.

When the prime minister asked Geddes to move to the Admiralty: 'He undertook to consider the matter and to reply as soon as possible.'[73] Geddes and Lloyd George went to France to discuss it with Haig, who was agreeable as long as Geddes also continued to consult on railway matters with Haig's staff. Geddes was given control of all shipbuilding: naval, merchant, and inland waterway. Of course those responsible for building merchantmen were opposed. The prime minister told them that 'there is no better driver in the United Kingdom.' And Hankey added 'that Sir Eric Geddes is one of the easiest of men to work with ...'[74]

Geddes was appointed civilian lord and commissioned as a vice-admiral. He strode into the Admiralty, delighted with his gold braid—he enjoyed uniforms—and asked to inspect their inventory of the resources of the British shipyards. They did not have one. Geddes had their measure. He was not trained in science, but worked with numbers and careful analysis, and soon skippered a cadre of bright civilian doers recruited into the Admiralty. They were staring disaster in the face. U-boats were sinking even more shipping than the German admirals had promised. In April 1917 881,000 tons went to the bottom, 48 per cent were British and 1,125 seamen died. Geddes wrote to Haig:

> That the Admiralty expects to win without fighting or running risks, that old inefficient officers are seldom removed, and that altogether our Naval arrangements are most unsatisfactory.

Bragg's anti-submarine equation predicted why convoying surely would help, though he may never had pointed this out. A convoy might increase the range at which a U-boat can spot victims two- or three-fold, but that was more than offset because clumping 40 or 50 merchantmen in a convoy dramatically reduces a U-boat's opportunity to spot prey. Karl Dönitz (who led the Germany Navy in the Second World War) saw what it did to the U-boats: the

> ... introduction of the convoy system in 1917 robbed it of its opportunity to become a decisive factor. The oceans at once became bare and empty; for long periods at a time the U-boats, operating individually, could see nothing at all; and then suddenly up would loom a huge concourse of ships, thirty or fifty or more of them, surrounded by a strong escort of warships of all types.[75]

Geddes responded to the Bragg memo with a crash program to build 13 knot trawlers, fast enough to hunt while stopping and starting.[76] The Navy mapped out patrolled lanes for shipping to enter four major British ports, which only made it easier for U-boats to find their quarry, so soon they were abandoned. Jellicoe intended to beat the U-boats by attacking them at sea and in their anchorages.[77] The army must occupy the U-boat pens on the Belgian coast.

Ryan was still regarded in the Admiralty as *the* hydrophone expert. Edith Beatty kept praising him to her husband, now far off in the Orkneys, writing that 'Blinker' Hall had visited Hawkcraig and was impressed with Ryan's work. By May 1917 more than 1,000 hydrophones had gone into use since the beginning of the year and 1,500 unidirectional hydrophones were on order.[78] Then the Navy arbitrarily cancelled an order for 200 of the BIR's directional hydrophones and instead opted for 700 of Ryan's Mark II instruments, without bothering with comparative tests of the two designs.[79]

New initiatives

WHB now had the means to try new initiatives. When WL came home on leave he told father how they localized German artillery pieces by recording the inputs from six microphones spaced along 9,000 yards of front, which is the subject of the next chapter. Loud underwater sounds might be located similarly. The BIR tried a line of six hydrophones distributed over a baseline of several miles.[80] (At first they used the hot wire microphones used in France which are described in the next chapter but soon found that their hydrophones did just as well.) It worked beautifully. The sound wave set up by the explosion of 300 lb of TNT was detected 230 miles away.[81] When an enemy mine detonated they could pinpoint the minefield. By setting off their own charges they could plot the positions of lightships, buoys, ships floundering in the fog, and the like. They located the exact position of each of the monitors that anchored off Zeebrugge in 1918 to bombard the U-boat pens, which enabled the ships to fire accurately from their maps.[82] According to the Admiralty:

> It has been estimated that the saving of expense in making the hydrographical survey of the North Sea using the new method of location could alone cover the cost of the experimental station at Parkeston Quay.[83]

By the end of the war there were six underwater sound-ranging stations.

They also devised 'detector loops': lengths of cable laid on the sea bottom. A metal ship passing over the loop induces a tiny electrical current, which they detected with newly-available vacuum tube amplifiers.[84] Their first major project was a huge loop that would detect U-boats passing through the English Channel. It was useless. The earth's magnetic field fluctuates randomly; in long loops this masks smaller signals. Random noise is not a problem with small loops with a diameter of 100 yards or so. They were used to sense vessels entering mine fields. Larger loops, enclosing an area of a square mile detected vessels sailing though harbour mouths. Random fluctuations were dealt with by installing an identical loop nearby but outside of the channel. The two loops were connected so that random fluctuations induced equal but opposite currents—cancelling out the noise. This worked even with the loop in the River Clyde, which had to cope with added interference from the electric trams in Glasgow. On 29 August 1918 a submerged intruder was detected by a loop in the channel off Folkestone. A mine was detonated and the *UB-109* was no more.[85]

Turning the loop idea 180 degrees, they set up 'leader gear': cables along the sea bed supplied with alternating current at an audio frequency which vessels equipped with receivers followed into port. One of them led into Felixstowe from 40 miles out to sea.

American science

The US entered the war in April 1917. Part of the credit went to Commodore Hall, whose code breakers in Room 40 decoded an intercepted wireless from the German foreign office to their ambassador in Mexico outlining plots against the US: the famous Zimmerman telegram. They showed the intercept to the Americans only after creating a false trail suggesting that it was decoded by a German recipient and then stolen by British spies.[86]

American science was ready to go. At a meeting of the National Academy of Sciences (NAS) a year previously, their president, the astronomer George Ellery Hale, proposed that they offer their services to President Woodrow Wilson in the 'interests of national preparedness'[87] His motion was approved unanimously. Ten days later Academy officers met in the White House with Wilson. A former university president, Wilson was comfortable with scientists and backed their project. Two months later they established the National Research Council (NRC), to which Wilson appointed representatives from the armed forces and from the national laboratories.

The president of the NAS and the chair of the NRC organizing committee sailed over to learn what problems their French and British colleagues were tackling.[88] The military representatives suggested useful lines of research. Detectors for submarines topped their wish list, so the NRC started to work with the American Telegraph and Telephone Company and Western Electric, supported by private monies. At the end of March 1917, before the US declared war, the NRC sent a nine man committee to Europe to coordinate research with the Allies. When they went to war most of the members of the NRC were given reserve commissions.

By this time NRC scientists could hear submarines at 9,000 yards. They suggested that research on submarine sound localization should be centralized at Nahant, an island off the coast of Massachusetts, where the Submarine Signal Company had a station. Their proposal was submitted on 6 May and was approved by the Secretary of the Navy three days later. The staff was enlarged with workers from other companies but to avoid potential problems with patents no academics were on the staff.

A French-led mission visited the US to exchange ideas with the NRC. The French sent four academics now serving in the army and the eminent chemist Victor Grignard (Nobel laureate 1912).[89] By request from the Admiralty Rutherford came with them. He was just the man for the job, vast prestige along with a booming, colonial style that radiated candour and enthusiasm. The visitors participated in a conference on submarine detection at which Langevin's work was presented in detail. They also dined with Newton Baker, the secretary of the army, and five of his bureau chiefs. In July, the US Navy set up a civilian, non-commercial hydrophone research unit at the submarine base at New London, Connecticut, staffed by ten eminent, volunteer physicists, who were equipped with a surface vessel and a submarine.

They began working with the French Walzer apparatus, which is essentially a nautical version of the physician's stethoscope: a diaphragm covers an air-filled chamber that is connected to the ears by rubber tubing, no microphone is needed. The diaphragm was mounted on the exterior of the hull on a hemispherical blister several feet across. Each side of the hull held a blister. When the source was on one side of the vessel the hull blocked some of the sound from reaching the other side, which enabled experienced listeners to localize the source—our own everyday localization of low frequency sounds is based in the same principle, with the skull as the blocker.

The Americans modified the Walzer apparatus by placing a several blisters on each side and connecting them with tubing of carefully calculated lengths, so that the sound from all of the blisters reached the listener's ear in phase, amplifying the signal. Ultimately they strung 30 to 60 blisters in two rows on either side of the keel.[90]

Transforming the Admiralty

The Admiralty was in turmoil. On 19 June 1917 Jellicoe told the War Cabinet that they were losing, soon they would run out of merchantmen. (His pessimism was not recorded in their minutes.[91]) The naval appreciation issued the following day announced that in the week ending on 17 June they had swept up 116 German moored mines, about average, while losing 32 British and 34 Allied and neutral civilian vessels. There were 23 encounters with submarines, in which two probably were sunk. Almost as an aside it announced that convoys would be tried in the Mediterranean.[92]

Field Marshal Haig was visiting London and was told about Jellicoe's loser's mentality. According to Haig, Jellicoe had told them: 'There is no good discussing plans for next Spring—we cannot go on.' Haig discussed their quandary with Geddes, who he now cheerily addressed as 'Admiral'. Geddes:

> is most anxious about the state of affairs at the Admiralty. The first Lord (Carson)
> has recently married, is very tired, and leaves everything to a number of incompetent

sailors! Jellicoe, he says, is feeble to a degree and vacillating ... There is no fixed policy; they don't know where the submarines are sinking our ships, or the type of ships ... to build.[93]

Haig asked Geddes to go with him to see the prime minister. If he would not intervene they would take their disquiet to King George.

After the next War Cabinet meeting, Haig drew Lloyd George aside to express his views on the 'inefficient state of the Admiralty'. Lloyd George asked Geddes and Haig to breakfast at 09:15 the next morning, where they began by disparaging Sir Edward Carson. He was an eminent lawyer who had made his name in the courtroom by savaging Oscar Wilde during the famous libel trial. Now 63, with a wife half of his age, he was letting the Admiralty run itself. Haig regarded Jellicoe as 'an old woman'. (Sims regarded Jellicoe as '... a profound student of everything which pertained to ships and gunnery, and a man who joined to a splendid intellect the real ability of command.')

Lloyd George agreed that 'Carson was not cut out for a mule driver' and said that 'he was firmly determined to take immediate action to improve matters.' So Haig and Geddes did not have to appeal to the King, though Haig easily could have done so; his career was stoked by intimacy with the royal family. His older sister Henrietta, ten years his senior, at age 18 married William Jameson, uniting Britain's foremost distilling families. Jameson was a *bon vivant* yachtsman in Edward Prince of Wale's circle—they took to his young bride. She was childless and after their mother's death looked after Douglas: she introduced him into the highest society and helped to pay the bills. He graduated first in his class from Sandhurst, but later failed the mathematics examination for the staff college and was not admitted. Three years later he gained a place thanks to a personal nomination by the Duke of Cambridge, then in his 39th and final year as commander of the British Army. After the Boer War, Haig served as aide-de-camp to Edward VII. In 1905 he was invited to Windsor Castle for Ascot week. On the Thursday he met one of the Queen's attendants, who accepted his proposal of marriage on Saturday morning. They married in the private chapel in Buckingham Palace.[94] He called on the King during his frequent visits to London throughout the war, and they corresponded, with some of Haig's letters marked 'secret'. Haig treated the King as commander-in-chief.

On 6 July 1917 Carson was elevated to the War Cabinet and Geddes became First Lord of the Admiralty. For the first time the Admiralty Board met with an agenda, minutes were kept and decisions noted. Only MPs could serve in the Cabinet, Geddes was elected by the University of Cambridge. He decided not to rock the Admiralty further and retained Jellicoe as First Sea Lord. At the War Cabinet meeting on 20 July Admiral Duff reported that by the end of August they would have seven convoys operating, bringing in 120 to 130 ships per week. Three salvage tugs would join each convoy when they entered the danger zone. Geddes nodded approvingly and Commander Henderson was there to present his ideas.[95]

The War Cabinet report of 28 July evaluated their situation bleakly. In the following year they hoped 300,000 tons of merchant shipping would be added each month, but the Germans were currently sinking twice as much. The British had 3,000 vessels on anti-submarine patrol, but they made few contacts and more U-boats were launched than sunk: '… no fully effective hydrophone or magnetic detector has yet been discovered.'[96] In August 1917 43 ships of more than 500 tons were sunk. The only good news was that only seven were in convoys and five of these were stragglers.

Geddes relaxed the strict secrecy maintained within the Navy, seeing that information got to those who could profitably use it. For example, the commander of the Grand Fleet now received all decoded enemy radio messages, so that his intelligence staff learned how the German Navy set about with their daily business. Geddes set up a committee to recommend how to make the BIR more effective. He choose three men who worked with Lord Moulton on explosives: Sir Robert Sothern Holland and Sir H. Ross Skinner, two skilled administrators, and A. C. G. Egerton, a chemist. In a month they visited all of the BIR establishments and interviewed 40 naval officers and scientists, including WHB and Paget.[97]

Their report is a model: lucid and damning. Able scientists squandered too much time in committee meetings, the BIR and Admiralty were not interacting effectively, and the Admiralty was needlessly multiplying experimental establishments. In time they should be brought together as a central laboratory. Scientists were walled off from the end users; they should not be confined to the laboratory and should be encouraged to treat 'tactical problems from a scientific and mathematical standpoint.' (WHB had made his points.) On anti-submarine warfare:

> Even at this late stage of the war it is not considered that the problem is now being grappled with sufficient earnestness or with sufficient vigour.

They advocated abolishing the BIR and establishing a Director of Experiment and Research (DER) in the Admiralty, advised by a committee of distinguished scientists. Jellicoe's rejoinder was that the scientists were only interested in personal and professional advancement.[98]

The enforced candour of the Admiralty's communiqués entered German politics. Mathias Erzberger, a leading deputy from the Catholic Centre Party, was promoting a Vatican peace initiative by trying to convince the Reichstag to pass a resolution calling for peace without annexations or indemnities. In July 1917 he strongly criticized the Naval General Staff's sinking claims—their numbers were far higher than the British, who had earned a reputation for truthfulness. U-boats would not win the war. (The German figures came from U-boat captains peering through periscopes who sometimes mistook damage for sinking and surely estimated tonnages on the high side.) The Reichstag voted overwhelmingly for the peace resolution on 19 July: 212 to 126. At the same session, to support their fighting men, they voted the credits needed to keep the war going. The money was spent, the resolution was flouted.[99] (Erzberger signed the armistice in 1918; three years later he was assassinated by right-wing zealots. OHL deployed Colonel Max Bauer to torpedo or defang the peace resolution.)

When Rutherford returned from the US he allowed himself a scientific break. On 8 September he started a new laboratory notebook with the title: 'Range of high-speed atoms in air and other gases'.[100] He and the laboratory 'boy' Kay shot alpha-particles from radium into nitrogen gas. The irradiated gas emitted energy that they detected as flashes on a fluorescent screen. They deflected the path of the emitted energy with an electric field and proved that the flashes were produced by protons. When a nitrogen atom is hit by an alpha-particle it splits apart, one of the by-products is a proton. He called it the 'artificial disintegration' of atoms—they were the first atom smashers.

The DER

The transformation of the Admiralty continued when Geddes met with Jellicoe on Christmas Eve. Jellicoe left on extended leave and was soon an earl, replaced by Admiral Wemyss.

The DER was established in January 1918, directed by C. H. Merz, a distinguished electrical engineer.[101] WHB was the DER's representative to the Anti-Submarine Division (ASD) of the Admiralty. He was in charge of experimental stations at Parkeston Quay, Dartmouth, Portland, Wemyss Bay, Stratford, Shannon and Malta. Scientists had been brought from the margin into the centre of power. The BIR remained as a paper organization without sub-committees; Fisher stayed but defanged. WHB settled into office 22S in the Admiralty building, next door to the director of the ASD.[102] The family moved back to Notting Hill.

He was succeeded at Parkeston Quay by Arthur Stewart Eve, a 55-year-old Major in the Canadian Army.[103] A 17th Wrangler, while teaching at Marlborough School he received military training and continued as a part-time soldier after moving to Canada, where for a time he worked with Rutherford. When WHB had proposed that he be seconded to the BIR the Admiralty had dug in their heels because they would have to pay his salary; it took several months to oblige them to give way.

The pressure was easing—convoys worked. A total of 2,084,000 American soldiers reached Europe; only 113 were lost to U-boats. Convoys in home waters lost only 1.25 per cent of their ships.[104] As soon as they were within flying range they were joined by aerial escorts. In the Mediterranean U-boats 60 to 90 feet below the surface could be seen from the air; though in the muddy waters of the English Channel they were hard to see at periscope depth.[105] By April 1918 the British deployed 2,949 aeroplanes and 103 airships against U-boats, the French added another 1,000. Convoys with air support were rarely attacked, and aerial patrols also saved many fishing boats, which surfaced U-boats sank by gunfire.

Edith Beatty kept her finger in the pie. Her husband wrote to Wemyss:

And I state emphatically that if Captain Ryan's talents were fully utilized their value to the State would be incalculable.[106]

The ASD set up hunter units, each with three trawlers towing 'fish hydrophones' and a destroyer. The fish were developed for the Admiralty by G. H. Nash of the Western Electric Company, who had insisted that his experiments be kept secret from the BIR because they had turned down one of his earlier proposals. It was a container shaped like a small torpedo, made of a wood framework covered with a thin layer of German silver and filled with water. Each fish contained two hydrophones that could be rotated by listener-controlled motors: one bi-directional and the second directional, which was used to make the final determination of the target's bearing. Fish did not solve the speed problem: top operational speed was only three to four knots.[107] One hundred and ninety nine Nash fish were deployed.

In April 1918 278,000 tons of shipping was sunk, 77 per cent was British and 215 men died. Heavy losses, but not compared to the year before.

The ASD issued a monthly report divided into eleven sections, one was hydrophones; invariably it was one of the longest and included a table showing the types and numbers in operation.[108] The Navy had 38 hydrophone officers and 200 qualified listeners who were paid an extra 4*d* per day. WHB also wrote a more detailed monthly report of the experimental work done at the DER stations and in America—but there was no input from France.[109] The Americans were testing improved versions of the Walzer blisters, which worked better than hydrophones when the vessel was moving. A skilled operator could localize a submarine within a few degrees, and could tell when they were directly above a submarine with running engines. The latest model had 348 blisters, each coupled to a carbon microphone. The contraption weighed two tons so it could not be used on vessels smaller than destroyers.[110]

The Admiralty also received advice from America's preeminent inventor, Thomas Alva Edison, in a long letter in his copperplate handwriting transmitted directly to Geddes by the US ambassador.[111] Edison concluded that the most effective tactic was to make it harder for the U-boats to spot their prey, by entering and leaving port at night, reducing the height of unneeded masts and the like. Geddes noted that all of Edison ideas had been already tested by his anti-submariners, but of course wrote an effusive thank you.

In April, they completed tests on a mine triggered to explode by the sound of a nearby vessel. The output of a hydrophone was rectified and if the DC current exceeded a threshold level it detonated the mine. Several thousand were in place by the end of the war and they were used extensively in the Second World War.[112]

Data gathered after the war proved that the Admiralty had made gratifying progress. In March 1917 U-boats on patrol destroyed 0.55 ships per submarine per day; while in June 1918 the figure fell to 0.07.

The Braggs rented a cottage in rural Kent for July, and WHB had a week's leave, his first since he had started fulltime with the BIR.

In March 1918 they distinctly heard an echo from a submarine 450 yards distant. The codename for the device was Allied Submarine Detection Investigation Committee (ASDIC).[113] In June, the Admiralty ordered twenty ASDIC sets and began to train operators. The war ended just before ASDIC could be put into use.

ASDIC was desperately needed. The sailors valued hydrophones and used them extensively and there are many descriptions of exciting hunts—largely unsuccessful.[114] As an example take the Allied barrage set up to pen enemy U-boats into the Adriatic. It extended 71 km from Otranto on the coast of Italy to Corfu. Dotted along its length were 38 trawlers with hydrophones. From April to August 1918 U-boats attempted to sneak through 141 times. The defenders made 198 contacts by all media; they attacked 58 intruders but sank only two.[115] The hydrophones on the U-boats told them when it was safe to surface to slip over the barrier.[116]

The ASD believed that in the first eight months of the year attacks relying on hydrophones sank two U-boats. Minefields sank one or possibly two, seriously damaged five and lightly damaged 17.[117] The convoy statistics to September were as follows. The coal trade to France since March 1917 convoyed 37,221 ships and lost 53. Since April 1917, 6,475 vessels were convoyed to Scandinavia with 75 lost. On the North Atlantic since the end of May 1917, 306 convoys sailed eastward with 5,416 vessels; 40 were lost.

The last U-boat attack

The Germans asked for an armistice on 21 October and stopped sinking merchantmen. The skipper of *UB-166*, Lieutenant Commander Emsmann, requested permission to undertake a final mission for the honour of Imperial Germany: an attack on the British capital ships in Scapa Flow.[118] He was allowed to take volunteers who must be told that return was unlikely. Emsmann had prepared for that stipulation by sounding out officers from other U-boats, so he would not be short of skilled hands. This was unnecessary because when he laid out his plan to the *UB-166* crew they all volunteered. They added one extra officer who had shipped on her before.

Submarines were habitats that bonded men into unshakable brotherhoods, living cheek by jowl day after day, enduring together the pounding of the diesels, the dank air seasoned with the stench of their shipmates and oil fumes, and the likelihood that they would die together. All submariners were volunteers; there were long queues of hopefuls. Many men—including noted scientists—enjoy war. John Burdon Sanderson Haldane, the son of John Burdon, nephew of Lord Haldane, and later an eminent biologist in his own right, was unusually frank:

> He enjoyed the opportunity of killing people and regarded this as a respectable relic of primitive man...[119]

On 28 October *UB-166* slipped into Scapa Flow. She was heard by hydrophones along the channel and the current was turned on in a detector loop positioned under a nearby minefield. When the U-boat passed over the loop the mines fired.[120] The scattered remains of the last U-boat sunk in the war are now an attraction for scuba divers. The crew of *UB-166* never appreciated the irony in their quest—they had no prey, months before the Grand Fleet had moved to a new anchorage.

The end of the naval war

The Armistice terms required the Germans to surrender 160 submarines, they turned over 176. Fifteen others were blown up by their crews. All told, the Germans had lost 192 submarines, many to the perils of the sea rather than Allied action. Five hundred and fifteen officers and 4,894 ratings perished. [121] The British Merchant Navy lost almost three times as many: 15,313. As Admiral Jameson points out, the volunteer crews of the merchantmen were the Allied heroes of the U-boat war.[122] When he left ASD, WHB gave a glowing account of his experiences:

> Finally, it does not seem out of place to refer to the less tangible but very real and important benefits that are following from the unusual association of so many varieties of men on one common and urgent purpose. Officers of the Navy, engineers and scientists have learnt to know each other's methods of working. The mutual recognition of the help that each can give and the methods of co-operation that have been worked out, may well prove to be some of the most lasting and important consequences of the experimental and research work carried on during the war. [123]

He did not mention how long the war had dragged on before British scientists were allowed to show what they could do. If the war had gone on a few months longer they would have given the U-boats a real licking with ASDICs. WHB was awarded the CBE in 1917 and made KBE in 1920. The Admiralty assured him that:

> The success of the experimental establishments created during the war has been largely due to your efforts …

The armistice specified that the German High Seas Fleet was to be interned in a neutral port; they were ordered to Scapa Flow. Seventy German warships arrived on 21 November 1918, steaming in between two rows of British ships with crews at battle stations and guns ready. Boarders found that the German ships were missing powder, shell, rangefinders, gun sights and breach blocks.

The great ships bobbed at anchor until 21 June 1919, a warm, sunny day, a week before the peace treaty was to be signed. A party of 200 English schoolchildren on an excursion was boating among the German ships, waving derisively and throwing candy wrappers. The ships were silent. At 11:20 the flagship raised a flag signal, 'Paragraph eleven! Acknowledge!' Crews raced below to the sea cocks. A few minutes later the signal from the flagship was, 'Condition Z-scuttle'. The valves were twisted open, their keys and handles wrenched off and hurled overboard. New battle flags were raised. The bands played as the seamen manned the boats. Some British sailors fired on the boats, killing six and wounding ten, while 70 ships went to the bottom. It did not bode well for the future.

1 HMS *Victory* in Portsmouth Harbour in late 1918. Launched in 1765, she was Nelson's flagship at Trafalgar in 1805, where she was badly mauled. She remained on active service until 1812. In the left foreground is a newly-surrendered German U-boat. The two epitomise the almost fantastic changes produced by the growth of science in the intervening century.

2 HMS *Iron Duke* was commissioned in 1914 and was the flagship at the Battle of Jutland in 1916, where she fired 90 rounds from her main battery, early on hitting an enemy battleship with seven shells at a range of 24,000 m. Warfare had been transformed by expending massive amounts of energy on killing. The consequence was the staggering horror of the Great War.

3 Alfred Nobel (1833–1896). His father invented plywood and made explosives in Sweden. Alfred was taught mostly by tutors, even when he studied in the US. An explosion of nitroglycerine at the plant killed four, including his younger brother. At age-29 Alfred solved that problem by inventing dynamite, ultimately he had 350 patents. He moved about Europe, always setting up a private laboratory nearby. His estate funds the prizes.

4 John Arbuthnot 'Jackie' Fisher (1841–1920). One of those who transformed the military by utilizing science, as first sea lord he led the construction of the dreadnoughts. In 1916 he returned from retirement as chair of a new committee to give the Admiralty scientific advice. His pugnacious personality delayed progress; finally in late 1917 his scientists were moved into the Admiralty.

5 Students of radioactivity at a meeting in 1910. Otto Hahn (1879–1968), the American Bertram B. Boltwood (1870–1927), and Ernest Rutherford (1871–1937). Hahn had worked in Rutherford's laboratory in Montreal. Rutherford was the greatest experimental physicist of the age, discovering radioactive decay, the nucleus of the atom, and in 1917 smashing an atom. During the war he was on Fisher's committee, trying to detect submerged submarines.

6 Lise Meitner (1878–1968) and Hahn in their laboratory at the Kaiser Wilhelm Institute for Chemistry in 1913. When the war broke out he was recalled to the army, leading a machine gun platoon fighting in Flanders. She served as an x-ray technician in the Austrian army. But as the war dragged on she left the service to return to the laboratory. Whenever possible he joined her to isolate new radioactive elements and isotopes.

7 Capt. Fritz Haber (1868–1934) was director of the Kaiser Wilhelm Institute for Physical Chemistry and Electrochemistry. He discovered how to transform nitrogen from the air into compounds essential for fertilizers and explosives, which enabled blockaded Germany to wage the war. In 1915 he proposed to break the stalemate in the trenches by releasing a cloud of chlorine gas in a favourable wind. For assistance he assembled a cadre of brilliant scientists, including Hahn. The cloud gas attacks on both western and eastern fronts were relatively ineffectual.

8 Troops needed to be protected from gas. The German mask was sealed to the face with rubber edging. The wearer breathed through a multilayer filter screwed on the front of the mask that absorbed all of the poisons in use. Hahn tested filters in gas filled chambers. By 1918 they no longer had rubber for the seal.

9 Gas warfare was changed by the British Liven's projector: a tube buried in the ground that fired a canister like the one being loaded. The German version were called a *gaswurfenminen*. An array of 894 were fired simultaneously by electricity. to cloak the Italian trenches at Caporetto with a mixture of chlorine and phosgene as the first step in the breakthrough in late 1917. The site of the gas attack was selected by a small group led by Hahn, by then on the General Staff.

10 Ernest Starling (1866–1927) in his laboratory after the war, photographed by A. V. Hill. A great physiologist and scientific statesman, despite his age he enlisted early in the war. Serving in a London hospital, after the introduction of gas he was given responsibility for teaching gas protection to troops training in England. *(Churchill College Archives, Cambridge)*

11 For protection the British moved from nose pads to the bag respirator, which was soaked in an absorbent solution before use. Starling's instructors taught how to prepare the bag and how to don it by the steps shown. It was fastened to the tunic with safety pins. The photographer was an instructor, the physiologist Charles Lovatt Evans.

12 The bag was replaced in 1916 by the British box respirator. The filter is in the container at the waist, connected to the mask by the flexible tube. The user's nose is clamped and he breathes and expires through a mouthpiece. This is the artillery version with a larger filter and separate goggles instead of eyepieces in the mask.

13 William Maddock Bayliss (1860–1924) was a physiologist at UCL who often collaborated with his brother-in-law Starling. Early in the war he began to experiment on wound shock, building on Starling's work on the heart and circulation. He devised a transfusion solution that saved shocked animals. It was brought to human use by a group headed by Starling, who resigned from the army in 1917 to do more weighty work. *(Wellcome Library, London)*

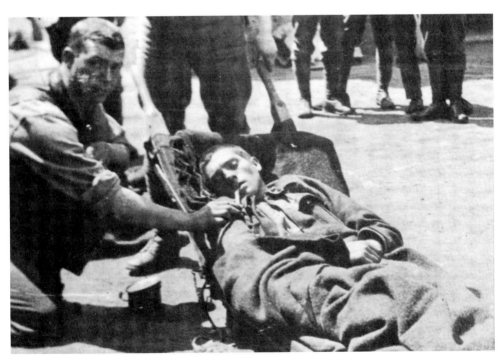

14 A gassed soldier. He is breathing oxygen and is wrapped in a blanket although obviously it was a warm day. Bright young physicians at the front had discovered that keeping the wounded warm helps prevent shock. By 1918 they were treating shock effectively by transfusing blood or Bayliss's solution.

15 Harriette Chick (1875–1977) in her laboratory at the Lister Institute, London, where during the war she worked on nutrition. Starling became scientific advisor to the Food Ministry, specifying how many calories were needed and what foods contained the trace nutrients that were just being discovered. In 1919 Chick and two colleagues went to starving Vienna where they demonstrated that cod-liver oil (containing vitamin D) cures rickets in babies and older children. *(Wellcome Library, London)*

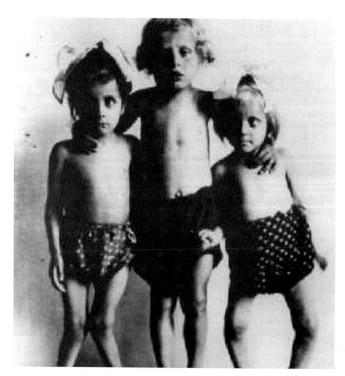

16 Viennese children with rickets. An endemic disease in the north made worse by near starvation, the Lister group showed that it is caused by a deficiency of vitamin D. A German physician discovered that it can also be treated with UV light, which accounts for its absence in sunny climates.

17 Chaim Weizmann (1874–1952) in his laboratory in the Chemistry Department at Manchester University, well dressed as usual for work. He had come to England to promote Zionism while also continuing his academic career. He was working on obtaining precursors for synthesizing rubber from bacterial fermentations.

18 C. P. Scott (1846–1932) on his way to work at the *Manchester Guardian*, which he edited from 1872–1929. He was a Liberal who knew all major politicians and was a friend of Lloyd George. He became Weizmann's friend and an ardent Zionist. He helped Weizmann contact the political establishment and also was his scientific agent, negotiating positions, salary, and royalties.

19 Lord Justice of Appeal
John Fletcher Moulton
(1844–1921) was a brilliant
mathematician, an FRS
for research on electricity,
an advocate and a judge.
At age-70 in 1914 he was
appointed to produce
explosives. He mobilized
chemists, engineers, and
administrators, who
'never left a shell unfilled'.
Weizmann was assigned to
his group, providing acetone
needed for making cordite.

20 Arthur James Balfour (1848–1935) the foreign secretary and Weizmann in
Jerusalem after the war. Balfour was for Zionism on its merits and as a lever for
the British to obtain Palestine. Working closely with Weizmann, they succeeded in
1917 when the Balfour Declaration adopted. Weizmann then gave up explosives
and worked for the Foreign Office.

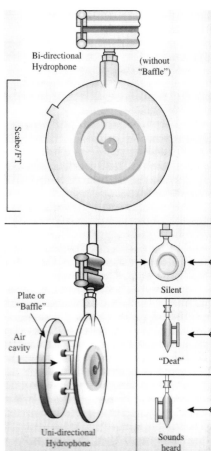

21 *Above left:* William Henry Bragg (1862–1942) working at his x-ray spectrometer. With his elder son they used it to measure the wavelengths of x-rays and to determine the structures of simple crystals. They shared a Nobel Prize in 1915. W. H. Bragg and Rutherford were appointed to Fisher's committee to advise the admiralty, charged with locating submerged U-boats. Bragg became more and more involved, by the end of the war he was in the Admiralty. His unit collaborated with the French to develop echo location by sonar. *(Bridgeman Art Library)*

22 *Above right:* W. H. Bragg's diagrams of the underwater microphones or hydrophones that were developed to hear U-boats. Above is the initial version, with a microphone connected to a brass diaphragm. Because of the long wavelength of underwater sounds it responds equally well to sounds from all directions. Below is the directional hydrophone his group developed. One side is shielded with a baffle that absorbs sound which hits it before reaching the diaphragm. The rub was that vessels traveling at the speed of a submarine make too much noise for effective listening.

23 Eric Geddes (1875–1937), one of the wonder men of the war. A railway man who was recruited by the Ministry of Munitions, he skyrocketed shell production. Then he was sent to get the failing railways in the British sector in France working, becoming a major general. The next crisis was the U-boat campaign of 1917. He was transferred to the Admiralty; in a few months he was first lord. To get science working effectively he brought W. H. Bragg into the Admiralty.

24 William Lawrence Bragg (1890–1971) shared the 1915 Nobel physics prize with his father. In 1915 he was transferred to the Royal Engineers to pinpoint the position of enemy guns from the boom of their firing. There were formidable difficulties, but by 1917 they succeeded and sound ranging was done all along the fronts. When the Americans came into the war they adopted the British method. *(Nobel Foundation)*

25 The six input string galvanometer developed by Lucien Bull in Paris was one of the keys to sound ranging. The inputs from six widely-spaced, hot-wire microphones were recorded on fast moving photographic film, from which the position of the enemy gun was determined. Later a similar system localized underwater explosions.

26 A bearing picket (in Palestine). British artillery techniques evolved markedly during the war. By late 1917 whenever possible a gun was sited at a precisely surveyed position and nearby was a precisely surveyed bearing picket. Working from a specially prepared map, the gun was set at the proper angle to the picket so that it was trained on target. This eliminated the need for preliminary registration fire. The cross on this picket was illuminated for night use.

27 A. V. Hill (1886–1977) in 1914 when he was working on the heat production of contracting muscles at Cambridge. He was an infantry officer until asked for advice on AA gunnery. He showed them how to use two widely separated mirrors to determine accurately the position of an object in the sky in three dimensions *(Archives of Churchill College, Cambridge)*

28 To exploit his mirrors Hill recruited about 100 scientists and mathematicians, who became known as Hill's brigands. Those shown were at the naval gunnery school in Portsmouth harbour. They fired shells with different fuse settings from AA guns, determining where they burst with the mirrors. Hill is second from the right; Cdr Bowering is on the right. Richmond is tipping his boater on the left, next to him is Fowler. *(Archives of Churchill College, Cambridge)*

29 A British mobile anti-aircraft gun in action. The brigands provided the tables they used to set the gun and the fuse timing. The man in the foreground is using a Barr-Stroud rangefinder, so the photograph was taken toward the end of the war when enough were available to be used by AA; until then they used simpler methods developed by the brigands.

30 A zeppelin that had been hit by AA fire while bombing London in 1916 made it to the sea before coming down. Zeppelin attacks were abandoned after the British introduced incendiary machine gun bullets that ignited the hydrogen providing lift.

31 An Austrian search light combined with a sound detector. One operator listens to the sound captured by the cones in the horizontal plane and adjusts the light to point where the sound is loudest. The second operator does the same in the vertical plane. The brigands developed the British sound detectors.

32 A German Gotha bomber like those that bombed London in 1917. They flew over at high altitude with crews breathing oxygen but came down to bomb. At the end of the year the Germans decided that results did not justify losses; in 1918 they targeted ammunition dumps and the like in France.

6

Sound Ranging
William Lawrence Bragg

For WL the war ended a glorious era: 'It was a wonderful time, like discovering a new goldfield where nuggets could be picked up on the ground, with thrilling new results almost every week, until the war stopped our work together'.[1] But behind it all he was bitter. Their work was based on the equation WL wrote while he was a research student strolling the Backs along the river Cam, where green meadows and brindled cows enhance the glory of the medieval buildings in the background:

> I can remember the exact spot on the Backs where the idea suddenly leapt into my mind that Laue's spots were reflections of x-ray pulses by sheets of atoms in the crystal.

From this insight WL wrote the equation describing the relationship between the wavelength of an x-ray, the distance separating the sheets of atoms and the angle at which the x-ray beam must strike the face of the crystal to be reflected. Together the Braggs deduced the structures of seven crystals, including sodium chloride and diamond. They measured the wavelengths of x-rays emitted by platinum, nickel, tungsten, and iridium anti-cathodes.

> The results with the reflection angles, especially the solution of the diamond structure, were far more striking and far easier to follow than the elaborate analysis of the Laue photographs, and it was my father who announced the new results to the British Association, the Solvay conference, lectures up and down the country, while I remained at home. My father more than gave me full credit for my part, but I had some heart-aches.

WHB's presentation at the Second Solvay Conference in 1913 to Einstein, Laue, Rutherford, Marie Curie and the other greats of international physics was especially galling. Father described their results, giving his son credit for the equation. The distinguished attendees sent WL a postcard with their congratulations—meagre recompense for not presenting his own idea. The incident was '... remembered 60 years later with pain ... '.[2]

After the conference father published two brief reports or 'letters' in the prestigious weekly scientific journal *Nature*. In each he attributed the equation to his 'son', not giving his name, let alone making him a co-author. Later that year, WL published his own letter in *Nature*. It was entitled: 'The diffraction of short electromagnetic waves by a crystal', not mentioning x-rays so as 'not to assert that my father was wrong in thinking that x-rays were particles'.[3] His paper introduced the idea that in sodium chloride each Na atom is surrounded by six chlorides and vice versa—the celebrated sodium chloride molecule never exists.

As Gwendy wrote years later:

> It was difficult for the young WL; father and son never managed to discuss the situation. WHB was very reserved and WL inclined to bottle up his feelings … he felt things strongly but he could not hurt his father by telling him what he felt.[4]

Passing years did not dim his resentment. In 1966 in the First Nobel Guest Lecture WL wrote:

> It is sometimes said that my father and I started x-ray analysis together, but actually this was not the case.[5]

As Cambridge undergraduates WL and his brother Bob enlisted in a Territorial Force unit for men from the colonies, King Edward's Horse. Soon after the war began Bob was called for active duty with the Horse and then was commissioned in the RFA. (The Royal Regiment of Artillery had three branches: Field (RFA), Horse (RHA), and Garrison Artillery (RGA). WL had retired from the Horse. He applied to the War Office and on 26 August was commissioned as a second lieutenant in the Leicester RHA. After what seemed a never-ending wait, he was ordered to Diss in Norfolk for further training.[6] Happily for us, his mother kept every letter he wrote home and its envelope.[7]

The French field artillery took a genuine interest in guns, which they planned to fight at short range. Each battery had merely 500 m of telephone wire; the maximum range for their sound-powered field telephones was 1 km.[8] The British and German field artillery focused on the horses who hauled their guns into position at a gallop; after which they fired over open sights. Tables of logarithms were seldom consulted. It was not WL's element:

> … my knowledge of horses was not at all extensive and my fellow officers and men were Leicestershire hunting enthusiasts.

Training was monotonous and repetitive, as was the officer's mess with seemingly endless discussions of stifles, fetlocks and the like; the weary months dragged by while they languished far from the battlefront assiduously training to fight the last war. For example one day they galloped to site their guns to fire at 'enemy cavalry advancing, represented by a cow'. WL wrote to mother:

I get very sick sometimes because I am slack with the men, and get moments of awful despondency, and then again I feel I am much better than anyone else.

But usually his letters home were upbeat, relating how cheery his fellow officers were and requesting cake.[9]

The Bragg's book *X-rays and Crystal Structure* was published in early 1915.[10] In May father and son were jointly awarded the Barnard Medal of Columbia University; reported prominently in *The Times* as 'American Medal for British savants'.[11] WL wrote to mother: 'I am so awfully braced about that gold medal, what a score it is for us.' His mess insisted that he stand them a bottle of best port. On the strength of the award he was negotiating for some free time to do scientific work, but did not want to leave his battery: '… as I am awfully keen on it now and like the others so much.'

The Royal Engineers

The publicity given the medal may account for what happened next. In July 1915, he was ordered to report at the War Office to Colonel Coote Hedley, a Royal Engineer (RE) who headed the Geographical Section of the General Staff. WL had no idea why he was wanted. The Germans had caught their foes flatfooted by bringing 105-mm and 150-mm howitzers into action: they had almost one of them for every two of their 77-mm field guns.[12] Field guns as a rule fought close to the front, firing shrapnel canisters that exploded after a pre-set time, pelting out lead bullets like a massive shotgun. They were murderous against men in the open but relatively ineffectual against men shielded by a dirt rampart. The howitzers fired at high trajectories. Hidden well behind the front they hurled high explosive shells that exploded on contact, discharging a dense cloud of noxious black smoke and hurling off jagged metal splinters that struck men far from the explosion. The pressure wave itself killed. They tore up trenches and men. To be fought these guns must be found.

Hedley learned that the French were trying to pinpoint hidden enemy cannon from the sound of their firing. Excited by the concept but sceptical of the efficacy of memoranda, Hedley went to GHQ in Flanders to persuade them to try the idea. There was 'much apathy and some opposition', but he prevailed. To evaluate the French techniques GHQ set up a three man committee: experts on artillery, electricity, and topography. The theory was simple. The boom when the gun fires travels in all directions, moving across the ground as an expanding circle with the gun at its centre. If you accurately measure the times when the sound arrives at a series of widely spaced points, it is easy to extrapolate back to the sound's origin. The French were trying to make the measurements by three methods: 1). Observers at widely spaced points started stop watches when they saw a gun's flash and stopped them when they heard the boom. It was like estimating how far away a lightning bolt hit the earth from the time between flash and thunderclap; with several observers the hit's location can be determined. This was simple, but inaccurate because of variations in observer's reaction times. 2). Spacing microphones along the front and recording their output on moving smoked paper, the time delays are measured from the record. 3). Recording the output from the microphones with a 'string galvanometer'—one of the most advanced scientific instruments of the day.[13] This approach was being tried by Charles Nordmann, an astronomer serving at the front as a NCO.

The string galvanometer was invented by Willem Einthoven (Nobel laureate, 1924) for recording from the surface of the body the weak electrical signals generated by the contracting heart, the electrocardiograph. The principle is that a tiny electric current flows through a thin strand of silver-coated quartz that passes between the two poles of a massive magnet. (Molten quartz can be drawn into a strong thin wire and the silver coating conducts electricity.) A current generates a magnetic field in the strand so it moves in the permanent magnet's field. The shadow of the strand is projected through prisms onto a moving strip of photographic film. They were constructed at the Institute Marey in Paris by Lucien Bull, a skilful Briton who resided in France. Now he was constructing galvanometers with six strands running between the magnets, so six inputs could be recorded simultaneously. The light projected on the wires was interrupted 100 times per second by a spinning, toothed wheel, producing precise time marks on the film. The galvanometers were heavy, delicate, and very expensive, but the evaluation committee thought them most promising. Since sound travels at about 344 m per sec, the time differences between when the sound wave reached different microphones had to be measured precisely. GHQ was not convinced, and sent the committee back to observe the rival methods in action. Again they opted for the costly galvanometer. Their recommendation was forwarded to the GHQ Experiments Committee, who rejected the idea because it had not been proven to work—obviously their definition of 'experiment' was whimsical. The head of the topographical sub-section at GHQ, Major Ewan Maclean Jack RE, 42-years-old, did not let the matter rest. 'After some discussion' the rejection was rescinded and a six string galvanometer was ordered. It would be delivered in October. The RE's attitude toward scientists was vastly different from the Navy's. Now they needed an officer who could use it properly. Would WL be interested? Indeed he was. He left the interview with Hedley overjoyed; it made him:

> walk on air ... To have a job where my science was of use, after feeling so inefficient at the battery, seemed too good to be true ....

On 19 July 1915, he was seconded for special duty to the topographical sub-section of GHQ in France—'maps GHQ'. That night he came down with a nasty cold; ten days later he took the cross-channel ferry.

In Paris he was briefed by French officers and visited the Institute Marey to meet Bull and to see their galvanometer being built. Then he went to GHQ to report to Major Jack.[14] If Jack feared that his new subordinate would be a cartoon scientist— the scrawny, introverted, short-sighted chap with a bulbous forehead—he had a pleasant surprise. WL was a sturdy, good-looking young fellow of medium height with a rectangular face, forehead of normal dimensions—usually partially covered with a thick lock of hair that persisted in tumbling forward—frank brown eyes, a moustache proper for an officer, and a relaxed and friendly manner. He instructed in simple terms and showed no irritation if his pupil was a bit slow. Jack ordered WL to return to England to acquire helpers.

WHB wrote to Rutherford about his sons:

> The elder I want to write to you about. He is seconded for special scientific service and is collecting men for his 'staff'.

He needed an instrument maker and a mathematician—they might already be serving in the army. 'I dare say you know what the job is; if you don't I'll tell you when I see you'.[15] Henry Roper Robinson was selected. He had worked with Rutherford at Manchester University before he was commissioned in the RGA. He was a year older than WL but junior on the army list. He added visibility to British sound ranging by standing 6 feet 4 inches and was habitually enveloped in a dense cloud of pungent smoke; he liked rough, flavourful pipe tobacco like 'half-dark nailrod'.[16] He and an enlisted instrument maker and an electrician were sent to France.[17] Early in September WL sailed across to Havre, where he was greeted by Robinson. 'Robinson is the cheeriest fellow he is such fun.' The French bundled them into a car for a nine-hour drive to the front in the Vosges Mountains. The troops they encountered coming from back from the trenches: '... looked like awful ragamuffins but so cheery and fit.' They were quartered in a hut with a French lieutenant and his men. From a nearby height they saw German trenches and a woman tending two cows grazing in no-man's-land. Once in a while a rifle shot. The cannon were silent; the nearest shell hole was half a mile away. Both sides were extremely short of shells. French gunners laid out their wash on their emplacements. The visitors' British uniforms created a stir: usually the first guess was that they were Belgians. At long last a German gun or two fired, so they could see some data. It gave precise locations, but there was no confirmation that there was a gun at the predicted point—scarcely an ironclad test. They returned to GHQ in Flanders.

In October WL went to Paris, where he cemented friendly relations with Lucien Bull and picked up their galvanometer. It was trucked up to the Fifth Army area where Robinson had been settling them in. Their unit had added a lorry, with its driver and mate, one lineman and one NCO, two drivers of Singer cars for the officers, and by Lieutenant Bocquet RGA, a regular who had experimented with sound ranging. Their officers' servant, Stanforth had 'brought a large cooking book with him and is determined to do his worst'. WL wrote to Dad that a Lieutenant Nash would come to England to obtain sensitive microphones:

> he will explain what he wishes to do ... Send me a large cake and some cigarettes in tins.

They improved the directionality of their carbon microphones with paper horns. Every morning each microphone was tapped firmly with a heavy mallet to loosen packed carbon granules.

Maps GHQ

They set up near to GHQ in Belgium, close to Mount Kemmel, where they overlooked the battlefield and had adequate maps. Pre-war British military planners supposed that a continental war would be brief, bloody, and fought in Belgium and on the French frontier. They stockpiled excellent 1/20,000 maps of Belgium and of the French frontiers. They did not anticipate further typographical needs, so surveyors were given other duties.

Major Jack had arrived with the Expeditionary Force in August 1914 commanding three men: an assistant who remained at GHQ and two surveyors with theodolites. He had graduated from the Military School at Woolwich in 1893, where the three-year course included intensive training in trigonometry and surveying, and afterwards worked in the field, including a stint with the Anglo-Congolese Border Commission. (Despite brains and training, his pay was 80 per cent that of an infantry officer of the same rank.) His tiny command was supposed to locate hidden German batteries by triangulating smoke puffs released by bombs dropped onto them from British aircraft. The results were almost useless because the aviators found it difficult to drop bombs close to the guns while being shot at. In April 1915 Jack was reassigned to GHQ, where he was handed a daunting job.

When the warriors dug in much of the battle line was deep in France, where only 1/80,000 maps were available.[18] Better maps became vital when 'granny' arrived: she was the first British 9.2-inch howitzer in France. How could they map behind the German lines? Jack discovered that the French held 'cadastral plans', at 1/2,500. They were maps of property lines drawn for local governments in the early years of the French revolution. He obtained some for localities along the British front. When flown over the lines map in hand he saw that major features like roads, streams, churches and even many buildings were unchanged. Only woods had moved because they were felled periodically and replanted in new locations. The maps could be updated from aerial photographs. Jack assembled a team of cartographers and printers to turn them out.[19]

On the British side of the line, surveyors fixed and marked the 'trig points', precisely fixed positions on which a survey is based. Infuriatingly their trig point markers frequently took the fancy of passers-by who appropriated them for other uses. Jack's remedy was to mark each trig point with a cross inscribed 'Grave of an unknown soldier of the __ Field Survey Battalion', which made them sacrosanct. With the mapping work well in hand Jack was ready to get back to pinpointing enemy guns with WL as his point man.

WL received the dreadful news that his brother Bob had died at Gallipoli on 15 August. He was given a brief leave to grieve with his parents and little sister. To add to his depression, it took far too long to set up their equipment. Finding all the bits and pieces was like a treasure hunt. In October he wrote home:

> Tremendous complications unfold themselves as one penetrates further into our job; but I am sure that it will work all right.

In November WHB and WL were awarded the Nobel Prize in physics. WL later wrote that he could not remember how he first heard the news, he thought that some acquaintance at GHQ saw it in a newspaper and 'sent me a message'.[20] He did not receive an official letter because the Swedish Academy did not know his address. Finally:

> Just got Dads letter and yours, with the cheery news in it. You can imagine how I felt, really I am the most lucky fellow in the world I think.

Months later he learned that his monetary award was in the bank:

> That's great news about all of the Kroner, I shall never be tempted to do any more work again.

WL was the youngest laureate ever and they were the only father–son team ever to share a Nobel Prize. He was billeted in the home of a Curé, where he slept on the floor. The host broke out a hoarded bottle of *Lachryma Christi* to celebrate. But even glory has its downside. Robinson wrote to Rutherford that their mess president threatened to cut off WL's beer ration as unsuitable for anyone so exalted, and he was given the 'unpleasing nickname of "The Nobbler"'.[21] Robinson wrote Rutherford that he and WL had been under heavy shellfire for half an hour.

> Bragg kept cheerful though it all—by the way, I don't think that he has said anything to his people about it, they would be worried if they knew; anyhow I don't think it will happen again for some time.

WL did not tell his parents.

Failure

They moved from the Curé's to a wooden hut near to where they would have their first trial. Six microphones were connected to the galvanometer in its lorry. They spent days playing out miles of connecting wires, by good chance mist hid them from the enemy. A 3,000 yards baseline used all of their cable. They placed the microphones at convenient sites and surveyed their exact positions. There were two forward observers. When either saw the flash of an enemy gun he telephoned the lorry where they turned on the galvanometer's film transport. Once the strip of film was developed they could calculate the cannon's position. They had their first record of an enemy gun in November, with Bocquet and WL as forward observers. Results were bitterly disappointing. Despite incontestable physics the answer was often absurd—in the worst cases enemy guns seemed to be behind their own line.

They soon realized what was wrong. When a shell leaves a cannon's mouth it produces a low frequency sound—the 'gun-wave'. A field gun bellows at 25 Hertz. Larger pieces, 'crumps', boom at 10 Hertz. Even a youngster cannot hear sound waves below 20 Hertz. Carbon microphones were no better, their diaphragms move feebly in response to low frequency sounds, so at best gun-waves gave tiny deflections on the photographic record. But the crux of the problem was that most shells were fired at velocities faster than sound—more than twice as fast from heavy guns they most wanted to pinpoint. As it flies toward its target a supersonic shell produces a loud, higher frequency clap, the 'shell-crack', which records splendidly. The crack vigorously waggled microphone diaphragms and they were still quivering when the gun-wave arrived—the crack 'washed-out' the wave. As if that were not problem enough, the microphones were too sensitive to rifle shots, buzzing insects and the like, so records were very noisy. Only small German howitzers had muzzle velocities below the speed of sound, so they could be found.

They saw the problem, not the answer. They followed the French by measuring where a shell cracked and where it exploded. Then they tried to extrapolate backward to the gun's position, a procedure known as 'caustics'; very tricky maths.[22] They had to know what type of gun had fired so that they could obtain its muzzle velocity from captured range tables. Nonetheless the exercise was futile because they assumed that the crack was midway along the trajectory.[23] This is not true. In 1952 a bright young physicist showed that an object moving at supersonic speed generates a bang when the rate at which it approaches the observer just equals the speed of sound.[24] Therefore the sound is not heard at a fixed point on the trajectory, it varies with the position of the listener. They struggled on, but they had hit a dead end.

It was especially exasperating because gun-waves are so energetic. In WL's billet the latrine was in a small sealed chamber, when in use the only sizable opening was beneath the seat. WL noticed that his bottom was elevated 'slightly but perceptibly' every time a nearby heavy gun fired, even though he heard nothing.

Though they had few successes, the sanguine Lieutenant Colonel Jack decided that they had met 'just satisfactory requirements', so he ordered WL to set up additional sound ranging sections and purchased seven more Bull galvanometers. WL must have had mixed feelings about expanding a failure. He searched the army list for familiar names and was authorized to attend parades of combat units, where he would order: 'All Bachelors of Science step forward'. He sent WHB a list of nine men he had asked for, including Charles Galton Darwin (son of the mathematician George Howard and grandson of Charles.)[25]

Scientific recruits, regardless of rank, were treated as members of the team. Like any research group they had periodic meetings to hash over successes, failures, bits of gossip, and the like; followed by what WL called a 'binge of heroic magnitude'. Each sound ranging section had three officers and 18 others: one Sergeant, one instrument repairer, one photographer, three linemen, two telephonists, three forward observers, three bat-men and four motor transport drivers. The sections were designated by letter, working backward down the alphabet starting with 'W'—presumably for 'Willy', as he was known in the army. New personnel were all trained in section W.

Batman Stanforth's hours of study proved themselves when he cooked a fine Christmas dinner. Later in the war he was promoted to observer, replaced by a new servant.

Bull visited early in 1916. Fast talk was needed to get him off the train talk because he had none of the required passes. He slept in WL's bed while his host took the floor. Then WL had a jaunt to England to obtain stores. He returned with Jenkinson, who was on loan and 'very proud because he wasn't sick coming over'. They visited Bull's manufacturing facility. The two workmen wore white gowns and hats—with the galvanometers cleanliness was indispensable—and there also was a boy paid by the day. Jenkinson returned home carrying a music book as a gift from WL to Gwendy. Unhappily he was ill on the return passage. In future more of the equipment would be manufactured in Britain; WL must have had qualms whether the cost was justified, but he put on a confident face for his troops.

Flash spotting

About this time Bragg had a letter from a stranger, Harold Howard Hemming. They were of an age, civilians in uniform and colonials. Hemming was a Canadian, with a BA from McGill, where he also obtained a commission after training in heavy artillery—'slide rule gunners'.[26] After graduation he was awarded a fellowship to study at the *École des Sciences Politiques* in Paris, arriving just in time to watch the troops march off to war. He was commissioned in the RGA. Toward end of 1915 Hemming was stationed in an OP (observation post) searching for enemy guns when he was confronted by an indignant infantry colonel, who demanded to know why the artillery did not take on a German battery that was roughing up his trenches. Hemming recalled replying:

> For three reasons, sir. I don't know where he is; he is probably out of range; and I have only shrapnel, which will not hurt him.

The red-faced Colonel responded:

> Well I can tell you exactly where he is. He is just over the first crest—one can see the sky-flash when he fires at night and one hears the bang almost immediately.[27]

Hemming obtained permission to try to locate German guns by triangulating on their flashes. In flat country the flash often was seen in daylight; on a night with low cloud they were easy to spot. The idea had been tried in previous wars, and now both the French and Germans were doing so.[28] Hemming's results were promising, so he was seconded to the RE and the delighted Lieutenant Colonel Jack added another string to his bow. OPs were carefully selected. After a shakedown period the observers were equipped with excellent French telescopes, with oculars giving three levels of magnification, but mounted on sturdy British stands. Snipers hunted observers, so on bright days they wore dark masks.[29]

The observers and their controller shared an open telephone line. An observer who saw a flash would alert them all, giving his rough bearing. If the controller though it a promising target he ordered them all to look in that direction, giving each his estimate of the bearing from their post. When they all reported the same flash the gun was considered pinpointed. Too often the locations were bogus. Observers, suggestible like all of us, were likely to think that they had seen a flash when it was called in from another post. Hemming tried replacing the open telephone line with a system he modified from the French, called a 'flash board'. When an observer saw a flash he closed a key in his OP. This sounded a buzzer in each of the other OPs and in the control post sounded a buzzer and lit a lamp. If the controller thought it a likely lead, he obtained the bearing from the first observer by telephone and directed all of his observers toward it. When all posts buzzed and lit almost synchronously, they may have been on the same target. The crucial test was when the controller cut off the buzzers in the OPs. If they still pushed their keys in synchrony, they had it.

A brilliant idea, but hard to implement; too often the long cables could not carry enough electrical current to light the lights and sound the buzzers. Hemming was advised to write to WL for help; he recommended that they use electrical relays, in which a small current closes a switch through which large currents can flow. Relays were sold in London electrical kit shops clustered in High Holborn. Hemming applied for leave and returned in four days with relays. His fellow officers thought him either a criminal or a cad: his leave had been for fourteen days. With relays, flash boards worked like a charm, soon they were manufactured by the General Post Office. In favourable weather flash spotting sections located four to five guns a day. The boards were also 'used to enthral and amuse countless Generals and other V.I.P.s'.[30] Of course some of the Brass were not pleased by what they saw. Hemming was told by a visiting Brigadier that:

> You dammed surveyors with your co-ordinates and angles and all the rest have taken the fun out of war; in my day we galloped into action and got the first round off in thirty seconds.

To which Hemming would have liked to have replied, 'Yes, sir, and you hit nothing with it except possibly the backs of your infantry.'[31]

Field Service Companies

Flash spotting, sound ranging, typography and surveying were brought together as Royal Engineering Field Survey Companies, one for each army, all reporting to

Colonel Jack at GHQ. Being officially transferred into the RE eliminated a hazard for those sound rangers who had begun military life in other formations: some wore kilts, some were ANZACs and there was even an able-bodied-seaman from the Royal Naval Division. While roaming about in such a potpourri of garb they were liable to be arrested as spies, which they quite enjoyed but which did interfere with work.

Now they wore RE uniforms with an F.S.C. patch on the right arm. They entertained those curious about its meaning with imaginative inventions—perhaps the gem was 'First Serving Conscripts'. The timeliest explanation was improvised when a small party was apprehended by a staff officer while illicitly removing timber from a supply dump. The NCO in charge pointed to his badge and declared that they were from the 'Field Salvage Corps'.

Vans were too unsteady for the galvanometers, so most sections housed theirs with other necessities in a building, which over the years became increasing home-like, even with the luxury of bookshelves.

In March 1916 WL was in Paris, where he visited the Duc Maurice de Broglie and lunched with his family. The Duchesse told wonderful jokes. 'You should hear me talk French now, I am simply wonderful.' When he wrote home about the visit he also discussed his concerns about the sound ranging equipment:

> Colonel Jack is madly keen to get it ready; we want all of the sections badly, at once, and we were rather counting on having it at the end of the month … It is the prisms and recorders that are wanted … I don't want to worry Jenkinson, I know he is doing his damnedest, but perhaps you could arrange to relieve him of a little of the work by having it done out.

The first 20 galvanometers were Bull's, the rest were manufactured by the Cambridge Instrument Company.[32] They still were unable to get reliable localizations of the guns they most wanted.

He had a letter from his dearest friend at Cambridge, Cecil Hopkinson, who had been gravely wounded on Gallipoli, and was now in hospital in England, hopefully on the mend. Later that month WL wrote:

> I can't imagine myself as 26 … it seems a fearful age … we are all looking forward to the birthday cake.

Happily, there was a steady flow of food parcels. Meat pies came over in good nick, but fruit did not ship well. Wine and spirits were bought in France at low cost: 'so we get drunk very cheaply'. C. G. Darwin was with him, a 'delight'. Pre-war Darwin had had trained in the Manchester OTC. He had been in France since 1914 serving as a censor and a railway officer until Bragg snagged him. WL's lectures for new sound rangers sometimes were distracted by the war.

> There is a dickens of a row going on because our batteries are all blazing away at the Bosches and all the while there is a stream of fat shells trundling overhead. At the same

time the Germans are firing at two of our planes that are observing for the batteries and the cracks in the air add to the general excitement.

Of course their work was top secret and never discussed in letters. Many of his envelopes were stamped by the censor. But occasionally security was breached.

> When did that notice appear in the Cambridge papers and how did they get to know about it? I would be awfully glad to know, it really ought to be enquired into if it gives the show away. I am sick about it.
>   I am so sorry Dad is having such a worry with the navy. People are fearfully pig-headed about being helped always. I am having a dreadful time doing everything wrong and altogether sure that anybody else whosoever could do it all better that I do.

The breakthrough

His self-evaluation was that the first year of sound ranging 'was really a wash-out, though we tried to pretend it was not.'[33] Finally the dawn:

> We were living in tarred felt huts in bitterly cold weather at the time and we noticed that whereas the shell-wave was a deafening crack, the faint gun-wave blew jets of very cold air through the readily available holes in the sides of our hut. Now I had in my unit a certain corporal W. S. Tucker, who before being conscripted was a lecturer at Imperial College and who had made experiments on the cooling of heated fine platinum wires by currents of air.

Thirteen-years-older than WL, he:

> ... rather smiles at you with his head on one side but is really very decent. ... The joint brainwave came to us, I think mainly to him, that we could use this effect.[34]

(More likely it was WL's brainwave.) They tested the method by stretching the finest copper wire they could find across the opening of a rum jar. When they blew on the wire it cooled, which increased its resistance so less current flowed. With a simple electrical circuit they could record the resistance change with the galvanometer. WL sent to England for thin platinum wire, 10 μm diameter, used for wind detectors because it is so strong. When it arrived it had to be mounted. There were plenty of empty wooden ammunition boxes lying about, so they took one, ran the wire the length of the box and drilled a hole in a side for gun-waves to enter. You can imagine WL's delight when they recorded a well-defined gun-wave following a shell-crack too small to distort the tracing. It was a delicate measurement because the signal generated was only about 0.01 V. Most battlefield noises were not recorded because they were higher frequency. The device was named the Tucker microphone and he was commissioned. Now WL could write home: 'What cheers me up is that our experiments are getting on so well.'

They were not there yet: even a gentle, gusty wind made the microphone unusable. They tried to block the gusts by covering the hole in the ammunition box with every wrapping that came to hand, but those that stopped gusts blocked gun-waves as well. Finally they found that several layers of standard issue camouflage netting did the trick. They also stacked brushwood around the boxes, which filtered out gusts and camouflaged the boxes. (Late in the war the Germans experimented with hot wires but never solved the wind problem.[35] In the Second World War the boxes were lowered into pits.) Another problem was that small insects were attracted to the warm wire; if they landed they incinerated and the flame broke the thin wire. Fine copper screening was requisitioned to protect the aperture. On the army stores list it became 'protector, Earwig, Mark I'

With these refinements the Tucker microphone worked brilliantly. Of course there were insoluble limitations; no sound ranging system would work when the wind was blowing toward the German lines. Gun-sounds would be pushed up above the wind, sometimes audible in London when not heard in Flanders. As WL noted: 'due to the 'principle of maximum cussedness' the wind in Flanders and Artois was usually westerly. After the initial success, Tucker microphones were manufactured in England by the General Post Office. They strung the wires through neat metal boxes, which performed poorly. Just as the effectiveness of a high fidelity speaker depends on its enclosure, by chance the sturdy ammunition box had the low resonance best for gun-waves.

On 16 June 1916, WL was mentioned in dispatches and four days later he was promoted to Lieutenant 'to remain seconded'. A week later he was off on leave. He picked up some needed clothing in London and then went up to Hawkcraig, Scotland. The added distance entitled him to an extra day of leave. He presented Gwendy with an elegant box of Parisian chocolates and described the pleasures of the glorious city which glistened at night as in peacetime, unlike blacked out London or Flanders. He had written her entertaining letters about the animals living at his quarters and pictured in charming drawings—though not up to father's high standard. She loved hearing about Section W's animals. He had been collecting souvenirs and was pleased to see how well an almost intact shell he had dug out had been polished up by the household staff. Soon after he returned he proudly snagged a piece of the canvas from a German kite observation balloon that had been shot down and fell on the British side.

The attack on the Somme

He was still on leave when the French and British launched a joint attack to break through the enemy lines in the valley of the Somme. The attack had no noteworthy strategic objective; the sector was selected because it was at the junction of the two allied armies. The artillery preparation was the most extensive yet undertaken, but as noted in the official history: 'Flash spotting and sound ranging were still in an experimental stage'.[36] The British concentrated more than 1,537 guns along a twelve mile front. Of these 269 were six-inch or larger.[37] Firing began at dawn on 24 June 1916. The primary targets were the enemy trenches and belts of barbed wire, which were also showered with explosive by Stokes mortars. Some heavy guns were assigned to counter-battery work, but they were handicapped because the fall of shell had to be observed by aviators braving AA guns and hindered by low clouds.[38] The German infantry sheltered in deep dugouts in the chalk, but were traumatized by days of bombardment and weakened because it was difficult and dangerous to bring up rations and water.[39] Two sound ranging sections were along the Somme front. One did some useful pinpointing before the bombardment; once the thunder began it was hopeless.[40] Their cables were supported on stakes above ground and often cut. After this disappointment the sound rangers were issued higher quality cable that could be laid directly on the ground—burying made it too hard to locate breaks. There were also difficulties with inquisitive Australians brought in for the assault, who could not resist poking about the microphones. Therefore, signs were attached: DANGER 3000 VOLTS.[41] Haig warned the Australian commander Birdwood:

> You're not fighting Bashi-Bazouks now—this is serious scientific war, and you are up against the most scientific and military nation in Europe.[42]

During the preliminary bombardment flash observers were ordered to fix the positions of enemy kite balloons every day at 12:00. It was not easy. Each balloon was tethered at a different site every day and they bobbed so violently that it could be tricky for two posts to be confident they were fixing on the same balloon. HQ collected the data with a daily priority call. As the days passed the observers griped about another senseless boondoggle. Finally one afternoon at 12:30 a squadron of British fighting planes swept over the front. They zeroed in with machine gun tracer bullets and then fired their rockets. Nine balloons went down in flames.

Just after dawn on 1 July 1916 in one hour the British fired 250,000 shells at the German trenches. At 07:28 ten mines were exploded under the enemy. Ten minutes later the infantry climbed out of their frontline trenches, formed lines and began to walk toward the enemy, preceded by a barrage that skipped ahead in 100 yards steps. GHQ thought that new army men could not cope with more intricate tactics and wanted them to reach the enemy in line for an overpowering bayonet attack. In one sector 8,000 men in the British 8th Division assaulted the 1,880 men in the German 180th Infantry Regiment. Seventy per cent of the attackers were casualties compared to 18 per cent of the defenders.[43] The 1,627,824 shells had failed to take out the German infantry or most of their guns and some places even their wire was uncut.

WL travelled from England to Flanders on 3 July:

Just a note to say that I am very fit though feeling rather exhausted. We have been having some quite decent results lately, which always cheers one up.

WL was wearing too many hats:

Had Bull staying ... I am sort of consulting engineer and experimenter and O C section all in one.

He reassured Father:

I have a dugout now, with steel girders, two feet of concrete, four feet of earth, and then bags full of flints ....

He was appointed 'Acting Captain whilst holding a special appointment'. He corresponded in veiled terms with father about data recording. It took too long to develop their film. A visit to the French showed him the advantages of having a continuous record, which they obtained from ink writers that responded too slowly for Tucker microphones.

Hemming's duties changed. The Third Army was reorganized when General Edmund Allenby left for the Middle East. His successor, General Julian Byng, assigned an officer to the HQ of each Corps to coordinate reconnaissance. Hemming was promoted to staff captain and sent to VI Corp at Arras. A staff captain was paid twice as much as a RE captain, but coordinating was less fun than spotting enemy guns. He passed along flash and sound localizations to the kite balloon observers who sometimes saw the gun but for safety from shellfire were tethered well behind the front and usually were dancing too vigorously to mark gun pits accurately on a map. In the evening Hemming went to the airfield to debrief the aviators, going over their aerial photographs asking them where they had seen flashes.

WL was thriving.

Everyone is bucked with us at present, and then again the weather is bad and we cannot work they say we are no good, so I go through terrible times of ups and downs for you know what a fearful fellow I am for taking my tone from everyone round about ... We have been flourishing lately and think ourselves tremendous dogs ... I saw Colonel Jack yesterday, and he is very pleased with our work which is encouraging ... I am doing great things just now, I can tell you!

His friend Cecil had gone downhill and his pals were moving off, Robinson and Darwin to new sections, Tucker and others to establish an experimental section on Salisbury Plain. W section was left with nine officers and 56 men, enough to keep him occupied:

In our line, Dad's and mine, we are always wondering about the reason for things and are not used to the immense amount of organizing it takes to make a good idea actually useful in practice.

The attacks on the Somme were finally shut down by dreadful October weather. WL toured the other sound ranging sections. He spent a couple of days with Darwin and then went on to the section commanded by Bocquet, where Robinson was assigned. Regular army, Bocquet ran a tight, disciplined unit. He was a vegetarian, who discouraged meat at lunch and limited tea to baked beans on toast. Robinson had only been allowed to shop in a sizable town twice in the past eight months, but bore his cross with usual good cheer.

As the days shortened the elation of success seeped away:

> I am not really so fearfully depressed as I suppose I seemed in my letters. One is never really depressed because one is bad oneself, it is the hopelessness of other people that makes one wild.

He was hoping that Professor Bayliss might come over to demonstrate his ink recorder. 'Professor Bayliss' experiment looks awfully good now.' However it turned out to respond too slowly, so they fed the film coming out of the galvanometer directly into a pool of developer followed by a pool of fixative, so it emerged wet but ready for reading. They trapped 28 rats in one of their OPs.

At the end of November he visited the experimental unit on Salisbury Plain. His family would soon have the chance to entertain Tucker: 'He does enjoy himself so easily if he has a cheery girl to meet …'.

The official history of the RA in the First World War lauds sound ranging as the outstanding technical innovation in 1916.[44]

A new year

On New Year's Day 1917, Haig became a field marshal and '… the guns gave the Germans a few rounds to cheer them up …'. Twenty sound ranging sections were in action, covering the entire British front at least adequately, except for the Somme and the Ypres salient, 'in which two areas there was considerable difficulty in working.' [45]

Reginald W. James, a newly minted RE lieutenant came over to join them.[46] He and WL had the only two firsts in physics given in their year. James was un-social and un-athletic but devoted to science. His fellows were astounded when after a ten minute interview he signed on as physicist for Sir Ernest Shackleton's ill-fated expedition to cross the Antarctic from sea to sea by way of the Pole. After their vessel was trapped on the ice, he was one of those who lived precariously on a flow while Shackleton and a few seamen sailed a small boat to South Georgia to organize a rescue—they did not lose a man. He was commissioned soon after the heroes return to England.

WL was cheery:

> Our show is going famously, my only fear is lest the war should end before it has reached its full stage of perfection…. My car now is most luxurious, a

very long Sunbeam with deep springy seats and I have two immense fur rugs to cover me, it is just great.

Mother wrote that he had been mentioned in dispatches. Conditions at the front were appalling:

Imagine walking for three miles along a road with mud over your knees, up to your waist in parts, in the dark, and with tree trunks floating in it which used to be part of the corduroy.

He was busy:

Its hard because there is always a such a crowd of fellows around all asking for something and so on.

Then there was a bitter cold spell, ghastly for the men in the trenches. Even in WL's heated quarters:

My shaving brush froze between wipes this morning although I had got hot water to put it in.

His prized Sunbeam automobile fractured its cylinder block in the cold, and he had to make do with a borrowed Ford.

In February the Germans began to withdraw from a large salient jutting out from their front to a new line of fortifications constructed across its base, which the Allies regarded as part of the Hindenburg line. It was the first opportunity for sound rangers to tramp over what had been enemy ground to see where their heavy guns had been dug in. They had located 87 per cent of them. Surely some glasses were raised in celebration.

Then tragic news: Cyril Hopkinson died. WL called on mother for help:

I have been trying ever so hard to write something for Mrs Hopkinson about Cyril ... it is almost impossible. Do tell me what sort of thing I should write; I am in such despair over it.

In March, he was sent to England to consult with Tucker, give a lecture at the War Office, and then had leave, so he finally wrote the Hopkinson letter at the family home, probably with some maternal assistance. It is a heartfelt nine page letter, eulogizing his friend, notably for his love of travel, exploration and maps.

When WL arrived back in France, he was pleased to be met at the boat by a car sent to bring him and two others officers up to GHQ. Colonel Jack had decided that he should set up a training school and research centre, while still keeping an eye on W section. His address was now 'Map Section. G.H.Q.' and he was billeted in a French hotel. He described to Gwendy his breakfasts: a large bowl of coffee, a 'piece of bread about a yard long like this [drawing] and lots of butter and nothing else. I rather like it'. His school was also in the hotel. He had 100 poster boards made up with examples of recordings and localizations. Effective localization depended on the ability of the film reader or 'computer' and the alertness and judgment of the observers who turned on the film transport.

One of the students was a New Zealander, Lieutenant Ernest Marsden, who had worked with Geiger and Rutherford. In early 1914, Rutherford was visiting his homeland when the Professorship of Physics in Wellington became open. He recommended Marsden, who was given the position without further search or advertisement. He was a success in the lecture hall and was also commissioned in the New Zealand territorial force—he had attended an OTC in England. He volunteered for service overseas, arrived in France in the middle of 1916 and eventually was co-opted by WL. Again he did well and was promoted to temporary captain a few months later. His friends described him as a man with 'expressive eyes and a brain like a needle'.[47]

WL inspected the other sound ranging sections and discussed problems with Colonel Jack—naturally some of their men did not work out. In June Edward Andrade, another of Rutherford's chaps, was transferred to the Ministry of Munitions to work on explosives.[48] WL wrote to father:

Andrade got jolly well kicked out of the show here as he became absolutely the limit. He is a hopeless chap. I am sorry for him too sometimes, but he has a bad kink in him somewhere. There was an awful to-do about it all; the officers in his section refused to work with him any longer and told the colonel so.

Mother was told:

He is a garrulous fierce conceited self-opinionated Scotchman.

(Years later Andrade wrote WHB's obituary for the Royal Society and took over his position at the Royal Institution—where again he caused trouble.)

WL was mentioned in dispatches again on 1 April 1917. He had an agreeable break in Paris with Lucien Bull, his sister and his aunt, who now seemed like family. They lived in a tiny apartment overlooking the Seine and were full of good cheer. Help from home was still welcome:

My underpants are rather thin in patches. I would like three pairs medium for spring …But really the British Army is getting a lot better and more reasonable.

Passchendaele

The first major attacks of 1917 were by the British at Arras and by the Canadians at Vimy Ridge. Their artillery fire was more deadly because they had a more sensitive contact fuse that exploded before the shell buried itself in the mud. For the first time sound rangers were working across all of the front to be attacked.[49] During the preliminary bombardment at Arras two rounds were fired for every yard of enemy trench and one for every yard of protective barbed wire. More of the heavy guns did counter battery work. Now and again the bombardment lifted from the German trenches, their infantry rushed to man their parapets and then the fire rained down again. The British infantry advanced behind a rolling shrapnel barrage, moving forward at 25 yards per min. (The rolling barrage was the brainchild of Major Alan Brooke, who in the Second World War was Chief of the Imperial General Staff.) Almost all of the German frontline trench system was taken in 45 minutes along with 5,600 prisoners and the second line was secured two hours later. Ludendorff was so upset that he spurned his birthday dinner. They were stopped at the third enemy position, which was beyond the range of the British field guns. They did not try to advance further because their assault was merely a diversion for a massive French attack planned along the Aisne by the new French Commander General Robert Nivelle. OHL was reassured when they learned that their commander at Arras had not adopted the elastic defence tactics they now advocated and had crammed his forces in the front line where they were overwhelmed.[50] He was replaced.

Flash and sound training were shifted to a new school at Merlimont-Plage, 40 km south of Boulogne, where they built an elaborate dummy range with electric lights to provide the flashes. Novice observers were flown over the fighting lines to see enemy battery positions and the lie of the land they would be watching. In November a newly formed company was sent to Italy; the following year companies went to Salonika and Egypt. There was a sound ranging conference every two months, attended by at least one officer from each section. A group photograph was taken at the closing party. Technical papers written by officers and other ranks were published and circulated.

The artillery was delighted with sound ranging:

> At first a certain amount of incredulity, quite natural under the circumstances, prevented the results from exerting their natural influence.[51]

And by this time they had enough heavy guns and sufficient ammunition to target enemy artillery. An RA counter-battery staff officer—the 'counterblaster'—was assigned to each corps HQ. He compared the map coordinates of enemy batteries located by flash and sound rangers to aerial photographs; on every flying day they took 100–400 photographs along each army front. Their quality had been vastly improved and they were analysed by experts—another new military specialty, challenged by constantly improved camouflage. The counterblaster passed along the map coordinates of verified or suspected enemy gun positions and coordinated attacks on the most promising targets. The rule of thumb was that firing the same gun with the same settings repeatedly would drop shells in a zone 100 to 200 yards long and 20 yards across.[52] On this basis, a six-inch howitzer would fire 100 shells on the enemy position, an eight-inch would fire 80, or a 9.2-inch would fire 60. During the barrage, they would pause for a few minutes and then fire a few shrapnel shells, hoping that they had lured the gun crew out from shelter. Not surprisingly in a budding bureaucracy, there was still an RE reconnaissance officer in each corps despite the overlap with the counterblaster.

The French attack along the Aisne was another murderous failure. After a few futile days many French regiments refused to attack. Gen. Henri Pétain was given command and set to nursing their mutinous army. Meanwhile, to distract the Germans—who vastly underestimated the turmoil in the French camp—Field Marshal Haig was authorized to attack in Flanders. This time there was an important strategic objective: occupying the Belgian ports used as U-boat bases. Step one was to occupy the Messines Ridge by a brilliant set-piece attack, which began with the detonation of almost one million pounds of high explosive in 21 mines—the largest man-made explosion to date.[53] (Less than four per cent the power of the Hiroshima atomic bomb.) The explosives had been in place for months, so the Germans were not alerted by hearing miners at work. German batteries had been located by the counterblaster during a period of excellent weather before the attack. They were suppressed by some of the 756 British heavy guns. The German retreat allowed the British to see how well they had pinpointed enemy gun pits. Over 90 per cent were 'absolutely accurately localized'; wherever there had been disagreement the sound rangers were correct.

With the Ridge taken, they were ready to break through further north. The first objective was the Passchendaele Ridge, east of Ypres. Then there would be amphibious landings along the coast. General Gough, commander of the attacking Army, planned to advance 5,000 yards in the first eight hours. Therefore he insisted that microphones and flash and sound OPs were placed just behind the start line, which made it difficult to work effectively. His artillery had 752 heavy or medium and 1,422 light guns or howitzers. In the days before the attack the wind was blowing so strongly from the west that sound ranging was almost impossible, even when the noise of the bombardment permitted: they located less than five per cent of the enemy batteries.[54] Heavy clouds kept aeroplanes grounded. Despite these snags, the official history states that before D-day 50 per cent of the enemy heavy guns were hit, but—mysteriously—almost all were promptly replaced.[55] The number of hits may have been exaggerated because each enemy gun rotated between three or more pits. On D-day the British had about 27,000 casualties—fewer than on the first day on the Somme—but the German's were so satisfied by their defence that Col. Lossberg, the responsible staff officer, was immediately promoted to major general.

During the battle the British fired 4,283,550 shells, almost two-and-a-half times the number fired on the Somme. The torrent of fire often made sound ranging impossible. Haig's intelligence staff kept reporting that German casualties far exceeded British. Their count was based on how often the Germans relieved their divisions.[56] In the Somme battle a division was relieved after they sustained 4,000 casualties, which usually took about 14 days. Now the German army group commander, Crown Prince Rupprecht, found that: 'It is proving very difficult to transport food, rations and trench stores forward because of the amount of gas the enemy is using', and his miserable troops huddled in 'flooded trenches or shell holes'.[57] Hence, divisions were relieved after a few days, even though they had taken only 1,500 to 2,000 casualties, which threw off the British bookkeeping. Actually the British had 1.6 casualties for each German.[58]

The hail of shells destroyed the drainage in the low-lying fields, the rains came, men drowned in a sea of mud. The artillery fire was only stilled briefly in the morning, when Red Cross flags flew and both sides ceased fire for an hour while medical teams and their search dogs brought in the wounded.[59]

Curiously, the British Official History judges German defensive tactics a failure. [60] Eventually the British gave up trying to break through, instead using limited bite-and-hold actions with carefully rehearsed troops. The defenders responded by beefing up their front line. A second division was keep close behind; if ordered to counterattack it came under the command of the division holding the front. The agonizing creep toward Passchendaele finally ended in November. They had advanced 9,000 yards, less than twice the distance they had intended to advance in the first eight hours.

Crown Prince Rupprecht's assessment was:

> Despite the deployment of immense quantities of men and material, the enemy achieved absolutely nothing. A narrow, utterly smashed strip of ground represents his entire gain. He has bought this outcome at the cost of extraordinarily heavy casualties; whereas our losses were far fewer than in any previous defensive battle.[61]

Field Marshal Haig saw it differently:

> It is certain that the enemy's losses considerably exceeded ours. Most important of all, our new and hastily trained Armies have shown once again that they are capable of meeting and beating the enemies best troops, even under conditions which favoured his defence to a degree which it required the greatest endurance, determination and heroism to overcome.[62]

Hindsight provided a more balanced appraisal. After the war, Rupprecht's chief of staff, Hermann von Kuhl wrote:

> Today, now that we are fully aware of the critical situation in which the French army found itself during the summer of 1917, there can be no doubt that through its tenacity, the British army bridged the crisis in France. The French army gained time to recover its strength; the German reserves were drawn toward Flanders. The sacrifices that the British made for the Entente were fully justified.[63]

Haig lauded his Field Survey Companies:

Their assistance has also been invaluable to our artillery in locating the enemy's new battery positions during the actual progress of the battle.[64]

The sound rangers were more realistic:

The experiences of the Passchendaele battle did a great deal to discredit the capabilities of sound ranging in a battle.[65]

But this is overcritical, because they kept improving their techniques. Examination of ground captured in September suggested that the Germans were faking flashes to mislead observers. Thereafter, sound and flash rangers swapped detailed information. Flash ranger's work was hamstrung when the Germans copied the British and began bombardments with only half of their batteries firing. As soon as the horizon became an unbroken vivid red streak, the other guns joined in. When counter batteries fired at a visible target, flash rangers observed their fall of shot. The observer would centre his telescope on the target, and quickly read the deviation of errant shell bursts from a graticule in his eyepiece. The flash observers also helped to calibrate the British guns, which was becoming increasingly important. At a pre-agreed time the gun would fire ten shells at the same elevation and pointing. The observers recorded the coordinates of each explosion. From the mean distance travelled the muzzle velocity was calculated from the range table. Often the muzzle velocity was painted on the gun's barrel. Toward the end of the war, visual calibration was improved by firing shells with time fuses that burst just before hitting the ground.

Sound rangers also calibrated British guns by measuring the distance between the gun position and the exploding shell. For precise measurements WL set up a station at a firing range near the channel where guns fired out to sea. The shell ripped through two webs of wire 100 yards apart. The novel aspect of his method was that the electrical signal generated by breaking the wires was recorded on galvanometer film moving at 1 m per sec.

Their recordings of enemy firings often showed the shell-crack, the gun-wave and finally the detonation of the shell. From the flight time of the shell and the distance travelled the computer could guess the gun's calibre. His guess could be tested by sending a party to the site of the shell burst to pick through the crater until they found the fuse. If they could not find it they estimated calibre from the size of the shell hole. Casual observers on the scene also reported shell hole sizes, but WL pointed out that:

for determining the calibre of a gun such 'local information' is useful, but only if one divides by two the estimate of the calibre formed by those on the spot.

Their calculations required the velocity of sound. It is about 335 m per sec (367 yards per sec), but varies with air temperature and wind direction. At first they used values listed in tables. Then they set up 'wind sections' behind their lines in which a ring of microphones recorded test charges fired in their centre, from which they calculated sound velocity and wind corrections. A wind section was a major undertaking, using much equipment and personnel spread over 35 square miles. So they compared their data to the temperatures, velocities and wind directions recorded by the 'meteor' (meteorology) sections at each Army's HQ. The meteor data was satisfactory, so the wind sections were shut down.

When they started microphones were placed at convenient, roughly equidistant locations; then their exact positions were surveyed. Usually the microphones were about 3,000 yards behind the British front and the galvanometer another 3,000 yards further back. Later some sound rangers proposed that it would be better if the microphones were separated by exactly equal distances. WL was sceptical because this would not add any information; it would merely present it differently—but he gave it a try. With regular microphone spacing the film pattern made it easier for a skilled computer to recognize which gun had fired and therefore to count the number firing. Equal spacing was adopted by all sections.

A German order was captured:

In consequence of the excellent Sound ranging of the English, I forbid any battery to fire when the whole sector is quiet, especially in east wind. Should there be occasion to fire, the adjoining battery must always be called on, either directly or through the Group, to fire a few rounds.[66]

The Germans were underestimating their foes:

... we could record almost any number of guns firing at once, the more the merrier.[67]

The sound rangers also helped to 'walk-in' counter battery fire. According to Colonel Jack:

An ingenious mechanical plotter was devised by Bragg whereby the necessary corrections could be supplied to our gunners in a very short time, in terms of yards short or over, minutes right or left.[68]

Their ultimate exploit was when they used three sections simultaneously to pinpoint a giant German railway gun firing at the Canadian troops on Vimy Ridge from the shelter of a wood eleven miles behind the lines.[69]

American sound ranging

After the US declared war two French physicists brought over the designs of four sound ranging devices for the NRC to consider.[70] The French detected gun-waves by using modified aneroid barometers or electromagnetic microphones and vacuum valve amplifiers.[71] When quizzed about the relative merits of their approaches, the French conceded that comparative tests had not been done. On the recommendation of the NRC Augustus Trowbridge, a Princeton physicist, was commissioned as a major and assigned as technical director for flash and sound ranging.[72] He assembled a cadre to build and test the most promising French design and the British system. Meantime, he went to France to see them in action. His team at home cabled that the French Dufour system was best.[73] At the front Trowbridge found that the bulky Dufour microphones were often put out of action and that their recording apparatus was frail.[74] Then he visited WL. He cabled his team that they would follow the British, who would get them started with Tucker microphones and galvanometers. WL wrote:

> They have decided to take up our show anyhow which is rather a score ...

Remember that in 1917 the US public regarded Great Britain in a far different light than today. The English were still the ruthless antagonists of the revolution and the War of 1812, supporters of the Confederacy during the Civil War, and Machiavellian imperialists who occupied a quarter of the globe. Hence the Americans turned to the French—allies in the war for independence—for military tuition and arms and deployed their army on the French right wing, far from the British front. Trowbridge's opting for the British system was an oddity. He established a one-month training school in France and the graduates did their operational training with the British. At the armistice the Americans had five flash and sound sections, with 83 officers and 1,068 other ranks.

Cambrai and artillery boards

In September 1917 WL asked father whether Jenkinson might come over to France, because they were having problems with instrument fabrication. WL obviously gave his work higher priority than father's efforts against the U-boats, which had the Royal Navy rocking on its heels. Jenkinson did not come.

As the Passchendaele offensive was winding down, Haig decided to attack the Hindenburg line west of the German-occupied city of Cambrai. The germ of the idea came from his tank commanders who had been bogged down in the Flanders morass. To test tactics they wanted to carry out a large-scale raid. GHQ beefed-up the proposal into an attempted breakthrough spearheaded by tanks. First they had to move the men and guns south on the sly, which depended on meticulous staff work that had been wanting in the past. This time the roads were scheduled effectively; food, hay and petrol were where needed; the crosswise traffic to the immediate front was maintained; and every gun was smuggled into a prepared position opposite Cambrai. The newly dug gun pits showed how the RE had transformed artillery practice. Each pit was precisely surveyed. Each battery commander was handed an 'artillery board', an idea taken from the French 'planchettes'.[75] It was plywood board with a zinc plate attached. A map, showing major landmarks and known enemy positions, was glued to the plate. The solid mounting was needed because on a 1/20,000 map a millimetre on the paper represents 20 metres; changes in temperature could expand or contract the paper by at least this amount introducing unacceptable error. One end of a string was glued on the position of the British pit. When the other end of the string was placed on a target its length gave the range, and its bearing was read from a scale on the top of the map. During the war the RE supplied 11,379 artillery boards.

Compasses were useless for setting guns, because they were outrageously inexact on the battlefields where iron was scattered everywhere. Pre-war artillery procedure was for a battery commander to select a conspicuous feature in the landscape—steeple, tree, or the like—which was designated as the aiming point. The gun layer zeroed his dial sight on the aiming point, and then set on target by traversing his barrel to the angle between it and the target provided by the battery commander. French batteries carted along poles in case there was not a useable feature. When they arrived at Cambrai the British gunners found at each position one or two precisely surveyed metal stakes, called 'bearing pickets'. They had been devised by Major B. F. E. Keeling RE. At night one side of the picket was illuminated by an ammunition box with a slit cut in one side containing a lantern.

Once the gun's muzzle velocity, its position and that of the bearing picket were known, it was feasible to fire at a target on the map with a fair chance of hitting close, doing away with the customary hunt-and-peck registration fire that tipped an attacker's hand. At dawn on 20 November the British guns opened—most firing their first shot from their position—with an intense bombardment directed at German guns located by flash and sound rangers. Many shells contained tear gas which, without falling precisely on target, forced the German gunners to don gas masks, which impeded their work. Then the barrage shifted and began to creep across no-man's-land, firing equal proportions of high explosive, shrapnel and smoke, so that the ground would not be tossed into a moonscape of craters problematic for tanks.[76] The noise, the smoke and a heavy morning mist hid 381 tanks rumbling across no-man's-land ploughing gaps through the German wire.

The Germans expected that their trenches would stop the tanks because they were four metres wide, further than a tank could leapfrog. But tied on the front of each tank was a fascine: a hefty bundle of brush-wood. The leading tank dumped its fascine into the trench. Then the three tanks in the section rolled over the trench and the second in line took the lead, ready to bridge the next trench. Most of the German infantry ran. The main opposition was a few anti-tank guns and their intrepid crews. They did not fire routinely and hence were not on the British artillery boards. On the first day the British advanced two to four miles into the German positions, sustaining 4,000 casualties while taking as many prisoners. The church bells rang in London. As Erich Maria Remarque wrote:

From a mockery the tanks have become a terrible weapon. Armoured they come rolling in long lines, more than anything else they embody for us the horror of war.[77]

Field Marshal Haig had five cavalry divisions ready to exploit a breakthrough. With hindsight the British Official History put it:

You can't make a cavalry charge until you have captured the enemy's last machine gun.

Pétain had three French infantry divisions available; they could not be deployed because the approach roads were jammed with useless horses. The British leaders still did not understand the war they were fighting; Lieutenant-General Sir Lancelot Kiggell, Haig's chief-of-staff until February 1918, still maintained that the bayonet was the decisive weapon. Such wanton ignorance is almost incompressible.

The successful advance meant that sound rangers and flash spotters had to leapfrog forward. This was not easy; each flash group needed to lay 25 miles of telephone line and a sound ranging section required 40 miles of highest quality electrical cable, with low resistance and without leaks to ground. Nonetheless 'H section' moved forward and went into action after 56 hours.

The artillery also had to move up. In newly dug pits without bearing pickets or artillery boards they could not fire accurately from their map, so they had to observe the fall of shell. The British tanks were finally stopped by anti-aircraft guns pressed into a new role and their infantry was unable to take the final German trench line, which was manned by a division that fortuitously had just arrived from Russia and later with reserves rushed in on their excellent railway network. On 30 November the Germans launched a hurricane bombardment on the British positions, using many gas shells. They had precise map coordinates for their former fieldworks, now sheltering exhausted British survivors. German planes swept over at low level, bombing, machine gunning—keeping the defenders engaged. Meanwhile storm troops slipped through weak points and jumped into the former German trenches, which they rolled up in both directions. Their planes kept the artillery up-to-date about where their infantry were. On the first day of their counter-offensive the Germans took 6,000 prisoners, 103 field guns, 11 howitzers, and 55 heavy pieces. The British artillery was blind so long as the infantry of the two armies were mixed together in the web of trenches. The Germans recovered all they had lost and part of the former British line as well.

Much has been written about how starting in the autumn of 1917 the Germans surprised defenders with artillery firing by the map.[78] Usually these writers do not note that the British did the same at the same time.

By late November GHQ had grown so large that WL had to move his billet to a village four miles out. Haig, with his silver pencil, built an increasingly effective administrative staff for the BEF, which swelled from 200,000 men in 1914 to 2,000,000 in 1917.

The German assault

WL was given leave to celebrate the 1918 New Year. Back at HQ he fretted that he had unintentionally trifled with a young lady's affections, surely not a unique problem for a dashing wartime captain. As usual he was self-critical:

> I am just realizing what an awful mess I've made of all my jobs lately and beginning to pull up to scratch again. I am an ass.

To the intellectually adventurous sound ranging had 'reached such a pitch that there are no new ideas in it'. C. G. Darwin transferred to an RAF research station to work on aeroplane noise. WL could think of few improvements:

> I expect that the Americans will absolutely revolutionize the whole show when they get going ....

(They did not.)

With Serbia, Russia and Romania trounced, the outnumbered Allies steeled themselves for a devastating German assault. Railway lines across Central Europe were jammed with trains bringing the fittest men and their artillery parks from the east to west. It was not a question of whether but of where and when. In early March, Field Marshall Haig visited VI Corps HQ. The commander, General Rotton, assured him that the enemy could not break through. Haig responded briskly:

> Of course he will break through. Any army with sufficient artillery and tanks can break through if it is willing to pay the price and the Germans are ready. The point is at what point you can stop them.[79]

Then he asked to speak privately with the reconnaissance officer, so soon he was closeted with Hemming. He asked 'whether the Germans were ready to attack? No. Why do you say that?' Hemming explained that to attack they would want one gun for every two-and-a-half yards of front. They had only one-third that number on VI Corps front and Hemming was confident of this figure thanks to excellent aerial photographs of the barren, wasted German rear areas.[80] He had so many photographs because the Germans were deliberately allowing British observations planes to work unimpeded.[81] Haig instructed Hemming to report directly to him by telegram when the Germans reached the critical number. Hemming sent the telegram on 18 March 1918. The German guns were brought in at the last moment at night.

On 21 March, almost 6,000 German guns—Ludendorff's battering ram—opened fire on the fronts of the British Third and Fifth Armies in the Somme, firing from maps. All along the 40 mile front the Germans penetrated the British first line, so OPs and sound ranging apparatus had to be hastily withdrawn; each section had only a single two-wheeled cart; everything that could not be evacuated was blown up. As the attack continued the second and third positions were overwhelmed along parts of the line; the British Fifth Army was routed but strong resistance by the Third Army prevented the Germans from attaining their strategic objective, which was to snare them in a pocket. Nonetheless the Germans, elated by their success, decided to try for the railway hub of Amiens. To defend the city Field Survey troops were drafted into a scratch RE formation, 'Carey's Force'. It included two companies of American and one of Canadian engineers.[82] The engineers resented cavalrymen with naked sabres lined up behind them to cut off retreat, but nonetheless fought bravely and suffered heavily. The Germans could not take Amiens. OPs, microphone positions and guns then had to be surveyed in along the new defensive lines, in some places 40 miles back from where they had been two weeks before.

When the attack began WL was off visiting the Americans in Lorraine. He returned to GHQ, shaken by the German gains and afraid that he might have missed WHB, who was in France to inspect a piece of apparatus being made for him. They did connect so WHB saw sound ranging in action and WL learned more about father's naval establishment. One sound ranging section commander and a new officer had been killed. WL was busy replacing lost equipment. Later he wrote:

> I have been seeing a lot of our people back from the front, they have been having a hairy time. They dug themselves in and held the Bosches back for four days, but they had a lot of casualties.

Marsden was wounded at the end of March and was mentioned in dispatches for gallant service. He recovered quickly, was given command of a Field Survey Battalion and promoted to temporary major. About this time he received a letter from Hans Geiger, who had introduced him to research at Manchester, belatedly congratulating him on his professorship in New Zealand. Geiger was in the German artillery; the letter was forwarded by Niels Bohr.

At the beginning of April WL and Hemming were transferred to GHQ to oversee and coordinate the work of all sound ranging and flash spotting units. Their first meeting led to an enduring friendship. Both had distinguished themselves. WL had been awarded the Military Cross (MC) at the first of the year, was appointed an Officer of the Most Excellent Order of the British Empire (OBE) in March and was mentioned in dispatches for a third time. Mother was in charge of sewing the ribbons on the dress tunic kept in his closet at home.

The Germans would strike next in Flanders, in W section's neighbourhood. They had planned a massive attack codenamed *St George* on both shoulders of the Ypres salient. However they had committed so many reserves in the unsuccessful push toward Amiens that the next attack was scaled down to hit only the south shoulder and was re-christened *Georgette*—so much for the non-existent German sense of humour. The blow fell on 9 April; a massive bombardment along the River Lys paved the way for storm troops slipping forward through a mist. Part of the line there was held by two Portuguese divisions that were being relieved. The Germans swept them aside.

On the southern edge of their *schwerpunkt* the Bragg boy's old unit, King Edward's Horse, was deployed as infantry to keep that flank from being rolled up. That afternoon WL looked south from the OP on Mt Kemmel, watching the Germans pulling guns across the former Allied line and shells falling on Armentières, which until that morning had been bustling with civilians. The Germans did not occupy the town; instead they dowsed it with mustard gas so that it was out of bounds for both sides. WL wore his gas mask because even the crest was in such a cloud of gas that pilots above the battlefield smelt it.

The Germans were coming straight toward him. They planned to take Mt Kemmel, then the entire ridge line stretching north to Passchendaele and finally the major railway junction in Flanders. The sound ranging section retreated 7,000 yards and was functioning again in five hours, because they had surveyed microphone positions beforehand. The British moved men south from the Ypres salient to plug the hole. The Germans riposted by shifting north to hit the thinned line. On 11 April Haig issued a Special Order of the Day. The memorable section is:

> There is no course open to us but to fight it out. Every position must be held to the last man: there must be no retirement. With our backs to the wall and believing in the justice of our cause, each of us must fight to the end.

Unconstrained by rhetoric, the able commander of the salient, General Sir Herbert Plumer, retreated four days later, ceding all of the blood-soaked ground they had taken the previous autumn. A new defence line was set up on chosen ground just outside of Ypres. The Germans lost momentum as they followed, dragging guns and stores across the moonscape of the old battlefield. On 18 April a French division took over the lines on Kemmel. A week later the Germans pushed them off the hill. W section evacuated their equipment; leaving behind the snug quarters they had put together piece by piece in two-and-a-half years.

All of the evacuated ranging units were surveyed into new positions. On 29 April the Germans made their final push in Flanders, they were stopped short of the vital railway junction. Not planning retreat, WL was building a four hole golf course on a piece of waste land near GHQ. Despite thistles and mole hills it was great fun. Clubs were purchased in England, carefully camouflaged, and shipped over. They were 'absolutely topping'. One evening, WL trounced both RE colonels who were his superiors, 'a very impolitic thing to do.'

Ludendorff's battering ram shifted south to Champagne to let fly a diversionary feint toward Paris; then they intended to return to Flanders to finish off the British. The Allies in Champagne were caught napping. The Germans smashed through their lines and crossed the Marne. OHL was delighted; surely by pushing once more they would reach Paris. The tables turned when their attack to widen their salient was repelled.

In mid-June WL had a short trip to England. In Leeds he visited Bob's old unit. They spoke highly of his dead brother. When he arrived back at GHQ he found that the week before he had been promoted to temporary major. He was sorry not to have known earlier: 'Think how I could have swanked around in town!' Maj. Bragg toured his sections all along the British front and visited Paris, driving the 250 km on a dusty day. 'I'm glad to be getting there before the Bosche get there.'

Then the French and Americans turned the tide by counterattacking the Marne salient, driving the Germans back to their starting line with heavy losses. Hindenburg began a measured retreat to a shorter, defensible line. WL was enjoying after-dinner bridge games as well as golf. He also took a weekly French lesson from a chemist's wife who turned her fees over to a French army relief fund. He visited the Belgian sound rangers and had another spin down to Paris, where he enjoyed the Bulls. Bull came back with him for a few days.

Flash spotting's days were numbered, because the Germans were eliminating the flash with cooler-burning propellant explosives produced by adding nitroguanidine or ammonium nitrate and trapping some of the heat with added potassium chloride. They did not get into general use during the remaining months of the war. Sound ranging was improved when they discovered that German artillery observation planes now radioed the order to fire. The sound stations eavesdropped, when they heard the order they switched on the film transport. The short length of exposed film was developed immediately and the computer was measuring the data within minutes.

Colonel Jack hosted a gay dinner for the Americans working at GHQ. They had ample meat and vegetables but had not seen a crumb of bread or biscuit for five days. Food was rationed in England; his mother had lost two stone.

Amiens

In July the British began planning an attack along the front east of Amiens—it would come out of the blue; another chance for the British staffs to demonstrate how skilful they had become. Every planning conference was held at a different location. Two Canadian battalions were sent to a conspicuous sector north of Mount Kemmel where a busy wireless station spewed out messages from a make-believe Canadian HQ. Naturally the Germans anticipated a wallop up there. The bulk of the Canadians and the 1st Australian Division were billeted behind Amiens. Six hundred and four tanks were concealed nearby. A thousand additional guns and their ammunition were smuggled into position at night, camouflaged before daybreak, surveyed in and given their boards. The stealthy build-up was made easier because in the final week the entire region was clothed in heavy fog that prevented aerial reconnaissance. The Germans took advantage of the fog to shift their batteries to new positions. Heavy mist in dead calm is ideal for sound ranging, so their cannons were easily tracked. It was the sound ranger's finest hour.

The attack began before daybreak on the morning of 8 August. British planes roared low over the German lines, firing machine guns and drowning out the motors of the tanks as they drove forward along lanes marked with white tape. When the bombardment began at 04:20 two-thirds of the British heavy guns targeted enemy batteries. The new German gun pits were smothered with gas and high explosive shells, so they were unable to keep the tanks from tearing broad gaps in the wire in no-man's-land. Tanks trailed by small infantry units clawed deep gashes into the German lines. Then British cavalry charged the gaps; losing heavily and accomplishing nothing. Nonetheless, overall the day was a triumph, especially for the Canadians and Australians—Hemming and Bragg bragged shamelessly. They broke through fifteen miles of German front, to a maximum depth of seven miles. Entire units flew the white flag and marched into captivity. Thirteen thousand prisoners were in the cages and 334 guns captured.

When Winston Churchill, the minister of munitions, visited the next day he was struck by the 'almost cheerful countenances of the rank and file' prisoners. Ludendorff was distraught:

> August 8th was the black day of the German Army. It put the decline of our fighting powers beyond all doubt. The Army ceased to be a perfect fighting instrument.[83]

Morale was crumbling; their soldiers were '*zur Hölle betrübt*' (depressed to hell). Some of the captured German guns still had their muzzle covers on because accurate, unanticipated British fire had prevented their crews from getting into action.[84] The British did not repeat the mistake of Cambrai by recklessly pushing onward. The infantry stopped at specified lines and defended themselves against counterattacks. Meanwhile the artillery moved up, many into prepared, surveyed positions just north of the first attack, where they marked time until all was ready for the next surge forward. WL toured the battlefield, which was covered with swelling horse corpses, all nearing the 'explosion stage'.

The end

During the last hundred days of the war the British Army could be slowed but not stopped. WL realized that the war would not go on forever. He wrote to father:

> Has any new work on our job come out lately? What do you mean to go on with? I don't know quite what line to take up.

He was shown captured German apparatus and questioned prisoners about their artillery localization techniques. Like father he had no German, so his translator was Captain Reginald James, now the commander of the sound ranging school. He had 'lived in Boschland for a few months but was terribly rusty …'. They also examined captured German daily ammunition returns, which were written on YMCA paper captured during the drive toward Amiens. The Germans also used sound ranging, but the best apparatus they developed relied on skilled listeners, who would try to get the bearings by auditory localization from amplified signals. They located shell-cracks, and tried to locate the gun by caustics, the method the Allies had found unworkable. They had set up artillery survey sections in the fall of 1915; two years later they had 177 of them. Germans flash-spotters were trained at a school near Cologne. At first the sound ranging units were separate, by the end of the war there were 119 of them.[85] One of the physicists working on the German side was Max Born (Nobel laureate, 1954). He wrote little about sound ranging and seems to have spent as much time as he could free up calculating the internal energy of ionic crystals.[86]

In August WL was visited by his French opposite number, who spoke no English. WL was chuffed that his French did the job. In September, Colonel Jack went on leave, delegating WL to exercise his pony. He enjoyed their jaunts, though after his first morning in the saddle he was painfully creaky. Then he was off on a visit to the French. With the Americans they had attempted unsuccessfully to locate guns from the tremor of the earth from the recoil. WL would never have wasted the time. Sound conduction in the soil varied even more from place to place than in the air.

He wrote home about what he might do after the war. 'I am not meant for a job which means, as part of it, getting hundreds of other people to do their jobs too.' At the same time, he cautioned them that the men at the front were upset by the peace talk at home and asked for a pair of winter gloves. Haig expected the war to go on into 1919. The enemy rear-guard fought so intrepidly they hid the truth that the German army was falling apart.

WL drove up to inspect the liberated area; again the drive was spoiled by the reek of dead horses.

> The captured guns were jolly interesting, we must have given the Bosche beans by the way his battery positions had been knocked about … You would love to see the joy of the civilians who have got amongst friends again. The people say the German men were generally not too bad but their officers were the absolute outside edge.

He moved quarters into a nice house that had been occupied by the Germans for four years. The invaders had made off with all of the carpets and pictures.

Dad wrote about two job offers but WL was not interested. He did not want to go to the US, though few would anticipate his reason: 'Americans are much too intelligent and too polite and I feel a clumsy idiot when I am with them.' He would write to J.J. about prospects at Trinity. Finally on 8 November he wrote: '… the old Bosche has been beaten handsomely in the end.'

Early in December, he had a brief home leave, with a rough crossing on the return and he left his ration book in his bedroom in London. He was busy writing books on sound ranging and helping his friends find jobs so they could be discharged. The New Year began with a motor trip through Belgium to Cologne, accompanied by Hemming and another Canadian. Hemming, like WL, had been mentioned in dispatches three times, wore the MC and was a major. His additional reward was £100 from the War Inventions Board for his flash spotting board, which was a godsend for starting back in civilian life. They found Brussels very expensive; it had been a German playground. In Cologne they had excellent abundant meals for little money (surely in the British officers' mess). Local train and tram services were notably good, and the houses well-constructed.

The Germans were 'frightfully keen' to be polite, even the many men wearing field grey topped with civilian hats. WL found them all frightfully ugly, even the children were unappealing. The highpoint of his visit was an aeroplane flight along the Rhine, up to Bonn and back. He wrote to Gwendy that: 'It made one feel frightfully tummy-ey at times...', but thought it a great event in his life. He examined German sound ranging manuals, which James tried to translate.

His observations in Germany contrast strongly with other reports. Most thought the trains and trams in frightful shape, after four years without paint owing to the lack of oils. The food blockade was still on. General Plumer, commander of the occupation army, went to Paris to tell Lloyd George that his troops wanted to go home because they were so disgusted by watching: 'hordes of skinny and bloated children pawing over the offal from the British cantonments'.

Major Bragg was—in that wonderful British term —disestablished by the army at the end of January.

The British Association for the Advancement of Science met in Bournemouth that year. The Presidential Address was given by Sir Charles Parsons and his subject was science in the war.[87] He began by extolling the enormous amounts of energy released in steam turbines and by exploding chemical, products of science. Then he lauded:

> The sound ranging apparatus developed by Professor Bragg and his son ... which in 1917 located some 30,000 guns to within 50 feet at 7,000 yards range.

Poor WL, life in the shadow went on and on. WHB wrote to *The Times* to correct the record. Parsons also discussed the hydrophones developed by Captain Ryan and Professor Bragg, and Professor Bragg's pinpointing underwater explosions.

Anti-aircraft
A. V. Hill

In the last week of 1915, Captain Hill (Third Wrangler 1907) was convalescing at home in Cambridge.[1] He was on sick leave from the newly formed 3/1/ East Midland Infantry Brigade with 'a nasty attack of flu'. Despite sniffles and aches, he celebrated the holidays with his young wife and infant daughter, with both of their families nearby. He had married Margaret Keynes in 1913:

> Our friends, and many descendants, agree that it was the cleverest thing I ever did, though I cannot take all of the credit.[2]

They honeymooned on AV's motorcycle, Margaret bundled up in the sidecar as they raced about the countryside. Soon they also acquired a motorboat. Her parents had given them the house.

Her father was the university registrary, having resigned from a fellowship back in the days when a fellow could not marry; her mother was an author and social activist. His two brothers-in-laws were John Maynard (Twelfth Wrangler 1904) now an economist at King's College Cambridge and Geoffrey, a tyro physician.

His mother and younger sister Muriel had settled in Cambridge in 1905 when he went up to Trinity College on scholarship. When he was three-years-old mother ordered father out from the family home. He never saw father again or discussed him with mother. Father, a prosperous timber merchant, provided for his family and followed his brilliant, unseen children's careers with pride. To give her brood the best, resolute mother moved to Devon to be near a first-rate school. The lad was inspired by his mathematics teacher (Fourth Wrangler 1883):

> At the end of the first term there the best teacher I have ever known reported, 'I like his work very much'. My comment could well have been that I liked his even better.

Hill had joined an OTC at Cambridge, perhaps for the fun of firing off Government cartridges—at school he had become a crack rifle shot. He was promoted to sergeant, and in 1908 was posted to a three weeks course in musketry.

It proved also to be a course in the traditional linguistics of obscenity, conducted day and night by some of my fellow sergeants.[3]

He was commissioned the following year. When war came, Hill, now 28-years-old, volunteered for service in the Cambridgeshire Regiment, where he was the musketry officer.

I was aware that there were other tasks I could undertake that were really more essential, but that was not the sort of thing one talked about when other chaps were killed.[4]

He was a capable teacher; so once the recruits swapped broomsticks for rifles he ran an effective training program. The British Army stressed fast, accurate rifle fire, 'ten rounds rapid', at distances up to 800 yards. They were so confident in the killing power of their riflemen that they deployed few machine guns, because hauling the heavy guns and ammunition slowed an army on the march.

On New Year's Day 1916, Captain A. V. Hill received a letter at his home.[5] The use of his initials showed that it came from someone he knew. He detested his Christian names Archibald and Vivian, so he insisted on being addressed as AV.[6] The letter was from Horace Darwin, the fifth son and ninth child of the great biologist and his wife Emma. Born in 1851, he had his share of Darwin–Wedgewood brains.[7] Despite delicate health Horace graduated from Trinity College as a Senior Optime (the category below Wrangler) and served a three-year engineering apprenticeship in a prominent firm before settling in Cambridge. The Darwin wealth—Charles left £146,911—allowed their children to be casual about earning.

The Ministry of Munitions

The letterhead was from the Munitions Inventions Department (MID), a component of the Ministry of Munitions (MM). The history of the MID again drives home how incompetently the British mobilized their scientific talent. In November 1914, the Royal Society set up a General War Committee, with specialized subcommittees. The War Office ignored them until they requested input from the Chemical Committee after the German gas attack of 1915. Later that spring, the British attempted to seize Neuve Chapelle, a village perched on a low ridge. They failed. Sir John French, the BEF commander, publically blamed his defeat on the scarcity of artillery shells. The press fanned outraged public protests. In self-defence, the Government established the MM under the leadership of David Lloyd George, who had been Chancellor of the Exchequer.[8] He supplied dynamic energy and fresh ideas, recruiting men who 'were pushers and doers' to mobilize British industry. The MM was to make what the War Office ordered. In June, Sir John French established an Experimental Committee at GHQ, just at the time when A. J. Balfour at the Admiralty set up the BIR.

The MID

In July 1915 Lloyd George set up the MID as a component in the MM. One of their responsibilities was to respond to the torrent of recommendations and designs pouring in from the public. It was headed by Ernest Moir, a distinguished engineer who held a Territorial Army commission in the RE; he was assisted by a panel of 48 scientific consultants. The establishment of the MID did not mollify critics who had been campaigning for using science for war. For instance, H. G. Wells's fictional mouthpiece Mr Britling was indignant:

> A press clamour for invention and scientific initiative was stifled under a committee of elderly celebrities and eminent dufferdom: from the outset the Ministry of Munitions seemed under the influence of the businessman.[9]

The MID began with a staff of fourteen, which grew to more than 300. Two artillery experts, Colonels Goold-Adams and Heffernan, were seconded from the Ordnance Board at Woolwich. In October, they were ordered to return to Woolwich where they were needed. Lloyd George's hand was strengthened a few weeks later when General Du Cane, the head of the Experiments Committee at GHQ in France, reported that they had lost 36 guns during the past month from premature explosions owing to faulty high explosive shells: 1 in every 4,000 to 5,000 exploded prematurely. The French premature explosion rate was 1 in 120,000. Du Cane described the Ordnance Board as 'mentally exhausted' and their experimental department at Shoeburyness as 'hopelessly congested'. His timing was propitious because Kitchener was away at Gallipoli, leaving Prime Minister Asquith as acting secretary of state for war. Despite strong objections from the War Office, Asquith made the MM responsible for 'designs, patterns and specifications' of arms and ammunition. General Du Cane and the entire Research Department at Woolwich were transferred to the MID and the Ordnance Board was reconstituted as a Committee with diminished responsibilities. Moir was sent to the US to negotiate arms production and Colonel Goold-Adams became the comptroller of the MID.

Bureaucratic crossfire was not quashed. As Lloyd George put it:

> Whatever else the War Office failed to do, at least they lived up to the old tradition of the British Army of never knowing when they were beaten.[10]

The War Office maintained that they were still responsible for testing the MM's products; only weapons that passed their tests might see service. Lloyd George brought the issue to the War Cabinet, which on 3 February 1916 mandated:

> The responsibility for designs, patterns, and specifications and for testing arms and ammunition rests with the Ministry of Munitions.

The MID was allocated their share of the letters and proposals that flooded the Government's mailboxes. By November, they had received 6,671 ideas and inventions, 5,281 of them were examined. Some were easily dumped. One bright idea was to eliminate reflected light from the waters of the Thames, which guided German night bombers, by covering the surface with sawdust. 'Hopeless because sawdust does not float.'[11] Air defence was a popular subject matter because in 1915 German dirigibles dropped 34 tons of bombs on England, killing 181 people and wounding 455. The public demanded protection. In response the MID established a new division: (iv), Anti-Aircraft Experimental Section.

This brought in Horace Darwin, who surely did not fit into Wells's pigeonhole of 'eminent dufferdom'. He had founded and managed the Cambridge Instrument Company.[12] In 1909 he was appointed to the Advisory Committee for Aeronautics, set up by R. B. Haldane, who also had a wind tunnel built at the National Physical Laboratory at Teddington.[13] Haldane's effective championship of science is often overlooked because he did so much in so many spheres. Darwin invented an aircraft turn indicator and delivered the Wilbur Wright lecture to the Royal Aeronautical Society in 1913. The Horace Darwins had two daughters; their son was killed in 1915 in the Second Battle of Ypres.

Anti-aircraft gunnery

Physiologist Hill was approached because he was 'known to Horace Darwin and had shown signs of the unpleasant habit of inventing things'. So early in the New Year, Hill motor biked to the MID offices in the Whitehall Club on Princes Street.[14] Darwin briefed Hill on the 'problem of coping with enemy aircraft'. The combatants began the war with modest numbers of aeroplanes and airships, used for scouting and spotting the fall of shot. They were so useful that more were obtained and specialized bombers, fighters, and observation planes were hurriedly developed. The armies began with only a few specialized artillery pieces mounted for high angle fire to target kite balloons and dirigibles. Now they needed anti-aircraft (AA) guns. Darwin was working on a device for training AA gunners without expending scarce ammunition; Hill was asked to suggest improvements.

They met a few days later at the Central Flying School at Upavon, Wiltshire. Horace's idea came from his older brother Leonard, who as a RE in the 1880s experimented on the use of a camera obscura for observing aerial targets, like balloons. The camera obscura gave the X and Y coordinates of the target; its height, Z, was determined from the angle of the gun barrel when the target was centred in the layer's sight. For training, an aeroplane flew overhead, tracked by the AA gun. When ordered to 'fire' an electrical signal was generated and the gun setting was recorded. The electrical signal started a metronome in the camera obscura ticking every second. At each tick, the observer marked the position of the aeroplane on the image. After enough time had passed for the imaginary shell to explode, the calculated position of its burst was compared to that of the target. At the time, Hill did not ask how they knew where the imaginary shell would burst. In fact they did not know, they speculated.

The camera obscura was a large, immobile dome with a small lens at the top, which focused a faint image of the sky on the floor. Hill was next shown another experimental apparatus, a horizontal mirror that was viewed through an eyehole placed above it. The reflection of a bombing plane was observed and the point where it released its bomb was marked on the mirror.

Hill urged them to replace the camera obscura with two identical, flat, horizontal mirrors, each engraved with a calibration grid. The two mirrors would be placed at the ends of a long, measured baseline. Observers looking at the mirror through eyeholes—to keep the distance between eye and mirror fixed—would follow the reflection of an aeroplane. On a telephoned command, they would mark its position on their mirror with a dot of coloured glycerine ink. From the coordinates of the ink marks, the distance between eyehole and mirror, and the length of the base line it is easy to calculate the X–Y–Z coordinates of the target.[15] Hill diagrammed the apparatus and wrote down the equations. His presentation was compelling. His handsome face sparkled when he discussed science. He looked at home in uniform, even in old age his military bearing was notable. Despite prematurely greying hair, he exuded a compelling, boyish enthusiasm. He made science good fun.

Persuaded, Darwin ordered the mirrors, their supporting tables and viewing eyeholes from the Cambridge Scientific Company for £70. He requisitioned telephone wire and telephones and located an airdrome where they could test the mirrors. The MID obtained a short extension of Hill's leave and applied for his transfer.

Hill's physiology

An eyebrow at the War Office may have been elevated when the MID asked for a physiologist, but Hill's background was unusual. He had started brilliantly at Trinity in mathematics but questioned whether it was the right choice. His tutor was a physiologist, Walter Morley Fletcher (later head of the MRC).[16] They became friendly while running together, so Hill was open about his uncertainties. Fletcher and Frederick Gowland Hopkins[17] were working on chemical changes in isolated, contracting frog muscle. They found that lactic acid accumulates in the contracting muscle and then—if oxygen is available—disappears during rest. They thought that lactic acid might trigger contraction. Hill left maths and prepared for the Natural Science Tripos in 1907, studying chemistry, physics and physiology. Two years later, he was awarded a George Henry Lewes studentship, established by the novelist George Eliot to commemorate her polymath extramarital companion; they had been leaders in the campaign to establish physiology in Cambridge. When Hill started work in the physiology department, their quarters were modest and dingy, but were illuminated by the most accomplished band of physiologists that ever graced a department.[18]

After some initial investigations that will be described later, the professor, John N. Langley, suggested that Hill take advantage of his math to investigate frog muscle as a thermodynamic machine.[19] Langley supplied a thermocouple and a mirror galvanometer, left behind by a Swedish visitor.[20] Junctions between wires of two different metals generate an electrical potential proportional to its temperature. Hill usually used a junction—or 'couple'—between constantan (a copper-nickel alloy) and silver.

Hill set up the delicate apparatus in the cellar of the physiology laboratory, alongside the cages for the rats Gowland Hopkins was using to discover vitamins. Hill experimented on a thin muscle, the sartorius, from the inner surface of the leg. It gives a single short twitch in response to an electrical shock, or a sustained contracture in response to a rapid burst of shocks. In 1910 Hill was elected a Research Fellow of Trinity for a set term. He published his first thermal paper, which showed that even a single twitch of a frog muscle produces heat. It was an impressive technical feat: the temperature rose only 0.003 degree C. Hill improved his measurements by using five thermocouples rather than one, and by working at low temperature. He and his sister also measured heat production by intact animals.

On a trip to German laboratories he saw several student duels, concluding:

> They seemed to me a grotesque and tragic mixture of stupidity and brutality; a great people who could allow, or encourage, their children to go on like that were not safe neighbours.[21]

Hill and Darwin desperately needed more clever hands and minds. Conscription made it difficult; there were only lads or elders. Hill sounded out the eminent Cambridge mathematician G. H. Hardy, hoping he might volunteer.

> He was always an odd fish and I remember him expressing great indignation and saying that although he was ready to go off and have his body shot at he was not prepared to prostitute his brains for purposes of war.[22]

Hardy did suggest Arthur Milne, a student from Hull who had made the highest mark ever on the scholarship exam:

> Apparently he was ready to have Milne's Brains prostituted.

Milne was a slight, pale, 20-year-old mathematics student on a scholarship worth £80 yearly.[23] He had tried to enlist, but was rejected because of his abysmal eyesight; his thick glasses gave him a pop-eyed, slightly bewildered expression. He listened quietly to Hill. He started his reply hesitatingly, in low tones, but as he warmed up, flashes of brainpower, keenness, and quick grasp convinced Hill that he was a find. Milne was put on the MID payroll at 25s per week.

A contemporary of Hill's, Ralph Howard Fowler, was back in Cambridge. A fellow Wrangler, he was recovering from a nasty shoulder wound received on Gallipoli.[24] Fowler had been commissioned in the Royal Marine Artillery at the outbreak of the war, possibly winning such a coveted preferment for his celebrated prowess on cricket pitch and golf links. Now he was a first lieutenant. He was delighted to do something useful while waiting to be declared fit.

The finished mirrors were two feet square and ruled in both directions with a one centimetre grid, mounted on a table that could level them precisely. They were tested on a radio wireless mast in Cambridge whose height was also measured with a theodolite and chain. The two estimates agreed nicely. Then Hill, Fowler, and Milne went to Northolt Aerodrome for more demanding tests. Hill's transfer was approved and he went on the MID payroll. His military servant, Freeman, a former plumber, was also transferred.

The MID acquired two miles of telephone wire, which was in short supply, partly used but 'in good order' and constructed two huts to shelter the mirrors in nasty weather. The wire was threaded along a hedge on the airfield's boundary. The first test with an aeroplane was done less than a month after the Darwin–Hill meeting, with the mirrors separated by 4,000 feet. The height of the first aeroplane they followed was unknown; they marked points at intervals of three to five seconds. Their results were 1,810 feet, 1,800, 1,820, 1,845, ... 1,905, 1,935—obviously the aeroplane was climbing. The next flight was put on for them: the pilot was instructed to fly at constant altitude and to measure height with his aneroid barometer. On the first run, the determinations were 3,840 feet, 3,820, and 3,800. The altitude measured by the flyer was 4,000 feet. After the measurements Hill teased Fowler about lavish use of physical strength, claiming that he repeatedly heard on the telephone line from the second mirror, 'I have broke my pen'.[25] It was a great first step, as Hill often said: 'A thing never becomes so real as when one measures it ...'.

Colonel Goold-Adams, the eminent engineer Sir Alexander Kennedy, and Mr Bolton of the MID came to see the mirrors on Thursday 10 March. The base was lengthened to 6,650 feet. The results were excellent, and Hill enthusiastically reeled off a list of what the team could do:

> training AA crews, speed tests and measuring wind velocity, checking aneroid readings, used in field to observe target and burst and hence used for spotting.

You may wonder why they did not use conventional optical rangefinders. They were loaned a standard Barr & Stroud instrument, modified so that it could be tilted to point at aerial targets. A skilled operator who was able to keep focused on a rapidly moving aeroplane obtained good results, but few were available, it had taken many months to train additional instrument makers and lens grinders to increase production. For the time being AA must find simpler options.

Hill next wrote to William Hartree (Eighteenth Wrangler, 1892) in Guildford, asking him to come, 'on ridiculously short notice', to Northolt Aerodrome the following day. Suggested by his brother-in-law, the director of the NPL, Hartree was a 45-year-old engineer, with ample income from a family marine engineering business. He had given up lecturing at Cambridge to experiment with wireless transmission. Hartree could not come on the designated day because he was a war worker, testing local telephone lines for the Post Office. Several letters went back and forth until he was released by the Post Office and came to Northolt by train the next day with his bicycle, so he could search for local accommodation. Hill was not impressed when he first saw this 'shabby, middle-aged linesman'.

Then Hill had gratifying news: he had been elected as a fellow at King's College, Cambridge. His academic future was secure. After he dined with his new colleagues he received a letter from a distinguished, 58-year-old Kings' mathematician, William Herbert Richmond FRS (Third Wrangler 1885), who volunteered.[26] Richmond worked on algebraic geometry and also was a musician and naturalist. Perhaps his greatest attribute was: 'his genius for friendships with men of all academic generations'. He spiced life with good humour.

Another older recruit was Geoffrey Thomas Bennett FRS, 47-years- old.[27] He was Senior Wrangler in 1890. (In fact, Miss Fawcett had outdone him but women had no standing in the competition). Now he was a fellow of Emmanuel College, Cambridge. His competitive personality is reflected by his rankings the three times he pedalled in the University Bicycle Club 50 mile race: third, second, and first. By 1915, he sported an elegant, greying beard, barbered in the style of King George V, shaped much like Horace Darwin's darker version. Bennett was an accomplished pianist—he would improvise by the hour. (He later transferred to the gyrocompass division of the Admiralty, where they needed his mastery of dynamics.)

Height finders

When Horace Darwin had asked Bennett for ideas, the answer was that they needed a simple way to measure a target's height.[28] An aeroplane's range changes constantly, but usually it keeps at the same elevation. Bennett determined height with a simple two-station method. The stations are separated by a substantial distance. The angle to the target is measured by each operator, using a rectangular panel the size of a small table. The panel is elevated so that its lower edge is convenient for the operator's eye; it is rotated to face the target and tilted so that the panel's face lines up with the target. The angles of the two panels and the distance between them give the height of the target. Once the target's height is known its range from an AA gun can be calculated from the elevation angle of the barrel. They tested the height finder with the mirrors. It did well, but the panels were heavy, cumbersome and difficult to move about.

William Hartree suggested replacing the panels with a pair of cables mounted on poles at right angles to one another, one cable strung several feet above the other. Each observer obtains the angle by sliding a simple sight along the lower cable until the target is in line with the sight and the upper cable. Hill purloined a few old gas pipes, added some wire and tape, and they assembled a prototype. It worked. Their second instrument was made honestly at a cost of 2s 6d. The gunners were delighted with the easily used height finder. [29]

William was visited by his 19-year-old son, Douglas Rayner Hartree, who had just begun mathematics at St John's College, Cambridge. Hill asked him to join. He was a quiet, self-effacing youth with bright intelligence and interests in railways and music. All of his family were musical; he was an amateur conductor and percussionist. Some of his co-workers referred to him as Hartree II.[30] The little troop was based at the NPL. Later, Hartree's second son, Colin, was transferred from the RA: Hartree III.

The mirrors, placed a mile apart, were used to determine the path taken by bombs released from aircraft. The aviator fired a Very pistol when he released his bomb, and its position at set intervals was marked on the two mirrors. They worked far better than the camera obscura (which workers on bombsights nonetheless continued to use). Hill wanted to locate aerial shrapnel bursts, but ammunition was so scarce that there were few test firings.

Smoke and mirrors

Horace Darwin learned that Commander 'Barmy' Gilbert of the Royal Navy had devised a new AA gun sight; a prototype was mounted on a 6-inch gun on a monitor stationed at Great Yarmouth. Monitors were shallow-draft craft mounting very large guns, designed to provide firepower for amphibious landings along the shallow Baltic coast, one of the favourite pipe dreams in the pre-war Admiralty. (Some saw action on D-Day 1944.) The gun was scheduled to fire a series of shots with different time fuse settings. Darwin arranged for Hill's group to be there. They set up the mirrors. On their first day four shots were fired, they located the smoke from three explosions but the fourth was lost in the clouds because the weather was turning foul. Over the next days the clouds occasionally parted and they had 20 more chances. Finally, there was a gloriously clear day, perfect except that it was the Sabbath which the monitor's captain refused to violate with gunfire. The rains came again. To pass the time William Hartree wrote a poem about AA gunnery, Hill responded with a poem in the style of W. Hartree. It was three weeks before the tests were completed.

Now they had measurements of where shells fired with different fuse settings exploded. Those fired with the barrel at the same angle—known to the gunners as the quadrant elevation—marked points along the shell's trajectory. The mirrors had supplied a set of data almost unique in the history of ballistics. One of Hill's precepts was that: 'The secret of science is to ask the right question ...'.[31] He realized that if they could fit the points with equations describing the path taken by the fired shell, the change in its path produced by gravity and wind, and its slowing by the air resistance—which varies with velocity, altitude and temperature—they could calculate accurate range tables for AA guns and know where the shrapnel would burst.

Hill had made his scientific mark by fitting equations to data. His first publication was 'The mode of action of nicotine and curare', a topic suggested by Langley.[32] They studied an atypical muscle, the rectus abdominis of the frog, a thin muscle covering the belly. An isolated rectus gives a sustained contraction when the solution it is bathed in contains nicotine. The shortening increases as the nicotine concentration increases until it reaches a maximum. He fit the points relating nicotine concentration to shortening with an equation based on Langley's hypothesis that the drug acts by reversibly binding to a receptor—then a novel idea. The extent of the contraction depends on the amount of drug-receptor complex formed and reaches a maximum when all receptor is occupied. Charles Galton Darwin (Horace's nephew), a friend and contemporary at Trinity, helped with the fitting. Low concentrations of the arrow poison curare reduce the efficacy of nicotine. Hill fit this data by assuming that curare binds to the receptor without eliciting contraction, thereby reducing the number of binding sites for nicotine. You can imagine how impressed his fellow physiologists, who then rarely used mathematics, were by the 'Hill equation'. (Subsequently others did similar mathematical modelling on the interactions of substrates with enzymes, the blocking of sites by enzyme inhibitors, and on the absorption of molecules onto binding sites.) As Galileo taught: 'Mathematics is the language of nature'.

His next two papers fit curves to data obtained by Joseph Barcroft on the disassociation of oxygen from haemoglobin. These papers:

> ... are alight with new and sometimes brilliant ideas, and already show signs of A.V.'s main contribution to physiological science, the introduction of physical-chemical concepts and the emphasis on quantitative, numerical treatment that became the distinguishing features of his particular brand of physiology, usually called 'biophysics'.[33]

HMS *Excellent*

After the Yarmouth trials Hill was sent to Portsmouth to show their data to a Royal Navy ordnance expert, who invited him to dinner. Another guest was the experimental officer at HMS *Excellent*, the Royal Navy Gunnery School in Portsmouth harbour. He appreciated the value of Hill's trajectory points, agreed that more data was needed and suggested that they come to *Excellent* where they fired most days despite the ammunition shortage. A chance meeting at an unanticipated dinner opened the door to AA ballistics.

Excellent is on Whale Island and is entered over a bridge. The School started aboard ship but when the short-range broadside became obsolete, she moved onto the island. Ship's captain was Commander Vincent Lewin Bowering, a merry companion who claimed that he detested the roar of gunfire because it inhibited the growth of his flowers and vegetables. According to Hill, Bowering's duties were:

> To look after pigs, fowls, old horse and dogs, grow oats and vegetables, produce chickens and eggs, look after the welfare of some 2,000 officers and men, and several gardens; and weekly inspect some 65 women W.R.N.S. to see that their clothes were properly worn.[34]

Without waiting for approval from his superiors, on the first clear day after the mirrors were surveyed into position Bowering had a 3-inch gun on an experimental mounting fire smoke shell with varying fuse settings. As Hill put it: '... it was my luck my party was standing about in the neighbourhood during this trial—with their instruments'.[35] One mirror was on the beach at Eastney, just east of Portsmouth, and the second was on Hayling Island. The connecting telephone wire ran under the inlet separating them.

Bowering provided living quarters, a large office up under the eaves, and meals in the officers' mess. Naturally, their messmates speculated about this incongruous working party: an army and a marine officer plus boys and elderly civilians. Some inspired wag—most probably Bowering—decided that they were best categorized as a band of brigands. Henceforth, they were 'Hill's Brigands'.

Initially seven Brigands were stationed at *Excellent*, not counting Hill who was often away seeing to other units, which will be introduced later, or at meetings in London or France. Fowler led the Portsmouth group. His credentials were admirable: exuberant good humour, infectious laugh, sporting fame and frame, and a wound stripe—scarcely the stereotypical reclusive scientist. He was soon gone. Despite MID pleas, the Navy yanked him away to serve as an inspector of steel at a shipyard. Horace Darwin went straight to the top: writing to First Lord Arthur Balfour, a contemporary at Trinity. It worked:

> Fowler turned up for duty with my gang in two or three days.[36]

Now they had to fit their data points with the equations. It was far more difficult than oxygen binding to haemoglobin. Many eminent mathematicians had tried to simplify trajectory calculations. No single equation gives a projectile's position and velocity at a time after firing. The Italian Francisco Siacci devised a set of approximate equations that after a lengthy chain of calculations give points on the trajectory.[37] There are a number of modifications of his method, but all are only useful for quadrant elevations less than 20 degrees. This is a minor restriction when firing at ground targets where the crucial questions are how far the projectile travels and how long that takes.

The alternative to Siacci was to solve the equations by the arduous 'small arc method'. The shell's angle, velocity, the resistance of the atmosphere, its x and y coordinates, and time of flight time are calculated one after the other at short steps.

If wind is considered a z-coordinate is added. A skilled computer needed many tedious days to calculate a single trajectory. (Now, it all can be done with a PC in a second.)

Hill learned that some AA trajectories had been plotted at the Ballistics Office by a novel method devised by Lieutenant J. E. Littlewood (Bracketed Senior Wrangler, 1905), so he was asked for advice.[38] Hill and Darwin knew Littlewood from Trinity, where he was elected a fellow in 1910 when he was 25-years-old, and every Brigand knew him by reputation. He had been on active duty in the RGA, stationed at a large camp where he trained gun crews and enjoyed almost daily horseback rides. Off duty he worked on mathematics—in 1915 he and his co-worker G. H. Hardy published three papers and from 1914 to 1918 Littlewood published twelve, eleven with Hardy as a co-author. Distance did not hamper their collaboration; even when both were in Cambridge they exchanged ideas in letters conveyed by college servants.

One night in the autumn of 1915 Littlewood was orderly officer, idling away his watch in the early hours of the morning.[39] On an office table, he saw a diagram of a trajectory fired at a high quadrant elevation. Someone had been thinking about AA gunnery. A point was marked at the maximum height. He gave it a quick thought. A few days later, his colonel saw the diagram and asked Littlewood whether the maximum height could be calculated. Littlewood showed him that this was easily done for the sketch in which rise and fall were mirror images because air resistance had been neglected. The colonel was impressed.

The exchange started Littlewood thinking about how to calculate AA trajectories less painfully than with small arcs. He devised an indirect method, first calculating by small arcs the time-height points for vertical (90 degree) fire, estimating the change in air resistance as it rose into lighter air. This could be done relatively quickly because the shell was going straight up and coming straight down. The time-height-distance points for horizontal (0 degree) fire were obtained from the Siacci equations. Then he created an interpolation to calculate the trajectory at any desired quadrant elevation between the two extremes. There were still many tedious steps, but fewer than with small arcs. His colonel arranged for him to show his method to Captain Douglas, a regular army officer at the Ballistics Office who was responsible for range tables. Littlewood was seconded to the Ordnance Committee at Woolwich. This brought about a most agreeable change in living arrangements: he was permitted to lodge with friends in London and no comment was made when he appeared in uniform carrying his umbrella. Littlewood's method did not impress Hardy: 'Even Littlewood could not make ballistics respectable'.[40] The rub was that there was no data to test how well his calculated trajectories matched reality.

Fitting trajectories to shell bursts

The Brigands used Littlewood's method to try to fit trajectories to their measurements of shell bursts. Ordinary 10-inch slide rules were too inaccurate, so they used calculating machines and circular Fuller slide rules, which had an effective length of 50 feet, so accuracy was 1/10,000.[41] They began by assuming values for shell resistance, the effect of velocity on resistance and the like. If they saw they were not going to fit the points, they guessed at better parameters and started over again— tedious is an understatement. The relation between velocity (v) and resistance was problematical. Some thought it proportional to v^2, some preferred v^3, while others varied the power at different parts of the trajectory.[42] Using v^2 fitted their points poorly. Using v^3 was excellent, but then the resistance they calculated was in senseless units. Even Hill just shook his head. Milne was a quiet lad who kept silent until he had an idea, which then spilled out excitedly. He suggested that the third v must be a ratio to another velocity, so units would cancel out properly, and suggested cubing the ratio of v to the speed of sound. It worked. It is a measure of lack of effective interchange that the French used v^2 throughout the war.[43]

Sometimes Fowler was a bit much, as Milne wrote to his mother:

> Fowler comes fussing around, ordering everybody about without considering whether it is the best thing they can do. He always means astonishingly well, but I think he would get rather a shock if he knew how he annoys us sometimes.

Hill restored good feelings on his next visit. The tiffs should not obscure the intellectual pleasures Fowler provided. As Milne later wrote:

> It was always tremendous 'fun' collaborating with Fowler. Usually it was not he (to be quite just) who produced the first original idea; but he tossed it back with lightning speed; and you had to be very agile to field it properly. There was a thrill about the investigation—it was as though one were physically in love with a particular problem, when Fowler was present. [44]

At war's end Fowler commanded 15 Brigands on *Excellent*: eight officers and seven civilians. He enhanced their welcome in the officers' mess by obtaining fine vintage ports from the cellars of Cambridge colleges, for example, an 1887 at a thrifty *2s 6d* a bottle.[45]

Richmond was the oldest Brigand but was always willing to bike to the mirrors to help with the measurements—a nasty chore on nasty days. As Milne wrote to his younger brother Geoff:

> ... coldish job standing in a half-gale of wind without a hat with a telephone headpiece on, to say nothing of being strafed at intervals by each of the other three observers at other places on the line. Be content that you know so little of the fiendish trouble of a telephone-observer.

Richmond also took his share in the prolonged, tedious calculations to fit each successful data set. Despite his shyness, he fitted in easily. He and Milne, one of the youngest, were roommates.

By mid-November, they had located bursts from 150 rounds of smoke shell fired from a 4-inch gun at different quadrant elevations and had begun a series of 600 rounds from a 3-inch gun. They used three mirrors, half, two-and-a-half, and five miles from the gun, but were frustrated by the plethora of overcast days on the English south coast. The 3-inch 20-cwt gun was the backbone of the British AA and was so good that it was used in the Second World War. It fired a 16 lb shell with a muzzle velocity of 2,500 feet per sec, which could send a shell up to 11,000 yards—well above the ceiling of aeroplanes of that time. The shrapnel canister had to explode within 36 yards to damage an aeroplane, so good shooting was a must.[46]

William Hartree (Hartree I) was an invaluable member of the team because: 'Nobody could see shell-bursts so nearly into the sun ...'.[47] Hartree II, who displayed what others regarded as a perverse pleasure in tedious numerical computations, kept devising tricks to make the computations easier.[48] Traditionally numerical ballistic calculations had been done starting with changes in the angle of the flying shell; Hartree II showed them it was easier if they worked with small time steps.[49] Throughout his life, his face would go beet red when he offered up an idea. In later life he often travelled back and forth to London on the train, invariably taking a numerical problem to work on *en route*. Once he apologized to the colleague whose problem he was solving; there were no free seats so he calculated while standing and progress was slow because often his elbow was jogged.

The MID work on height finders was first done at Farnborough, Hampshire, by an army lieutenant and fifteen 'light-duty' men. Later, they moved to Rochford, Essex. In May 1916, twenty Hartree instruments were sent to the army in France. Subsequent models were improved with supports to keep the cables from sagging. German dirigibles travelled 60 mph or faster, so in the time a shell might take to reach their altitude the target might move 320 yards. To speed up the calculations the Hartrees placed a second scale on the lower wire. When the angle was telephoned from the apparatus at the other end of the base line, the operator set this value on the second scale and then read off the height of the target directly. As the AA gunners acquired optical range finders, height finders lost importance; by the end of the war only one officer and one man were working at Rochford.

The MID began to liaise with the French in May 1916. The British representative in Paris, Captain Sir Henry Norman Bt, MP,[50] was provided with an office in the *Direction des Inventions, des Etudes, et des Experiences Techniques*. His reports were mostly about patents French inventors wanted to sell.[51] The *Directions* representative in London, the Marquis de Chasseloup-Laubat, was not given an office in the BIR. He was supplied with the BIR monthly reports and his reports home must have been informative. (They included all of the Brigand's range tables.)

Fowler's younger brother was killed on the Somme in July 1916.

In October, the Brigands had a demonstration of a French device, the Brocq electro-magnetic predicting apparatus. (The imaginative Francois Brocq was a director of the *Compagnie Pour La Fabrication Des Compteurs Et Materiel D'usines A Gaz*.) The British had requisitioned six of them. It had eyepieces for two observers; each kept the target fixed in his telescope's crosshairs, one following in the x-coordinate and the other in the y-coordinate. A simple electrical circuit used the rate at which they turned their knobs to compute target velocity. Target height and fuse timing were dialled into the apparatus, the reading was corrected for wind velocity, and the results were passed along to men standing beside the gun, who adjusted the pointer's sights to make the needed corrections for anticipating the movement of the target between the moment of firing and the arrival of the shell. The apparatus evolved over time. In the next model, the corrections were output directly to dials viewed by the pointers. Still later, the Brocq instrument adjusted the gun sights directly by electro-mechanical coupling. The Germans used a similar apparatus.[52]

Hill persuaded the MM that AA guns should fire heavier shells, containing more shrapnel bullets, even though extra weight decreased the muzzle velocity. (For instance, a 3-inch 20-cwt gun with 12.5 lb shell had a muzzle velocity of 2,500 feet per sec. A 16 lb shell reduced the muzzle velocity to 2,100 feet per sec.) Lower muzzle velocity was advantageous, because the higher the velocity the faster the rifling in the gun barrel erodes and wear was a serious problem with guns firing 30 rounds per minute. The MID also placed all 3-inch guns in Britain into a single pool, whether manned by Army or Navy, so guns were rotated between very active and less active batteries to even out wear.

Young Brigands were called-up for military service. Hill reported that:

> Mr E. A. Milne is still lacking an exemption certificate, it would be disaster to the present work if Mr. Milne were taken away & put in the Army as a Private Soldier to do garrison work. The best resolution would be to give Hartree and Milne temporary commissions.

While his proposal worked its way through the bureaucracy, jolly Capt. Bowering claimed that he ordered *Excellent's* watch to arrest any recruiting sergeant who dared set foot on the bridge to the island.

While they waited for a scheduled aeroplane to appear or for a gun to fire, they measured the speed and heights of clouds. Their velocity startled them. To make sure that their values were not ridiculous Hill wrote to meteorologists and other Brigands called on them. Fowler and Milne visited a venerable, distinguished expert, W. H. Dines. Milne was impressed by him, '… a cadaverous, bearded, ancient man, every whit the savant.' Fowler loved to recount how early in the visit the study door swung open and a large dog strolled into the room. Dines introduced a member of the forecast division of the Meteorological Office. Astonished Fowler thought he meant the dog. In fact, Dines' son was obscured behind the opened door. The officers' mess at Whale Island was frequently regaled with this adventure and the narration always concluded with peals of Fowler's exuberant laughter.[53]

Hill purchased balloons manufactured to display advertising slogans and they followed them as they rose to the heights while buffeted by the winds, a procedure that became routine for gunners. Wind forces and directions vary with altitude.

They could account for the deviations in a shell's path by the force and direction of the winds it encountered along its way, but such calculations were too complicated to be useful for gunners. Richmond and Milne devised an elegant integral giving an 'equivalent constant wind': a single number that gunners used to correct for wind velocity and direction.

Hill travelled between MID meetings in London and experimental stations and AA batteries in England and France. Some nights were spent at home in Cambridge—his three younger children were fathered during the war. He came up with most of the ideas that the Brigands followed up. His self-control helped keep his men on even keel. He also touched their feelings. He was 'slightly humorous about the Germans.'[54] One might marvel at their misbegotten ideas, but hate was not helpful. Hill's self-control crumbled only when he found something truly funny—tears would stream down his cheeks.[55]

The aerial assault on Britain

During 1916, the Germans dropped 116 tons of bombs on Britain, thinking that at best terrorized citizens would demand peace; at least British interceptor aircraft and AA guns would be kept at home.[56] Total casualties in Britain for the year were 293 killed and 651 wounded, some by shrapnel balls and fragments of AA shells that pelted down during the actions. On 2 September, sixteen dirigibles attacked London. One was shot down by a British night fighter using incendiary machine gun bullets invented by Richard Threlfall. The bullet won Threlfall a knighthood. It was Gwendoline Bragg who stopped him from 'appearing at Buckingham Palace for the ceremony in a soft trilby hat, tweed coat and brown shoes!'[57]

On 19 October, the mirrors at Portsmouth showed the highest clouds were scudding across the sky at 150 mph. Hill assured Fowler, 'There won't be an air raid tonight'. Assuming that the Germans must measure wind velocity at high altitudes before authorizing an attack, he gave them too much credit. Eleven navy Zeppelins attacked. Pummelled by the brutal wind, four were lost at sea or destroyed in the south of France.

In the last three months of 1916, the Germans lost six dirigibles in attacks on England, five to AA fire or to machine gun bullets from interceptors.[58] The German army turned over their surviving airships to the navy. The post-war German evaluation was that these assaults: 'yielded practically no results and entailed heavy loss of airships'.[59]

In October, the new German commander, Hindenburg, formed a *Luftstreitkräfte* (Air Force), commanded by cavalry General Ernst von Hoeppner, responsible for both air attack and defence, including AA guns. They started the war with an 88 mm high elevation gun, developed by the navy, and 77 mm anti-balloon guns mounted on lorries. They began work on the special problems of AA gunnery in late 1915, focusing on:

measuring apparatus for determining the range, flying speed, direction and altitude of flight and special devices for facilitating range conversion.[60]

The Brigands completed a 'trajectory time & fuse chart (Graphical Range Table) for fuse 65A fired from a 3-inch 20-cwt gun for up to 30 seconds time of flight'. The graph showed trajectories marked with points where the shell would explode with fuses set for different time delays. Many more tables were needed: one for each type of gun, shell, and fuse and at a number of quadrant elevations. They needed help. Hill wrote to friends who might recommend talented youngsters too young for conscription. Professor Karl Pearson FRS had a son, but he was not available. Pearson volunteered himself and his group, the National Eugenics Laboratory at UCL, so Hill reported in December:

> An offer of assistance in Computation has been made to me ... he has 8 efficient computers & suitable calculating machines, which he has very kindly offered to utilize for our work.[61]

Pearson (Third Wrangler, 1879), 59-years-old, was a remarkable polymath with an arresting personality.[62] He took a mathematics degree, then studied literature in Germany for two years before being called to the bar in the Inner Temple. He practiced law and deputized as a professor of mathematics at UCL before becoming a full time academic. He was cut off from his scientific peers because he was too hot-tempered to attend scientific meetings; if he went there were nasty shouting matches. He was deeply interested in social problems: he changed the spelling of his forename from Carl after meeting Karl Marx. Concerned about the role of women in society, he began to work on problems in evolutionary biology. This led to collaboration with Charles Darwin's half-cousin, Francis Galton FRS.

The Galton Laboratory

Galton was another polymath.[63] He had not sat the mathematical tripos because of illness but was projected to do well. He made the first weather map, pioneered regression methods in statistics, devised a system to classify fingerprints, studied identical twins, and invented the field of eugenics. He feared that human society interfered with natural selection and therefore the unsuitable would be flourishing at the expense of the fit. Pearson became Galton's protégé and made numerous, lasting advances in statistics, for example the Chi Square test. When Galton died, leaving an estate of £104,487 5s 1p he endowed a Chair in Eugenics at UCL with the provision that Pearson should be its first incumbent. Included in the bequest were funds for a eugenics laboratory, which later was named after Galton. (For years the president of the Eugenics Society was Leonard Darwin, who had retired from the Royal Engineers to become an MP.)

Hill sent Milne to UCL, he 'had a sort of photographic mind and could repeat pages he had read or speeches he had heard'—he had the wits to meet Pearson head-on.[64] Nonetheless, soon there was a squabble. Milne provided them with a flow sheet for the modified Littlewood method and they started calculating range tables for the 3-inch gun. On 25 January, Pearson was agonized by a discrepancy between formulae written in two different instruction sets from Littlewood. Littlewood responded that it was only a slight modification. At $x=22,568.3$ feet the first estimate of y was $14,485.9$ feet and the second was $14,489.4$, but that the second method was better because it gave a more accurate figure for the time of flight. Pearson was appalled at such sloppiness but was induced to carry on regardless.

When the graphical range tables for the 3-inch gun were submitted, Comptroller Goold-Adams wrote to thank Pearson and to tell him that tables were needed for other guns. Pearson agreed to do the computations for the 4-inch Mark V gun, with a muzzle velocity of 2,550 feet per sec for quadrant elevations at 5 degree steps.

Hill and Pearson soon arrived at agreeable intimacy in their correspondence; it was no longer 'Dear Professor Pearson' and 'Dear Captain Hill' but simply 'Dear Pearson' and 'Dear Hill', exchanging mutual expressions of satisfaction on such intimacy. Hill had to apologize for slowness in responding to Pearson's needs:

> But everything we do is held up & every kind of obstacle is continually put in the way by the Comptroller. Perhaps that is too much to say, as sometimes he is very good & ready to help. But he suffers from timidity, & has no imagination to see the possibilities of things. … It is about time he should be promoted.

Later Hill expanded on this theme:

> Nature is easy to investigate being merely inanimate and reluctant: but to persuade military officers of high standing to unlearn their prejudices & to give one—especially if one is a junior officer—the credit for knowing one's job, is infinitely harder & requires tact and patience beyond understanding.

He was still duelling with his superiors about measuring height rather than range.

The next eruption was when Pearson saw that the tables printed by the MID were initialled 'K. P.', rather than the 'G. L.' (Galton Laboratory) specified—his colleagues had been dismissively snubbed. Hill apologized abjectly.

Hill arranged for three male and three female computers at the Galton to be paid three month's salary by the MID to work during the long vacation, based on their salaries of £100 to £150 annually. In July, they appealed to the readers of *Nature* for the loan of calculating machines. They were only offered a 'Millionaire' calculating machine, which was limited to six figures, and a small American machine that multiplied but could not divide.

Unexpectedly the next crisis was triggered by the affable Richmond. While Fowler was away in October, Richmond wrote to Pearson. The Brigands always took

Pearson's list of numbers for the coordinates and subtracted the preceding number from each, giving the '1st differences'. From them they obtained the 2nd, 3rd, and 4th. If the differences did not follow one another smoothly, there was an error, often because a number had been garbled. Richmond found that in the latest table the differences became highly irregular after 37 s. There had been a mistake. Pearson hit the roof. His honour and that of his laboratory had been assailed. He was finished with their sloppy operation. Richmond grovelled:

> Last January Milne told you everything we knew of Littlewood's method and small arcs. ... I ask you to believe that when Milne went to you, it was plainly understood by us how much we were asking of you, in wishing you to accept dogmatic rules without explanations or reasons ... . There is no ground for your statement that I have brought a general charge against the laboratory ...

(The discrepancy came about because some of the values sent to Whale Island had been read from a graph rather than from the table of figures used to plot the graph.)

Hill was unable to appease Pearson. Finally Colonel Goold-Adams called; he was persuasive; the computations continued and the MID bought them several new calculating machines.

Milne and Douglas Hartree finally were commissioned as lieutenants in the wavy navy (RNVR), pleased with their 'pair of curly gold bands, surmounted by a loop' on their sleeves. The down side was that their pay dropped by £30 annually.

Locating aeroplanes by sound

Work on devices to locate aircraft by sound had begun before Hill appeared on the scene, but he took over and the researchers became Brigands. Their starting point was that humans can localize the azimuth of a sound source quite accurately, working primarily from the difference between the arrival times of sound waves at each ear. We are less successful in estimating the elevation of a sound; we try to do so by cocking our heads up and down. For aeroplane localization they listened through a wooden trumpet, connected to the listener's ear by a rubber tube and an earplug, like the physician uses with a stethoscope. The trumpets amplified sound intensity seven to tenfold. Localization is best using two trumpets five feet apart. The trumpets did not improve height estimates. Cleverly, they added a second pair of horns mounted on a vertical axis directing sound to a second listener. Each listener adjusted his horns so that the sound seemed to be directly ahead, and the azimuth and height were read from dials.[65]

Field tests of the apparatus started at Farnborough in February 1917, in April they moved this work to Rochford and by October were testing in France. They were accurate to 0.5 degree. Hill realized that greater precision would not pay off because:

Airplanes are moving at half of the speed of sound and air is never a clear medium, ... hearing through the open air is more like seeing through a pane of ribbed glass; the inequalities of the density of the air bend the rays of sound out of their straight path.[66]

Fuse burning times

The Brigands observed that shells on high trajectories often burst later than expected and sometimes even failed to explode. They concluded that: 'much of the "bad-shooting" by AA guns was really due to unanticipated variations in the fuse burning times'. They set out to gather the data needed to write an equation describing how altitude alters burning time.

Fuses are screwed into the front of a shell. The time fuse was an arc machined into the fuse's steel that was filled with gunpowder. When the shell is fired, acceleration drives a firing pin onto a cap, which ignites the gunpowder at the beginning of the arc. The gases generated by the burning powder leave the arc via a narrow passageway to the outside: the fuse hole. The powder burns its way along the arc until it reaches a channel leading to the shell's magazine, which then detonates. A gunner set the fuse time by using a spanner called a fuse key to rotate the gunpowder-filled arc to alter its position to the channel leading to the magazine.

An obvious hypothesis is that the cold at high altitude slows the rate of powder burning. The NPL had a low temperature room and a pressure chamber. The three Brigands stationed there found that burning was not markedly slowed by the cold. However, fuses burn slower when the barometric pressure is decreased. The situation is more complicated for a flying shell, because the pressure in the fuse hole depends both on the external air pressure and on the shell's velocity—the higher the velocity the higher the pressure. It also depends on the position of the fuse hole, which differs in different models. As the data came in, the Brigands gave up on a unified theory and satisfied the need by measuring detonation times for each model of fuse fired with different time settings at different quadrant elevations.

They stumbled across a further complication. Fuses burn more slowly when the shells are fired at a higher muzzle velocity. Due to the rifling of the barrel, higher muzzle velocity increases the rate the shell spins when it leaves the muzzle. The air does not resist spin very much, so shells spin throughout flight. Hill requisitioned two custom-built 3-inch guns with altered rifling. One had more twist than usual. Shells fired from it at high quadrant elevations did not explode. Some of the shells fired from a gun with usual twist also failed. All those fired from a gun with decreased twist exploded. The trajectory was almost unaltered by the changes in spin. Henceforth the rifling in the 3-inch gun was altered to lower spinning rates.

Further work on the effects of spin on the burning of the gunpowder were done the laboratory of Professor Goudie at UCL, with a turbine that could spin fuses at speeds up to 30,000 rpm. The rate of fuse burning decreases as the rate of spinning increases, due to centrifugal effects on the burning slag. Three Brigands were in the UCL laboratory.

They needed to know air temperatures and pressures at high altitudes. Selected brigands bicycled over to the aerodrome at nearby Gosport to hitch rides on aeroplanes flown up to their maximum elevation. Fowler had the first flight, but according to Hill, Milne '… had a great capacity to induce the pilots of the Royal Flying Corps (as it then was) to fly where we wanted and to do what was needed.'[67] Hence he was a frequent flyer even though with his poor eyesight he could scarcely read the thermometer dangling from the aeroplane's upper wing, 'I never had quite enough definition to be sure of my readings'. He loved flying up to 13,500 or 14,000 feet, despite the bitter cold, and wrote enthusiastic descriptions to Brother Geoff, asking him to 'keep it squat' [secret] so as not to worry their parents.

On the way down the pilots often entertained their passenger by stunting. Milne looked like he might be easily terrified, but relished everything they threw at him. Once, the pilot deliberately threw his craft into a spin, hurtling straight toward the earth. There is a lovely fable, resounding to the credit of science, which claims that a few weeks earlier they would have been dead men, because no one knew how to get out of a spin. Frederick Lindemann (FRS 1920) had solved the problem.[68] An Englishman, he had a doctorate from Berlin, working under Nernst. Now he was at the Royal Aircraft Factory at Farnborough. He developed a mathematical description of aeroplane spin, which showed how to stop it. Then he learned to fly and personally proved his theory. Lindemann did work out the physics of the spin and did learn to fly and to spin, but the manoeuvre to regain control had been discovered earlier by a clever and lucky flight instructor.

Once they had the data, the Brigands prepared tables that enabled the gunners to adjust fuse timing according to the barometric pressure on the ground. Showing how to set fuses properly was probably the Brigand's major contribution.

German heavy bombers

The AA gunners faced a new challenge when the *Luftstreitkräfte* struck at England in 1917 with large, long-range bombing planes. They started with two-engine 'G-planes', customarily known as Gothas, after one of their manufacturers. They also were building four-engine giant bombers or 'R-planes'.

The Gothas began bombing in daylight for maximum psychological effect, targeting Government buildings in Whitehall and newspaper headquarters on Fleet Street.[69] They flew to London at 16,000 feet with their crews breathing oxygen. They bombed from lower altitudes. Top speed was 80 mph but in a strong headwind they were lucky to reach 50 mph—it was a long trip.

On 25 May, 23 Gothas attacked killing 95 and wounding 195. On 13 June, 18 bombers came. Forty-six children died when a bomb hit a kindergarten; all told 162 Londoners were killed and 432 wounded. The next strike by 20 Gothas was on 7 July, killing 54 and wounding 196. As the bombers were heading home, they surprised Henry Tizard (FRS 1926), who was flying at 16,000 feet testing a Sopwith

Camel. He was an Oxford chemist who had been commissioned and assigned to aeronautical research at Upavon. He insisted on learning to fly so that he could have a feel for the questions they were asked to solve. Now out of the blue he was in action. He fired about 100 rounds at the trailing Gotha. Both guns then jammed so he could only wave farewell. The enemy waved back.[70] Then they shifted to night raids to minimize their losses.

The Gothas flew so high that the interceptors needed appreciable lead-time to climb up to meet them. A Sopwith Camel, the latest British fighter, required 25 minutes. Ground observers on the coasts often missed attackers who were above the clouds. William Tucker, of hot wire microphone fame, turned his hand to long-range sound detection. Parabolic sound reflectors were built from concrete above ground or were carved into the white chalk cliffs along the coast.[71] Tucker microphones were mounted at the focus to hear approaching bombers. They also mounted microphones in pits along the coastline, to catch the sound when the enemy passed overhead. Hot wire microphones were too quirky for the task and long-range warning only became effective in 1918 when they were able to amplify the output of magnetic microphones with vacuum tube amplifiers.[72]

The Germans invented a phosphorus incendiary bomb that could not be extinguished with water. The *Luftstreitkräfte* expected that they would crack British morale. They were not dropped because Hindenburg ruled that: 'the civilian population might unintentionally be made to suffer too'.[73] (Both sides used them indiscriminately in the Second World War.)

Geoff Milne was not impressed by the AA defences. His brother replied:

> Your reflexions on my department pain me more, pain me that you should so follow the lead of our yap-yap press in raising a hue-and-cry against our AA defences.

He argued that GHQ panicked by trying to defend the capital with barrage fire rather than aimed shots. 'The result is that <u>nearly all 3" A.A. guns in London have been condemned as worn out</u> (a 3" will only stand 1500 rounds).' In France in daylight, the AA gunners brought down one foe with every 3,000–4,000 rounds. This triggered back and forth squabbles between the brothers that escalated to harsh language. Geoff was reminded that Arthur worked nine hours a day, with only an occasional Saturday afternoon off. Sundays were especially busy because the naval students were not using the ranges. Fellow Brigands had learned that Milne was apt to take scientific disputes as personal attacks, and were suitably cautious. In later life, Milne engaged in some memorable scientific dustups.

The fun of reading the brother's back-and-forth vanishes whenever they pass news about the death or wounding of schoolmates.

Milne was shifted to sound localization, travelling about 'carrying to the ends of the earth the gospel of trumpets'. He was sure that with proper tactics they could bring down every Gotha on a night raid by using the bearings provided by sound localizers to aim searchlights. Once an interloper is fixed by two searchlights a known distance apart, it is easy to calculate height, range and speed for the gunners. Milne insisted that only the stupidity and in-fighting of the generals prevented them from doing this effectively.

Travelling circuses

The Brigands had solved the major questions; now they must get the answers to the AA gunners. Hill started by creating a travelling detachment of three officers and four other ranks. They would set up the mirrors near an AA battery. One gun would fire a smoke shell. Then every gun in the battery would fire eight or ten rounds at the smoke puff—the days were long past from when ammunition was in short supply. The results enabled the gunners to adjust their sights. Hill wrote to Pearson:

> Fowler and Milne are now in Scotland going around with our so-called travelling circus, recording high angle 'battle practices' with great success.[74]

Fowler led a circus to France to demonstrate height finders, and to visit Brocq. Soon two bands of Brigands were based there and Hill was trying to obtain additional men to establish a third. AA gunners had given up shooting at a plane, instead batteries fired together to set up a wall of shrapnel in the path of their target. Often they fired 20 shots before the first exploded. Hill summarized the best tactic as:

> ... to fire a very large number of shots in a very short period of time distributed more or less evenly over a large region through which it is known that the target must pass.[75]

To set up the wall all of the guns in an area were controlled from a central command post.

The Germans learned another use of AA guns in late November 1917. The British army launched a surprise tank attack to take the city of Cambrai. The tank force overwhelmed the front-line defenders and rumbled on through the German reserve positions, entering the suburbs of the city. They were on the cusp of the long-sought breakthrough. They bumped into a German battery of lorry-mounted AA guns, which promptly put three tanks out of action; the rest turned tail. The tanks were followed by two squadrons of British cavalry. They galloped forward but were no match for the guns.[76] In the Second World War dual-purpose AA guns served them well.

In December, Milne wrote to Geoff, who was at an NCO training camp:

> Father told me you have written home for a book on sound. Are you after sound-ranging? Get it if you can. At one time or another I have heard details about it. One L. Bragg, son of Professor H. Bragg, late of Leeds, the aforesaid L. Bragg being fellow of Trinity, was in charge of a sound-ranging section in France for sometime.

He also narrated some of his own adventures:

> We had an exciting time shooting yesterday. Shells set to burst at 20 or 30 secs burst after 5 secs, and two were prematures, i.e. burst 50 yds or so off the muzzle. We had to send a seaman out to search the shore for bodies, dead or alive. No one, however, was bagged.

He closed with the news that he hoped to be off to France before too long.

In early 1918, Hill allocated more Brigands to travelling circuses. Tactics had been modified. Usually the intruder would be spotted at 7,000 yards distance. Range finders provided height and range measurements. The battery commander used a special slide rule to obtain fuse settings and quadrant elevations for his guns. They opened fire when the range fell to 6,000 yards, each gun firing four rounds in quick succession. The commander observed the shell bursts through binoculars equipped with a graticule, so he could estimate the error, and issue new settings for the next burst of four rounds. If they got a firewall in place, the interloper would usually turn tail.[77]

The British were shaken to the core in March when the Germans broke through their Fifth Army's front. Geoff was a sound ranger stationed near the breakthrough. Arthur Milne encouraged their parents:

> Of course we ought to be good at retreats—we have had sufficient practice.

He was also worried about father, who had been ill, on sick leave from the headmastership of a Church of England school, and now was called up for induction—the age had been raised to 51. Geoff fought in Carey's Force and came through unharmed; father was not conscripted.

Pearson finally withdrew in disgust, but the computers in the Galton Laboratory remained employees of the MID, supervised by a deputy responsible to Hill. Four more calculating machines were bought for £25 each. On 23 April, they handed over their 100th Graphical Range Table.

Attacking cities

London was defended by 266 AA guns, 159 day fighters, 353 searchlights and 123 night fighters.[78] The heaviest attack was in May 1918 with 38 Gothas and three giants. Ten Gothas aborted but all of the others reached their targets. The British air defence commander sat in a gallery looking down at a map on which markers for the attackers were manoeuvred by staff with elongated croupier's rakes, as information from observers came in by telephone and two-way radio. The commander telephoned his orders.

In May the Germans made their last air raids on England. They had lost 137 aviators. They believed that six Gothas were brought down by AA fire (the British claimed 23), four were lost in air combat (the British reported eleven). Five planes crashed *en route*.[79] Landing was their greatest peril. They flew handily when ballasted by their bomb load, but atrociously when the bay was empty—32 crashed when landing.

The Germans concluded that their attacks on civilian centres were not worth continuing. Morale was unbroken. The resources the British had devoted to defence were likely to stay in place regardless of whether they were attacked again. Roughly half of their AA guns were in Britain. The results did not justify means expended. Instead, their heavy bombers plastered railway yards in France at night, preparing for the massive German attacks and unnerving men recovering from a bout at the front.

In 1918, 352 RAF bombers were lost bombing German cities. They planned to increase the attacks massively if the war continued into 1919.[80] After the armistice, the Allies made little effort to determine how worthwhile this sacrifice had been. The British and Americans were firmly convinced that bombing civilian targets would be decisive in future wars and invested heavily in constructing and manning heavy bombers for 'strategic bombing'.

Hill was still short of men. James G. Crowther, nineteen-years-old, was another recruit from Trinity. The College provided him with a list of opportunities for wartime scientific work; too many brilliant minds had already been lost in the trenches. He came from a modest home in Yorkshire and his politics were to the left. At *Excellent* he saw an 'immense and absolute' gap between officers and ratings, as well as a subtler dividing line between engineering and line officers. Line officers regarded dinner table conversation as indispensable while engineers often ate silently. Neither talked at breakfast; where each officer was presented first with a wire holder containing a newspaper and then his meal. If either was slow in arriving the aggrieved officer would bellow 'Gather round, gather round'.[81]

There were two entrances to the officers' mess. When the dinner bell rang, ship's company filed in through one door, in strict order of seniority, while trainees entered though the other. On weekends, many wore dress uniform. They also dressed when the Brigands were visited by two Frenchmen: a colonel and a noted mathematician, Haag. Formality vanished when the colonel led them in jolly sport, shooting little bullets of bread at well-dressed dinner companions. For Crowther, *Excellent's* great resource was its well-stocked library.

Crowther found that D. W. Hartree (II):

Had an insatiable appetite for tedious and routine observations and arithmetical calculations … . The father and son did not seem to understand each other very well. W. Hartree used to appear in the workroom on the stroke of nine every morning, and sometimes before. His son did not have the same sense of order, and was sometimes late. Only … to be suddenly carpeted before the whole office by his father. The situation was comic, because D. R. Hartree was probably the most important man at Portsmouth so far as the theory of gunnery was concerned.[82]

Hartree II transcribed this passage by pen; it is with his papers at Christ's College, Cambridge. Crowther thought Hartree III charming, but not a key player in the group. Incidentally, Crowther's time as a Brigand taught him that he was not suited for high-powered mathematics; he became a leading science journalist.[83]

While the military Brigands were off in the field, the shyest Brigand, Richmond, was assigned to host two visiting American officers, but was given no information about their provenance. He missed their names during the introductions, so he tried to explain trajectory calculations in simple terms. Frustrated, he asked if they knew the calculus. They nodded, so he went into slightly more detail. When he ended his exposition, their questions showed how badly he had blundered. One was Major Oswald Veblen, the American authority in geometry and topology, precisely Richmond's own area. Major Veblen was currently director of experimental ballistics at the Aberdeen Proving Ground. When the visitor's identity dawned on Richmond, he jumped from his chair 'murmuring a series of inarticulate "Oh's"'.[84]

Milne became the advisor to the general commanding the AA guns of the First Army and taught a course for the AA officers. By August 1918, the British had a belt of searchlights, two or three deep, extending from the River Scarpe south to the River Somme. Germans scouts flew ahead of their night bombers to machine-gun the searchlights. According to the British from January to September their AA guns destroyed 151 enemy planes and damaged 67. Another 26 were brought down by infantry fire.

German night bombers hit Paris 44 times in 1918, to keep French interceptors and AA guns away from the front. The French fenced the city with fixed barrage balloons, which kept the attackers above 3,000 m, so they were unable to target military objectives. Attacking a fortified city, like Paris, was legal under international law. They dropped fifteen tons of explosives.

The German Navy delivered the most astonishing attacks on Paris—shells fired from long-range guns 120 km away. They were modified 380 millimetre guns of twice-usual length kept straight by overhead trusses and mounted on railway cars so that the recoil shot them backward along the tracks.[85] Muzzle velocity was 1,524 mps. They always fired at a quadrant elevation of 50 degrees, to get their 103 kg shells into the thin air of the upper atmosphere by the shortest route. Maximum height was 38,000 m, more than four times the height of Mt Everest, and the shells travelled for 176 seconds, so aim was corrected for the spin of the earth during flight. Distance travelled was determined by the amount of propellant placed into the breech, inserted as two bags of fixed size and a metal case that contained the weight calculated for each shot. The pressure developed in the chamber was measured with two gauges screwed into the breech; each contained a carefully machined copper pellet, which was compressed by the explosion; compression was measured with a micrometer. The amount of propellant for the next shot was then taken from range tables computed under the direction of Professor von Eberhardt, head of research at Krupp's, where they had done ballistic calculations for decades, but the histories do not tell how the calculations were done. Resistance was calculated from v^3. Perhaps they used the F. Krupp-Gross equations, which were derived from Sciacca.[86] They were not concerned about points on the trajectory, only the distance travelled until impact and they had an extensive target. The enormous detonation wore down the barrels so rapidly that shells were numbered, each slightly larger than the one before. Sixty shots wore out a barrel.

It was suicidal to fly over Paris in daylight, so they did not observe the fall of shot, boasting that their gunnery was so precise that observation was unnecessary. In fact, spies on the spot did the observing, their reports arrived in Switzerland by nightfall. Accuracy was poor: 183 shells fell within the walls of the city, and 120 in the suburbs. They killed 256 people and injured 620.[87] Hindenburg felt sure that these great guns would destroy enemy morale and diverted scarce resources to them (this is inconsistent with his prohibition of incendiary bombs). He planned to fire on the ports of southern England once they occupied Calais, but his offensives were stopped far short of the channel coast. The long-range guns squandered scarce resources and made newspaper headlines.

After the armistice Hill took leave in August to bike in Devon with his wife. Milne was on leave in Paris, able to join the celebration on 11 November.

Hill issued more than 100 certificates—which he drew for printing by the Ordinance Committee at Woolwich—licensing recipients to practice as a Brigand. There were restrictions:

> This license is valid between the hours of 7 a.m. and midnight on week-days and Sundays alike, except at the Sister University [Oxford], where it is valid only from 9 a.m. to 11 p.m. on weekdays and not on Sundays.

Hill allotted ranks; for instance, Bowering was a 'Friend and Counsellor Brigand'.[88] There were 'Unprincipled Brigands' as well as 'Unprincipled Pickpockets'. Strained humour for an intellectually distinguished body: four Brigands were Senior Wranglers.

Hill also sat down with each Brigand to discuss post-war plans and to ask how he might help. Milne was a challenge. He maintained that at age-23 he was too old to return as an undergraduate. He was contracted to edit a book on sound localization for the Ministry of Defence and would look for other work. He did not mention that his family's finances were straitened by father's illness, or that they had quarrelled bitterly over the son's agnosticism. Hill firmly told Milne that he was 'being silly', and persuaded him to return to Trinity under a special program allowing veterans to obtain a war degree without the usual examinations. Hill wrote to Milne's father:

> I have great hopes for him, for he possesses not only the highest ability but also the human nature, the courage, the modesty, & the sympathy which are even more valuable.

There was admiration of both sides. Milne later wrote about Hill and Fowler:

At directing research, both were superb; to behold the way they set about a new problem, often in a new terrain with new material, to see the way they made inferences and came to conclusions and sound judgements and to take part in it all, was far better training than most universities can offer to aspirants in research. The present writer desires to put on record his realization that this three-years' period under Hill and Fowler, at the most formative period of his life (age twenty to twenty-three) was a most vivid, enjoyable and valuable experience; to both of them he can never be sufficiently grateful for that schooling in research.[89]

William Hartree had never had more fun than when working with Hill. Hill's talk had interested him in muscle energetics. They agreed that Hartree would move back to Cambridge to join Hill as a volunteer working on heat production.

A striking affirmation of the intellectual fascination of ballistics was that Fowler, Richmond and two others stayed on at *Excellent* for months to finish the mathematics describing the motion of a spinning shell 'at velocities both greater than and less than the velocity of sound'.[90] They wanted to allow for the wobble of the shells, which they had to measure. Hill, with his 'inventiveness of physical ideas and devices ...' saw how. They obtained the data on three windless, clear days in January and February 1919; firing 3-inch guns on a flat trajectory out to sea. While crossing the 600 feet between gun and sea, the shell passed through a series of ten to twelve stiff pasteboard pistol targets, each two feet square and about 0.05 inches thick. The targets were set at right angles to the gun muzzle, so eccentricities in the shell's hole measured its yaw. The effect of yaw on a shell's air resistance for velocities below the speed of sound was measured in the wind tunnel at the NPL.

They arrived at two separate solutions for the equations of motion for shells treated as rigid bodies; the second solution coped with any degree of yaw. From wind tunnel data, they could estimate the drift and stability of any type of shell.

Major Hill was awarded an OBE. Before the war, he was about to become a lecturer in physical chemistry at Cambridge to support his family, but now he was a fellow of King's and free to return to physiology.

His brother-in-laws also served. When John Maynard Keynes consulted at the Treasury during the financial crisis just before the war, he persuaded Lloyd George to maintain the gold standard by spending gold to support the paper currency. It worked. Some months later, he accepted a position in the Treasury, delighted to have a finger in public affairs. He negotiated contracts for food and goods, and arranged gold transfers from the Allies to Britain and from Britain to the US. He rose in the Treasury hierarchy, living agreeably in London with his friends, who he called the 'Bloomsberries'. They deplored his participation in the war machine and were aghast when he was made a Companion of the Bath Third Class, but he was too charming and interesting to shun. The massive war expenditures eroded the British economy. At the beginning of 1917, he calculated that the nation would be bankrupt in four weeks. They were saved when the Germans declared unrestricted submarine warfare and the Americans loaned freely without passable security. Keynes became head of the foreign division of the Treasury. After the armistice, he was appointed principal financial advisor in the British delegation to the peace conference.

His brother Geoffrey was cut from different cloth. From an early age, Geoffrey thought of his older brother as 'an eminent acquaintance to whom I looked up to as a superior and somewhat distant being'.[91] He was cool to Bloomsberries, though he did notable service when he pumped Virginia Woolf's stomach after she took an overdose of a barbiturate in 1913, while he was completing his medical training at St Bartholomew's Hospital. He entered the RAMC in 1914. Before the end of August, he was stationed at a makeshift British Army Hospital in a Versailles hotel just outside the palace gates. Next, he was assigned to a hospital train, where his major task was injecting narcotics. Then he became medical officer to an artillery brigade, in seven months half of his fellow officers were casualties. Thanks to a friend, he was transferred to a large CCS. He wanted to be a surgeon; now he did plenty of cutting.

In May 1917, he was granted leave to marry Margaret Darwin. Her late father, George Howard Darwin FRS (Second Wrangler 1868), Charles' second son, was a pioneer geophysicist. She was working in what had started as an all-female code-breaking team in the Admiralty, chosen for her excellent German and sharp brain.

Geoffrey's most eminent patient during the war was Prince Friedrich of Prussia, a cousin of the Kaiser who was also related to the British royal family. A flyer, he had been shot down with a machine gun bullet in his abdomen. Geoffrey was disgusted when 'a bi-lingual British officer, disguised as a German, was placed in the bed next to the Prince, so that he could engage him in conversation'. Every day Geoffrey had to take part in the trickery by dressing fake wounds. The deceit produced nothing of military value. The prince seemed to be recovering nicely. He was sent along to a base hospital, where he died from a secondary haemorrhage. If Geoffrey had been there, he might have saved the prince, because he had become adept with blood transfusions.

8

Lessons Learnt: 1919-1971

In the Treaty of Versailles the victors dictated terms to a pariah nation that had almost succeeded in destroying Western civilization—according to the winner's propagandists. The Germans were compelled to accept full responsibility for starting the war. The harsh, non-negotiable terms undermined the new, revolutionary social democratic Government.

Hill's brother-in-law, John Maynard Keynes, became an international celebrity for his blistering attack on the treaty in his book *The Economic Consequences of the Peace*. By continuing to wage economic warfare against their thrashed foes the victors were ripping apart a delicate web: the European economic order which in the past half century had created vast wealth.[1] Keynes did not mention international science, even though it is a key cog in the clockwork that was being shattered.

In 1920 the Swedish Royal Academy of Sciences invited the wartime laureates to a celebration in Stockholm. Among them were the Germans Planck, Haber, Willstätter, and Johannes Stark (physics, 1919). The Braggs—still stung by Bob's death—were outraged that barbarians were invited. They declined. Barkla attended and presented their lame excuses.

In the same year an International Physiological Congress was held in Paris. Germans were barred from attending. In protest Starling, Bayliss, and Hill stayed away and let everybody know why. The next Congress was in Edinburgh in 1923. French and Belgian physiologists declared that if Germans came they would not. Starling and Hill led a British group who pledged to boycott the meeting unless Germans were welcomed. They carried the day. The following year, Starling outraged the haters further by inviting a former U-boat commander to his laboratory as a collaborator.

The neutral Dutch worked to promote international scientific reconciliation; in 1922 they invited small groups from abroad to meet to exchange ideas. Hahn was one of three German chemists who met with representatives from five other countries, his first international meeting in eight years.

Starling and WHB were vocal critics of classical education, which did not train minds for: 'new kinds of work and new methods of working.'[2] They wrote a joint letter to *The Times* urging prompt implementation of the Haldane commission reforms of the University of London. They cheered a small step in 1919 when Cambridge eliminated the Greek requirement.[3]

Over the next decade it gradually dawned on many British that German did not necessarily equal Hun. This change could be measured by the cooling of the vicious hatred for Richard Burdon Haldane. He urged the public to judge the German people fairly and to reflect that the peace had been made when blood was still hot.[4] In 1924 he again became lord chancellor in the new Labour government. A diabetic, he profited from the science he had supported so wholeheartedly as one of the first in England to control his blood sugar with insulin, discovered in Canada by Fredrick Banting (Nobel laureate, 1923), John Macleod (Nobel laureate, 1923), and Charles Best (Banting wrote to the newspapers urging the Nobel committee to include Best). Haldane died in 1928.

The Braggs

WHB and Jenkinson returned to their laboratory at UCL. WL was back at a bench in the Cavendish blowing his own glassware. Soon J. J. Thomson was elected master of Trinity College. Rutherford succeeded him as Cavendish Professor at Cambridge, vacating the Langworthy Chair in Physics at Manchester University which went to WL—academic musical chairs.

The war taught WHB how productive a well-supported group of investigators could be and how well he could lead them; it was ludicrous to think that just he and Jenkinson could remain on the cutting edge of physics. A £1,905 grant from the DSIR paid for five research assistants and two students. He pinched pennies to equip them properly. UCL would not or could not help.

WL did not get off to a good start at Manchester.[5] He had never lectured to undergraduates, many of them were returning servicemen who gave him no mercy. 'In one dramatic incident a student set off a firework under the reading desk and Bragg boxed his ears.' Letters were sent to the University authorities accusing him of incompetence, containing enough truth to make them particularly wounding.

> ... in the end it drove me into what was really a nervous breakdown. Curiously enough, I recovered when the letters began to attack my father and Rutherford as well ...[6]

On the plus side, he recruited an outstanding research group, including former sound rangers. C. G. Darwin developed an advanced mathematical model for diffraction from crystals. The experimenters substantiated his model and used it to determine the structures of complicated crystals. It was still a long drawn-out game: they had to guess a structure, predict its x-ray pattern and keep reiterating until their prediction fit the data.

WL was elected to the Royal Society in 1921. One congratulatory letter was from Alice Hopkinson, a cousin of the late Cyril. She was reading history at Cambridge, where they met shortly after the war. She had not warmed to his hesitant advances;

she was just beginning to stand on her own feet and may have feared being trampled under by a war hero nine years older and already famous. Two years later she knew how sturdy her legs were.

> I replied asking when I could come to see her and she arranged a tea date in Newnham …We became engaged the next day.[7]

They married late in 1921. They had four children.

In the Christmas holidays of 1921, WHB delivered an acclaimed series of popular lectures on sound at the Royal Institution on Albemarle Street, London. It had been established in 1799 to teach the public about science. His lectures also appeared as a short, successful book.[8] Two years later the elderly director died and WHL succeeded him. His get-up-and-go revived the Institution. The family moved into the resident professor's elegant fifteen-room flat and with a small group of excellent collaborators WHB deciphered the structures of organic compounds. He continued to deliver memorable popular lectures and then vastly expanded his listeners by lecturing on the BBC. In a letter concerning a joint hydrophone patent, Ryan wrote: 'I listen to your lectures and often think of that hopeless war'.[9]

Toward the end of the 1920s WL negotiated possible moves to Cambridge or to ICL; he found it so harrowing that he broke down. Strongly supported by his wife and sister, he recovered in a few months and went to Munich on sabbatical, no longer ostracising Germans. Back home, they made a great advance by analysing diffraction data as frequencies instead of distances between dots (by using Fourier series, a mathematical transformation). Now they could determine crystal structures directly from the x- ray data, without the former repeated guesses. It was a nice example of one his favourite adages:

> You either have nasty physics and nice mathematics, or nice physics and nasty mathematics.[10]

He opted for nice physics. The opposing view was articulated by Paul Dirac (Nobel laureate 1933), the Lucasian Professor of mathematics at Cambridge:

> It is more important to have beauty in one's equations than to have them fit experiment.

Gwendoline Bragg died in 1929, so they lost one:

> … who was so warm and vital; if sometimes she wore her family down in her efforts to look after countless friends and lame dogs …[11]

Two years later Gwendy married Alban Caroe. Eighteen months later, the young couple moved into the Royal Institution with father. A few years later WHB could walk his grandchildren to school in the mornings, sharpening his talent for elucidating scientific ideas by trying to answer their often thorny questions.

In 1931, WHB was awarded the Order of Merit (OM), a personal gift of the sovereign limited to 24 members; Admiral Beatty was a fellow member. Naturally enough, the Braggs followed with interest the careers of their former military commanders. Beatty was promoted to admiral of the fleet and became First Sea Lord.[12] A parliamentary grant of £100,000 provided his luxuries without relying on Edith. He had become intimate with Eugenie Godfrey-Faussett, the young wife of a naval captain. Edith Beatty continued to revel in multiplicity and wrote erotic fairy tales for private circulation. She broke down in the 1920s and somehow Beatty coaxed Eugenie to help with her care.[13]

Jellicoe was promoted to admiral of the fleet and was rewarded with £50,000. Beatty was promoted to the same rank on the same day; he became Governor-General of New Zealand. Fisher loyally followed the Nelson tradition by embarking on a flamboyant affair with the Duchess of Hamilton. His two volumes of memoirs earned him £4,000, some of which went for a Rolls-Royce for his Duchess.[14]

Jack retired as a brigadier general and then for ten years directed the Ordnance Survey, where he updated the maps by using aerial photographs. Many history books praise middle-level officers in the German Army: for instance Bauer at OHL and Lossberg's innovations in defensive tactics. Jack deserves similar recognition for solving the map problem in France and setting up the Field Service Companies, which enabled the Royal Artillery to slug it out on equal terms with their skilful opponents. After the war, sound ranging and flash spotting were handed over to the Royal Artillery.

The physiologists

In 1920, Hill became professor at Manchester, reviving an almost moribund department. He studied the physiology of human exercise, working on what he named the 'oxygen debt'. The debt accumulates during spurts of intense activity, like a 100 m dash, during which you use up the energy-donating compounds stored in the tissues. Afterwards you pant as the store is replenished with energy provided by oxidative metabolism. Throughout his active life he ran daily from 07:45 to 10:30. William Hartree kept on with their muscle heat measurements in Cambridge.

Starling was busy rebuilding his department and strengthening scientific medical education at UCL, where he was also the pre-clinical dean. At long last the Royal Commission Report on the University of London was being implemented. The *British Medical Journal* reported that Starling would head a brand-new, scientific clinical unit in medicine at St Thomas's Hospital, just what he had ardently advocated. A few days later a delegation from the Rockefeller Foundation arrived for a brief stay in London. They had come to offer UCL £1 million to improve clinical and pre-clinical medicine, following Starling's objectives and presupposing that he would implement them. With his dreams for UCL in sight, red-faced Starling retreated from St Thomas's.

Despite such exhilarating changes, he was listless and had pains in his abdomen. He asked his old chief at Guy's, William Hale-White, for an opinion. Nothing serious, he did not have appendicitis but should cut down on his smoking. He stopped for two days. When he returned from an advisory trip to India he consulted a surgeon, who diagnosed a cancer on his ascending colon and removed that loop. He recovered sufficiently to take dancing lessons, but whereas before the war he appeared younger than his age, now he could be taken as older.

Bayliss was knighted in 1922. Famously, he declined to appear for his investiture because the date conflicted with a meeting of his beloved Physiological Society, but finally he relented. Soon after the sword touched his shoulder Sir William became ill with a malignancy. He died in 1924 at the age of 64.

One might think that he would be remembered for his brilliant work on the role of colloid osmotic pressure in counteracting wound shock. Not so, Bayliss's and Cowell's breakthroughs faded into obscurity. Neither man is even mentioned in Alfred Blalock's influential 1940 book on shock.[15] Blalock rejected gum acacia solutions because a friend told him that they had killed a number of patients in France in 1918. In the Second World War most infusions were done with blood plasma or whenever possible with whole blood. The enthusiasm for blood waned later when many transfused patients were inadvertently infected with viruses and it was gradually appreciated that a transfusion—like other transplants—elicits immunological reactions with long-term consequences for the host. Today dextran, a high molecular weight polymer of glucose produced by lactobacteria, provides the colloid osmotic pressure in some infusion solutions.

Starling was working on the kidney. In 1922, the Royal Society used a generous bequest to establish two research professorships each paying £1,400 for five-year, renewable terms. A search committee chaired by W. B. Hardy selected Starling for one of them. He relocated to spanking new quarters at UCL paid for with Rockefeller dollars.

A. V. Hill succeeded him as Jodrell Professor. In his inaugural lecture, he recounted how that while considering the offer from Manchester he wrote to Starling for advice, concerned because he knew so little classical physiology. The reply was: 'My dear Hill, you don't know a word of physiology, but I think you ought to go there.'[16] Shortly after moving to London Hill was awarded the Nobel Prize. The UCL students celebrated:

I was carried around the College on their shoulders, they finally took me to the top of the building where Starling was working. When Starling appeared they loudly demanded, "who says he doesn't know a word of physiology?" To which Starling retorted, and insisted, "I did—he doesn't know a damned word". After which they let us go'.[17]

He was given the prize for demonstrating that contracting muscles generate heat, but relaxing muscles do not, so therefore relaxation is a passive process. After contracting the muscle produces 'recovery heat'. In the absence of oxygen there still is contraction heat, but no recovery heat. The prize was shared with the German Otto Meyerhof, who studied the formation of lactic acid during contraction. When oxygen is available, the lactic acid disappears during recovery. We now know that ATP (adenosine triphosphate) provides the energy for contraction when it is broken down to ADP, the diphosphate. A falling ATP concentration increases the rate at which glucose and other carbohydrates are broken down by the fermentation pathway to lactic acid. The energy released in the breakdown is used to convert ADP back to ATP—2 ATPs are made from each glucose molecule metabolized. If oxygen is available, lactic acid is broken down in the mitochondria to carbon dioxide and water, producing from 30 to 36 ATPs. Remaining lactic acid is converted back into carbohydrates. Dealing with the lactic acid accounts for the recovery heat.

Hill began his Nobel banquet speech:

> The War tore asunder two parts of the world as essential to one another as man and wife. Physiology, I am glad to know, was the first science to forget the hatreds and follies of the War and to revive a truly international Congress: my own country, I am proud to boast, was happy to be its meeting-ground.

The Royal Society's investments did so well that in 1925 Hill became the second research professor at UCL, while Charles Lovett Evans became head of department. The three professors coexisted amicably.

In 1927, Starling took a banana boat to the West Indies, hoping his health would improve. He died aboard ship in the harbour of Kingston, Jamaica at the age of 61.

Gowland Hopkins became the first professor of biochemistry at Cambridge in 1914 and in 1929 received the Nobel Prize for his work on vitamins. Charles Martin retired from the Lister Institute at the mandated age, and became the director of a nutrition institute in Adelaide, Australia. After his second retirement he moved to Cambridge where he experimented productively for years. His last paper appeared in 1948. He eulogized his dear friend Starling: 'He loved music, he loved beauty, he loved a fight; in fact, he loved life'.[18]

The brigands

William Hartree enjoyed working on muscle, publishing his first paper at age 50. He constructed thermopiles with 100 junctions. In 1933, when age made the long experiments too demanding, he volunteered to help his son, undertaking to solve 34 simultaneous differential equations. He published his last paper at age 71.[19]

Fowler returned to Trinity, rewarded for his war services with an OBE. He golfed with Rutherford and married his daughter. Ballistics had shifted his interests from pure mathematics to solving physical problems. He collaborated with C. G. Darwin on the partitioning of energy in physical systems and with Milne on absorption bands in space. According to Milne: 'he turned a scientific research into a matter of glorious gaiety, and made collaboration with him the finest thing in the world'.[20] He became Plummer Professor of Mathematical Physics at Cambridge.

In his first year back at Trinity Milne prepared three theses: on the maximum value of integrals, on sound waves in the atmosphere, and on the ionization and viscosity of the stratosphere. Strongly supported by Hill and Richmond, he was elected a fellow of Trinity and he also became assistant director of the Solar Physics Laboratory. When his father died he could help support his family. Then he was infected with encephalitis. The William Hartrees nursed him through, but he never recovered completely, he had severe motor problems in later life. In 1924, he moved to Manchester as professor of applied mathematics and four years later took a similar position at Oxford.

Douglas Hartree returned as a student to St John's College, Cambridge. He took a PhD working under Fowler and later succeeded Milne at Manchester, in time becoming professor of mathematical physics there. He pioneered in numerical analysis, applying his methods to quantum models of atomic structure.[21] He became interested in analogue machines to perform integrations, pioneered by Vannevar Bush in the US, and after a visit built the first analogue computer in the UK, using parts from Meccano sets. (It is displayed in the Science Museum, London).

Littlewood returned to his bachelor rooms at Trinity, still frequently collaborating with Hardy. Nothing changed when Hardy moved to a professorship at Oxford, only now their letters went by post rather than by college servant. A Danish colleague claimed: 'Nowadays, there are only three really great English mathematicians: Hardy, Littlewood, and Hardy-Littlewood.' He was dogged by depression, and his life was transformed in 1957 when he was prescribed an effective anti-depressant. He published his last paper at age-87—on ballistics—and died at 92.[22]

Weizmann

The post-war boom in automobile manufacturing made Weizmann very rich because the oleoresinous lacquer they used as paint was a bottleneck—it took three weeks to dry. The problem was solved by the discovery of nitrocellulose lacquers—relatives of guncotton—dissolved in fast drying butyl acetate. The demand for butyl alcohol consumed the stockpile accumulated in the war, Commercial Solvents expanded, and the royalties poured in. Strange and Fernbach challenged his patent unsuccessfully in the British and then in the US courts.

Lord Samuel was the first high commissioner for Mandate Palestine. His appointment outraged the Palestinians—it was stacking the deck. There were bloody riots. Neither Samuel nor his successors could reconcile the Palestinians to their fate. Gradually the British realized that they had dealt themselves a difficult hand.

In 1921 Weizmann was elected president of the World Zionist Organization. According to Isaiah Berlin: 'In politics he suffered neither fools nor equals gladly'.[23] Year after year he clashed with adversaries about how to make the most of the

Balfour Declaration. The Hebrew University's first building was dedicated by Balfour in 1923. Six years later the Zionists set up the Jewish Agency to promote development in Palestine and to negotiate with the British. Its headquarters were in London and Weizmann was elected leader. Following a riot in which hundreds died, the British began to restrict Jewish expansion in Palestine. Many Zionists blamed this setback on Weizmann, who resigned as president of the Agency.

He returned to science after fourteen fallow years. In 1931 he set up a private laboratory in rented space in London. Shortly thereafter Richard Willstätter visited London to accept a medal from the Royal Society. They met and discussed Weizmann's scientific resurrection. Willstätter was studying enzymes that break proteins into smaller pieces. Their talk stimulated Weizmann to work on converting poorly digested plant proteins to more readily assimilated molecules by using yeast enzymes. The dried product is a nutritious powder with an 'agreeable meat-like taste'. He obtained three patents for the process. 'Blitz broth' supplemented diets in Britain during the Second World War.[24]

In 1934 a scientific research institute was opened in Rehovoth in Palestine. In the 1920s Simon Marks and Israel Sieff had taken on the management of Marks and Spencer, setting 5s as top price for any item. Soon they dominated British retailing. There was a family tragedy when Daniel Sieff, a son who had studied at Cambridge for a career in medical research, killed himself. The families endowed the Sieff Institute in his memory. Richard Willstätter spoke at the dedication, but declined the directorship. After the ceremony they attended a *Seder* at Weizmann's mother's house along with 35 members of his family living in Palestine. Weizmann became president of the Institute and began to spend part of each year in Rehovoth, where they built a lovely home and garden.

One of the Sieff Institute's goals was to provide for notable scientists driven out of Germany by the Nazis. Weizmann invited many; only Fritz Haber accepted and he died *en route*. It is a measure of how well Weizmann and his colleagues developed science on the edge of the bleak desert that in a comparable situation today they would be overwhelmed by applicants.

Looking for a way out, a British commission recommended partitioning Palestine. Weizmann supported the idea: 'I know that God promised Palestine to the children of Israel, but I do not know what boundaries He set.'[25] To many Zionists this was betrayal. In 1939 the British published a White Paper severely restricting Jewish immigration and land purchases, in effect ripping up the Balfour Declaration.

Otto Hahn

On 19 January 1919, 33 million Germans voted in an election that legitimized the revolutionary government. The Social Democrats won 38 per cent of the seats in the Reichstag; the right-wing Nationalists had 10 per cent; the Independent Socialists 5 per cent. Some right and left wingers still challenged the elected government with arms in the streets. The nation was officially in a state of siege from March until December 1919. Allied troops occupied the west bank of the Rhine.

Willstätter was visited by Harold Brewer Hartley, a chemist who years before had worked for a summer in his laboratory. Now Hartley was head of an Allied commission interviewing leading German gas warriors. Willstätter found it hilarious that Hartley was a brigadier general while Haber had never risen above captain.

Early in 1919, Hahn published the work done with his student Rothenbach, who had been killed in 1914, along with four papers with Meitner. There is no way to quantify the scientific talent lost in the war. In France from 1911–1913 there were 161 graduates from the *École Normale Superieur*: 61 of them were wounded and 81 killed.[26]

Shortly after the war the German army—with customary thoroughness—critically evaluated their performance. Fifty-seven questions were set; each was answered by a committee formed from a cadre of 400 officers. They reported that tactics for using of gas were difficult to evaluate because there were so many variables; with this caveat they rated wartime operations highly.[27]

After eight years of marriage the Hahn's only child, a boy named Hanno, was born. Meitner was Godmother and thenceforth addressed Hahn with the informal 'du'. He was a major figure in world science, frequently nominated for the Nobel Prize and honoured with medals and awards. Perhaps his most treasured trophy came when the governing body of the German Student Societies adopted his National Scientific and Medical Association as a full member. He received a jaunty blue cap that he wore to the annual reunion where they drank beer and sang the old songs.

In 1925 when his old comrades Franck and Hertz were awarded the Nobel Prize in Physics for their study of electron movement through vapours of metal ions.[28] The results fit perfectly with Bohr's model of the atom, in which orbital electrons move between different quantal energy levels and are shifted to a higher energy level if struck by an electron with sufficient energy. In 1928, Hahn became director of the KWI for chemistry.

After he moved to Munich during the war, Willstätter was told that as the Bavarian king Ludwig III signed his appointment he remarked that he hoped this would be the last Jew. This rankled even though the king entertained him at a pleasant, informal lunch. In 1924 the faculty senate was debating the appointment of a professor of geology, the leading candidate was Jewish. One senator pontificated that they did not need another 'foreigner'. Willstätter left the meeting and resigned his chair. He refused to reconsider, left his comfortable professorial house next to the laboratory and moved to a small dwelling on the other side of town too small for much of his library. He did not enter a lab again but kept some work going with assistants who telephoned each night with their results.[29]

When Hitler came to power, academics were prime targets. He held the whip hand because the faculty were civil servants. The Government decreed that no Jews could teach in universities unless they had served in the war. The dispensation was based on the Nazi slur that Jews had been shirkers. In fact, 100,000 Jews had been in the army, 78,000 at the front, 30,000 had been decorated for bravery and 12,000 killed.[30] About one per cent of the Germans were Jews and Jews made up roughly one per cent of the army and of the casualties. When Hitler learned how many Jews had served he rescinded the exemption. Those Jews who could emigrated. Old comrade James Franck was one of the first to leave; he completed his career at the University of Chicago. Hertz went to the USSR. Of the six laureates who had worked on gas warfare only Hahn remained in Germany.

Karl Bosch, now directing I. G. Farben, met with Hitler in the summer of 1933. He delivered a dire warning: they had already lost 26 per cent of their physicists including eleven Nobel laureates and thirteen per cent of their chemists. It did not ruffle Hitler: 'Germany could get along for another hundred years without any physics or chemistry'.[31] Even the arms industry was hit. The Jewish head of research at Krupp, Benno Schmidt, was retired early (he died in a labour camp in 1944).[32] Hitler assigned the engineer Fritz Todt to direct science.

Nernst retired after the Jews were ejected from his chemistry department. Haber, a Lutheran of Jewish ancestry, left the country for a temporary post at the University of Cambridge, arranged by British colleagues who also had worked on war gases.[33] He died while on his way to Palestine. Hahn and Planck defied strong Nazi opposition by holding a memorial service in Berlin. Next, the Nazis decreed that no Jew could be a member of a student society. Hahn resigned and sent back his beloved blue cap, issuing a public statement that he refused to be part of a bigoted clique.

Lisa Meitner was a Lutheran of Jewish ancestry. An Austrian citizen, she was allowed to work at the KWI without interference. Then in March 1938 Hitler incorporated Austria into the Third Reich. An ardent Nazi in the KWI who coveted Hahn's job denounced her, naturally she appealed to Hahn. After consulting lawyers and bureaucrats he advised her to leave the lab and go home. She was incredulous and deeply hurt: 'He has, in essence, thrown me out'.[34] The next day was the Hahn's 25th wedding anniversary. She attended the celebration but her coolness was obvious. She was denied permission to leave the country. The Nazis did not want another well-known refugee speaking out. If she left illegally, she would lose her pension and all her possessions. Meanwhile Edith Hahn was becoming more and more disturbed. Meitner tried to calm her and often took care of Hanno, but in June, Edith was admitted to a psychiatric hospital.

Hahn and other friends begged colleagues abroad to find a place for Meitner. Dutch scientists arranged for her to enter the Netherlands illegally without a visa. She was slipped across the border in 1938, carrying a small valise containing only light summer clothing and in case of need a diamond ring Hahn had inherited from his mother. From a minor, temporary position in the Netherlands, thanks to Niels Bohr she moved to a physics institute that was just opening in Stockholm.

She and Hahn had been trying to find the product formed when uranium was struck by a neutron. Their hypothesis was that the neutron was incorporated into the nucleus, creating a different, unstable, radioactive element. Finally Hahn and Fritz Strassmann came up with the revolutionary idea that the neuron split uranium into two smaller elements; one of them a radioactive isotope of barium. Their evidence is that every insoluble salt that precipitated the radioactivity also precipitated added barium.

Hahn sent a draft of their paper to Meitner in Sweden, asking her to think about it and if '… you could publish, then it would still in a way be work by the three of us'.[35] Two days after the data arrived Meitner and her nephew Otto Frisch, who was working with Bohr in Copenhagen, travelled to the west coast of Sweden to spend Christmas with friends. She showed Frisch the draft. He thought: '… that this was no chipping or cracking of the nucleus but rather a process to be explained by Bohr's idea that the nucleus is like a drop of liquid; such a drop might elongate and divide itself …'.[36] The next day, out walking in a snowy forest, they sat on a tree trunk and started to scribble on bits of paper. He calculated that if the nucleus was like a liquid droplet, when it divided a great deal of energy would be released—about 200 million electron volts. Meitner calculated that if two new nuclei were formed they would be lighter than their parent by one fifth of the mass of a proton. Since $E=mc^2$, this would be about 200 million electron volts. A tantalizing fit. (The fission of a kilo of uranium releases about 2.5 million times the energy released by burning a kilo of coal.)[37] After chatting with a biologist friend, Frisch named the splitting 'nuclear fission', after the term for cell division.

The two papers opened a new world. By the end of the year more than 100 papers on fission had appeared. One showed that only the isotope uranium-235 undergoes fission. Irène and Frédéric Joliet Curie (Nobel laureates 1935) showed that at least two neutrons were released by the fission, potentially enough to trigger further fissions—a chain reaction.

The British

In 1932 and 1933 a committee of British Army officers published their report: *Notes on Certain Lessons of the Great War*.[38] The chair was Lt-Gen. Walter M. St. G. Kirke.[39] the seven members were colonels or generals. Unlike the German inquiry a decade earlier, the Kirke Committee was not asked questions but were to make their proposals after examining the official histories. Their common sense recommendations suggest that their own experiences carried more weight than their reading. They concluded that trench raids undertaken to control no-man's-land cost the attackers more than the enemy. Too often troops massed to attack were exhausted from prolonged trudging and lack of sleep, hungry and thirsty, often wet and cold, in no fit state for a charge. Attacks should be done at night or with a heavy smoke screen, but even then infantry armed only with rifles, grenades, and machine guns are likely to fail. Tanks and mortars are the key offensive weapons and should be included in every infantry division, rather than concentrated in specialized armoured formations (as the Germans were doing). In most situations high explosive is more effective than shrapnel.

Astonishingly, since science is scarcely mentioned in the official histories, their first recommendation is the vital need to keep:

abreast of modern scientific developments.... There is always the danger that a new war may find us surprised again by new scientific weapons.

They listed the German firsts. They point out that:

A conscript army, which is recruited from every class and profession, has an advantage over a professional army such as ours in keeping abreast of modern scientific developments.

Hence:

Close co-operation with civilian experts is therefore very necessary in peace-time.

Hill led groups who assisted scientists driven out of Germany. He kept an unsightly plastic comic figurine of the saluting Führer fixed to a laboratory shelf with Plasticine. Bemused German visitors were told that the statuette was there to remind him to thank for the superb scientists they were driving abroad. One of Hill's precepts is that 'Laughter is the best detergent for nonsense.'[40]

He continued to work on heat production in muscle, training young investigators who became major contributors. They measured heat production during the passage of nerve impulses, a difficult technical feat that had eluded him for years but which added little to our understanding.

H. E. Wimperis, director of research in the Air Ministry, had invented a course-setting bombsight during the War. Now he needed biophysical advice, so he invited Hill to lunch on Oct 15 1934 at the Athenaeum, the London club whose ethos is established by the life-sized portrait of Charles Darwin hanging behind the bar. [41] His question was whether a beam of energy could incapacitate an enemy aviator miles away—science fiction's death ray. Hill told him how the question could be answered. Wimperis then contacted Robert Watson-Watt, the radio expert of the NPL, who asked his assistant Arnold Wilkens to calculate how powerful a radio beam must be to raise the temperature of a litre of water at increasing distances from the transmitter. The needed power was gargantuan. Wilkens also calculated that an object the size of an airplane would reflect about 10^{-19} of the power of a radio wave that struck it. Their amplifiers were good enough to detect a reflection of that magnitude.

Wimperis also inspected the latest long range sound warning apparatus, a sound mirror 200 feet long and 25 feet high facing the Channel. It was impressive but would be of little use. Sound travels relatively slowly and aircraft would approach at half the speed of sound.[42] W. S. Tucker had remained in Government service working on long range sound detection. With war approaching he was thunderstruck when his contract was not renewed. He finally understood when the secret of radar was revealed.

Wimperis set up a small scientific committee on air defence in early 1935. It was chaired by the former RAF Lt-Col. Henry Tizard, who as a civil servant had appointed Wimperis and now was the rector of ICL. Wimperis was a member; the others were officer-scientists: Army Major Hill and Navy Lieutenant P. M. S. Blackett (Nobel laureate 1948). They could communicate with military men. The committee was impressed by the report from the NPL, perhaps echolocation would work in the air as in the sea. They arranged for a test flight past a powerful BBC transmitter in the Midlands. An echo was detected when the target was eight miles away. They recommended a generous investment in radio echolocation.[43] The Treasury began secretly to allocate millions of pounds.

Winston Churchill was rasping in the Commons about the secret expansion of the Luftwaffe, revealing secret Government intelligence leaked to him by plucky, whistle-blowing civil servants. Hence the ministry felt obliged to add to the committee his crony and scientific guru F. A. Lindemann (later Lord Cherwell). The 'Prof' was a wealthy bachelor, charming when he chose and an outstanding tennis player—once the Swedish champion. He was elected Dr Lee's professor of experimental philosophy at Oxford in 1919, nominated by his friend Tizard. Every weekend he was a guest at a stately home, arriving impressively in his chauffeured Rolls. He bitterly disputed his seating at his college's high table, finally suing—and losing. He was brilliant, but contemptuous of other's ideas.

Committee meetings became nightmares. The Prof endlessly criticized their wager on radar and argued for equal attention to infrared detection of intruders and to parachute bombs to be dropped on bombers, all intermingled with nasty personal assaults on Tizard. The language became so fierce that at one meeting the secretaries were asked to leave the room. Finally Hill and Blackett resigned in protest. Hill had learned:

> … that it never (repeat never!) pays to lose one's temper, but that occasionally, in a good cause, it is useful to pretend to lose it.[44]

The committee was dissolved. A new committee was appointed several months later: Tizard, Wimperis, Hill, Blackett, and an expert on radio waves. The committee closely followed the development of the electronics and worked on how radar should best be integrated into the air defence network. They discussed the opportunities with RAF and AA officers, briefing them on what the promised equipment could and could not do and inviting criticisms of the plans for implementation. They would link the future radar sites into the communications network feeding into the HQ where the commanders looked down on a map on which emblems of attackers and defenders were moved as the battle developed. The committee identified young civilians capable of keeping radars operating; they were taught during school vacations. A small group of civilian scientists was stationed at the RAF fighter aerodrome at Biggin Hill to study interception under central control, just as the Brigand's had studied AA operations two decades before. Radar and the central direction of the defence were decisive in the Battle of Britain.

WHB was elected president of the Royal Society in 1935 at age 73, Hill was the biological secretary, and a year later A. C. G. 'Jack' Egerton became physical secretary. He was a chemist who had worked on explosives in Lord Moulton's shop during the First World War. They shared a vision: in the next war science must be well organized, not turned to grudgingly and then extemporized. They urged the Ministry of Labour to prepare for war, and the Ministry agreed to have Hill represent the Royal Society. The Society assembled a central register of qualified men, which enabled the Government to tap needed talent and also kept indispensable men out of the firing line. It would be stupid to sacrifice another Marsden.

When war came Tizard asked Hill to try to get American scientists into the war, even though they were neutrals. Tizard had him posted as a supernumerary air attaché at the embassy in Washington. He arrived in March 1940. The Americans were friendly; but both sides were hamstrung by the cult of secrecy. They tried trading secrets, but this is dicey: how do you know that the secret you will learn is as valuable as the one you divulge in exchange? Hill realized that to get things moving the British must throw their cupboard open, revealing everything. He returned to London with this outlandish proposition.

Tizard had the imagination to grasp the idea and obtained permission to lead a small mission to Washington. His brief was:

> To tell them what they want to know, to give all assistance I can on behalf of the British Government to enable the armed forces of the U.S.A. to reach the highest level of technical efficiency.[45]

It seems astonishing that secrecy-obsessed Prime Minister Churchill would sign away his jewels, but at the time he was distracted by the fall of France.

Tizard, R. W. Fowler, and J. D. Cockcroft arrived in Washington that summer with a suitcase containing secret devices, which they handed over for inspection. The most impressive was a magnetron, an electronic valve capable of generating short, powerful pulses at high frequency. It was top, top secret. (In fact, the Germans already knew about the magnetron from work published in Leningrad in 1936.[46]) It was tested at MIT and found to be 1,000 times more powerful than their best vacuum tube. It was the basis for high frequency radar and now millions are used in microwave ovens. The Tizard mission was a *tour de force* of scientific diplomacy. Neither side mentioned the atom. The Americans also held back their greatest secret, the Norden bombsight, which did not live up to expectations when it came into action.

Hill and Egerton wanted to make it harder for scientific pitchmen, like the Prof, to hawk dubious goods. In the early summer of 1939 they proposed that the Committee on Imperial Defence should establish a small scientific subcommittee to advise how to tackle new scientific opportunities facing the nation and identify those scientists who could be most helpful.[47] WHB wrote to the prime minister advocating a small subcommittee of six FRSs. This idea was rejected and there was an inconclusive debate about what to do. Months passed and the nation was at war.

When Churchill became prime minister in May 1940 he proposed that Lord Hankey, then a Minister without Portfolio, should coordinate and prioritize scientific support for the war. WHB submitted a new, modified proposal for an advisory committee chaired by a cabinet minister and made up of the president and two secretaries of the Royal Society and the secretaries of the three research councils.

Meantime the discontent of rank and file scientists was displayed impressively. A dining club known as the Tot and Quot, chaired by the Oxford anatomist Solly Zuckerman, decided to protest in print. One month later *Science in War* was in the bookstores, published by Penguin. It sold so well that there was a second printing. It charged that: 'The scientific societies, which might have integrated the scientific effort of the country, have almost gone into hibernation ...'.[48] Examples of scientific successes in the last war were contrasted with the current failure to mobilize for solving problems like wound shock. They slammed food policy, which seemed to ignore the advances in vitamins and trace elements made since the First World War, and praised the work of the Royal Society Food [War] Committee in the last war. Churchill did not respond to WHB's proposal. The Prof, without an official position but whose office was in No. 10, set science policy singlehanded. In June 1940 Tizard and Hill resigned from the committee advising the air staff. Hill's political position was now stronger because he was an MP from the University of Cambridge. As he wrote: 'I propose to make myself a nuisance until something is done or I am squashed'.[49] He raised questions in the House of Commons, arguing that the numerous problems arising from the Luftwaffe's blitz of the British cities showed that the 'full resources of science are needed'. Bowing to the pressure, WHB's proposal was re-examined. Hankey thought that yet another committee was overkill, but nonetheless it was needed to cool down the scientists. His Scientific Advisory Committee to the War Cabinet first met on 10 October 1940. Immediately they were confronted by a crucial question.

Four days after the publication of the paper by the Joliet-Curies showing that uranium fission triggered by a neutron produced at least two more neutrons, WL and G. P. Thomson (Nobel laureate 1937; son of J. J. Thomson) wrote to Tizard pointing out that a chain reaction could liberate huge amounts of energy. Tizard and his advisors thought it a long shot and did nothing.

Otto Frisch and Rudolf Peierls, who had studied with Werner Heisenberg (Nobel laureate 1932) in Germany and worked with Ralph Fowler, were at the University of Birmingham. They thought deeply about the science, calculating that the critical mass of uranium-235 to sustain a chain reaction was only a few kilos (too low), so an atomic bomb was feasible. They suspected that the first-rate German physicists were already well on the way. Britain must have its own bomb as a <u>deterrent.</u> Their memo was sent to Tizard in March 1940. Impressed by their calculations, he set up a committee: P. M. S. Blackett (Manchester), Mark Oliphant (Birmingham) and G. P. Thomson (ICL). At their first meeting they were sceptical, even when they learned that the Germans were acquiring heavy water from Norway, which could be used to slow neutrons so they were more likely to trigger fission. They asked for James Chadwick (Liverpool) to be added to the committee. Chadwick also calculated that a chain reaction was possible. The second meeting strongly endorsed the memo. They recommended that the British should get to work.

There was a second route to an atom bomb. Hahn demonstrated that when uranium-238 captures a neutron it is transformed into radioactive uranium-239, which decays by releasing a beta particle. A young physicist, Carl von Weizsäcker, proposed that the decay product is element 93, which does not occur in nature. Element 93 was made in the cyclotron at Berkeley and named neptunium. It decays with a half-life of 2.3 days, into element 94, also not found in nature. Element 94 was made in the Berkeley cyclotron and found to have a slow-neutron fission rate twice that of uranium-235. It was named plutonium. A chain reaction in a uranium reactor would produce plutonium as a side product, which could be separated readily because its chemistry differs from uranium. A critical mass of plutonium would detonate.

Hankey's committee, on which the Royal Society was now represented by president Henry Dale and biological secretary Edward Mellanby, met with Tizard's committee on 16 September 1941. After a meticulous review of the proposal and the data, they recommended that the uranium-235 project be given the highest priority. Hankey's private secretary—the spy John Cairncross—let his Russian handler know.

The Americans had started a year beforehand after President Roosevelt read a letter from Einstein. Within weeks they ordered 50 tons of uranium oxide and four tons of highly purified graphite to slow the neutrons. Even after they entered the war the Americans and British exchanged little information about the atom. In 1943 Lindemann visited and made it clear that the British intended to continue their independent program after the war. This was interpreted as a move to hold the Empire together with the glue of atom bombs, which most Americans wanted no part of. A few months later the British clarified their position, post-war they only wanted an independent deterrent. Then Chadwick was invited to bring a small group over to join the Manhattan Project, which will always be the archetypical military-academic-industrial complex. The group included Frisch, who was made a British subject. Meitner was also invited, but she would have nothing to do with bomb-making.

Meanwhile WHB closely followed the battle against the U-boats. Initially he was sure that sonar had stacked the odds for the convoys. Hitler seemed to agree; he poured the monies for German navel rearmament into fast surface vessels to raid commerce. Some U-boat men still thought that U-boats could beat convoys and sonar with novel tactics. A flotilla of U-boats would fan out over a trade route to scout for a convoy. When one was found the flotilla concentrated as a 'wolf-pack' to attack at night on the surface, where the U-boats were faster than their prey and barely visible because their conning towers had such low profiles. In 1942 the U-boats seemed likely to win the war, sinking 600,000 tons per month.

However the British and Americans were developing micro-wave radars whose beams would echo from relatively small objects. By April 1941 they were able to detect conning towers ten miles distant and periscopes at 1,300 yards.[50] Once compact micro-wave radars entered active service convoys could fight back on the darkest night because they could see the attackers. Micro-wave radar won the Battle of the

Atlantic.[51] ·By 1943 less than 50,000 tons per month were sunk. The next step was to develop micro-wave radars small enough to be mounted in night fighters, they helped to whittle away the Luftwaffe until the Allies commanded the air over Europe.

In early spring 1942 a cabinet paper was issued on the probable effects of bombing Germany for the next 18 months.[52] The British had discovered that their night bombers were incapable of hitting specific targets like factories; they turned to carpet bombing of working-class homes. The Prof calculated that 50 per cent of the housing in cities with populations of 50,000 or higher could be destroyed if Britain poured its resources into bombing. Tizard and Blackett independently examined the mathematics and both concluded that his estimate was at least five times too high because all of the bombers that would be built during the 18 months were taken as engaged from the start. Their contrary calculations were ignored and resources were poured into saturation bombing. It achieved even less than the Prof's opponents calculated. Tizard realized that now he was powerless in Whitehall; he became president of Magdalene College Oxford.

WHB's term at the Royal Society finished in 1940. He died in 1942.

When the war came the British interned all enemy aliens, including the refugee scientists. As an MP, Hill pressed vigorously to free them. He helped to establish a group to work on aiming AA guns with radar, which included P. M. S. Blackett, Andrew Huxley (Nobel laureate, 1963), and Hill's son David. The radar-directed guns were especially effective against the V1 flying bombs. Later in the war he was sent to India to advise on their scientific development. He did not seek re-election to the House of Commons. He detested politician's lies and backdoor manipulations.

Milne gave up astrophysics during the war, working for the Ordnance Board on ballistics and AA gunnery. Hartree worked in the Ministry of Supply. The first digital computer, ENIAC, was built in the US for ballistic calculations and the designers asked Hartree to come over to advise them on its use:

> I do not think it would be any exaggeration to say that it was he who taught them the way in which advantage could be taken of its supreme rapidity of action.[53]

At the outbreak of the war Queen Mary College and Bedford College were relocated to Cambridge to teach radar trainees. The professor at Queen Mary was Harold Robinson, who lodged with the Braggs—his pipe smoke mingled with their cigarette smoke. WL continued to consult with the Sound Ranging Section of the Army on Salisbury Plain where some of his old comrades, like Hemming, were back in service. Later he used data from a group of radars to plot the trajectories of the V2 rockets hurtling toward the British Isles. He also served as an advisor on the implementation of sonar, regularly visiting the research station on the Clyde where the scientists enjoyed talking with someone who knew what they were trying to do and appreciated their problems.[54]

He was investigating the structure of metals and developed a useful bubble model of their structure. He also served as the scientific advisory committee of the Ministry of Supply, as Chairman of the General Physics Committee and as a member of the Metallurgy Committee. In 1941 the newly-dubbed Sir Lawrence succeeded R. W. Fowler for a six month term as the scientific liaison officer in Canada, sailing over with C. G. Darwin who was going to the same job in Washington.

Throughout the war Lady Bragg was intensively involved in the Woman's Voluntary Service which made her a prominent figure in Cambridge. The year after the war ended she was elected mayor.

Max Hastings, who has written a series of brilliant books on campaigns in the Second World War, has now published an overall history of the war, in which he makes frank, telling and often scathing evaluations of statesmen, generals, campaigns and the like. His view on our topic is unequivocal:

> ... mobilization of the best civilian brains, and their integration into the war effort at the
> highest levels, was an outstanding British success story.[55]

When war came Weizmann was appointed honorary scientific advisor to the Ministry of Supply and provided with a small laboratory and group of collaborators. Both of their boys were Cambridge graduates. Their younger son Michael joined the RAF the day after Neville Chamberlain returned from Munich. When war came Benjy enlisted and was assigned to an AA aircraft battery commanded by a leading Zionist. The US needed butyl alcohol for synthetic rubber, so the Weizmanns went there in 1941. They tried fermenting molasses, wood pulp, and straw for chemicals to use as high octane aircraft fuels. He obtained a patent on methods for separating butadiene from mixtures. However the US decided to make to make synthetic rubber from petroleum, which Weizmann thought a blunder owing to the political muscle of the oil companies. He no longer relied on scientific fame to open doors. As Zionist leader he was invited to meet President Roosevelt; in the oval office he delivered a personal message from his friend Winston Churchill. Soon he had a network of supporters in the US Government as well as a network of wealthy, influential American Zionists. He cultivated both groups with customary skill.

In 1942 the Air Ministry listed Michael as missing on a patrol flight over the Bay of Biscay. Benjy had an emotional breakdown after his battery was attacked from the air. He was hospitalized and then discharged.

Germany and uranium

In the spring of 1939 the Reich Research Council founded an *Uranverein* (nuclear association) to coordinate work on fission. Hahn and Werner Heisenberg (Nobel laureate, 1932) were members.[56] When war came the *Uranverein* was assigned to German Army Ordnance, and was directed by Todt, who built Hitler's highways. Heisenberg proposed to build a uranium reactor by slowing down released neutrons so that they would fission uranium-235. They needed a large supply of uranium ore and also a substance to slow the neutrons. They tried using graphite, which did not work because their supply contained trace impurities. Therefore the Army requisitioned heavy water, a by-product of a Norwegian nitrogen-fixing factory.

Starting in 1941 Heisenberg's small group built a series of circular containers containing layers of uranium and heavy water. Each try was larger than its predecessor, but still they did not obtain a chain reaction. Todt was killed in an air crash in 1942 and the architect Albert Speer became minister for armaments. He met with the *Uranverein* to discuss their work. Their requested budget was modest. He assured Hitler that there would be no atomic super-weapon in the present war. Hahn, in the Chemical Institute, kept following his own nose, publishing 57 papers between 1940 and 1944, about his usual rate of production. In 1943 he visited Meitner in Stockholm, predicting that fission would stay in the laboratory for many years. Of course the Allies feared that the redoubtable German physicists were working all out on a bomb. Norwegian resistance fighters blew up part of the heavy water plant and then sank a ferry transporting the heavy water that had been produced to Germany. In 1944 the US Army Air Force targeted Dahlem at the request of General Groves, the commander of the Manhattan Project. The Chemistry Institute was destroyed and the Physics Institute badly damaged.

Planck's only surviving son from his first marriage, a leading civil servant, was executed after the failure of the bomb planted in Hitler's bunker.

The displaced KWI chemists moved into a converted textile factory at Hechingen in the Black Forest, with Hahn were his wife, his son Hanno who had lost an arm in Russia and Hanno's girlfriend Ilse, a nurse who had met Hanno while assisting with his amputation. Nearby, the physicists continued their unsuccessful atomic pile building. On 25 April 1945, the French army took Hechingen. On the following day, a special American unit—Operation Humbug—roared into town to arrest the scientists. They were from operation ALSOS, set up by the Manhattan Project to keep an eye on the Germans. Its scientific head was Samuel Goudsmit.[57] ALSOS was confident that the Germans were a long way from a bomb, but they wanted to debrief the German atomic scientists and to keep them from the Russians. Hahn and nine other scientists were turned over to a British unit commanded by Major T. H. Rittner.[58]

In their first days of captivity, Hahn and Max von Laue (Nobel laureate, 1914) lived cheek by jowl. Both were born in 1879 and soon they were using 'du' and Christian names. The others could not understand why Laue was there. He did not work with uranium and was an outspoken anti-Nazi; naturally he was furious at being gaoled. Goudsmit had put him on the list for discussions about post-war international physics.

After a short migratory period, the captives were moved to England where they were housed in a well-prepared, secure house near Cambridge called Hall Farm. Before the new occupants arrived microphones were hidden in all of the rooms and around the gardens. Some of the prisoners speculated that they might be bugged, but Heisenberg pooh-poohed the idea, it was quite un-English. Five German POWs served as servants and cooks. The prisoners were frustrated. No one would tell them why they were in prison and even minor decisions were made in Washington. They were well-treated and well-fed, but did not know what had happened to their loved ones, who they were not permitted to contact. Hahn kept his equanimity: 'Also I don't take life too seriously in that I always look at the bright side of things.' Major Rittner:

> Shortly before dinner on 6th August I informed Professor HAHN that an announcement had been made by the B.B.C. that an atomic bomb had been dropped. HAHN was completely shattered by the news and said that he felt personally responsible for the deaths of hundreds of thousands of people, as it was his original discovery which had made the bomb possible ... With the help of considerable alcoholic stimulant he was calmed down and we went down to dinner where he announced the news to the assembled guests.[59]

The prisoners could scarcely believe that the Anglo-Americans had done it. They struggled with back of the envelope calculations to see how much uranium-235 would be needed for a chain reaction and speculated about how it had been separated. Heisenberg was stymied:

> Well how have they actually done it? I find it a disgrace that we, the Professors who have worked on it, cannot at least work out how they did it.

On another occasion, Hahn asked Walther Gerlach, professor of experimental physics at Munich who was a strong supporter of the war:

> Are you upset because we did not make the uranium bomb? I thank God on my bended knee that we did not make a uranium bomb. Or are you depressed because the Americans could do it better than we could?

Gerlach's answer was an ambiguous 'yes'.

After four months they received their first letters from home. Hanno and Ilse had married. In August they were visited by C. G. Darwin, and in early September by P. M. S. Blackett.[60] He had served as a naval officer in the First World War before studying physics with Rutherford. After the war he was the first British physicist to work in Germany: in 1924 he was with James Franck and made many German friends. Perhaps they also knew that he was a long-time Labour supporter who had the ear of Prime Minister Attlee. They talked about how to restore and reintegrate German science, but Blackett made it clear that the decisions would be made by higher-ups.

At the end of September, Hahn had a letter from Planck with the news that the President of the KWG had committed suicide. Planck would act temporarily but the directors wanted Hahn as president. The same mail brought his first letter from Meitner; she was pleased finally to have news from him.

On Tuesday 2 October, Hahn, von Laue, and Heisenberg were taken to the Royal Institution in London to confer with senior British scientists: Sir Henry Dale, WL, Sir George Thomson, and A. V. Hill.

During tea and afterwards we were able to talk about all we had at heart. We learned that the Americans had agreed to allow us to return to Germany ... We got the impression that we were being treated with particular benevolence and that everything possible was to be done for German science.[61]

On 16 November, Hahn read in the *Daily Telegraph* that he had been awarded the Nobel Prize for Chemistry. He had not been notified because the Swedes were unable to obtain his address. After anxious days in which he heard nothing more, during which he begged his captors to ask WL for verification, finally the official notification was forwarded to him. He had to respond that he would be unable to attend the ceremony on 10 December, giving no hint of his location, but captors and captives celebrated merrily with drinks, poems and songs.

On Christmas Eve 1945 Hahn ran 11.5 km in 67 minutes; he was very pleased— not bad at the age of 66. Early in the New Year they returned to Germany, still in custody. It was months before Hahn was allowed to see his son and even longer before he could visit Ilse to be introduced to his new-born grandson. He took over as president of the KWG. The British agreed to allow it to continue in their occupation sector, but only with a new name. Hahn persuaded Planck to agree to renaming it the *Max Planck Gesellschaft* (MPG). Later the Americans agreed to allow it in their zone also.

He was allowed to attend the Nobel ceremonies in 1946 to receive his prize, accompanied by a British minder. At a dinner before the ceremony Meitner berated him for sending her out of Germany. He shared the Nobel money with Strassmann. Meitner was bitterly disappointed that in his interviews and speeches in Stockholm he did not mention her contributions. He focused on the message that there were German scientists with clean hands who deserved readmission to the international fellowship. Perhaps Meitner did not totally agree. She never lived in Germany again.

The MPG was formally inaugurated in 1948. Hahn was as good an administrator as he was a scientist, playing a major role in the recovery of German science from the Nazis and the war. He campaigned against the spread of nuclear weapons. His wife collapsed again in 1952. She was hospitalized, given electric shock treatments, but never fully recovered and had little short-term memory. In 1960, he retired as president of the MPG. A few months later his son and daughter-in-law were killed in an automobile accident. His longevity—he died at 90—is especially remarkable considering how few precautions he took during his years working with highly radioactive substances. He would stir solutions with the little finger of his left hand; later in life this nail would not grow, but that seemed the only ill effect. Meitner moved to Cambridge, England, to be near her surviving family members. She died a few months after Hahn—she had not been told of his death.

Hahn has a remarkable position in the history of 'weapons of mass destruction': having a prominent role in the development of both poison gas and atomic bombs. But it is propagandists who lump these two weapon systems together. Gas was an effective weapon in the mole warfare of the First World War, but it was relatively humane. In 1918 on the Western Front only 2.3 per cent of the British hospitalized for gas poisoning died, compared to 7.6 per cent of those ripped into by metals. We do not know how many died at the front by gas, but there is good data for the British horses because they were accompanied by handlers. From July 1916, 44 per cent of the horses with gunshot wounds died compared to 9.5 per cent of those gassed.[62] Poison gas was scarcely used militarily in the Second World War because it is unsuitable for mobile warfare or for bombarding cities from the air because it would take so many bombs to reach lethal gas concentrations; explosive and incendiary bombs did their ghastly work far more efficiently.[63] Gas became a weapon of mass destruction in the confined spaces of the death factories of the Second World War. Zyklon B killed more than one million people at Auschwitz-Birkenau alone. Herded into closed rooms they were textbook victims for poison gas.

Britain post-war

Back in his laboratory after a five-and-a-half year gap, Hill celebrated his 60th birthday by recording the heat of muscle contraction on a new cathode ray oscilloscope, the first time he saw it undistorted by a galvanometer's time lag. UCL established a Biophysics Department in 1951 with Hill as head. He retired a few months later, and his protégé Bernard Katz (Nobel laureate, 1954) took over. Hill had provided this brilliant refugee from Germany with a place to work and helped to bring his parents to safety. Hill gave up his laboratory in 1967 and moved back to Cambridge. He was losing use of his legs. He died ten years later. To the end, he maintained:

> The pursuit of natural knowledge, the investigation of the world—mental and material—in which we live, is not a dull and spiritless affair: rather is it a voyage of adventure of the human mind, a holiday for reckless and imaginative souls.

The mechanism of muscle contraction was worked out. Two proteins actin and myosin form the bulk of the machinery. They cooperate to release energy from ATP. In muscle there are two types of filaments, one containing actin and the other myosin. The muscle shortens when the filaments slide past one another. The filaments account for the increase in contraction when the muscle is stretched—the basis of Starling's Law—because stretching brings them into optimal alignment for interacting. Andrew Huxley was prominent in the discovery of the sliding filaments; he became Jodrell Professor at UCL.

Milne was a major contributor to astrophysics and cosmology. He died before being able to write Hill's obituary; 'He had a genius for writing such notices about his friends…'[64]

Shortly after the war D. R. Hartree returned to Cambridge to succeed Fowler as Plummer Professor of Mathematical Physics. He wrote a widely consulted book on numerical methods.[65] Many of his methods are used today as algorithms for mathematical calculations by digital computers.

WL and molecular biology

In 1947 WL became director of the NPL, a year later he succeeded Rutherford at Cambridge. (Fowler would have succeeded WL as director of the NPL had he not died at age 55.) When WL arrived he appraised the research groups working in the department. Most were working on the fine structure of the atom. On the other extreme a young refugee from central Europe, Max Perutz, hoped to determine the structure of giant biological macromolecules by x-ray diffraction.[66] He had some data from haemoglobin. At best it would take years but WL thought it might be done, so he obtained a grant from the Rockefeller foundation and began to work on the needed mathematics. Next he convinced the Medical Research Council to support two investigators and two assistants for five years as a unit studying biological macro molecules with, which was named the LMB (Laboratory of Molecular Biology). The grant continued to be renewed. The LMB reached it apogee in 1962. The two investigators shared the Nobel Prize for Chemistry: Perutz for determining the structure of haemoglobin and Andrew Kendrew for the structure of another oxygen-carrying protein, myoglobin. Francis Crick and Jim Watson, who had worked in the LMB, shared the Physiology and Medicine prize with Maurice Wilkins from Kings College, London for solving the structure of DNA. WL had given molecular biology a firm footing. Today almost every issue of *Nature* or *Science* shows the structure of a least one huge biological molecule revealed by x-rays.

In 1953 WL and his group moved to the Royal Institution in London where he became the Resident Professor. He succeeded Andrade, who had been forced to resign after two tumultuous years. WL relocated to what many considered an inferior position in part to restore the Royal Institution to what his father had made of it. He retired in 1966 and died in 1971.

Weizmann and Israel

The Labour Government elected in 1945 prohibited further Jewish immigration to Palestine, even by the miserable homeless survivors in the European refugee camps. Weizmann was defeated at the Zionist Congress in 1946—no one was elected president. Jewish terrorists attacked the British in Palestine. His heart was failing and glaucoma was dimming his vision. Without an official title he went to New York as *de facto* leader of the Zionist delegation for the United Nations debate on Palestine. He had to speak about the terrorist attacks on the British, which he called un-Jewish: 'Thou shalt not kill'.[67] They were shameful but those who had torn up the Balfour Declaration were responsible. His romantic dream of how the Jews would peacefully recover their patrimony was an illusion.

On 14 May 1948 Israel declared its independence. Weizmann was one of those who persuaded President Truman to recognize the new state. He became president of Israel. It was a ceremonial position: he was not even permitted to see the minutes of Cabinet meetings. They lived at Rehovoth and most days he went to his laboratory. In 1949 the Sieff Institute became a component of a new Weizmann Institute that was built on the same site in honour of his 70th birthday. He is buried there—he died in 1952. The Institute and the Hebrew University are monuments to his vision of how to develop barren Palestine.

The military-academic –industrial complex

Our protagonists were deeply involved in the emergence of the complex in the Great War, since then the complex has thrived. It is a two-edged sword, because the economic interests of all three participants continually press for improved weapons for use against perceived potential foes. Time and time again the weakness of the academic link has been painfully obvious. Some scientists come up with first-rate ideas, while others—less wise and biased by their interests—sell fantasies to political leaders. As Starling cogently argued, most political leaders have no idea of what science can or cannot do. The development of the atom bomb and the other highly visible successes in the Second World War enormously boosted science in the public's and politician's eyes. It was boosted further by landing men on the moon. Before taking on that enormously expensive venture President Kennedy made sure that his sagest scientific advisors agreed that the journey was feasible.

It was different in 1983 when President Regan proposed a strategic defence initiative to build a shield against intercontinental ballistic missiles. He thought that anyone able to pay the bill could order any science wanted. Many knowledgeable scientists pointed out the daunting hurdles facing successful interception—for instance, being overwhelmed by a flood of cheaper, unarmed incoming missiles or by a shower of decoys released by an incoming missile. Even trying to build a shield is destabilizing. But a small group, led by Edward Teller, eagerly promised to fulfil Reagan's dream, even reviving hopes of the death ray. They were championed by small army of lobbyists from companies that stood to profit. Billions of dollars have been spent, but 30 years later the shield is still being developed and the end is not in sight.[68]

On almost any issue there are some scientists who disagree with the consensus. Such dissidents help to insure that science advances only on impeccable evidence but they can be cherry-picked to support political illusions. 'My scientist says' is not enough. In a better world politicians will be educated to know that they are not qualified to pick their scientific advisors, the point argued so cogently by WHB and A. V. Hill.

Notes and References

Preface

Van der Kloot, W., 'April 1915: Five future Nobel Prize winners inaugurate weapons of mass destruction and the academic-industrial-military complex.' Notes Rec. R. Soc. 58: 149–160 (2004)

Chapter 1. From *Victory* to *Iron Duke*

Barnett, E. de B., *Explosives* (London: Ballière, Tindall and Cox, 1919)

Bergenren, E., *Alfred Nobel. The Man and His Work* (London: Thomas Nelson and Sons, 1962)

Brooke, C. N. L. (ed.), A *History of the University of Cambridge. Volume IV 1870-1990* (Cambridge University Press, 1993)

Davis, L. E. and R. Huttenback, Mammon and the Pursuit of Empire. The Political Economy of British Imperialism, 1860–1912. (Cambridge University Press, 1986)

Fenwick, K., *H.M.S. Victory* (London: Cassell, 1959)

Gray, R. (ed.), *Conway›s All the World›s Fighting Ships. 1906–1921.* (London: Conway Maritime Press, 1986)

Gray, R. and C. Argyle, *Chronicle of the First World War* (Oxford University Press, 1990–91)

Hindenburg, Marshal von, *Out of My Life* (Tran., F. A. Holt) (New York: Harper and Brothers, 1921)

Hobson, J. M., 'The Military-Extraction Gap and the Wary Titan: the Fiscal Sociology of British Defence Policy 1870–1913' (*J. Euro. Econ. Hist* 22, 1993: 461–506)

Hogg, Brig. O. F. G., *The Royal Arsenal. Its Background, Origin, and Subsequent History* (London: Oxford University Press, 1963)

Marder, A. J., *From the Dreadnought to Scapa Flow, Vol. 2.* (Oxford University Press, 1965)

Marder, A. J., *British Naval Policy 1880–1905* (London: Putnam & Co, 1941)

Morris, J., *Fisher's Face* (New York: Random House, 1995)

Massie, R. K., *Dreadnought. Britain, Germany, and the Coming of the Great War* (London: Jonathan Cape, 1992)

Mitchell, B. R., *Abstract of British Historical Statistics* (Cambridge University Press, 1962)

Morris, J., *Fisher's Face* (New York: Random House, 1995)

Moulton, Lord, *Science and the War* (Cambridge University Press, 1919)

Musson, A. E., and E. Robinson, *Science and Technology in the Industrial Revolution* (Manchester: Manchester University Press, 1969)

Parsons, R. H., *The Steam Turbine and Other Inventions of Sir Charles Parsons, OM* (London: Longmans, Green and Co., 1942)

Trebilcock, C., *The Vickers Brothers. Armaments and Enterprise 1854–1914* (London: Europa Publications, 1977)

Van Creveld, M., *Command in War.* (Cambridge, MA: Harvard University Press, 1985)

Van der Kloot, W., *A World War 1 Fact Book* (Stroud: Amberley, 2010)

Van der Kloot, W., 'Lord Justice of Appeal John Fletcher Moulton and explosives production in World War I : 'the mathematical mind triumphant' (*Notes Rec. R. Soc.* 68: 161-186 (2014).

Wadsworth, A., 'Newspaper Circulation 1800–1954.' (*Trans. Manchester Stat. Soc. 1-15 (1955)*

Wolff, L., In Flanders Fields (New York: Viking Press, 1958)

Yerkes, R. M. (ed.), The New World of Science. Its Development During the War (New York: The Century Co., 1920)

1. Moulton, 1919, p 7.
2. Van der Kloot, 2010, p. 9.
3. www.ggdc.net/maddison.
4. Wadsworth, 1955, p. 13.
5. Bergenren, 1962.
6. Barnett, 1919.
7. Marder, 1941. Nicholas, 1999.
8. Hobson, 1993.
9. Mitchell, 1962.
10. Davis and Huttenback, 1986.
11. Marder, 1941. Sumida, 1989.
12. Trebilcock, 1977.
13. Hogg, 1963.
14. Brooke, 1993.
15. Musson and Robinson, 1969.
16. Parsons, 1942.
17. Davis and Huttenback, 1986.
18. Gray and Argyle, 1990-91.
19. Hindenburg, 1921.
20. Wolff, 1958, p. 253.
21. Van Creveld, 1985.
22. Yerkes, 1920.

Chapter 2. Gas Warfare. Otto Hahn.

Barkan, D. K. K., *Walther Nernst and the Transition to Modern Physical Science.* (Cambridge University Press, 1999)

Barrow, C., *The Life of General Sir Charles Carmichael Monro* (London: Hutchinson, 1931)

Bartel, H-G., *Walther Nernst.* (Leipzig: BSB B. G. Teubner, 1989)

Bauer, Oberst, *Der Grosse Krieg im Feld und Heimat* (Tübingen: Oftander'sche Buchhandlung, 1922)

Blake, R. (ed.), *The Private Papers of Douglas Haig 1914–1919* (London: Eyre & Spottiswoode, 1952)

Charles, D., *Between Genius and Genocide. The Tragedy of Fritz Haber, Father of Chemical Warfare* (London: Jonathan Cape, 2005)

Cherwell, and F. Simon. 'Hermann Walther Nernst 1864–1941.' *Obit. Not. Fell. Roy. Soc* 4, 101-112 (1942–44)

Cobb, I. S., *The Red Glutton. Impressions of War near or at the Front* (London: Hudder & Stoughton, 1915)

Corum, J. S., *The Roots of Blitzkrieg. Hans Von Seekt and German Military Reform*
(Lawrence: The University Press of Kansas, 1992)

Cron, H., *Imperial German Army 1914–18. Organization, Structure, and Order of Battle*
(Solihull, West Midlands: Helion and Co., 2002)

Devons, S., 'Rutherford and the Science of His Day.' *Notes Rec. R. Soc.* 45, no. 2, 221-242
(1991)

Duguid, Colonel A F., *The Canadian Forces in the Great War 1914–1919* (Ottawa: J. D.
Patenaude, 1938)

Edmonds, Brig.-Gen. J. E. *Military Operations France and Belgium, 1914.* (vol. 2.)
(London: Macmillan, 1925)

Edmonds, J. E., 'Two German Books on Field Fortifications.' *Roy. Eng. J.* 32, 164-66
(1920)

Eve, A. S., *Rutherford., Being the Life and Letters of the Rt. Hon. Lord Rutherford*
(Cambridge University Press, 1939)

Falkenhayn, E. von, *General Headquarters 1914–1916 and Its Critical Decisions* (London:
Hutchinson & Co., 1919)

Falls, C., *Caporetto 1917* (London: Weidenfeld & Nicholson, 1966)

Farrar-Hockley, A., *Death of an Army* (New York: William Morrow & Co., 1968)

Feather, N., *Lord Rutherford* (London: Blackie & Son, 1940)

Foulkes, Maj,-Gen. C. H. *"Gas!" The Story of the Special Brigade* (Edinburgh: William
Blackwood, 1934)

Gerlack, W. and D. Hahn, *Otto Hahn. Ein Forscherleben Unserer* Zeit (Stuttgart:
Wissenschaftliche Verlagsgesellschaft, 1984)

Glaise-Horstenau, E. (ed.), *Österrich-Ungarns Letzer Kreig 1914–1918* (Wein: Verlag der
Militärwissenschaftlichen Mittelilunge, vol. 6, 1936)

Graves, R., *Goodbye to All That* (London: Doubleday Anchor, 1957)

Greenfield, R. A., I. M. Brown, J. B. Hutchins, J. J. Landolo, R. Jackson, L. N. Slater, and
M. S. Bronze., 'Microbiological, Biological, and Chemical Weapons of Warfare and
Terrorism.' *Amer. J. Med. Sci.* 323, 326-340 (2002)

Haber, L. F., *The Poisonous Cloud: Chemical Warfare in the First World War* (Oxford:
Clarendon Press, 1986)

Hahn, O., *A Scientific Autobiography* (Tran. Willy Ley). (New York: Charles Scribner›s
Sons, 1966)

Hahn, O., *My Life* (Trans E. Kaiser and E. Wilkins) (London: MacDonald, 1970)

Harris, R. and J. Paxman, *A Higher Form of Killing* (New York: Hill and Wang, 2002)

Hartley, Brig H., 'A General Comparison of British and German Methods of Gas Warfare.'
J. Roy. Artill. 46, 492-509 (1919–20)

Hastings, M., *Catastrophe: Europe goes to war 1914* (London: HarperPress, 2013)

Herwig, H. H., *The Marne, 1914* (New York: Random House, 2009)

Hoffmann, K., *Otto Hahn. Stationen Aus Dem Leben* (Berlin: Verlag Neues Leben, 1978)

Hoffmann, K., *Otto Hahn: Achievement and Responsibility* (Tran. J. M. Cole.) (New York:
Springer Verlag, 2001)

Hutchison, K., J. A. Gray, and H. Massey, 'Charles Drummond Ellis. 11 August 1895–10
January 1980.' *Biogr. Mem. Fell, R.S.* 27, 199-233 (1981)

Killian, H., *Wir Stürmten Durchs Friaul* (Neckargemünd: Vowinckel, 1978)

Falls, C., *Caporetto 1917* (London: Weidenfeld & Nicholson, 1966)

Kitchen, M., *The German Offensives of 1918* (Stroud: Tempus, 2001)

Kuczeera, J., *Gustav Hertz* (Postdam: B. G. Teubner Verlagsgesellschaft, 1985)

Kuhn, H.G., 'James Franck (1882–1965).' *Biogr. Mem. Fell. R. Soc.*11, 53-74 (1966)

Liddell Hart, B., *History of the First World War.* (London: Book Club Associates, 1973)

Ludendorff, E. von., *Ludendorff's Own Story* (New York: Harper and Brothers, 1919)

Lutz, R. H., *The Causes of the German Collapse in 1918* (Tran. W. L. Campbell) (Stanford:
Stanford University Press, 1934)

Marion G., *A Strange and Formidable Weapon : British Responses to World War I Poison Gas* (Lincoln: University of Nebraska Press, 2008)

Medical Department of the United States Army in the World War., *Medical Aspects of Gas Warfare* (ed. by Maj.-Gen. M. W. Ireland) (Washington: Government Printing Office, vol. XIV, 1926)

Meitner, L., 'Looking Back.' *Bull. Atomic Sci.* November 2–7 (1964)

Mendelsohn, K., *The World of Walther Nernst. The Rise and Fall of German Science, 1864–1941* (London: MacMillan, 1973)

Middlebrook, M., *The Kaiser's Battle. 21 March 1918: The First Day of the German Spring Offensive* (London: Penguin Books, 1983)

Moyer, L. V., *Victory Must Be Ours* (New York: Hippocrene Books, 1995)

Oliphant, M., 'Some Personal Recollections of Rutherford, the Man.' *Notes Rec. R. Soc.* 27, 7-23 (1972).

Perutz, M. F., 'The Cabinet of Dr. Haber.' *NY Rev Books* 43, no. 11, 31-36 (1996)

Read, J. M., *Atrocity Propaganda* (New Haven: Yale University Press, 1941)

Rutherford, E., *Radio-Activity* (Cambridge University Press, 1904)

Prentiss, A. M., *Chemicals in War* (New York: McGraw-Hill, 1937)

Sabine, E., *Lise Meitner an Otto Hahn. Breife aus den Jahren 1912 bis 1924* (Stuttgart: Wissenschaftliche Verlagesellschaft, 1992)

Schindler, J. R., *Isonzo. The Forgotten Sacrifice of the Great War* (Westport, Ct: Praeger, 2001)

Sime, R. L., *Lise Meitner. A Life in Physics* (Berkeley: University California Press, 1997)

Stallings, L., *The Doughboys. The story of the AEF, 1918–1918* (New York: Harper and Row, 1963)

Stoltzenberg, D., *Fritz Haber. Chemist, Nobel Laureate, German, Jew* (Philadelphia: Chemical Heritage Press, 2004)

Szöllösi-Janze, M., *Fritz Haber 1868–1934* (München: C.H.Beck, 1998)

Vogt, A., *Oberst Max Bauer. Generalstabsoffizier Im Zwieliecht* (Osnabrüch: Biblio Verlag, 1974)

Zabecki, D. T., *Steel Wind* (Westport CT: Greenwood, 1994)

Zweig, S., *The World of Yesterday (New York: Viking Press, 1943)*

1. Thoughts and quotes attributed to Hahn are from Hahn, 1970.
2. Sime, 1997. Meitner, 1964.
3. Rutherford, 1904. Rutherford, 1911. Hahn, 1966.
4. Eve, 1939. Feather, 1940. Devons, 1991. http://nobelprize.org/nobel_prizes/nobelprize_facts.html
5. Zweig, 1943, p. 235.
6. Kuczeera, 1985. Kuhn, 1964. Nobel Foundation: http://nobelprize.org/nobel_prizes/nobelprize_facts.html.
7. Van der Kloot, 2010.
8. Herwig, 2009.
9. Hutchison, 1981.
10. Cobb, 1915. Read, 1941.
11. Meitner's letters to Hahn are in Sabine, 1992.
12. Edmonds, 1925. Farrar-Hockley, 1968.
13. Blake, 1952.
14. Falkenhayn, 1919.
15. Hahn, 1970, p. 118.
16. Barkan, 1999. Bartel, 1989. Mendelsohn, 1973.
17. Bauer, 1922. Vogt, 1974.
18. Hoffmann, 1978.
19. Cron, 2002.
20. Hart, 1930. Foulkes, 1934.

21. Duguid, 1938.
22. Hartley 1919–20.
23. Medical Department of the United States Army, 1926. Greenfield et. al., 2002.
24. Public Record Office WO 32/5183.
25. Graves, 1957.
26. Foulkes, 1934.
27. Hasting, 2013, chapter 4.
28. Barrow, 1931.
29. Haber, 1986.
30. Haber, 1986, p. 217.
31. Stallings, 1963, p. 205.
32. Foulkes, 1934.
33. Edmonds, 1920.
34. Blake, 1952.
35. Stoltzenberg, 2004.
36. Hartley, 1919–20.
37. Information about the Caporetto attack comes from: Killian, 1978; Falls, 1966; Glaise-Horstenau, 1936; Schindler, 2001.
38. Cron, 2002, p. 167.
39. Moyer, 1995, p. 232.
40. Public Record Office MUN 5/386.
41. Information about the German attacks in 1918 comes from: Ludendorff, 1919; Lutz, 1934; Middlebrook, 1983; Kitchen, 2001.
42. Zabecki, 1994.
43. Haber, 1986, p. 144.

Chapter 3. Food and Wound Shock. Ernest Starling.

Addison, C., Politics from within 1911–1918. (3 vols.) (London: Herbert Jenkins, vol. 2, 1925)

B., J., 'Sir William Maddock Bayliss.' *Proc. R. Soc. B* 99, xxvii-xxxii (1926)

Bayliss, L. E., 'William Maddock Bayliss, 1860–1924: Life and Scientific Work.' *Persp. Biol. Med.* 4, 460-479 (1961)

Bayliss, W. M., 'Viscosity and Intra-Venous Injection of Saline Solutions.' *J. Physiol. Lond.* 50 xxiii-xxiv (1916)

Bayliss, W. M., *The physiology of food and economy in diet*, London: Longmans, Green & Co. 1917)

Bayliss, W. M., *Intravenous Injection in Wound Shock*. (London: Longmans, Green, & Co., 1918)

Bennison, S. A., C. Barger, and E. L. Wolfe, 'Walter B. Cannon and the Mystery of Shock: A Study of Anglo-American Co-opperation in World War I' *Medic. His.* 35, 217-249 (1991)

Bennison, S., A. C. Barger, and E. L. Wolfe., *Walter B. Cannon, Science and Society.* (Cambridge MA: Harvard University Press, 2000)

Beveridge, W. H., *British Food Control.* (New Haven: Yale University Press, 1928)

Bucholz, A. (ed.), *Delbrück›s Modern Military History.* (Lincoln: University of Nebraska Press, 1997)

Cannon, W. B., *Bodily Changes in Pain, Hunger, Fear and Rage: An Account of Recent Researches into the Function of Emotional Excitement.* (New York: Appleton, 1915)

Chick, H., 'Charles James Martin, 1866–1955' *Biogr. Mems Fell. R. Soc.* 2, 172-208 (1956)

Chick, H., E. J. Dalyell, E. M. Hume, H. M. M. Mackay, H. Smith and H. Wimberger, *Observations Upon the Prophylaxis and Cure of Rickets at The University Kinderklinik, Vienna* (London: HMSO, 1923)

Cowell, E. M., 'The Initiation of Wound Shock and Its Relation to Surgical Shock.' *Lancet* July 1–27 (1919)

Crowther, J. G., 'Richard Burdon Haldane 1856–1928.' In *Statesmen of Science*. (London: Cresset Press, 1965)

Dale, H. H., 'Frederick Gowland Hopkins.' *Obit. Not. Fell. Roy. Soc.* 6, 115-145 (1948)

Douglas, C. G., 'John Scott Haldane 1860–1936' *Obit. Not. Fell. Roy. Soc.* 2, 115-139 (1936–38)

Drummond, J. C. and A. Wilbraham, *The Englishman's Food*. (London: Jonathan Cape, 1957)

Eisenmenger, A., *Blockade. The Diary of a Middle-Class Woman 1914–1924*. (London: Constable & Co., 1932)

Evans, C. L., *Reminiscences of Bayliss and Starling*. (Cambridge University Press, 1964)

Feldberg, W. S., 'Henry Hallett Dale. 1875–1968.' *Biogr. Mem. Fell. Roy. Soc.* 16, 77-174 (1970)

Final Report of the Commissioners., *Royal Commission on University Education in London*. (London: HMSO, vol. XL 1913)

Flexner, A., *An Autobiography*. (New York: Simon and Schuster, 1960)

Ford, J. H., *Administration: American Expeditionary Forces* (The Medical Department of the United States Army in the World War, ed. C. Lynch, vol. II) (Washington: U. S. Govt. Print. Off., 1927)

Fullerton, A., G. Dreyer, and H. C. Bazett., 'Observations on the Direct Transfusion of Blood, with a Description of a Simple Method.' *Lancet* 715-17 (1917)

Haldane, R. B., *An Autobiography*. (London: Hodder and Stoughton, 1929)

Haber, L. F., *The Poisonous Cloud: Chemical Warfare in the First World War*. (Oxford: Clarendon Press, 1986)

Hardie, M. and A. Warber, *Our Italian Front*. (London: A & C Black, 1920)

Henderson, J., *A Life of Ernest Starling*. (Oxford University Press, 2005)

Henriksen, J. H., *Ernest Henry Starling*. (Copenhagen: Laegeforenings Forlag, 2000)

Hill, A. V., *Memories and Reflections*. (3 vols.) (London: Royal Society, 1974)

Hodgkin, A., 'Edgar Douglas Adrian, Baron Adrian of Cambridge. 30 November 1889–4 August 1977'. *Biogr. Mem. Fell. Roy. Soc.* 25, 1-73 (1979)

Hoover, H., *Memoirs of Herbert Hoover 1874–1920*. (London: Hollis and Carter, 1952)

M. C. J., 'Ernest Henry Starling — 1866–1927.' *Proc. R. Soc. B* 102, xvii-xxvii (1928)

Knowlton, F. P. 'The Influence of Colloids on Diuresis.' *J. Physiol. Lond.* 43, 219-231 (1911)

Liddell Hart, B. H., *History of the First World War*. (London: Book Club Associates, 1930)

Loewi, O., 'An Autobiographical Sketch.' *Persp. Biol. and Med.* 4, 3-25 (1960)

Logan, Sir D., *Haldane and the University of London*. (London: Birkbeck College, 1960)

Macpherson, W. G., A. A. Bowlby, C. Wallace, and C. English, *Medical Services. Surgery of the War*. (London: HMSO, vol. I, 1922)

Martin, C. J., 'Ernest Henry Starling, C.M.G., M.D., F.R.S.: Life and Work.' *Brit. Med. J.* 900-905 (1927)

Minutes of the War Cabinet 1915, in Gilbert, Martin. *The Churchill War Papers*. (6 vols.) (London: Heinemann, 1993)

Needham, J., 'Sir Frederick Gowland Hopkins, O.M., F.R.S. (1861–1947).' *Notes Rec. Roy. Soc.*. 17, 117-162 (1962)

Palmer, A., *The Gardeners of Salonika*. (London: Andre Deutsch, 1965)

Patterson, S. W., H. Piper, and E. H. Starling, 'The regulation of the heart beat'. *J. Physiol. Lond.* 14, 465-513 (1914)

Prentiss, A. M., *Chemicals in War*. (New York: McGraw-Hill, 1937)

Rous, P., and G. M. Wilson, 'Fluid Substitutes for Transfusion after Hemorrhage.' *JAMA* 70, 219-222 (1919)

Sinclair H. M. 'Chick, Dame Harriette (1875–1977)', in Oxford Dictionary of National Biography (ed. H. C. G. Matthew and Brian Harrison), vol. 4, pp. 458-459 (Oxford University Press, 2004).

Skalweit, A., *Die Deutsche Kreigsnährunswirtschaft*. (New Haven: Yale University Press, 1927)

Stansfield, A. E., 'An Apparatus for Transfusion of Blood by the Citrate Method.' *Lancet* . March 2 (1918)

Starling, E. H., *Principles of Human Physiology*. (London: J. & A. Churchill, 1912)

Starling, E. H., 'Wound Shock.' *Brit. Med. J.* 263 (1918)

Starling, E. H., *The Oliver-Sharpey Lectures on the Feeding of Nations. A Study in Applied Physiology*. (London: Longman, Green & Co., 1919)

Starling, E. H., 'The Food Supply of Germany During the War.' *J. R. Stat. Soc.* 83, 225-254 (1920)

Starling, E. H., 'Natural Science in Education.' *Lancet II*, 365-368 (1918)

Starling, E. H., and F. G. Hopkins, 'Note on the Urine in a Case of Phosphorus Poisoning.' *Guys Hosp. Rep.* 47, 275-278 (1890)

Sturdy, S., 'From the Trenches to the Hospitals at Home: Physiologists, Clinicians and Oxygen Therapy.' In *Medical Innovations in Historical Perspective*, (ed. J. V. Pickstone), pp. 104-123 (London: Macmillan, 1992)

Sturdy, S., 'War as Experiment. Physiology, Innovation and Administration in Britain, 1914–1918: The Case of Chemical Warfare.' In *War, Medicine and Modernity*, (ed. R. Cooter, M. Harrison and S. Sturdy), pp. 65-84 (Stroud: Sutton Publishing, 1998)

Tansey, E. M., 'Sir William Maddock Bayliss (1860–1924).' Oxford Dictionary of National Biography (ed. H. C. G. Matthew and B. Harrison), vol. 11, pp. 409-410 (Oxford University Press, 2004)

Van der Kloot, W., 'William Maddock Bayliss's therapy for wound shock'. *Notes Rec. R. Soc.* 64: 271-286. (2010)

1. Henderson, 2005. Henriksen, 2000. 'M. C. J. 1928.
2. Loewi, 1960, pp. 3-25.
3. Martin, 1927, p. 903.
4. Martin, 1927, p. 900.
5. Needham, 1962. Dale, 1948.
6. Starling andHopkins, 1890.
7. Bayliss, 1961.
8. Evans, 1964.
9. Haldane, 1929. Logan, 1960. Crowther, 1965.
10. Flexner, 1960, p. 92.
11. Final Report of the Commissioners, 1913.
12. Henderson 2005, p. 99.
13. Royal Society Archives Minutes of the War Committee, 1914.
14. Douglas, 1936–1938.
15. Wellcome Archives Starling letters in CLE 30.
16. Henriksen, 2000, p. 78.
17. Wellcome archives GC/223/B
18. Starling, 1912.
19. Drummond and Wilbraham, 1957, p. 426.
20. Chick, 1956.
21. Wellcome Archives GC/185/1.
22. Cowell, 1919,
23. The Times, 'Maj-Gen Sir Ernest Cowell; Wartime Medical Services in the Mediterranean. (Obituaries)'. 27 February 1971, p. 14.
24. Patterson *et. al.*, 1914.
25. Knowlton, 1911,
26. Bayliss, 1916.
27. Haber, 1986, p. 137.
28. Palmer, 1965.
29. Liddell Hart, 1930, p. 207.
30. Palmer, 1965, p. 70
31. Palmer, 1965, p. 132-135.
32. Minutes of the War Cabinet, 1993.

33. Archives of the Royal Society 19 February 1908.
34. Henderson, 2005, p. 115.
35. Hardie Allen. 1920.
36. Prentiss, 1937.
37. Haber, 1986, p. 118.
38. Public Record Office MUN 4/27/35.
39. Feldberg, 1970.
40. Public Record Office FD 1/5262.
41. Cannon, 1915.
42. Bennison *et. al.*, 1991 and 2000.
43. Fullerton, *et. al.* 1917.
44. Medical Research Committee, 1917.
45. Fullerton and Bazett, 1917.
46. Archives of the Royal Society Minutes of the food [war] committee.
47. Needham, 1962.
48. Hill, 1974, p. 71.
49. Starling, 1912.
50. Beveridge, 1928.
51. Archives of the Royal Society Minutes of the food [war] committee.
52. Archives of the Royal Society Minutes of the food [war] committee.
53. Drummond and Wilbraham, 1957, p. 433.
54. Chick *et. al.*, 1923.
55. Archives of the Royal Society Minutes of the food [war] committee.
56. Bayliss, 1917.
57. Archives of the Royal Society Minutes of the food [war] committee.
58. Archives of the Royal Society Minutes of the food [war] committee.
59. Stansfield, 1918.
60. Dale, 1947.
61. Starling, 1918, p. 263.
62. Public Record Office WO 142/7.
63. Evans, 1964.
64. Bayliss, 1918. p. 152.
65. Ford, 1927.
66. Rous and Wilson, 1919.
67. Macpherson, *et. al.*, 1922.
68. Ford, 1927.
69. Sturdy, 1992, 1998.
70. Hodgkin, 1979,
71. Drummond and Wilbraham, 1957, p. 225.
72. Drummond and Wilbraham, 1957.
73. Addison, 1925, p. 65.
74. Public Record Office MAF 60/149.
75. http://www.firstworldwar.com/source/armisticeterms.htm.
76. Archives of the Royal Society Minutes of the food [war] committee.
77. Hoover, 1952, p. 287.
78. Bucholz, A., 1997.
79. Eisenmenger, 1932.
80. Sinclair, 2005.
81. Public Record Office FO/608/267/17.
82. Starling, 1920.
83. Starling, 1920.
84. Skalweit, 1927
85. Starling, 1918.

Chapter 4. Explosives. Chaim Weizmann

Berlin, I., 'The Biographical Facts' in *Chaim Weizmann. A Biography by Several Hands,* (ed. M. W. Weisgal and J. Carmichael) (London: Weidenfield and Nicholson, 1962)

Berlin, I., *Personal Impressions* (London: Hogarth Press, 1980)

Cross, C. (ed.), *Life with Lloyd George, the Diary of A. J. Sylvester 1931–45* (London: Macmillan, 1975)

Delaunay, A., *L'institut Pasteur, Des Origines a` Aujourd'hui* (Paris: Interne de l'Hôpital de l'Institut Pasteur, 1962)

Fivel, T. R., 'Weizmann and the Balfour Declaration.' in *Chaim Weizmann. A Biography by Several Hands* (ed. M. W. Weisgal and J. Carmichael) (London: Weidenfield and Nicholson, 1962)

Furness, R., *The Fermentation Industries* (London: Ernest Benn, 1924)

Great Britain, *History of the Ministry of Munitions.* (12 vols.) (London: HMSO, 1920–22)

Gabriel, C. L., 'Butanol Fermentation Process.' *Indust. Eng. Chem.* 20, 1063-67 (1928)

Jones, T., *Lloyd George.* (London: Oxford University Press, 1951)

Levy, S. I., *Modern Explosives* (London: Sir Isaac Pitman & Sons 1920)

Lewis, G., *Balfour and Weizmann. The Zionist, the Zealot and the Emergence of Israel* (London: Continuum, 2009)

Lloyd George, D., *War Memoirs of David Lloyd George* (2 vols.) (London: Odhams Press, 1938)

Moulton, H. F., *The Life of Lord Moulton* (London: Nisbet, 1922)

Nicolson, H., 'People and Things.' *The Spectator*, May 26, 900 (1939)

Polkehn, K., 'Zionism and Kaiser Wilhelm.' *J. Palestine Stud.* 4, 76-90 (1975)

Reinharz, J., 'Chaim Weizmann and the Elusive Manchester Professorship.' *AJS Review*, 9, 215-46 (1984)

Samuel, Viscount, 'A Tribute by the First High Commissioner for Palestine.' in *Chaim Weizmann. A Tribute on His Seventieth Birthday* (ed. P. Goodman) (London: Victor Gollancz, 1945)

Samuel, Viscount, *Memoirs* (London: Cresset Press, 1945)

Seiff, I. M., 'The Manchester Period.' in *Chaim Weizmann. A Biography by Several Hands* (ed. M. W. Weisgal and J. Carmichael) (London: Weidenfield and Nicholson, 1962)

Sieff, I. M., *Memories* (London: Weidenfeld and Nicolson, 1970)

Skidelsky, R., *John Maynard Keynes; Hopes Betrayed 1893–1920* (London: Penguin Books. 1983)

Speakman, H. B., 'Dr Weizmann's Contribution to Microbiology' in *Chaim Weizmann. A Tribute on His Seventieth Birthday* (ed. P. Goodman) (London: Victor Gollancz, 1945)

Stevens, R. P., 'Smuts and Weizmann.' *J. Palestine Stud.* 3, 35-59 (1973)

Van der Kloot, W., 'Lord Justice of Appeal John Fletcher Moulton and Explosives Production in World War I: the Mathematical Mind Triumphant', *Notes Rec. R. Soc.* 68: 161-186 (2014)

Weizmann, C., 'Production of Acetone and Alcohol by Bacteriological Processes.' (US Patent Office, 1919)

Weisgal, M. W, *The Letters and Papers of Chaim Weizmann*, vol. V (London: Oxford University Press, 1974).

Weizmann, C., *Trial and Error* (London: Hamish Hamilton, 1949)

Wilson, T. (ed.), *The Political Diaries of C. P. Scott 1911–1928* (London: Collins, 1970)

1. Lloyd George, 1938, p. 348-349.
2. Cross, 1975, p. 87.
3. Weizmann, 1949, p.125.
4. Furness, 1924.

5. Speakman, 1945, pp. 130-37.
6. Weizmann, 1949, p. 190.
7. Berlin, 1962.
8. Weisgal 1974, p. 326.
9. Jones, 1951.
10. Samuel, 1945.
11. Van der Kloot, 2014.
12. Public Record Office NO 21073
13. Delaunay, 1962.
14. Wilson, 1970, p. 164.
15. Great Britain, 1921, vol. VII, p. 67.
16. Wilson, 1970, p. 255.
17. Public Record Office MUN/7/238
18. Weizmann, 1919.
19. Gabriel, 1928, pp. 1063-1067.
20. Weisgal, 1974, Letter to Nathan 17 February 1916.
21. Public Record Office MUN 192.
22. Great Britain, 1921, vol. XII, chap 4.
23. Great Britain, 1921, vol. VII, p. 67.
24. Public Record Office MUN/7/235.
25. Reinharz, 1984, pp. 215-246.
26. Public Record Office MUN/7/238.
27. Weisgal, 1974, Letter to Nathan 27 April 1916.
28. Weisgal, 1974,Letter to Nathan 24 May 1916.
29. Weisgal, 1974, Letters to Ahad 4 April 1916 and to Vera 14 April 1916.
30. Weisgal, 1974, Letters to Scott 1 March 1917 and to Adam 4 June 1917.
31. Weisgal, 1974, Letter to Scott 20 September 1917.
32. Weisgal, 1974, vol. V, p. 39.
33. Furness, 1924.
34. Levy, 1920.
35. Weizmann, 1949, p. 99.
36. Jones, 1951, p. 97.
37. Wilson, 1970, p. 255.
38. Sieff, 1970.
39. Skidelsky, 1983, p. 336.
40. Weizmann, 1949, p. 207.
41. Public Record Office FO145/805/1.
42. Stevens, 1973, p. 35-59.
43. Nicolson, 1939, p. 900.
44. Weizmann, 1949, p. 256.
45. Public Record Office, War Cabinet Minutes Curzon memo 26 October 1917.
46. Polkehn, 1975, pp. 76-90.
47. Weizmann, 1949, p. 150.
48. Great Britain, 1921, vol. VII, p. 68.
49. Gabriel, 1928.
50. Great Britain, 1920–1922 VII, pp. 69-70, pp. 98-99.
51. Public Record Office Mun 4/1097.
52. Weizmann, 1949, p. 275.
53. Berlin, 1980, p. 45.
54. Weizmann, 1949, p. 302

Chapter 5. Locating Submerged U-boats. William Henry Bragg

Allen, H. S., 'Charles Glover Barkla 1877–1944.', *Obit. Not. Fell. R. Soc.* 1, 341-366 (1947)

Andrade, E. N. d., ‹William Henry Bragg. 1862–1942.›, *Obit. Not. Fell. R. Soc.* 4, 277-300 (1942–1944)

Balfour, A. J., *Chapters of Autobiography* (London: Cassell & Company, 1930)

Beatty, D. (ed.), *The Beatty Papers: Selections from the Private and Official Correspondence of Admiral of the Fleet Earl Beatty* (Aldershot: Scholar Press for the Navy Records Society, 1989)

Bell, D. S., D. Johnson and P. Morris (ed.), *Biographical Dictionary of French Political Leaders since 1870.* (New York: Simon & Schuster, 1990)

Bragg, W. H., 'X-rays and crystalline structure.', *Proc. Roy. Instit.* 21, 198-207 (1914)

Black, N., *The British Naval Staff in the First World War* (Woodbridge: Boydell Press, 2009)

Blake, R. (ed.), *The Private Papers of Douglas Haig 1914–1919* (London: Eyre & Spottiswoode, 1952.

Bragg W. H. and W.L. Bragg, *X-rays and Crystal Structure* (London: G. Bell & Sons, 1915)

Bragg, W. L. and G.M. Caroe, ‹Sir William Bragg F.R.S. (1862–1952).›, *Notes Rec. R. Soc.* 17, 168-182 (1962)

Brian, D., *The Curies. A Biography of the Most Controversial Family in Science.* (New York: John Wiley, 2005)

Brock, M. and E. Brock (ed.), *H. H. Asquith. Letters to Venetia Stanley* (Oxford University Press, 1982)

Buchanan, L. R., *The Governmental Career of Sir Eric Campbell Geddes* (thesis, University of Virginia, 1979)

Campbell, J., *Jutland. An Analysis of the Fighting* (New York: Lyons Press, 1986)

Carlyon, L. A., *Gallipoli* (London: Doubleday, 2002.)

Caroe, G. M., *William Henry Bragg 1862–1942* (Cambridge University Press, 1978)

Chalmers, W. S., *The Life and Letters of David, Earl Beatty, Admiral of the Fleet, Viscount Borodale of Wexford, Baron Beatty of the North Sea and of Brooksby, P.C., G.C.B., O.M., G.C.V.O., D.S.O., D.C.L., Ll.D.* (London: Hodder and Stoughton, 1951)

Churchill, W. S. *The World Crisis 1911–1918* (2 vols.) (London: Odhams Press, 1939)

Doenitz, K., *Memoirs. Ten Years and Twenty Days.* (tran. R. H. Stevenson) New York: De Capo Press, 1997)

Dubinson, C., *Building Radar* (London: Methuen, 2010)

Eve A. S. and J. Chadwick, 'Lord Rutherford. 1871–1937.', *Obit. Not. Fell. R. Soc.* 2, 395-423 (1936–1938)

Eve, A. S., *Rutherford. Being the Life and Letters of the Rt. Hon. Lord Rutherford, O.M.* (Cambridge University Press, 1939)

Feather, N., *Lord Rutherford* (London: Blackie & Son, 1940)

Fleck, A., 'Frederick Soddy. Born Eastbourne 2 September 1877 Died Brighton 26 September 1956.', *Biogr. Mem. Fell. R. Soc.* 3, 203-216 (1957)

Fleming, C. A., 'Ernest Marsden. 1889–1970.', *Biogr. Mem. Fell. Roy. Soc.* 17, 463-496 (1971)

Foster, J. S., 'Arthur Stewart Eve 1862–1948.' *Obit. Not. Fell. Roy. Soc.* 6, 396-407 (1949)

Gaulle, Charles de, *The Enemy›s House Divided* (tran. R. Eden) (Chapel Hill: University of North Carolina Press, 2002)

Gibson, R. H. and M. Prendergast, *The German Submarine War 1914–1918* (London: Constable, 1931)

Gray, E. A., *The U-Boat War 1914–1918* (London: Leo Cooper, 1972)

Gretton, P., 'The U-Boat Campaign in Two World Wars.' in *Naval Warfare in the Twentieth Century. 1900–1935* (ed. by G. Jordan) (London: Croom Helm, 1977)

Grieves, K., *Sir Eric Geddes. Business and Government in War and Peace.* (Manchester: Manchester University Press, 1989)

Gusewelle, J. K., 'Science and the Admiralty during World War I: The Case of the Board of Invention and Research.' in *Naval Warfare in the Twentieth Century.* (ed. G. Jordan) (London: Croom Helm, 1977)

Hackmann, W., *Seek & Strike. Sonar, anti-submarine warfare and the Royal Navy 1914–1954* (London: HMSO, 1984)

Hunt, F. V., *Electroacoustics: The Analysis of Transduction and Its Historical Background* (Cambridge MA: Harvard University Press, 1954)

James, Adml Sir W., *The Eyes of the Navy. A Biographical Study of Admiral Sir Reginald Hall* (London: Methuen, 1955)

Jameson, W., *The Most Formidable Thing. The Story of the Submarine from the Earliest Days to the End of World War I* (London: Rupert Hart-Davis, 1965)

Jellicoe, Earl, *The Submarine Peril. The Admiralty Policy in 1917* (London: Cassel & Co., 1934)

Hamilton, Gen. Sir I., *The Commander* (ed. A. Farrar-Hockley) (London: Hollis & Carter, 1957)

Jenkin, J., *William and Lawrence Bragg, Father and Son* (Oxford University Press, 2008)

Katzir, S., 'Who Knew Piezoelectricity? Rutherford and Langevin on Submarine Detection and the Invention of Sonar. ' *Notes Rec. R. Soc.* 66, 141-157 (2012)

Lowery, H., 'Paget, Sir Richard Arthur Surtees, Second Baronet.' *Oxford Dictionary of National Biography* (ed. H. C. G. Matthew and B. Harrison), vol. 42, pp. 368-369 (Oxford University Press, 2004)

MacLeod, R M. and E. K. Andrews, 'Scientific advice in the war at sea, 1915–1917: The Board of Invention and Research.', *J. Contemp. Hist.* 6, 3-40 (1971)

Massie, R. K., *Castles of Steel* (New York: Random House, 2003)

Messimer, D. R., *Find and Destroy: Antisubmarine Warfare in World War I* (Annapolis: Naval Institute Press, 2001)

Millikan, R. A., *The Autobiography of Robert A. Millikan* (London: Macdonald, 1951)

Molinie, P. and S. Boudia, 'Mastering Picocoulombs in the 1890›s: The Curies Quartz-Electrometer,and How it Shaped Early Radioactivity Theory.' *J. Electrostatics* 67, 524-530 (2009)

Morris, J., *Fisher›s Face* (New York: Random House, 1995)

Moorehead, A., *Gallipoli* (Ware: Wordsworth Editions, 1997)

Rayleigh, *Lord Balfour in his Relation to Science* (Cambridge University Press, 1930)

Niemöller, M., *From U-Boat to Concentration Camp* (London: William Hodge, 1936)

Newbolt, H., *Naval Operations.* (vol. V) (London: Longman, Green & Co., 1931)

Rayleigh, ‹The Earl of Balfour (1848–1930).› *Proc. Roy. Soc. A* 129, xv-xxxiii (1930)

Rayleigh, *The Life of Sir J. J. Thomson* (Cambridge University Press, 1942)

Rutherford, E., 'Moseley, Henry Gwyn Jeffreys (1887–1915).' *Oxford Dictionary of National Biography* (ed. H. C. G. Matthew and B. Harrison), vol. 39, pp. 455-456 (Oxford University Press, 2004)

Scaife, W. G., *From Galaxies to Turbines. Science, Technology and the Parsons Family.* (Bristol: Institute of Physics Publishing, 2000)

Sims, Rear-Adml W. S., *The Victory at Sea* (London: John Murray, 1920)

Spindler, A., *Der Handelskreig Mit U-Booten* (Berlin: E. G. Mittler & Sohn, 1933)

Tarrant, V. E., *Jutland: The German Perspective* (Annapolis: Naval Institute Press, 1995)

Thomson, G. P., 'Charles Galton Darwin. 1887–1962.' *Biogr. Mem. Fell. Roy. Soc.* 9, 69-85 (1963)

Travers, T., *Gallipoli 1915* (Stroud: Tempus Publishing, 2001)

T. R. and H. T. T., 'William Symington McCormick.' *Proc. Roy. Soc. A*, 130, xv-xxiii (1931)

Tuchman, B. W., *The Zimmermann Telegram* (London: Constable, 1959)

Tyne, G. F. J., *Saga of the Vacuum Tube* (Indianapolis: Howard W. Sams, 1977)

Wilson, H. W., *Hush or the Hydrophone Service* (London: Mills & Boon, 1920)

Wood, A. B., *A Textbook of Sound* (London: G. Bell and Sons, 1949)

Wood, A. B., 'From B.I.R. To R.N.S.S. Part 1. Hawkcraig. Aberdour, 1915–1917.' *J Roy Naval Sci Service* 16, 123-134 (1961)

Wood, A. B. 'From Board of Invention and Research to Royal Naval Scientific Service.' *J Roy Naval Sci Service* 20, 16-41 (1965)

Zimmerman, D., 'Langevin and the Discovery of Active Sonar or Asdic.' *Northern Mariner* 12, 39-52 (2002)

Yerkes, R. M. (ed), *The New World of Science. Its Development During the War* (New York: The Century Co., 1920)

Young, K., *Balfour: the Happy Life of the Politician, Prime Minister, Statesman and Philosopher 1948–1930 (London: G. Bell and Sons, 1963)*

1. Bell, et. al. 1990, pp. 320-321. In March 1917 he became Minister of War and in September also became Prime Minister. He was replaced by Clemenceau in November 1917.
2. Balfour, 1930. Rayleigh, 1930. Young, 1963.
3. Spindler, 1933.
4. MacLeod and Andrews, 1971. Hackmann, 1984.
5. Rayleigh, 1942. Gibb and McConnell, 2004. Desch and Bosnell, 2004. Scaife, 2000.
6. Royal Institution MS WHB. WHB's handwritten autobiography is the source for unattributed quotes from him. The collection also includes correspondence with Rutherford, Fisher, and others and there are quotes from them as well. Other major sources of information about WHB are Bragg and Caroe, 1962, Andrade, 1942–1944), Jenkin, 2008.
7. Morris, 1995.
8. Brock and Brock, 1982.
9. MacLeod and Andrews, 1971.
10. Rayleigh, 1942, p. 179.
11. Rayleigh, 1942, p. 179.
12. Public Record Office ADM 293/5.
13. Caroe, 1978. His daughter's book is tells about his personality, his wife's, and his elder son's.
14. Eve and Chadwick, 1936–1938. Eve, 1939.
15. Fleck, 1957: 203-16.
16. Fleming, 1971.
17. Caroe, 1978, p. 81.
18. Jenkin, 2008, p. 365.
19. Moorehead, 2002. Travers, 2001.
20. Falconer, 2004.
21. Caroe, 1978, p. 73.
22. Bragg, 1914. Bragg and Bragg, 1915. WL Bragg's Nobel Lecture. http://www.nobel.se
23. Feather, 1940.
24. Thomson 1963.
25. Caroe, 1978, p. 98.
26. Wood, 1949, p. 158.
27. Wood, 1949.
28. Eve, 1939, p. 250.
29. Hackman, 1984, p. 21.
30. Wilson, 1920.
31. Public Record Office ADM 218/179.
32. Wood, 1961, 1964. Deacon, 1964,
33. Public Record Office ADM218/2.
34. Massie, 2003, p. 671.
35. Beatty, 1989, p. 271.
36. Lowery, 2004.
37. Public Record Office ADM131/107.
38. T. R. and H. T. T. 1931.
39. Churchill, 1939, pp. 630-658.

40. Chalmers, 1951.
41. Campbell, 1986. Tarrant, 1995.
42. Morris, 1995, p. 285.
43. Hackmann, 1984.
44. Chalmers, 1951, p. 271.
45. Public Record Office ADM212/1.
46. Wood, 1964.
47. Public Record Office ADM245/6.
48. Public Record Office 10886/1624.
49. Public Record Office ADM186/408.
50. Katzir, 2012.
51. Hackmann, 1984.
52. Zimmerman, 2002 includes a translation of Langevin's short account of his work.
53. Brian, 2005.
54. Tyne, 1977.
55. Hunt, 1954.
56. Caroe, 1978, p. 86.
57. Public Record Office ADM 186/429. After the war a copy was discovered by the British in the Ottoman archives.
58. Caroe, 1978, p. 86.
59. Public Record Office CAB 24/15.
60. Sims, 1920.
61. James, 1955.
62. Katzir, 2012.
63. Zimmerman, 2002.
64. Molinie and Boudia. 2009.
65. Lloyd George, 1938.
66. Jellicoe, 1934.
67. Gretton, 1977.
68. Sims, 1920.
69. Lloyd George, 1938.
70. Buchanan, 1979. Grieves, 1989.
71. Haig quotes are from Blake, 1952.
72. Hamilton, 1957, p. 137.
73. Public Record Office CAB 23/2.
74. Public Record Office CAB 24/12.
75. Doenitz, 1997.
76. Public Record Office Cab/23/3.
77. Public Record Office CAB24/21.
78. Public Record Office ADM 1/8490/131.
79. Jenkin, 2008, p. 391.
80. Public Record Office ADM 1/8490/131.
81. Wood, 1965.
82. Public Record Office ADM218/4.
83. Nature, 1919.
84. MacLeod and Andrews, 1971.
85. Messimer, 2001, p. 167.
86. Tuchman, 1959.
87. Millikan, 1951.
88. Yerkes, 1920.
89. Public Record Office ADM 116/1430, Case 5S45, Report by Rutherford and Commander Bridge on visit to US.
90. Messimer, 2001.

91. Public Record Office ADM118/179.
92. Public Record Office CAB 23/3.
93. Blake, 1952.
94. Blake 1952.
95. Public Record Office CAB 24/21.
96. Public Record Office CAB 23/3.
97. Public Record Office ADM 1/8480/131.
98. Jellicoe, 1934.
99. de Gaulle, 2002.
100. Wilson, 1920.
101. Gusewelle, 1977.
102. Black, 2009.
103. Feather, 1940. Foster, 1949.
104. Newbolt, 1931.
105. Public Record Office ADM 186/415.
106. Blake, 1952.
107. Public Record Office ADM 218/4.
108. Public Record Office ADM 218/4.
109. Public Record Office Adm186/410.
110. Messimer, 2001.
111. Public Record Office ADM 186/408.
112. Wood, 1965.
113. Dubinson, 2010.
114. Newbolt, 1931. Jellicoe, 1934.
115. Newbolt, 1931.
116. Niemöller, 1936.
117. Public Record Office ADM 186/408.
118. Gray, 1972.
119. Pirie. 1966.
120. Newbolt, 1931.
121. Gibson and Prendergast, 1931.
122. Jameson, 1965.
123. Public Record Office ADM 218/3.

Chapter 6. Sound Ranging. William Lawrence Bragg

Andrade, E.N. da C., 'Harold Roper Robinson 1889–1955' *Biogr. Mem. Fell. R. Soc.* 3, 161-179 (1957)

Boraston, J. H. (ed.), *Sir Douglas Haig's Despatches (December 1915 – April 1919).* (London & Toronto: J. M. Dent & Sons, 1919

Born, M., *My Life and My Views.* (New York: Charles Scribner's Sons, 1968)

Bragg, W. L., 'Reginald William James. 1891–1964.' *Biogr. Mem. Fell. R. Soc.* 11, 115-125 (1965)

Bragg, Sir L., 'Sound Ranging in France 1914–1918.', in *History of the Royal Regiment of Artillery. Western Front 1914–18*, (ed. Gen. Sir M. Farndale) (London: The Royal Artillery Institution, pp. 374-379, 1986)

Bragg, Sir L, Maj.-Gen. A.H. Dowson and Lt-Col. H. H. Hemming, *Artillery Survey in the First World War.* (London: Field Survey Association, 1971)

Bragg, W. H. and W. L. Bragg, *X Ray and Crystal Structure* (London: Bell & Sons, 1915)

Bragg, W. L., 'Half a Century of X-Ray Analysis. Nobel Guest Lecture I.' *Arkiv för Fysik.* 40, 585-603 (1966)

Bridland, T. and A. Morgan, *Tunnel-Master and Arsonist of the Great War.* The Norton-Griffiths Story. (Barnsley: Leo Cooper, 2003)

Broad, C. N. F., 'Artillery Intelligence and Counter Battery Work.' *J. Roy. Artill.* 49, 221-241 (1922)

Brooke, A. F., 'The Evolution of Artillery in the Great War.' *J. Roy. Artill.* 51, 250-68; 359-372 (1924–25)

Caroe, G. M., *William Henry Bragg 1862–1942.* (Cambridge University Press, 1978)

Charpentier-Morize, M., *Jean Perrin 1870–1942.* (Paris: Belin, 1997)

Charteris, J., *At G.H.Q.* (London: Cassell & Co., 1931)

Chasseaud, P., 'Sound ranging 1914–1918.' *Stand-to!* 30, 23-27 (1990)

Great Britain, War Office, *Report on Survey on the Western Front.* (London: HMSO, 1920)

Churchill, W., *The World Crisis.* (New York: Charles Scribner Sons, 1949)

Cottrell, A., 'Edward Neville Da Costa Andrade. 1887–1971.' *Biogr. Mem. Fell. R. Soc.* 18, 1-20 (1972)

Cron, H., *Imperial German Army 1914–18, Organization, Structure, and Order of Battle.* (Solihull, West Midlands: Helion and Co., 2002)

Edmonds, J. E., *Military Operations France and Belgium. 1916. Vol. I.* (London: Macmillan, 1932)

Edmonds, J. E., *Military Operations France and Belgium 1917. Vol. II.* (London: HMSO, 1948)

Farndale, Gen. Sir M., *History of the Royal Regiment of Artillery. Western Front 1914–18.* (London: Royal Artillery Institution, 1986)

Farrar-Hockley, A. H., *The Somme.* (London: Pan Books, 1966)

Fleming, C. A., 'Ernest Marsden. 1889–1970.' *Biogr. Mems Fell. R. Soc.* 17, 463-496 (1971)

Gold, T., 'The "Double Bang" of Supersonic Aircraft.' *Nature* 179, 79 (1952)

Great Britain, War Office, *Report on Survey on the Western Front.* (London: HMSO, 1920)

Innes, J. R. (ed.), *Flash Spotters and Sound Rangers.* (London: George Allen & Unwin Ltd, 1997)

Jack, Lt-Col. E. M., 'Survey in France During the War.' *Roy. Eng. J.* 30, 1-27 (1919)

Jenkin, J., *William and Lawrence Bragg, Father and Son.* (Oxford University Press, 2008)

Kevles, D. J., 'Flash and Sound in the AEF: The History of a Technical Service.' *Mil. Affairs* 33, 374-384 (1969)

Kitchen, M., *The German Offensives of 1918.* (Stroud: Tempus, 2001)

Ludendorff, E., *Ludendorff's Own Story.* (2 vols.) (New York: Harper and Brothers, 1919)

M. N. M., 'Brigadier E.M. Jack.' *Roy. Eng. J.* 65, 142-145 (1951).

Macloud, Maj. M. N., 'Survey Work in Modern War.' *J. Roy. Artill.* 48, 190-202 (1921)

Middlebrook, M., The Kaiser's Battle. 21 March 1918: The First Day of the German Spring Offensive. (London: Penguin Books, 1983)

Phillips, D., 'William Lawrence Bragg. 31 March 1890–1 July 1971.' *Biogr. Mems Fell. R. Soc.* 25, 75-143 (1979)

Prior, R. and T. Wilson., *Command on the Western Front. The Military Career of Sir Henry Rawlinson 1914–18.* (Oxford: Blackwell, 1992)

Remarque, E. M., *All Quiet on the Western Front.* (Tran. A. W. Wheen.) (Boston: Little Brown, 1996)

Sheffield, G. D., 'The Australians at Pozieres: Command and Control.' in *The British General Staff. Reform and Innovation 1890–1939* (ed. D. French and B. H. Reid) (London: Frank Cass, 2002)

Sheldon, J., *The German Army in the Somme. 1914–1916.* (Barnsley, South Yorkshire: Pen and Sword, 2005)

Sheldon, J., *The German Army at Passchendaele.* (Barnsley: Sword and Pen, 2007)

Swettenham, J., *Mcnaughton 1887–1939.* (Toronto: Ryerson Press, 1968)

Van der Kloot, W., 'Lawrence Bragg's Role in the Development of Sound ranging in World War I.' *Notes Rec. R. Soc.* 59, 273-284 (2005)

War Office, *Royal Warrant for the Pay, Appointment, Promotion, and Non-Effective Pay of the Army.* (London: HMSO, 1914) (reprinted 1917)

Winterbotham, H. S. L., 'British Survey on the Western Front.' *Geograph. J.* 53, 253-271 (1919)

Wynne, Capt. G. C., *If Germany Attacks. The Battle in Depth in the West.* (London: Faber and Faber, 1940)

Yerkes, R. M. (ed.), *The New World of Science. Its Development During the War.* (New York: The Century Co., 1920)

Zabecki, D. T., *Steel Wind. (Westport CT: Greenwood, 1994)*

1. W. L. Bragg's letters are in the archives of the Royal Institution. They are the source of the quotes attributed to him. Further information comes from Jenkin, 2001; Phillips, 1979; Phillips, 2004; Van der Kloot, 2005.
2. Caroe, G. M., 1978, p. 75.
3. Bragg, W. L., 1966, p. 587.
4. Caroe, 1978, pp. 77-78.
5. Bragg, 1966, p. 585.
6. Public Record Office WO374/8505.
7. Bragg, 1966.
8. Brooke, 1924–1925.
9. War Office, 1914.
10. Bragg and Bragg, 1915.
11. *The Times*, 20 May 1915, p. 5.
12. Zabecki, 1994, p. 11.
13. Bragg, 1986; Bragg, *el. al*, 1971.
14. M.N.M., 1951.
15. Royal Institution WHB 26.
16. Andrade, 1957.
17. Chasseaud, 1990.
18. Chasseaud, 1999.
19. Great Britain, 1920, p. 106.
20. Bragg, 1966, p. 585.
21. Jenkin, 2008, p. 377.
22. Public Record Office WO 297/73.
23. Bragg *et. al.*, 1971.
24. Gold, 1952.
25. Thomson, 1963.
26. Imperial War Museum Archives Hemming IWM PP/MER/155
27. Bragg *et. al.*, 1971, p. 17.
28. Sheldon, 2005, p. 48.
29. Winterbotham, 1919.
30. Hemming (note 26).
31. Bragg *et. al.*, 1971, p. 17.
32. Innes, 1997.
33. Bragg *et. al.*, 1971, p. 376.
34. Phillips, 1979, p. 94.
35. Bragg *et. al.*, 1979.
36. Edmonds, 1932, p. 295.
37. Farrar-Hockley, 1966, p. 87.
38. Brooke, 1924-25.
39. Sheldon, 2005.
40. Great Britain, 1920.
41. Chasseaud, 1990.
42. Sheffield, 2002, p. 124.
43. Churchill, 1949.
44. Farndale, 1986.
45. Great Britain, 1920, p. 107.

46. Bragg, 1965.
47. Fleming, ,1971.
48. Cottrell, 1972.
49. Prior and Wilson, 1992, p. 56.
50. Wynne, 1940.
51. Great Britain, 1920, p. 107.
52. Macloud, 1921. Broad, 1922.
53. Bridland and Morgan, 2003.
54. Prior and Wilson, 1992, p. 87.
55. Edmonds, 1948, p. 148.
56. Charteris, 1931.
57. Sheldon, 2007, p. 104.
58. Van der Kloot, 2005.
59. Sheldon, 2007, p. 152, p. 267.
60. Edmonds, 1948, p. 141.
61. Sheldon, 2007, p. 312.
62. Boraston, 1919, p. 133.
63. Sheldon, 2007, p. 315.
64. Boraston, 1919, p. 142.
65. Bragg, 1986.
66. Great Britain, 1920, p. 38.
67. Bragg, 1986, p. 378.
68. Jack, 1919.
69. Swettenham, 1968.
70. Yerkes, 1920.
71. Bragg *et. al.,* 1979.
72. Compton, 1937.
73. Kevles, 1969.
74. I do not know what microphone was used by the Dufour system. The French were using large rubber air-filled bladders lying on the ground for sound reception, so perhaps they used these. Charpentier-Morize, 1997.
75. Great Britain, 1920, pp. 86-90.
76. Brooke, 1924–25.
77. Remarque, 1996, p. 197.
78. For example Zabecki, 1994.
79. Middlebrook, 1983, p. 111.
80. Bragg et. al., 1979, p. 19.
81. Middlebrook, 1983, p. 334.
82. Kitchen, 2001.
83. Ludendorff, 1919.
84. Broad, 1922.
85. Cron, 2002.
86. Born, 1968.
87. 'British Association at Bournemouth.' *The Times,* 10 September 1919, p. 15.

Chapter 7. Anti-aircraft. A. V. Hill

Baker, H. F., 'Geoffrey Thomas Bennett. 1868–1943.' *Obit. Not. Fell. Roy. Soc.* 4, 596-615 (1944)
Becker, Capt., 'The 42 Cm Mortar: Fact and Fancy.' *Roy. Artill. J.* 44: 489-496, 1922–23)
Bull, G. and C. H. Murphy, *Paris Kanonen—the Paris Guns (Wilhelmgeschutze) Und Project Harp : The Application of Major Calibre Guns to Atmospheric and Space Research.* (Herford: Mittler, 1988)

Burkill, J.C., 'John Edensor Littlewood. 9 June 1885–6 September 1977.' *Biogr. Mems Fell. R. Soc.* 24, 322-367, (1978)

Caroe, G. M., *William Henry Bragg 1862–1942* (Cambridge University Press, 1978)

Cattermole, M. J. G. and A. F. Wolfe. *Horace Darwin's Shop. A History of the Cambridge Instrument Company 1878 to 1968* (Bristol and Boston: Adam Hilger, 1987).

Clark, R. W., *Tizard*. (London: Methuen, 1965)

Cowan, R. S. 'Galton, Sir Francis (1822–1911).' In *Oxford Dictionary of National Biography* (ed. H. C. G. Matthew and B. Harrison), vol. 21, pp. 346-349 (Oxford University Press, 2004)

Cranz, C. and Capt. K. Becker, *Handbook of Ballistics. Volume I. Exterior Ballistics Being a Theoretical Examination of the Motion of the Projectile from the Muzzle to the Target*. (London: HMSO, 1921)

Crowther, J.G., *Fifty Years with Science*. (London: Barrie & Jenkins, 1970)

Dale, H. H., 'Frederick Gowland Hopkins.' *Obit. Not. Fell*. Roy. Soc. 6, 115-45 (1948)

Darwin, C. G., 'Douglas Rayner Hartree. 1897–1958.' *Biogr. Mems Fell. R. Soc.* 4, 102-16 (1958)

Fischer, F., *Douglas Rayner Hartree. His Life in Science and Computing*. (Singapore: World Scientific Publishing, 2003)

French, P., 'Norman, Sir Henry, first Baronet (1858–1939)'. In *Oxford Dictionary of National Biography* (ed. H. C. G. Matthew and B. Harrison), vol. 41, p. 15 (Oxford University Press, 2004)

Fowler, R. H., E. G. Gallop, C. N. H. Lock and H.W. Richmond, 'The Aerodynamics of a Spinning Shell.' *Phil. Trans.* 221, 295-393 (1920)

Haldane, R. B., *An Autobiography* (London: Hodder and Stoughton, 1929)

Hill, A. V., 'The Mode of Action of Nicotine and Curari, Determined by the Form of the Contraction Curve and by the Method of Temperature Coefficients.' *J. Physiol. Lond.* 39, 361-73 (1909)

Hill, A. V., 'Mr. William Hartree, O.B.E.' *Nature* 152, 154-156 (1943)

Hill, A. V. 'Autobiographical Sketch.' *Persp. Biol. and Medicine* 14, 27-42 (1970)

Hill, A. V., *Memories and Reflections* (3 vol.) (London: Royal Society, 1974)

Katz, B., 'Archibald Vivian Hill.' *Biogr. Mems Fell. R. Soc.* 24, 71-149 (1978)

Kennett, L., *The First Air War. 1914–1918*. (New York: The Free Press, 1991)

Keynes, G., *The Gates of Memory* (Oxford: Clarendon Press, 1982)

Littlewood, J. E., 'Adventures in Ballistics.' *Math. Spectrum* 4, 31-38 (1971)

Loch, Capt. K. M., 'Anti-Aircraft Artillery.' *Roy. Artill. J.* 48, 433-442 (1921–22)

Lloyd George, D., *War Memoirs*. (2 vols.) (London: Oldmans Press, 1938)

McCrea, W. H. 'Edward Arthur Milne. 1896–1950.' *Obit. Not. Fell. Roy. Soc.* 7, 220-243 (1951)

Milne, E. A., 'Ralph Howard Fowler. 1889–1944.' *Obit. Not. Fell. Roy. Soc.* 5, 60-7 (1945)

Milne, E. A., and F. Puryer White, 'Herbert William Richmond 1863–1948.' *Obit. Not. Fell. Roy. Soc.* 6, 219-30 (1948)

Miller, H. W., *The Paris Gun*. (London: George G. Harrap, 1930)

Needham, J., 'Sir Frederick Gowland Hopkins, O.M., F.R.S. (1861–1947).' *Notes Rec. Roy. Soc.* 17, 117-62 (1962)

Pattison, M., 'Scientists, Inventors and the Military in Britain, 1915–19: The Munitions Inventions Department.' *Soc. Stud. Science* 13, 521-568 (1983)

R.T.G., 'Sir Horace Darwin.' *Proc. Roy. Soc. A* 122, xv-xviii (1929)

Scarth, R. N., *Echoes from the Sky. A Story of Acoustic Defence*. (Hythe, Kent: Hythe Civic Society, 1999)

Schwarte, M. (ed.) *Kriegstechnik der Gegenwart*. (Berlin: E. G. Mittler & Sohn, 1927)

Semmel, B., 'Karl Pearson: Socialist and Darwinist.' *Brit. J. Soc.* 9, 111-125 (1958)

Skidelsky, R., *John Maynard Keynes; Hopes Betrayed 1893–1920*. (London: Penguin Books, 1983)

Smith, M. W., *A Scholarship Boy, Sugar, and a Round Square*. (Beverley: Highgate, 1998)

Smith, M.W. 'E. A. Milne and the Creation of Air Defence: Some Letters from an Unprincipled Brigand' *Notes Rec. R. Soc.*44, 241-255 (1990)

Smith, M. W., *Beating the Odds.* (London: Imperial College Press, 2013)

Snow, C. P., *Science and Government* (Oxford University Press, 1961)

Terraine, J., *White Heat. The New Warfare 1914–18.* (London: Leo Cooper, 1992)

T. R. E., 'Sir Walter Morley Fletcher. 1873–1933.' *Obit. Not. Fell. Roy. Soc.* 1, 153-163 (1942–1944)

Tucker, S. C. (ed.), *The European Powers in the First World War. An Encyclopaedia.* London: Garland Publishing, 1996)

Van der Kloot, W. 'Soup or Sparks: The History of Drugs and Synapses.' in *Handbook of Contemporary Neuropharmacology* (ed. I. Hanin, D.R. Sibley, M. Kuhar and P. Skolnick), pp. 3-38 (New York: John Wiley & Sons, 2007)

Van der Kloot, W., 'Mirrors and Smoke: A. V. Hill, His Brigands, and the Science of Anti-Aircraft Gunnery in World War I.' *Notes Rec. R. Soc.* 65, 393-410 (2011)

Vigneron, H., *Les Applications de la physique pendant la guerre* (Paris, Masson et Cie, 1919)

War Office, *Textbook of anti-aircraft gunnery.* (London : HMSO. Vol. 1, 1925, Vol. 2, 1924)

Wells, H. G., *Mr. Britling Sees It Through* (London: Cassell and Company, 1917)

Yule, G. U., and Filon, L. N. G. ; 'Karl Pearson. 1957–1936.' *Obit. Not. Fell. Roy. Soc. 2*, 72-100 (1936)

1. Hill, 1974, Katz, 1978. Antiaircraft Experimental Section of the MID (1916–1918) in the Archives of Churchill College AVHL 1/37.
2. Hill, 1974, p. 33.
3. Hill 1974, p. 619
4. Hill, 1974, p. 39.
5. Hill's letters are the Archives of Churchill College Cambridge, AVHL1/1. The unattributed quotes that follow are taken from them.
6. Katz, 1978.
7. R.T.G., 1929 xv-xviii.
8. Lloyd George, 1938.
9. Wells, 1917, p. 343.
10. Lloyd George, 1938, p. 378.
11. Littlewood, 1971.
12. Cattermole and Wolfe, 1987.
13. Haldane, 1929.
14. Pattison, 1983.
15. Van der Kloot, 2011.
16. T.R.E, 1933.
17. Dale, 1948. Needham, 1962.
18. Van der Kloot, 2007.
19. Katz, 1978, p. 80.
20. Hill, 1970. p. 37.
21. Hill, 1970, p. 38.
22. McCrea, 1951.
23. Smith, 1998, 2013.
24. Milne, 1945.
25. Milne, 1945.
26. Milne and Puryer White, 1948.
27. Baker, 1944.
28. Public Record Office MUN 7/296.
29. Public Record Office MUN 7/343.
30. Milne's letters are at Oxford University in the Bodleian Library Special Collections and Western Manuscripts: CSAC 102.6.84. Otherwise unattributed Milne quotes are from them.

31. Hill, 1974, p. 117.
32. Hill, 1909.
33. Katz, 1978, p. 80.
34. Hill. 1974, 117.
35. Hill, 1974, p. 228.
36. Hill, 1974. p. 518.
37. www.exteriorballistics.com
38. Burkill, 1978.
39. Littlewood, 1971.
40. Hill, 1974, p. 525.
41. War Office, 1924–1925.
42. Becker, 1922–1923.
43. Vigneron, 1919, pp. 279-281.
44. Milne, 1945.
45. Hill, 1974, p. 519.
46. Loch, 1921–1922.
47. Hill, 1943.
48. Darwin, 1958. Fischer, 2003.
49. Darwin, 1958.
50. French, 2004.
51. Public Record Office MUN 7/327.
52. Schwarte, 1927.
53. Milne (note 30).
54. Milne, 1945.
55. Katz, 1978.
56. Public Record Office AIR 1/711/27/13/2214
57. Caroe, 1978.
58. Kennett, 1991, p. 58.
59. Public Record Office AIR 1/711/27/13/2214
60. Public Record Office AIR 1/711/27/13/2214.
61. Pearson's papers are in the UCL Archives of UCL boxes 909 and 610.
62. Semmel, 1958. Yule and Filon, 1936.
63. Cowan, 2004.
64. Letter from Hill to McCrae in Milne (note 30).
65. Public Record Office MUN 7/308.
66. Hill, 1974.
67. Smith, 1990.
68. Snow, 1961.
69. Public Record Office AIR 1/711/27/13/2214.
70. Clark, 1965. p.43.
71. Scarth, 1999.
72. Public Record Office MUN 7/303.
73. Public Record Office AIR 1/711/27/13/2214.
74. Pearson papers (note 61).
75. Hill, 1974.
76. Public Record Office MUN 7/303.
77. Public Record Office W0/ 33/270.
78. Terraine, 1992. p. 269.
79. Public Record Office MUN 7/303.
80. Crowther, 1970. p. 10.
81. Crowther, 1970.
82. Crowther, 1970.
83. http://www.archiveshub.ac.uk/news/02091301.htm.

84. Crowther, 1970, p. 16.
85. Miller, 1930. Bull and Murphy, 1988.
86. Cranz and Becker, 1921.
87. Tucker, 1996, p. 540.
88. Hill (note 5).
89. Milne. 1945, p. 66.
90. Fowler *et. al.* 1920.
91. Skidelsky, 1983. Keynes, 1982.

Chapter 8. Lessons Learnt: 1919–1971

Baggott, J., *Atomic. The First War of Physics and the Secret History of the Atom Bomb: 1939–49* (London: Icon Books, 2009)

Beatty, D., *The Beatty Papers: Selections from the Private and Official Correspondence of Admiral of the Fleet Earl Beatty.* (ed. B. McL. Ranft) (Aldershot: Scolar Press for the Navy Records Society, 1989)

Berlin, I., *Personal Impressions.* (London: Hogarth Press, 1980)

Blackett, P. M. S., 'Tizard and the Science of War.' *Nature* 185, 647-653 (1960)

Blalock, A., *Principles of Surgical Care. Shock and Other Problems.* (New York: Blenkinsop, T. J. and J. M. Rainer (eds). *Official History of the Veterinary Service.* (London: HMSO, 1925)

Blow, D. M., 'Max Ferdinand Perutz OM CH CBE 19 May 1914 – 6 February 2002.' *Biogr. Mem. Fell. R. Soc.* 50, 227-256 (2004)

Bragg, Sir W., *The World of Sound.* (London: G. Bell & Sons, 1920)

Caroe, G. M., *William Henry Bragg 1862–1942.* (Cambridge University Press, 1978)

Corum, J. S., *The Roots of Blitzkrieg. Hans Von Seekt and German Military Reform.* (Lawrence: The University Press of Kansas, 1992)

Chalmers, W. S., *The Life and Letters of David, Earl Beatty, Admiral of the Fleet, Viscount Borodale of Wexford, Baron Beatty of the North Sea and of Brooksby, P.C., G.C.B., O.M., G.C.V.O., D.S.O., D.C.L., Ll. D.* (London: Hodder and Stoughton, 1951)

Crowther, J. G., *Fifty Years with Science.* (London: Barrie & Jenkins,1970)

Darwin, C. G., 'Douglas Rayner Hartree. 1897–1958.' *Biogr. Mem. Fell. R. Soc.* 4, 102-116 (1958)

Evans, R. J., *The Third Reich in Power, 1933–1939.* (London: Alan Lane, 1995)

Fischer, F., Douglas Rayner Hartree, His Life in Science and Computing. (London: World Scientific, 2003)

Goudsmit, S. A., *Alsos: The Failure in German Science.* (London: Sigma Books, 1947)

Gretton, P., 'The U-Boat Campaign in Two World Wars.' in *Naval Warfare in the Twentieth Century. 1900–1935.* pp. 128-140 (ed. G. Jordan) (London: Croom Helm, 1977)

Hackmann, W., *Seek & Strike. Sonar, Anti-Submarine Warfare and the Royal Navy 1914–54.* (London: HMSO, 1984)

Hahn, O., *My Life.* (tran. E. Kaiser and E. Wilkins. (London: MacDonald, 1970)

Haldane, R. B., *An Autobiography.* (London: Hodder and Stoughton, 1929)

Haldane, J. B. S., *Callinicus. A Defence of Chemical Warfare.* (London: Kegan Paul, Trench, Trubner & Co., 1925)

Hartree, D. R., *Numerical Analysis.* (Oxford: Clarendon Press, 1952)

Hastings, M., *All Hell Let Loose: The World at War 1939–45.* (London: Harper, 2011)

Henderson, J., *A Life of Ernest Starling.* (Oxford University Press, 2005)

Hill, A. V., 'Mr. William Hartree, O.B.E.' *Nature* 152, 154-56 (1943)

Hill, A. V., *Memories and Reflections.* (3 vol.) (London: Royal Society, 1974)

Howse, D., *Radar at Sea. The Royal Navy in World War 2.* (London: Macmillan, 1993)

James, H., *Krupp. A History of the Legendary German Firm.* (Princeton: Princeton University Press, 2012)

Jenkin, J., *William and Lawrence Bragg, Father and Son.* (Oxford University Press, 2008).

Keynes, J. M., *The Economic Consequences of the Peace.* (London: Macmillan, 1919)

Kuhn, H.G., 'James Franck (1882–1965)', *Biogr. Mem. Fell. R. Soc.* 11, 53-74 (1965).

Lewin, R., *Lise Meitner. A Life in Physics.* (Berkeley: University of California Press, 1997)

Lovell, Sir B., 'The Cavity Magnetron in World War II: Was the Secrecy Justified?' *Notes Rec. R. Soc.* 58, 283-294 (2004)

McCrea. W. H., 'Edward Arthur Milne.' *Obit. Not. Fell. Roy. Soc.* 7, 421-443 (1950–51)

McGucken, W., 'The Royal Society and the Genesis of the Scientific Advisory Committee to Britain›s War Cabinet, 1939–1940.' *Notes Rec. R. Soc.* 33, 87-115 (1978)

Lovell, B., 'Patrick Maynard Stuart Blackett, Baron Blackett, of Chelsea. 18 November 1897–13 July 1974' *Biogr. Mem. Fell. R. Soc.* 21, 1-115 (1975)

Macksey, K., *Technology in War.* (New York: Prentice Hall, 1986)

Martin, C. J. 'Ernest Henry Starling, C.M.G., M.D., F.R.S.: Life and Work.' *Brit. Med. J.* 900-905 (1927)

Meitner, L. 'Looking Back.' *Bull. Atom, Sci.,* November 2-7(1964) .

Meitner, L. and O. R. Frisch., 'Disintegration of Uranium by Neutrons: A New Type of Nuclear Reaction.' *Nature* 143, 239-240 (1939)

Mendelsohn, E., 'Science, Scientists, and the Military.' in *Science in the Twentieth Century.* (ed. J. Krige and D. Pestre) pp. *175-202.* (Amsterdam: Harwood Academic Publishers,1997).

Milne, E.A., 'Ralph Howard Fowler. 1889–1944.' *Obit. Not. Fell. Roy. Soc.* 5, 60-78 (1945).

Morris, J., *Fisher›s Face.* (New York: Random House, 1995)

Operation Epsilon: The Farm Hall Transcripts. (Bristol: Institute of Physics Publishing, 1993)

Phillips, D., 'William Lawrence Bragg. 31 March 1890–1 July 1971.' Biogr. Mem. Fell. R. Soc. 25, 75-143 (1979)

Phelps, S., *The Tizard Mission.* (Yardley PA: Westholme Publishing, 2010)

Roskill, W., *The Navy at War. 1939–1945.* (London: Collins, 1960)

Sanderson, M., *The Universities and British Industry 1850–1970.* (London: Sime, Routledge & Kegan Paul, 1972)

Science in War. (Harmondsworth: Penguin Books, 1940)

Snow, C. P., *Science and Government.* (Oxford University Press, 1961).

Stoltzenberg, D., *Fritz Haber. Chemist, Nobel Laureate, German, Jew.* (Philadelphia: Chemical Heritage Press, 2004)

Van der Kloot, W., *World War I Fact Book.* (Stroud: Amberley Publishing, 2010)

Weizmann, C., *Trial and Error.* (London: Hamish Hamilton, 1949)

Willstätter, R., *From My Life.* (tran. L. S. Hornig) (New York: W.A. Benjamin, 1965)

1. Keynes, 1919, p. 278.
2. Royal Institution Archives W. H. Bragg letters.
3. Sanderson, 1972, p. 44.
4. Haldane, 1929.
5. Phillips, 1979. Jenkin, 2008.
6. Royal Institution Archives W. L. Bragg letters.
7. WL Bragg, note 6.
8. Bragg, W. H., 1920
9. Archives of Churchill College, Cambridge Hill letters. AVHL1/1
10. Bragg. 1920.
11. Caroe, 1978.
12. Beatty, 1989. Chalmers, 1951.
13. Beatty, 1989.
14. Morris, 1995.
15. Blalock, 1940.
16. Hill (note 9).
17. Henderson, 2005.

18. Martin, 1927.
19. Hill, 1943.
20. Milne, 1945.
21. Hartree, 1952.
22. Darwin, 1958. Fischer, 2003.
23. Berlin, 1980, p. 41.
24. Crowther, 1970. p.118.
25. Weizmann, 1949, p. 474.
26. Mendelsohn, 1997.
27. Corum, 1992.
28. Kuhn, 1965.
29. Willstätter, 1965.
30. Van der Kloot, 2010.
31. Evans, 1995, p. 426.
32. James, 2012. This is an official history written for the company.
33. Stoltzenberg, 2004.
34. Sime, 1997.
35. Sime, 1997.
36. Meitner, 1964.
37. Meitner, and Frisch, 1939.
38. Public Record Office WO 033/1305.
39. (1877–1949.) A Royal Artillery officer, he held a series of staff positions during WW1 and after the committee became head of the Territorial Army. The committee is not mentioned in his obituary in the *Times*.
40. Hill, 1974, p. 4.
41. Snow, 1961.
42. Phelps, 2010.
43. Blackett, 1960.
44. Hill, 1974.
45. Jones, 1961.
46. Lovell, 2004.
47. McGucken, 1978.
48. Science in War, 1940, p. 13.
49. McGucken, 1978, p. 105.
50. Macksey, 1986.
51. Roskill, 1960. Gretton, 1977. Hackmann, 1984. Howse, 1993.
52. Blackett, 1960.
53. Fischer. 2003.
54. Phillips, 1979, p. 114.
55. Hastings, 2011, p. 81.
56. Baggott, 2009.
57. Goudsmit, 1947.
58. Operation Epsilon, 1993.
59. Operation Epsilon, 1993, p. 70.
60. Lovell, 1975.
61. Hahn, 1970.
62. Blenkinsop and Rainer, 1925.
63. Haldane, J. B. S., 1925.
64. McCrea, 1950–51.
65. Hartree, 1952.
66. Blow, 2004.
67. Weizmann, 1949, p. 556.

People Index